# Mankind Evolving

403

# MANKIND EVOLVING

## THE EVOLUTION OF THE HUMAN SPECIES

by Theodosius Dobzhansky

New Haven and London, Yale University Press

Library of Congress catalog card number: 62–8243
ISBN: 0–300–00427–3 (cloth), 0–300–00070–7 (paper)

Set in Baskerville type and
printed in the United States of America by
The Colonial Press Inc.
Clinton, Massachusetts.

Published in Great Britain, Europe, and Africa by
Yale University Press, Ltd., London.
Distributed in Latin America by Kaiman & Polon,
Inc., New York City; in Australasia and Southeast
Asia by John Wiley & Sons Australasia Pty. Ltd.,
Sydney; in India by UBS Publishers' Distributors Pvt.,
Ltd., Delhi; in Japan by John Weatherhill, Inc., Tokyo.

Originally published as a Silliman Foundation
Lecture.

# Contents

# Preface

EINSTEIN said something that needed to be said and that has been said better by nobody else: "The most incomprehensible thing about the world is that it is comprehensible." He also said that "the most beautiful thing we can experience is the mysterious. . . . It is the source of all art and science." Man is the most mysterious of all experiences. This is why art and science strive to make him comprehensible.

Some light on the phenomenon of man is shed, to the surprise of many people, by the investigation of nonhuman and even non-living nature. Darwin was originally a student of animals, plants, and geological strata, and in his greatest work, *On the Origin of Species,* he judiciously refrained, except by implication, from discussing man; yet the storm of protest which greeted his book showed that the implication was duly perceived. The book contained perhaps the most revolutionary scientific idea of all time concerning the nature of man: man has evolved and is evolving. Today, more than a century after Darwin, the idea of evolution is becoming an integral part of man's image of himself. The idea has percolated to much wider circles than biologists or even scientists: understood or misunderstood, it is a part of mass culture.

Two rival trends vie constantly for influence in science—special-ization and synthesis. The former usually predominates. Scientists are specialists; a good specialist is able to master only some fraction or fragment of human knowledge. When a specialist writes, he feels the hot stares of his colleagues peering over his shoulder, ready to find and pounce upon any factual mistake or weakness of argument. This is, of course, as it should be, even though the privilege of criticism is sometimes abused. Attempts to synthesize knowledge are, however, indispensable. The need is the more keenly felt the more knowledge becomes splintered. Failure of synthesis would vindicate Albert Schweitzer's angry remark: "Our age has discov-ered how to divorce knowledge from thought, with the result that we have, indeed, a science which is free, but hardly any science left which reflects."

This book is an attempt to explore the possibilities of understanding mankind as a product of evolution and as an evolving whole. I am acutely aware that this is a perilous undertaking. The stores of knowledge concerning man and evolution have grown enormously, and are growing apace. This knowledge is now far in excess of the capacity of even the best brain to assimilate it. I have spent my life working in the field of genetics—of Drosophila flies, not of human beings. In the pages that follow I shall have to deal with some topics with which I possess only dilettantish familiarity. Nevertheless, when Yale University honored me with the invitation to join the distinguished roster of Silliman lecturers, I chose to explore how far the evolution of man can be understood from the vantage point of modern genetics and of the biological theory of evolution. The result is not likely to be of more than temporary utility, since the study of man happens to be at present in a period of rapid and, we hope, of deepening expansion.

Science is cumulative knowledge. This makes scientific theories relatively impermanent, especially during the epochs when knowledge piles up in something like geometric progression. Scientists should be conscious of the provisional and transient nature of their attainments. Any scientist worthy of his salt labors to bring about the obsolescence of his own work. In the pages that follow I shall deal with some topics which are controversial and concerning which many people hold emotionally charged opinions. It would be naive to hope that the facts and arguments which I have been able to muster will satisfy everybody. I can only re-echo the thoughts of Darwin, expressed some 90 years ago in the concluding chapter of *The Descent of Man:*

> Many of the views which have been advanced are highly speculative, and some no doubt will prove erroneous; but I have in every case given the reasons which have led to one view rather than to another. It seemed worth while to try how far the principle of evolution would throw light on some of the more complex problems in the natural history of man. False facts are highly injurious to the progress of science, for they often endure long; but false views, if supported by some evidence, do little harm, for everyone takes a salutary pleasure in proving their falseness; and when this is done, one path towards error is closed and the road to truth is often at the same time opened.

I am profoundly thankful to friends and colleagues for critical reading of my manuscript and for their suggestions, corrections, and emendations, by which I have profited enormously. In particular, I am obliged to M. D. Coe of Yale University and Mrs. Sophie Dobzhansky Coe, who have read all the chapters; to Charles Birch, University of Sydney (Chapters 1–10); Anne Anastasi, Fordham University (Chapters 1–4); G. E. Hutchinson, Yale University (Chapters 1–4); Howard Levene, Columbia University (Chapters 5, 6, 9, and 10); R. H. Osborne, Sloan–Kettering Institute (Chapter 5); Timothy Prout, University of California (Chapters 6 and 9); J. B. Birdsell, University of California (Chapters 7 and 8); N. K. Bose, Department of Anthropology, Government of India, Calcutta (a part of Chapter 9); C. S. Coon, University of Pennsylvania (Chapters 9 and 10); and I. M. Lerner, University of California (Chapters 6, 11, and 12). It goes without saying that the entire responsibility for the errors and defects which remain in the book are mine, the more so since not all the suggestions of my kind critics have been acted upon. Last but not least, I owe thanks to my wife, Mrs. N. Siverzev–Dobzhansky, who has not only typed almost the entire manuscript but by her patience and forbearance has made the work possible.

T. D.

*New York, N.Y.*
*May, 1961*

# 1. Biology and Culture in Human Evolution

So walk I on uplands unbounded, and
know that there is hope, for that
which Thou didst mold out of dust
to have consort with things eternal.
                    DEAD SEA SCROLL

THE APPEARANCE slightly more than a century ago, in 1859, of Darwin's *On the Origin of Species* marked a turning point in the intellectual history of mankind. Darwin ushered in a new understanding of man and his place in the universe. After him the fateful idea that all things change, that they evolve, has become one of the cornerstones on which the thinking of civilized man is based. The universe, inanimate as well as animate matter, human bodily frame as well as man's psyche, the structure of human societies and man's ideas—all have had a history and all are in the process of change at present. Moreover, the changes so far have been on the whole, though not always, progressive, tending toward what we men regard as betterment. Progress in the future is not inevitable; it is not vouchsafed by any law of nature; but it may be striven for.

It is hard for our generation to realize how novel the idea of evolution, in the broadest sense of universal and all-pervading change and development, really is. Marcus Aurelius, the "philosophical emperor" (A.D. 121–180), held that "a wise man considers the periodic destructions and rebirths of the universe, and reflects that our posterity will see nothing new, and that our ancestors saw nothing greater than we have seen."

Infinity is a notion which most people find hard to conceive of. Creation myths were accordingly constructed to show that man and the universe did have a beginning. Once created, they thought, things were established forever. Before the idea of universal change was thrust upon people by evolutionary science, whether they liked it or not, change was regarded with misgiving, as something more apt to result in deterioration than improvement. Deterioration was, indeed, the only kind of "evolution" people could imagine readily: the Age of Gold is far in the past, the Iron Age is our lot. Hindu sages combined this with the idea of eternal recurrence—the ages

of benevolent gods are succeeded by ages of less benevolent ones;
ours is the age of the terrible goddess Kali; this will end in a cata-
clysm; whereupon everything will be repeated from the beginning.
Even the ancient Greeks, whose wisdom we find so congenial, did
not think of evolution. Yes, the world had a start, they thought, but
it was not growing progressively better. Although man can aspire
to see the beauty of eternal ideas, these ideas are distorted, and only
dimly reflected in the things met in the world.

Christianity is a religion that is implicitly evolutionistic, in that
it believes history to be meaningful: its current flows from the Creation, through progressive revelation of God to Man, to Christ, and
from Christ to the Kingdom of God. Saint Augustine (354–430)
expressed this evolutionistic philosophy most clearly. But the Judeo–Christian tradition took over from oriental religions the idea
of the Garden of Eden and of the Fall as the beginning of the
world's history. Interpreted literally rather than symbolically, this
view is anti-evolutionistic. Moreover, almost two millennia of
Christian exegesis do not make it clear that the history of man
ought to be an evolutionary development, a collaboration of God
and Man, rather than a series of fitful interventions by God. Even
such forward-looking theologians and philosophers as Niebuhr
(1941) and Greene (1959b) accept scientific evolutionism as something irresistible but not exactly welcome. For a Catholic viewpoint, presented by a biologically informed author, see Aguirre
(1959); a not so orthodox but a lofty vision of evolution will be
found in the inspiring work of Teilhard de Chardin (1959).

## Evolution before Darwin

Evolutionism first developed as a secular and agnostic philosophy (Barzun 1937, Brinton 1953, 1959). Its starting point may
perhaps be apprehended in the "Quarrel of the Ancients and the
Moderns" which took place in France toward the end of the seventeenth century. One side to this dispute held the achievements of
the classic Greeks and Romans to be the apogee of history, while
the other side believed that these achievements could be equaled
and surpassed. The work of Newton (1642–1727) soon provided a
basis for the audacity of the "Moderns": Newton's vista of the universe was manifestly more satisfactory than Aristotle's. Then Gio-
vanni Battista Vico (1668–1744) announced the new and startling
view, which we hold almost self-evident now, that human society
and human history were the works of men, and products of grad-

ual development. To be sure, he combined this with the ancient idea that history repeats itself in cycles, but this idea is still very much alive—it was espoused in the nineteenth century by Nietzsche and Danilevsky, dramatized some 40 years ago by Spengler, and bolstered by the enormous erudition of Sorokin and Toynbee.

It was Condorcet (1743–1794) who explicitly stated the idea that man's history was a directional development from lower to higher states. The development was to have ten stages, from primitive savagery, through increasing enlightenment, to ultimate perfection. The tenth and perfect stage Condorcet assumed to be just around the corner as he wrote his essay. So cheerful a view might seem in our day an intolerable smugness, but it was nothing of the sort for Condorcet, who wrote his essay while awaiting execution as an alleged enemy of the French Revolution, which he had helped bring about. Echoes of Condorcet's views are audible in Jefferson, and perhaps in all the liberal thinkers who followed him.

A belief in progress was taken almost for granted by enlightened people in the West in the nineteenth century. The progress of human societies seemed to be a law of nature, inevitable, probably uninterrupted, which could at most be delayed somewhat by the stubbornness of reactionaries or speeded up by the well-meaning help of liberals. Indeed, many people were prospering, at least in the parts of the world swayed by the industrial revolution. The only point which remained in doubt was how soon general happiness would be reached. Those who reaped the improvements for themselves readily assumed that material comforts would eventually come to almost everybody, or at least to those capable of wanting and appreciating them; all that was needed to ensure this admirable prospect was completely free private enterprise and unrestricted competition. Marx, with a rather different view of the inevitability of progress but an equally strong belief in it, recommended rather different methods, which he believed to have been validated by Darwin's discoveries. Marxism is sometimes dubbed a Christian heresy because it promises a socialist City of God on earth, although it is curiously vague about just what this blessed state will be like.

The birth of the idea of the sociocultural evolution of man antedates only slightly that of the evolution of the cosmos. It may seem that there can be nothing more permanent than the celestial bodies. The ancients regarded them as perfect as well as permanent, and changes seem incompatible with perfection. The Newtonian cosmos was, if not perfect, at least perfectly orderly, and perfect orders need not contain provisions for changes. However, Kant (1724–1804) and Laplace (1749–1827) sketched a cosmogony according to which the solar system began as a gaseous cloud and gradually differentiated into the sun, planets, and moons, which subsequently solidified and assumed their present shapes. Basic improvement in this cosmogony was made only in our time.

The theory of uniformitarianism in geology and geography stems particularly from Lyell (1797–1875). He stated that mountains and plains and seas have acquired their present shapes very gradually, as a result of causes which continue to operate and are easily observable. The work of Lyell appears to have been the major formative influence in Darwin's scientific development, and Lyell's support of Darwin's theories a source of encouragement to the latter. Our current century has extended evolution down to inert matter itself. Under the new dispensation not even atoms are eternal and unchanging; they, too, have histories, and their histories and those of the near and distant universes are chapters of the same grand cosmic process. (Excellent general accounts are given by Gamow, Hoyle, and others.)

Theories of the evolution of life came on the scene last, after those of cultural and cosmic evolution. The history of the evolutionary idea in biology has been told frequently but not concordantly (see Eiseley 1958, 1959, Darlington 1959, Greene 1959b, Wilkie 1959, to mention only some of the recent writings). Matters of priority will always be debatable, and we need not enter this often unedifying debate. Because in the late eighteenth and the nineteenth centuries evolutionary ideas were clearly in the air, priority claims are hard to evaluate. Buffon, Blyth, Chambers, Erasmus Darwin, Lamarck, Maupertuis, Wallace, and others had many important insights. Lamarck is the author of the first self-consistent theory of evolution, but the mechanisms whereby he hoped to explain evolution are now known to be fanciful. It was Charles Darwin who was able so to marshal a great mass of evidence that evolution became intelligible, and the acceptance of the theory inescapable.

### Man's Animal Ancestry

Darwin supplied the keystone of the arch connecting our understanding of the destiny of the atom with that of the destiny of man. In *On the Origin of Species* he dealt with man only by implication;

in *The Descent of Man* (1871) he reluctantly took the inevitable step and showed that man is a part of nature and kin to all life.

The Darwinian revolution, like most revolutions, had to contend with an opposition. The resistance, desperate but pathetic, put up by religious and other conservatives is too well known to need detailing here. In this Age of Science it seems well-nigh incomprehensible that so many people found the idea of the animal ancestry of man insulting to human dignity. The attitude is well portrayed in the quaint story of the English lady who on being told of Darwin's theories exclaimed: "Descended from the apes! My dear, we hope it is not true. But if it is, let us pray that it may not become generally known." Apes and monkeys were held in low esteem in the folklore of Western peoples; creatures so dirty, ill-smelling, and lascivious did not deserve a place next to man even in the zoological system! Furthermore, to make Darwin's theory as shocking as possible the proposition "man and apes have descended from common ancestors" was garbled into "man has descended from the apes." This, of course, is obvious nonsense, since man's remote ancestors could not have descended from animals which are our contemporaries.

Darwin's successors had to labor to adduce proofs that the evolution of the biological world and of man had actually occurred. That was the paramount task which biologists faced in the closing decades of the nineteenth century. The task has been splendidly fulfilled, and the proofs of evolution are now a matter of elementary biology. They will be found summarized briefly in Chapter 7.

However, it is frequently asked, Is evolution a fact or a hypothesis? So stated, the question is meaningless and misleading. The enterprise of science is founded on the hope that all rational beings who investigate and ponder the same evidence, derived ultimately from sense impressions ("facts"), will be led to draw from this evidence the same conclusions. The evidence of biology means to most people familiar with it that the world of life, including man, is a product of an evolutionary development. But there are still a few persons not ignorant of the evidence who insist that evolution is a "mere" hypothesis, which they reject in favor of special creation (is special creation not another hypothesis?).

Nobody beheld the sight of man's ancestors giving rise to men, or of the ancestral horses transforming themselves into modern horses. We cannot re-enact these transformations in our laboratories. Evolutionary changes of this magnitude (sometimes called macro-evolution) take time intervals of much greater orders than the span of human life; they are accordingly not facts observed but events inferred from observed facts. In Lamarck's and Darwin's times evolution was a hypothesis; in our day it is proven. Another proven hypothesis is that the earth executes a complete revolution on its axis once every twenty-four hours.

When a hypothesis has been thoroughly verified, we may take it as a safe guide in our thinking and working activities. Those who are not satisfied that the existing evidence makes acceptance of the evolutionary origin of the living world inevitable are entitled to hold their opinions. The business of proving evolution has reached a stage when it is futile for biologists to work merely to discover more and more evidence of evolution. Those who choose to believe that God created every biological species separately in the state we observe them but made them in a way calculated to lead us to the conclusion that they are products of an evolutionary development are obviously not open to argument. All that can be said is that their belief is an implicit blasphemy, for it imputes to God appalling deviousness.

While the validity of the proposition that man's ancestors were not men cannot at present be reasonably doubted, this does not mean that we know enough about the appearance and habits of our ancestors who lived at different time levels in the past. Such knowledge can be gained with any degree of certainty only through human paleontology, the study of fossil ancestors and collateral relatives of now-living mankind. The available evidence, still very meager though rapidly growing, will be reviewed in Chapters 7 and 8. It should be stressed in this connection that in Darwin's time this evidence was practically nonexistent. The first skull of the Neanderthal race of fossil man was discovered in Germany in 1856, i.e., three years before *On the Origin of Species* and fifteen years before *The Descent of Man*. It was regarded by some outstanding anatomists (Virchow), however, as a pathological specimen, and its true significance was appreciated only much later. Similar doubts greeted the discovery in 1891 of an even more important human fossil—Java Man *(Homo erectus)*. It is really only in our century that the variety and number of human and prehuman fossils became great enough to warrant the first, though still hesitant, attempts to reconstruct human ancestry.

In our day the opposition to evolutionism has been thwarted. The notorious trial in 1925 at Dayton, Tennessee, was perhaps the final skirmish. A teacher named Scopes was found guilty of having broken a state law which prohibits the teaching of evolution; but the resulting ridicule heaped on this law produced a diametrically opposite verdict by the world. Strange to say, that law still remains on the statute books of Tennessee, although it is not being enforced. I broke it recently twice in succession within a little more than a month, by lecturing on evolutionistic subjects in institutions of higher learning in the state.

## The Evolution of Culture

Kroeber (1960) said that "Darwin's is a household name not because housewives and householders are deeply and clearly concerned about natural selection, but because Darwin is the symbol and was in large measure the agent of natural science finally achieving a historic approach, of being willing and able to operate without reservation or constraint in the dimension of time." In his books Darwin confined himself to biological matters, even in *The Descent of Man* and *The Expression of the Emotions in Man and Animals* (1872). But others were quite ready to apply his findings, or at least his phrases, to human society and human history. We have seen that Marx thought he was a Darwinist of sorts when he prophesied that human society will end in communism. Spencer (1820–1903), who speculated on evolutionary sociology even before *On the Origin of Species* was off the press, was among the first to jump on Darwin's band wagon, and he became a biologizing sociologist and sociologizing biologist with an enormous influence on the intellectual climate of his time (see Greene 1959a).

The "founding fathers" of evolutionary cultural anthropology are listed by Murdock (1959) and Kroeber (1960) as follows: Bachofen (1861), Maine (1861), Fustel de Coulanges (1864), McLennan (1865), Tylor (1865, 1871), Lubbock (1870), Morgan (1871), and Spencer (1874, 1896). Excepting Lubbock, who was a biologist, they were sociologists and jurists. But they viewed human societies and institutions in the way zoologists and botanists viewed animals and plants—the existing forms have descended by gradual modifications from very different antecedents.

Tylor staked out the field of cultural anthropology, as the study of culture, in 1871, the same year in which *The Descent of Man* was published. Culture is "that complex whole which includes knowledge, belief, art, morals, law, custom, and any other capabilities and habits acquired by man as a member of society" (for other definitions, see p. 59). The key word in this definition is "acquired"—not inherited biologically as is so much else in body structure, function, and behavior, both in man and in animals. Now, it cannot be too strongly emphasized that what is biologically inherited is not handed down ready-made from ancestors. On the contrary, the characteristics of an individual animal or of a person develop through long and complex interaction between heredity and environment (see Chapters 2–4). Culture, however, is something else. It is wholly acquired by human beings from other human beings, and not only by children from their parents as in biological heredity. Culture is acquired by imitation, training, and learning. To be sure, biological heredity may make the acquisition and transmission of culture, or of some of its aspects, more easy or more difficult, but it does not determine just what is acquired or transmitted. Heredity does determine that a person can learn to speak a language or languages, but it does not determine which language he will learn or what he will say. Biological heredity does not transmit characters which a human individual has acquired during his or her lifetime, but culture transmits *only* such characters.

To have founded the concept of culture is the enduring achievement of the pioneers of cultural evolutionism. But this current of thought has had an extraordinarily uneven career (see reviews in Steward 1953, 1960, Birdsell 1957a, and Murdock 1959). The founding fathers of cultural anthropology had at their disposal even scantier factual data than did their biologist contemporaries. Their speculative reconstructions of the origins and evolutionary changes of human societies were useful as working hypotheses which stimulated the collection of facts that eventually formed the basis of modern cultural anthropology. But the hypotheses themselves generally failed to stand the test of time. Their basic assumption was that the evolution of culture is unilineal, i.e., that all cultures necessarily progress through similar stages of development, which Morgan termed savagery, barbarism, and civilization. Among peoples living in the world at present some are still lingering in savagery, others have attained civilization; presumably the former may eventually also reach civilization, and the now-civilized ones were once upon a time like the present barbarians and savages. Just why the evolution of culture should always follow the same path was hard to explain; the unilineal character of this evolution was therefore declared a property of human nature—an easy but hardly satisfactory way out.

The theory soon met with difficulties. Cultures do not exist in complete isolation from each other; people may, and often do, borrow a culture ready-made from neighbors, conquerors, or the conquered, and thus skip over some "necessary" evolutionary stages. Cultures spread, or diffuse, from one people to another. For a time there was a diffusionist school which believed that culture arose only once, in ancient Egypt, and diffused from there in many directions, carried chiefly by Phoenician mariners.

Also, since savagery, barbarism, and civilization existed contemporaneously, the evolutionary changes obviously did not progress at similar rates in peoples in different parts of the world. Biological racism, which had many influential exponents during the late nineteenth and early twentieth centuries (see below), had an easy explanation—some peoples are by nature incapable of progressing beyond tribal savagery, while others are superior and develop civilizations.

Although cultural evolutionism has no necessary connection with biological racism, some social scientists felt suspicious of both. Nobody was more influential in bringing about a general repudiation of theories of cultural evolution than Franz Boas (1858–1942). Theories of cultural relativism came in vogue instead. No culture is really superior to any other; one should not talk about savagery or barbarism, or even about primitive and advanced cultures; euphemistic adjectives like "preliterate" and "literate" must be used instead. No one culture's way of life is better than another; people live differently, and that is all (see Benedict's *Patterns of Culture*, probably the most popular treatise on anthropology ever printed).

Cultural evolutionism probably reached an all-time low in popularity in the thirties, but a strong revival appears to have set in, especially in the postwar years. (It may be noted that the theory of savagery, barbarism, civilization, and socialism as successive stages of human development has enjoyed steady favor in the Soviet Union because it happened to have been mentioned favorably in the writings of Engels and in other communist scriptures.)

Cultural evolutionism has recently been espoused by White (1949, 1959), Childe (1951), Steward (1953, 1960), and Sahlins and Service (1960). This is not the place to attempt an analysis of their views; they are by no means in agreement on all points. Thus Steward proposes a theory of multilinear evolution: cultural developments occur differently in different "culture areas," of which the world has several. However, these different developments still pass through some broadly similar stages, which are stressed as significant. A modern form of unilineal evolutionism has been propounded by White, Sahlins, Service, and their collaborators, who argue that evolutionary changes of culture are of two kinds—general and specific. Their general unilineal evolution involves the passage of cultures from lower levels of development to higher levels; the levels are characterized best of all by the efficiency with which the energy resources of the environment are exploited. Specific evolution is adaptation of cultures to the diversity of local conditions; this is what historians are mainly concerned with.

A biologist cannot fail to note that "general evolution" sounds very much like what on the biological level is represented by the hypothesis of autogenesis or orthogenesis (see pp. 15–17). This notion proved to be unprofitable as a working hypothesis and is now a minority view. It might be better to distinguish evolutionary changes in cultures as analogous to anagenesis and cladogenesis in biological evolution (see Chapter 9). Perhaps Birdsell (1953, 1957b), Braidwood and Reed (1957), Braidwood (1958, 1960), Murdock (1959), and Willey (1960) are closest to a synthesis of the unilineal and multilineal views of the evolution of culture. The revival of evolutionism in cultural anthropology has not to date restored the mutual understanding between biologists and anthropologists which prevailed in the early post-Darwinian era, but the hope that it may yet do so should not be abandoned.

## Social Darwinism and Racism

Man's efforts to know himself are often frustrated by his propensity to deceive himself. The industrial revolution failed to benefit everybody equally. In cities of nineteenth-century Europe and America poverty and squalor persisted cheek by jowl with mounting comfort and luxury. This was nothing really new; disparities of wealth and social status have been increasingly a part of the social scene ever since simple food-gathering economies and low population densities gave way to more complex economic arrangements and growing populations. What was novel was the rapid carving up of the world into colonial empires. Most of mankind became "subject races," to be uplifted and perhaps even civilized; the pedagogic method was to put the subjects to work for the profit of their

white masters. If some of the latter felt a need to put their consciences at rest, a church hymn solved the problem:

> The rich man in his castle, the poor man at his gate
> God made them high and lowly. He ordered their estate.

To complement this with a scientific justification seemed, as
time went on, highly desirable to more and more people. Social
Darwinists found that Darwin, or his theory, accomplished the
purpose very nicely; all you needed to assume was that Darwin
had discovered not merely the laws of biological evolution but also
those governing the life of human societies. As will be shown in
more detail in Chapter 6, it was the phraseology more than the
essence of Darwinism which lent itself easily to abuse by social
Darwinists.

Actually, the "struggle" in the "struggle for life" was to Darwin
a metaphor. This struggle is not necessarily contention, warfare,
or bloodshed. Animals and plants "struggle" to avoid the perils of
cold, heat, desiccation, drowning, gale winds, etc., but they do not
freeze, burn, or drown other individuals of their own or of other
species. "Natural" in "natural selection" does not mean savagery
or conditions preceding or excluding man-made changes in the environment. Natural selection is going on in all human societies,
from the technologically most primitive to the most advanced (see
Chapters 6 and 11). Natural selection is simply the antonym of
artificial selection. The former means differential reproduction of
carriers of different genetic endowments owing to their adaptedness or shortcomings in a given environment, while the latter implies choice or culling of parents or of their progenies for some
purpose or with an end in view (Lerner 1950, 1958). Who is the
"fittest" in the evolutionary "survival of the fittest" is a most complex matter which has not been fully clarified even yet (see Chapter 6). One thing which is clear is that the fittest is not necessarily
a romantic figure, or a victorious conqueror, or a superman. He is
most likely to be merely a prolific parent.

Social Darwinists did not know, or did not want to know, any
of these subtleties and qualifications. They equated affluence and
occupation of the seats of the mighty with biological fitness, and
economic laissez faire, cut-throat competition, and rivalry with
natural selection (see Chapters 3 and 6). Solid and conservative citizens thought all along that success in business is a fair measure of
a person's worth; social Darwinists explained that it is also a meas-

ure of biological fitness. Sumner (1840–1910), an American ideologist of social Darwinism, taught that "the millionaires are a product of natural selection, acting on the whole body of men to pick out those who can meet the requirements of certain work to be done." On the other hand, "the strong and the weak are terms which admit of no definition unless they are made equivalent to the industrious and the idle, the frugal and the extravagant. . . . If we do not like the survival of the fittest, we have only one possible alternative, and that is the survival of the unfittest." John D. Rockefeller, Sr., wholeheartedly agreed. "The growth of a large business is merely a survival of the fittest. . . . It is merely the working-out of a law of nature and a law of God" (quoted after Hofstadter 1955). A good many lesser lights either welcomed these views or acquiesced in them. Such views became and continue to be the stock in trade of conservatives, but nowadays most people feel something awkward about them, and they are voiced in political discussions more often than committed to print.

Social Darwinism went beyond glorifying rugged individualism although man is too obviously a social animal and group loyalties may at times transcend individual self-interests. (Statesmen and politicians, too, are adept at utilizing these emotions.) Social Darwinists supposed that human progress demands a struggle and competition not only between individuals but also between social classes, nations, states, and races (see Chapter 6). This kind of struggle was regarded as the superior, specifically human, form of natural selection. Gobineau in fact anticipated social Darwinism by proclaiming the existence of a biological master race, the Nordics, while Darwin was still working on his theories in private (see Chapter 3). Talking about biologically superior and inferior races soon became popular with influential people. The proponents of such beliefs were most vociferous in Germany; among them were Houston Chamberlain, who was born an Englishman, and Wagner, who is better remembered as a composer of music. The climactic denouement of racist ideas occurred in Hitler's attempt to conquer the world for the Master Race.

Racism was far from endemic in Germany, however. An ideologist of the British Empire announced that "the English were by nature a people destined to rule the inferior races of the world to the benefit of both parties." The United States Senate was told in 1899 that "God has not been preparing the English-speaking and Teutonic peoples for a thousand years for nothing but vain and idle self-admiration. . . . He has made us adept in government that we may administer government among savages and senile people" (quoted after Hofstadter 1955). I always remember a "gentleman" from Alabama who argued with some eloquence the inadvisability of spreading education among Mexicans, a race biologically fitted solely to be servants. Nor have theories of this sort appealed exclusively to large and powerful nations; group pride goes easily with imagining oneself a member of a small, downtrodden, but superior elite.

## Equality or Identity

The popularity of social Darwinism and racism in America and elsewhere declined in the thirties, because of a revulsion against Hitlerism. But perhaps not unexpectedly, the movement went too far in its protest and led to the rejection of some sound, together with counterfeit, biology. The stated aim of the eugenic movement, since its foundation by Galton in 1883, has always been preservation and improvement of the genetic endowments of human populations. However, during at least the first quarter of the current century the movement was captured by social Darwinists and racists. Manuals of eugenics (such as Popenoe and Johnson 1918) do not make pleasant reading nowadays. Even as recently as 1949, Keith argued for the evolutionary virtues of war, nationalism, race and class prejudices, and conflicts as agencies of biological progress of mankind! In 1953 Darlington declared that "some men are born to command, others to obey, and others again are intermediate" and that imperial races and governing classes "derive their dominant position from the fitness of their genetic character to the conditions they find or make for themselves."

The race and class distortions of eugenics must certainly be rejected as a travesty of science. Osborn (1951), one of the leaders of modern eugenics, courageously admitted it: "But belief in the influence of heredity overreached itself when it was used—as it still is all too often—to justify the continued domination of some particular caste or group." Yet the opposite extreme, the notion that all men are born not only equal but also biologically alike, is likewise a fallacy, perhaps less vicious in its immediate effects but pernicious in the long run. The mighty vision of human equality belongs to the realms of ethics and politics, not to that of biology. To be equal before the law people need not be identical twins.

Equality means that all humans are entitled to equal opportunity to develop their capacities to the fullest, not that these capacities are identical. And yet Adler, one of the co-founders with Freud of the psychoanalytic movement, was able to write:

> Investigators who believe the characteristics of an adult are noticeable in his infancy are not far wrong; this accounts for the fact that character is often considered hereditary. But the concept that character and personality are inherited from one's parents is universally harmful because it hinders the educator in his task and cramps his confidence. The real reason for assuming that character is inherited lies elsewhere. This evasion enables anyone who has the task of education to escape his responsibilities by the simple gesture of blaming heredity for the pupil's failures. This, of course, is quite contrary to the purpose of education.

That is from Adler's *Understanding the Human Nature*. Adler is right that heredity has been used as specious justification of ungenerous human behavior, but had he been acquainted with some modern biology, he might perhaps have seen that knowledge of the genetic conditioning of character and personality traits is helpful rather than "universally harmful" for understanding human nature. That characteristics of the adult may be noticeable in infancy has nothing to do with their heritability. It is also not true that character and personality cannot be inherited because only anatomical structures can be inherited. Not even structures are transmitted through the sex cells, except some very special ones called genes! All other characteristics of the organism, including character and personality, develop gradually, through interaction between the heredity and the environment. The educator will be helped rather than hindered in his task if he knows that the success of the educational process depends upon the right environment being provided for the optimal realization of the hereditary endowment of every individual, and that diverse hereditary endowments require diverse environments if best results are to be obtained (see Chapters 2–4).

Despite having been temporarily perverted by racists, the eugenical idea has a sound core: human welfare, both with individuals and with societies, is predicated upon the health of the genetic endowment of human populations. Health and disease, physical and mental, depend upon heredity as upon environment (see Chapter 5). That an appalling amount of human misery is due to defective heredity cannot be gainsaid. Measures on both the genetic and environmental sides will have to be taken if this misery is to be alleviated rather than enhanced. Osborn (1951) has rightly said that "eugenics is not in opposition to efforts to improve the environment, but in many cases a necessary supplement to their success." What is needed before all else is a better knowledge of, not a conspicuous disinterest in, the diversity of human heredities and of their environmental requirements.

For several decades preceding 1930, or even 1940, the biological approach to man was dominated by varieties of social Darwinism. This is not to say that biologists failed to discern its hollowness; perhaps precisely because of this, many biologists thought with the geneticist Bateson (1928): "I never feel eugenics is my job. On and off I have definitely tried to keep clear of it." This facilitated the prostitution of biology in Nazi Germany and elsewhere, and widened the breach between the social and biological sciences studying man. The trend of social science was to favor the view that biological ideas are utterly useless in attempting to understand human societies.

### Ectogenetic, Autogenetic, and Biological Theories of Evolution

Change, whether in biological evolution or in human affairs, may come from without or from within, from external or from internal causes. The genetic endowment of a species or a population, or the structure of a society, may be shaped by the environment. Evolutionary changes imposed from without the organism are called ectogenetic. Autogenetic theories hold, on the contrary, that evolutionary changes stem from within the organism; the environment might play a minor role—it might perhaps speed the evolution up or slow it down, but would not determine just what kind of change takes place.

Genetic or social change may also result from interplay between an organism or a culture on the one hand and the environment on the other. This is the view espoused in biology by theories subsumed under the labels of Darwinism, Neo-Darwinism, and more recently the biological, or synthetic, theory of evolution. Marxists, too, have claimed that their ideas about the development of human societies somehow parallel the Darwinian theories of evolution, but these are remote analogies at best and they need not concern us here.

Early in the current century there was much discussion among biologists who preferred ectogenesis and those who favored autogenesis as an explanation of evolution. These early theories have been shown to be untenable and as this is largely a dead issue at present, we may deal with it only briefly. Lamarckism (or, more correctly, Neo-Lamarckism), though thoroughly discredited, has been revived under the names of Michurinism and Lysenkoism. The environment is believed to alter the heredity directly, and the sequence of such alterations is assumed to represent evolution. Thus the alterations induced in, say, the inhabitants of warm climates will differ from those in cold climates, and different races, species, genera, etc., will eventually emerge. This may seem plausible at first glance; indeed, since the environment can modify the phenotype, why not the genotype also? Experimental evidence shows unambiguously, however, that environmentally induced changes in the phenotype, so-called acquired traits, are not inherited. Another stumbling block of Lamarckian theories has been their inability to explain why so many environmentally induced changes happen to be adaptive, i.e., improve the harmony between the organism and its environment. Why, for example, should muscular exercise strengthen the muscles rather than weaken them? Believers in ectogenesis have to resort to explicit or implicit assumptions, ascribing to the organism an inscrutable capacity to react adaptively to environmental requirements. But this is verbiage, not explanation. No theory of evolution which leaves the phenomenon of adaptedness an unexplained mystery can be acceptable.

Autogenetic theories envisage the world of life as something like a music box, the spring of which was wound up on the day of creation and which can play the tunes stored in it from the beginning but no new ones. The authors of theories called orthogenesis, nomogenesis, aristogenesis, etc. claimed that it was precisely to explain the apparent purposefulness of life that they assumed that this purposefulness was an intrinsic property of life itself. But does this really explain anything? The primordial virus or the primeval amoeba are alleged to have contained, in a latent state, all the organic forms which developed from them, including man. Evolution was a kind of strip tease, peeling off one disguise after another, until its final, and perhaps most nearly perfect, product stood revealed. And this process of gradual unwrapping of organic forms happened miraculously to fit the environments which prevailed when these successive forms made their appearance! Some of the evolutionary theories of culture likewise assume "rectilinear evolution," unfolding of potentialities contained in the culture itself, i.e., a kind of autogenesis.

Many evolutionary lines ended in extinction. How do the autogenetic theories reconcile this with the belief in an intrinsic purposefulness of life? They have to make an additional assumption—that the primordial organism contained the seeds not only of evolutionary progress but also of evolutionary senescence and demise. The career of an evolutionary line is compared with the life of an individual—there are, supposedly, evolutionary birth, youth, maturity, senescence, and death. This is good enough as a metaphor but unsatisfactory as an explanation.

For a time the autogenetic theories of evolution were in vogue, especially among paleontologists and comparative morphologists. They had rather more adherents in continental Europe than in England or America, a fact which Northrop (1950) relates to basic philosophic trends in the respective countries. It has been a great achievement of Simpson (1944, 1953) and of Rensch (1947, 1959a) to show that there is nothing in the evidence gathered by paleontology and morphology that would warrant the assumption of autogenesis, and that the data at hand are quite compatible with the biological theory of evolution.

This theory, let us make it clear from the outset, recognizes that adaptation to the environment is the main causative agent of organic evolution. In this sense, evolutionary changes come from the environment. Assertions made by Lysenko and his henchmen, that geneticists deny that the genetic endowment of a living species can be changed by the environment, are nonsense. The point is, however, that the changes are mediated by natural selection. And it is because the changes are brought about by natural selection that most of them further the congruity between the organism and its environment (Chapter 6).

On the other hand, the environment does not impose changes on the organism. The biological theory of evolution is not so artlessly mechanistic as alleged by some followers of autogenesis. The relations in evolution between the environment and the organism are best epitomized by Toynbee's winged phrase—"challenge and response." It is a living species which may respond to the challenges of the environment by adaptive alterations. But on the other hand, it may not respond adequately and may die out or become less well adapted. The response depends on the availability at the proper time and place of suitable raw materials—mutations and gene combinations. This poses a problem, of which more in Chapters 6 and 11.

## Organic and Superorganic

Ortega y Gasset has epitomized the point of view of many social scientists and humanists as "Man has no nature, what he has is history" (quoted in Kluckhohn 1949). The polar opposite is the view of Darlington (1953): "The materials of heredity contained in the chromosomes are the solid stuff which ultimately determines the course of history," and "the structure of a society rests on the stuff in the chromosomes and on the changes it undergoes."

The thesis to be set forth in the present book is that man has both a nature and a "history." Human evolution has two components, the biological or organic, and the cultural or superorganic. These components are neither mutually exclusive nor independent, but interrelated and interdependent. Human evolution cannot be understood as a purely biological process, nor can it be adequately described as a history of culture. It is the interaction of biology and culture. There exists a feedback between biological and cultural processes.

Darwin's successors strove mightily and succeeded in satisfying themselves and in convincing others that man is a zoological species and kin to everything that lives. But scientists are humans, and they are tempted to think that their discoveries explain everything instead of something. Some biologists fancied that, since man's ancestors were animals, man also is "nothing but an animal," and that their findings confer upon them a competence to plan man's future "from here to eternity." This is a specimen of "genetic" fallacy, to which geneticists are, we may be assured, no more prone than other people. The fallacy has, however, made biology an easy prey to social Darwinists, racists, and unscrupulous politicians.

Social scientists reacted to the exaggerated biologism by a converse exaggeration. Human evolution is evolution of culture, and —although a human genetic endowment was needed to initiate the process—"cultural evolution is an extension of biological evolution only in a chronological sense" (Steward 1953). Closely related is the so-called hypothesis of the psychic unity of mankind (see Mead 1953, 1954, Howells 1955), one of the formulations of which is that "there are no known differences among races of men which either interfere with or facilitate the learning of cultural forms." A similar view is a part of the official creed in the Soviet Union. Biological evolution gave rise to a being capable of doing "work" (i.e., of making and using tools). This was a "sharp break," "saltation," and "discontinuity" in man's evolution; he no longer evolves biologically; biological evolution is entirely replaced by social evolution, the course of which is charted in Marxist scriptures (Nesturkh 1958). The view that man's biological evolution has come to a halt and that he now evolves only culturally has been adopted also by some eminent Western biologists (rather inconsistently with their other teachings).

Dichotomies are tempting; to dichotomize is one way to clarify an argument. But the dichotomy of biological and cultural evolution is misleading if pushed too far. Viewed in the perspective of time, the development of the human symbolic faculty and cultural transmission was certainly a radical innovation. Cassirer (1944) rightly said: "This new acquisition transforms the whole of human life. As compared with the other animals man lives not merely in a broader reality; he lives, so to speak, in a new *dimension* of reality." Having produced man, the evolution of the cosmos has perhaps entered a new eon. And yet, man's capacity for culture did not appear all at once, complete and finished. The germs of this capacity, or raw materials from which it could be formed, exist in the animal world (see Hallowell 1960, and Chapters 7 and 8). Nor is it in the least probable that this capacity, once formed, is fixed forever and can neither develop further nor retrogress (see Chapters 11 and 12).

Biological heredity is transmitted through the sex cells; and barring mutation, nobody can transmit to his descendants any genes other than those which he himself received from his parents. Acquired traits are not transmitted biologically. Culture is wholly acquired by learning and imitation, and transmitted entirely by teaching and precept. How can processes so profoundly different interact and influence one another? An imaginary example may illustrate this. Suppose that, through a genetic change, mankind comes to consist entirely of women capable of unisexual reproduction (by parthenogenesis); in Muller's utopia (see Chapter 12), it might be possible to perpetuate a mankind consisting only of males. An enormous number of cultural traits and processes connected with sex and the division of labor between women and men would then lapse or be modified, while new ones would probably be worked out. Or consider a perhaps less far-fetched possibility. Mutual attachment between parents and children may persist for the duration of their lives, or parents may be spurned by their children, or vice versa. If persistence of family cohesion were biologically more advantageous than its early dissolution, or vice versa, genetic factors might conceivably be selected to bolster one or the other of these tendencies.

The interrelations between the biological and the cultural components of human evolution may be brought out perhaps most clearly if we consider that they serve the same basic function—adaptation to and control of man's environments. Most contemporary evolutionists are of the opinion that adaptation of a living species to its environment is the chief agency impelling and directing biological evolution. As stated above, the adaptation takes place through natural selection, which promotes the survival and reproduction of the carriers of some genetic endowments and inhibits others. The construction of man's body and the conformation of his intellect developed as they did because they made our species biologically highly successful (which is not saying that man's biological frame is the acme of perfection in all respects; see Chapter 12). The genetic basis of man's capacity to acquire, develop or modify, and transmit culture emerged because of the adaptive advantages which this capacity conferred on its possessors (Chapter 8).

Culture is, however, an instrument of adaptation which is vastly more efficient than the biological processes which led to its inception and advancement. It is more efficient among other things because it is more rapid—changed genes are transmitted only to the direct descendants of the individuals in whom they first appear; to replace the old genes, the carriers of the new ones must gradually outbreed and supplant the former. Changed culture may be transmitted to anybody regardless of biological parentage, or borrowed ready-made from other peoples (see Chapters 2–4). In producing the genetic basis of culture, biological evolution has transcended itself—it has produced the superorganic.

Yet the superorganic has not annulled the organic. The hypothesis of the psychic unity of mankind is justified to the extent that all members of the species *Homo sapiens* free of overt pathology are capable of learning a symbolic language and a variety of cultural forms. This only means that the capacity has become established as a species characteristic, like the erect posture, ability to subsist on diverse diets, absence of a breeding season, a brain size exceeding that of other living primates, and much else besides (see Chapter 10). But it does not follow that the genetic variability affecting the capacity to learn has suddenly evaporated in human populations. This is unlikely on theoretical grounds, and is contradicted by much evidence (see Chapter 4).

Why do so many people insist that biological and cultural evolutions are absolutely independent? I suggest that this is due in large part to a widespread misunderstanding of the nature of heredity. As will be shown in more detail in the following chapters, biological heredity, which is the basis of biological evolution, does not transmit cultural, or for that matter physical, traits ready-made; what it does is determine the response of the developing organism to the environment in which the development takes place. To say that cancer runs in families does not mean that every member of these families dies of cancer, and the inheritance of longevity does not guarantee a long life to some and a short one to others—apart from accidents, one's life may be prolonged or shortened by the environmental hazards which one meets, and by how one chooses to live (but this choice may, in turn, be partly conditioned by one's genes).

The statement that the "intelligence" (or whatever it is that is measured by intelligence tests and expressed as IQ) is in part conditioned by heredity does not mean that some people are born clever and others stupid. It only means that, when brought up in certain environments, some persons come to possess higher IQ's than others. If the former were placed in conditions unfavorable for mental development, their IQ's might decline, while the latter might acquire higher IQ's in more favorable and stimulating environments. A group of persons who show in a certain environment a lower average IQ than another group may exhibit a higher intelligence in another environment. This is not merely a theoretical possibility. American Negro draftees during the First World War had a lower mean IQ than did the white draftees. Some people who were greatly pleased by this had their enthusiasm dampened by the finding that the mean IQ of the Negro draftees from Northern states was higher, not lower, than that of the white draftees from Southern states (Klineberg 1935, 1954). All of which does not signify that intelligence is either hereditary or environmental; it rather suggests that the observed variation in intelligence has both genetic and environmental components. (For further discussion, see Chapter 4.)

### Human Evolution as a Unified Process

Tax (1960) has stated succinctly the relationships between human biology and culture:

> Culture is part of the biology of man, of course, even though it is passed on socially and not through genes. It is a characteristic of our species, as characteristic as the long neck of the giraffe. The general biological questions asked about the giraffe's neck are also questions to be asked about the civilization of man. Culture is part of the evolution of man. Man is evolving continually as a species, perhaps more rapidly now than any other species.

Human evolution is not completed or discontinued. This is true of its biological and its cultural aspects. These aspects are different enough to make it legitimate, and indeed necessary, to study them with the aid of different methods. As pointed out above, our genes determine our ability to learn a language or languages, but they do not determine just what is said. The structure of neither the vocal cords nor the brain cells would explain the difference between the speeches of Billy Graham and of Julian Huxley. The fact which must be stressed, because it has frequently been missed or misrepresented, is that the biological and cultural evolutions are parts of the same natural process. This process, human evolution, must eventually be brought under human control. Here mankind will meet the greatest challenge of its biological and cultural histories. To deal with this challenge successfully, knowledge and understanding of evolution in general, and of the unique aspects of human evolution in particular, are essential.

# 2. Heredity

We are completely irreplaceable. We are
not merely cases of universal Being.

JASPERS

EVOLUTION is change. Mankind has evolved; it is evolving; if it
endures, it will continue to evolve. Human evolution has biological
and cultural components. Man's biological evolution changes his
nature; cultural evolution changes his nurture.

Almost everybody believes that he knows a lot about human nature. Uniformity of opinion is, nevertheless, conspicuously lacking.
There have always been optimists who held that people are naturally good and reasonable, and pessimists who regarded them as weak,
foolish, treacherous, and deceitful. What, if anything, has biology
to contribute toward a better understanding of this issue? Perhaps
the chief contribution is an assurance that human nature is not
singular but plural. Most human natures are inherently neither
good nor bad, but become so in different circumstances. How this
diversity of natures arises is the problem to be considered in the
pages that follow.

A person is what he is because of his nature and his nurture. His
genes are his nature, his upbringing is his nurture. The same is
true of mankind as a whole: its nature is its gene pool, its nurture
is its environment and its culture. In the present chapter we shall
consider some basic facts and concepts of genetics relevant to the
analysis of human biological nature. This is not intended to be a
one-chapter summary of genetics. The purpose is rather to bring
out those principles and ideas which will be useful in the discussion
to follow.

## Heredity and Inheritance

Galileo had difficulties convincing people that the earth revolves
around the sun because everybody could see so clearly that the sun

revolves around the earth. Everyday familiarity with a natural phenomenon may be a hindrance rather than a help in its scientific study. In a like manner, because everybody "knows" what heredity is, the distinction between two quite different "heredities"—the biological and the legal—is not perceived. Most languages use the same word for "inheriting" property and "inheriting" genes. (The only exception of which I am aware is the Malay–Indonesian language, in which the word *warisan* stands for inheritance of property and *keturunan* for biological inheritance, the latter word coming from a root meaning "copying.") It is perhaps because they confuse legal and biological heredities that most people accept the idea that acquired traits may be inherited. Descendants of the wealthy are wealthy because they inherit the opulence of their parents; children of the poor are poor because they do not inherit wealth. Occasionally an offshoot of a poor family acquires wealth; the acquired wealth is transmitted to his offspring. It would seem that physical, behavioral, and cultural traits are inherited in the same way as wealth. In this family a son has inherited the shape of his head, his gait, energy, and business acumen; in that family a daughter has inherited her blond curls, her musical talent, and her position in society. If a parent acquires a taste for good wines or good books, this too is sometimes passed on to his progeny.

Actually the notion that biological inheritance is the same as the inheritance of property is wrong and the habits of thought flowing from it hamper the understanding of heredity. Almost four centuries ago (1580), Montaigne had the sagacity to see not only that the notion was wrong but also that he was unable to set it right. He believed he had inherited gallstones from his father, but since his father first felt this condition some twenty-five years after Montaigne was born and Montaigne himself was free of it until past middle age, he wondered how a father could transmit to his son something he himself did not have at the time of conception and how stones could be transmitted in the semen, which is a liquid.

## Preformism and Epigenesis

Toward the close of the seventeenth century Leeuwenhoeck and other Dutch microscopists discovered spermatozoa in the seminal fluids of animals and men—the semen was not mere liquid. The discovery was a fundamental one but became confused. One of the microscopists imagined that he saw within the spermatozoon a homunculus, a miniature likeness of the human body. This discovery was certainly spurious, but it fitted nicely the popular notions about heredity: if the human body is preformed in the sex cells, then all the traits and characteristics of the body and spirit may indeed be handed down from parents to children ready-made except for size. Heredity is then essentially growth—the homunculus enlarges, expands, and assumes the adult body shape.

If the body is all preformed in the sex cells, what about the sex cells of the next generation? The early biologists, liking consistency, did not shrink from assuming that the homunculus contains within its sex cells very tiny homunculi, too small, of course, to be seen, and these have packed within them still more diminutive ones. As befits a philosopher, Leibnitz (1646–1716) drew the ultimate conclusion: "I would believe that the souls which will one day be human souls have been present in the semen of their ancestors down to Adam, and consequently existed since the beginning of things, always in organized bodies."

This is, of course, nonsense, because matter (if not the soul) is not infinitely divisible—the homunculi of a few generations hence would have to be smaller than atoms. But let us not treat the preformist speculations with patronizing smiles. In modern biology the preformist mode of thought is by no means dead; it only takes more sophisticated forms. And it has the virtue of making some very complex problems look simple. Although the simplicity is deceptive, the idea has inspired some very useful working hypotheses. An outstanding recent example is the "one gene–one enzyme" hypothesis of biochemical genetics, which postulates that the body is preformed in the sex cells as a battery of enzymes. Preformism is, after all, one of the manifestations of the basic human conviction that the present contains the seeds of the future, as the past carried the seeds of the present. "There is no new thing under the sun," said the writer of Ecclesiastes.

The homunculus-type preformism crumbled when embryologists from Wolff (1759) to von Baer (1827) demonstrated that neither sex cells nor early embryos resemble miniature adults. The development is, rather, epigenetic: the developing body goes through an orderly series of transformations which gradually increase in complexity. The adult is simply a stage in the succession of bodily forms.

But if this is so, then just what do the progeny inherit from their parents? The only physical connection between generations is the sex cells, hence the sum total of biological heredity must be contained in the sex cells. To visualize the nature of their contents Darwin went back to preformation, albeit showing his misgivings by naming his theory "the provisional hypothesis of pangenesis." He assumed that each cell of the adult body sheds into the blood or other body fluids some "gemmules" which are diminutive copies of the cell that produced them. The gemmules then assemble in the reproductive organs and there form the sex cells. When the sex cells give rise to an embryo, the gemmules become transformed into new body cells of the types that formed them originally.

Darwin's hypothesis of pangenesis had the virtue of being testable and Galton, making the test, found the hypothesis wanting. He transfused blood between white and black rabbits and ascertained that this produced no spotted or piebald progeny. Strange to behold, the same hypothesis of pangenesis has been reinvented in our days in the U.S.S.R. by Lysenko, who either does not know or does not acknowledge Darwin's authorship. Stranger still, some of Lysenko's followers claim to have confirmed the hypothesis by experiments of blood transfusion in poultry and in rabbits.

Weismann's theory of the "germ-plasm," which maintained the opposite view, was most influential at the turn of the century, when the then fledgling science of genetics was making its first thrusts into the unknown. This theory need not be considered in detail here, but it should be noted that Weismann believed the hereditary materials in the sex cells consist of "determinants" and "biophores," which he construed to be just as straightforwardly preformistic as Darwin's gemmules. But the gemmules were supposed to originate in the body cells (then lodge in the sex cells and expand again to form the body of the next generation), while the biophores, although they governed the development of the body cells, did not originate there. Instead they passed from the sex cells of the parents into those of the progeny by way of the "germ-line," which Weismann believed to be thoroughly insulated from influences emanating from the body. As a consequence, the gemmules could make the characters acquired by the body transmissible to the next generation, while the biophores could not. This is, of course, the reason why all believers in the inheritance of acquired characters and in Lamarckian evolutionary theories have to assume the existence of something like gemmules, and why Weismann was able to give the first reasonable explanation of the failure of acquired characters to be inherited. (An excellent discussion of the history of these views can be found in Zirkle 1946.)

## Mendel and the Gene Theory

The rediscovery of Mendel's laws in 1900 placed the study of heredity on an entirely new foundation. The gemmules, biophores, and other "elements" of heredity invented before 1900 were products of highly ingenious speculation. Mendel's evidence for the existence of genes, like that for the existence of molecules and atoms, came from brilliantly conceived and well-executed experiments in the tradition of Galileo and Lavoisier.

Mendel crossed varieties of peas which differed in clear-cut characters: color, shape, and size. He then carefully recorded the various characters and their combinations in the hybrid progenies. An account of his results can be found in any genetics or biology manual and will not be presented here. It is necessary, however, to realize clearly how the outlook on heredity that derived from the work of Mendel differs from pre-Mendelian notions, because the latter continue to be entertained by those unfamiliar with biology and some of them are even implicit in our everyday language.

First, since it is easy to see that children usually partake of the characteristics of both parents, it seems that the hereditary "bloods" of the parents commingle and blend in the offspring; the heredity of a child should then be a mixture, a solution, or an amalgam of the parental bloods. Mendel has shown that this is not so. The parental heredities do not mix in the progeny; when the descendants mature and proceed to form their own sex cells, the components of the parental heredities segregate, mutually uninfluenced and uncontaminated by their generation-long sojourn in the same body.

Second, the physical basis of heredity is not a continuum, not a "blood" every drop of which transports all the properties of the organism at once. Instead, heredity is particulate; the hereditary materials in the sex cells are arrays of more or less discrete units. For these units Johannsen suggested in 1909 the short word "gene." Exact counts of the number of genes an organism carries in its cells are not now possible. A human sex cell is conjectured, on the basis of very indirect and insecure evidence, to contain more than ten thousand but probably fewer than one hundred thousand genes.

Third, although a child gets half his genes from his mother and the other half from his father, he receives only half the total genes (never all) each parent possesses. This is again contrary to the popular notion that each child inherits from his parents, and even from remote ancestors, at least a particle of every one of the qualities they had. What other view can be the basis of family pride in having some illustrious or eminent ancestor? But it is actually a matter of chance alone which genes a child will inherit from his parents. It is even more of a gamble which, if any, genes he will inherit from ancestors several generations back.

Fourth and last, heredity seems notoriously capricious to a casual observer. A child may resemble one parent in one trait and the other in another trait, may be intermediate between the parents in a third, and resemble neither in a fourth. The gene theory discloses a system in this apparent caprice.

## The Rules of Inheritance

As stated above, a human sex cell *(gamete)* carries some tens of thousands of kinds of genes, A, B, C, D.... Fertilization results in the formation of a new individual *(zygote),* who has each kind of gene in duplicate (AA, BB, CC, DD...), i.e., some tens of thousands of *pairs* of genes. Now, the two members of a pair (derived respectively from the mother and from the father) may be alike, $A_1A_1$. The individual is then *homozygous* for the gene in question. Or else the members of a pair may be somewhat different; there may exist two or more variants, *alleles,* of a gene, $A_1$, $A_2$, $A_3$..., more or less different in their action. An individual carrying two different alleles of some genes, $A_1A_2$, $B_1B_2$..., is *heterozygous* for these genes.

When a heterozygous individual, $A_1A_2$, forms sex cells, half of these gametes receive the allele $A_1$ and the other half the allele $A_2$. Now suppose that the mother is heterozygous for the alleles $A_1$ and $A_2$ and the father for the alleles $A_3$ and $A_4$. Four combinations of the two pairs of alleles are possible and have the same probability of arising among their children: $A_1A_3$, $A_1A_4$, $A_2A_3$, and $A_2A_4$. Full brothers and sisters may receive different genes from their parents and will accordingly have different genetic endowments. This very obvious and often striking fact, that siblings are genetically different, was hard to understand on the basis of the pre-Mendelian "blood" theories of heredity, but it is easily explicable by the gene theory.

Let us now consider the genetic situation from the standpoint of the parents rather than from that of the offspring. Suppose that a parent is heterozygous for a series of genes, $A_1A_2B_1B_2C_1C_2$.... Any one sex cell formed by such a parent will contain either the gene $A_1$ or $A_2$, either $B_1$ or $B_2$, either $C_1$ or $C_2$, etc. As pointed out above, a child will have inherited half his parent's genes but will not inherit the other half. A second child will also receive half the parental genes, but it is a matter of chance whether the parent will transmit the allele $A_1$ or $A_2$, $B_1$ or $B_2$, etc. to either the first or the second child. It can be shown that a parent of two children will have transmitted about one-quarter of his genes to both children, about half his genes to one child, and about one-quarter of his genes to neither child. A parent of three children has transmitted $12\frac{1}{2}$ per cent of his genes thrice (i.e., to each of the three children), $37\frac{1}{2}$ per cent of his genes twice (to two children), $37\frac{1}{2}$ per cent of his genes once (to one child), and $12\frac{1}{2}$ per cent of his genes to none of the three children. No matter how large a family he may raise, he is unlikely to hand down to posterity all his genes, while some of his genes will have been implanted in more of his descendants than other genes. Which of the genes will be transmitted several times and which not at all is, at this level, a matter of chance and chance alone. (See, however, the discussion of natural selection in Chapter 6.)

### The Genetic Basis of Individuality

Even in these days of science and technology triumphant, some philosophers have the audacity to restrict the competence of science to something less than the totality of the universe. Science, they claim, is concerned only with properties which many things have in common, only with events which recur, return, or can be reconstructed and reproduced; the individual, the unique, the concrete happening, in other words the living reality of existence, is apprehended better by artistic, philosophic, and religious methods of cognition. Bergson has stated this view succinctly: "Science can work only on what is supposed to repeat itself." I confess a measure of sympathy for such an opinion, but must nevertheless point out that biology not only recognizes the absolute individuality and uniqueness of every person and every living being but in fact supplies evidence for a rational explanation of this uniqueness.

Let us consider first the situation in the species of organisms which reproduce by sexual union and in which the individuals who mate are usually not closely related. Mankind is one such sexual and outbreeding species. An individual heterozygous for one gene, $A_1A_2$, produces two kinds of gametes, those with $A_1$ and those with $A_2$. A double heterozygote, $A_1A_2$, $B_1B_2$, produces four kinds of gametes—$A_1B_1$, $A_1B_2$, $A_2B_1$, and $A_2B_2$. With three heterozygous genes, $A_1A_2$, $B_1B_2$, $C_1C_2$, eight kinds of gametes are produced, thus:

$A_1B_1C_1$      $A_1B_2C_1$      $A_1B_1C_2$      $A_1B_2C_2$
$A_2B_1C_1$      $A_2B_2C_1$      $A_2B_1C_2$      $A_2B_2C_2$

Generally, an individual heterozygous for $n$ genes has the potentiality of producing $2^n$ kinds of gametes, each kind carrying a different combination of the parental genes.

It is obvious that with increasing $n$ the number of possible kinds of gametes grows rapidly. A heterozygote for 9 genes is capable of giving rise to $2^9 = 512$ kinds of sex cells. A human female may produce at most 200–300 mature egg cells during her reproductive life, although the number of eggs that function is, of course, much smaller, being limited by the long pregnancy characteristic of mammalian females, not by the number of eggs that may mature. Anyway, with 9 heterozygous genes, some of the possible gene combinations will surely not be represented among the egg cells. The number of spermatozoa produced is vastly greater: in man a single ejaculation may contain about 200 million of them. However, an individual heterozygous for 31 pairs of genes could produce more than two billion kinds of spermatozoa with different complements of genes—a number as great as the number of human beings now living on earth. With 50 or 100 heterozygous genes, the potential number of gene combinations far exceeds not only the number of humans who ever lived but the number of all living organisms put together.

Now, since both parents are likely to be heterozygous for many genes, the potential number of genetic endowments among the progeny grows even faster than the potentially possible kinds of gametes. If both parents are heterozygous for the same $n$ genes, there may be produced $3^n$ genetically different individuals among the progeny. If the mother is heterozygous for $n$ genes and the father is heterozygous for $n$ different gene pairs, $4^n$ genetically different individuals are potentially possible among their offspring.

These calculations are not a mathematical pastime. They have a profound meaning when applied to sexual, outbreeding species. If populations of such species contain many genes each represented by two or more alleles, then the potentially possible genetic endowments are inexhaustible and a vast majority of them can never be realized. Their number far exceeds the number of individuals who are born in any one generation or in all generations combined. It is, therefore, in the highest degree unlikely that any two persons (other than identical twins), whether relatives or not known to be related, have ever had, or will ever have, the same constellation of genes.

The validity of this conclusion can hardly be questioned, even though there is unfortunately no way at present to specify for just how many genes an average individual, or any particular individual, is heterozygous. The adherents of the classical theory of population structure will generally be inclined to make lower estimates than those of the balance theory (see p. 295), but this is disputed ground which we need not enter here. What really matters is that the very lowest estimate of the number of variable genes in human populations will still be in the hundreds, and this is amply sufficient to make the potentially possible gene combinations far more numerous than can ever be realized in people now living or those to be born in the future.

The mechanism of the Mendelian recombination of genes thus confers upon a living species a capacity to produce a prodigious abundance of ever-new genetic endowments. Mendelian recombination is, in turn, a corollary to sexual reproduction. In a very real sense, genetic individuality is bestowed upon living things by sex. Sexual generation is, however, not the sole method of procreation in the living world. Many lower organisms propagate asexually, by fission of the parent body into two or more parts which then become independent individuals. An asexual progeny will in general be genetically uniform and also genetically identical with the parents. A single bacterium may, within a day or two, give rise to many millions of bacterial cells all of which will have, provided that mutation does not intervene, the same complement of genes. Such genetically uniform, pure races or *clones* may also arise through certain forms of uniparental reproduction, by virgin birth (parthenogenesis). This occurs among plants as well as among animals (e.g., aphids and certain other insects).

Strange to say, asexual reproduction happens also in man (a good trap question for biology students). Identical twins arise through fission (asexual) of a single zygote (sexually produced, of course) into two (or more, in cases of triplets, quadruplets, etc.) parts, each of which develops into a separate person. Identical twins (or triplets, etc.) are, technically, members of a clone and as such are expected to be genetically identical. Is the existence of identical twins an exception to the rule of absolute uniqueness and unrepeatability

of every person? This would be so only if there were no agents
other than genetic diversity causing differences in the developmental patterns of individuals. But there are other agents, and no
two persons, not even identical twins, live identical lives; everybody
meets a world different from everybody else's. Identical twins are
different persons, although their reactions to their environments
may be expected to be, and actually are, more similar than the reactions of persons who carry different gene complements (see
Chapter 4).

## Genes and Unit Characters

Mendel's enduring achievement is the demonstration that heredity is not a diffuse "blood" but is particulate; it is an aggregate of
more or less discrete units, genes. After 1900 the Mendelian discovery was confirmed, extended, and developed by many investigators who worked with numerous species of animals and plants,
of higher as well as lower organisms. Many human traits, both
normal and pathological, were shown to be inherited in the Mendelian manner. Of course, neither Mendel nor his successors have
actually seen the genes. What they have observed is the segregation
and recombination of characters in the crosses of various species.
Most diverse characters—colors, shapes, sizes, external and internal
structures, physiological reactions, chemical compositions, behav-
iors—were shown to segregate and to recombine in hybrid progenies. The existence of genes in sex cells and other cells was assumed
to account for these observations. Geneticists may be said to have
followed the example of chemists and physicists, who assumed the
existence of molecules, atoms, electrons, and numerous other units
and particles to account for observed chemical and physical phenomena.

The nature of the relationship between a gene transported in a
sex cell and a character of an adult organism is a separate problem
and has its own history. Remember that Mendel's laws were redis-
covered in 1900 when Weismann's preformistic theory of "determinants" and "biophores" had its greatest vogue. Pioneer geneticists fell back to preformistic models when they tried to explain
how the genes, the components of hereditary endowment transmitted in the sex cells, influenced the characters of their carriers.
It seemed justifiable to answer this question as Herbert (1910) did:
"It has become evident that the individual is an entity made up
of hereditary unit-characters. The aggregate of such units forms the

individual. During the process of inheritance the units segregate, and by recombination form new individuals."

The unit-characters of the early geneticists were less preformistic than Darwin's gemmules or Weismann's biophores only insofar as they were not so rigidly localized in the anatomy. Thus the unit-character of color is not usually confined to a single cell but may affect the whole body. If you suppose that the unit-characters are enzymes, the shadow of the homunculus seems to be exorcised. Nevertheless, it would appear that those who have inherited the unit-character for color will be pigmented, while those who have not inherited it will have no color; if there be such a thing as a unit-character for intelligence, those who inherit it cannot help being intelligent and those who do not are predestined to be dull. Heredity has, indeed, been described as "the dice of destiny."

The original conception of simple unit-characters had to be given up when it was discovered that the visible traits of organisms are mostly conditioned by the interaction of many genes and most genes have pleiotropic, or manifold, effects on many traits. The hereditary materials are particulate, the development is unitary. This was clearly stated by Morgan (1919): "Even if the whole germ-plasm—the sum of all the genes—acts in the formation of every detail of the body, still the evidence from heredity shows that this same material becomes segregated into two parts during the maturation of the egg and sperm, and that at this time individual elements separate from each other largely independently of the separation of other pairs of elements." This statement remains valid today, although modern genetic work has shown that the "elements" of heredity can be split, even as chemical elements can be.

Although geneticists no longer speak of unit-characters, others continue to do so, as exemplified by the statement of Adler quoted in the foregoing chapter. The academic lag goes far to explain why so many social scientists are repelled by the idea that intelligence, abilities, or attitudes may be conditioned by heredity. To suppose that a sex cell transports a particle called "intelligence" which will make its possessor smart and wise no matter what happens to him is, indeed, ridiculous. But it is evident that the people we meet are not all alike in intelligence, abilities, and attitudes, and it is not unreasonable to suppose that these *differences* are caused partly by the natures of these people and partly by their environments. As a matter of fact, this is substantiated by the evidence to be discussed below.

### Genes and Chromosomes

To account for the results of their experiments on plant and animal hybrids, Mendel and his successors after 1900 had to assume that the sex cells carried something which they called variously "factors," "unit-characters," or "genes." It could not be specified just what the factors or genes were. At least two of the pioneers of genetics in the early days, Bateson in England and Johannsen in Denmark, refused to have their chaste symbolic genes entangled with anything so crudely material as a microscopically visible body or a chemical substance. Johannsen wrote (1909) that "the word gene is fully free from every hypothesis; it expresses only the ascertained fact that at least many properties of the organism are determined by special separable and therefore independent conditions, bases, or materials, in short what we shall call genes, which are present in the germ cells."

Other geneticists had less puritanic tastes. As early as 1903, Sutton and Boveri independently concluded that the Mendelian "characters" must be borne in the chromosomes of the cell nuclei. Morgan and his school, chiefly in the years between 1910 and 1935, and using mainly the vinegar fly, *Drosophila melanogaster,* as their experimental material, were able to work out the connections between genes and chromosomes in detail. How the chromosomes would appear under a microscope could be predicted from experimental results of a statistical nature, and experimental results became predictable from microscopic observations of the chromosomes. According to Morgan:

> We are led, then, to the conclusion that there are elements in the germ-plasm that are sorted out independently of one another. . . . These elements we call genes, and what I wish to insist on is that their presence is directly deducible from the genetic results (segregation in hybrids), quite independently of any further attributes or localizations that we may assign to them. It is this evidence that justifies the theory of particulate inheritance.

But further attributes are assigned to the genes on the very next page:

> The gene is a certain amount of material in the chromosome that may separate from the chromosome in which it lies, and be

replaced by a corresponding part (and by none other) of the homologous chromosome.

Moreover, Morgan definitely broke away from the old preformist notion that a gene "represents" in the sex cell a part, or a character, of the adult body. He wrote:

> First, each gene may have manifold effects on the organism, and, second . . . every part of the body, and even each particular character, is the product of many genes. . . . It may also be well to point out that even if the whole germplasm, the sum of all the genes, acts in the formation of every detail of the body, still the evidence from heredity shows that this same material becomes segregated into two parts during the maturation of the egg and sperm, and that at this time individual elements separate from each other largely independently of the separation of other pairs of elements. It is in this sense, and in this sense only, that we are justified in speaking of the particulate composition of the germplasm and of particulate inheritance.

### The Genetic Code

The work of the Morgan school transformed the abstract symbol-gene of the early Mendelians into the chromosome-segment gene. Another major advance in understanding the mechanisms of the transmission of heredity has resulted from studies on the chemical composition of chromosomes. This advance is very recent. It is, however, of greatest interest, since it may conceivably suggest a resolution of the centuries-old preformation–epigenesis puzzle. The way toward the solution of this puzzle was thickly sown with false clues, and this has retarded the understanding of the phenomena of heredity and evolution, especially, perhaps, of human heredity and evolution.

The chromosomes of all organisms, from lowly bacteria to higher plants and animals and man, are rather similar in composition. This is a remarkable fact. Not only different genes of the same organism but also the genes of different organisms are made of the same class of chemical substances, called nucleoproteins. There is yet another notable fact—the viruses, the simplest living things known, standing almost athwart the dividing line between animate and inanimate nature, also consist of nucleoproteins. It can hardly be a mere coincidence that all chromosomes as well as the viruses are so similar. The chemical constitution of the nucleoproteins evidently permits a molecular entity to reproduce itself, to make its own copy from other materials in the cell or in the environment. Self-reproduction is, then, the basic property of both genes and viruses. It is, in fact, the basic characteristic of life.

The question that inevitably presents itself is, where does the

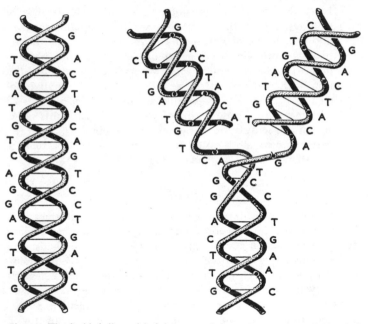

*Figure 1.* The double-helix model of the gene and chromosome structure *(left)* and of its replication *(right)* suggested by the Watson–Crick hypothesis. The genetic "alphabet" of four nucleotides: A—adenine, C—cytosine, G—guanine, and T—thymine.

gene specificity reside? What makes different genes influence the development of the organism in different ways? The protein fraction of the nucleoprotein has long been held the likely carrier of the specificity, but an overwhelming amount of recent evidence points rather to the nucleic acid fraction. The nucleic acid fraction of the nucleoproteins of all chromosomes consists predominantly, though not exclusively, of very remarkable substances called deoxyribonucleic acids (DNA). Only in the simplest plant viruses the

DNA is replaced by ribose nucleic acid (RNA). The chemical properties of DNA provide a possible basis for an exact copying of
every detail of the molecular structure. This is, of course, essential
for any gene. For no matter what other function a gene may have,
its most indispensable activity is to make a copy of itself in the interval between any two divisions of the cell that carries it. This is
necessary if all cells composing a body are to be provided with a
full gene complement.

Watson and Crick (1953) have proposed a hypothetical model
of the molecular structure of DNA that may explain how the reduplication of this structure takes place. A great amount of research by
many investigators has since given strong support to this hypothesis,
and although it will probably have to be modified in the future,
it is most likely correct in essentials, which are all that concern us
here. Molecules of DNA are double helices of polynucleotide
chains (Figure 1). Each nucleotide consists of a phosphate, a special
kind of sugar (deoxyribose), and a purine or a pyrimidine base.
Only two purines, namely adenine and guanine, and two pyrimidines, cytosine and thymine, are commonly found. The two chains
of the helix are held together by hydrogen bonds between the
bases. The crucial point is that an adenine base in one chain is
always bonded to thymine in the other and guanine is always linked
to cytosine. The two chains of a helix are thus exact complements
of each other. If the double helix separates into two single threads
each can re-form an exact copy of the original double structure by
the proper coupling of the four bases, adenine–thymine and guanine–cytosine.

An analogy may be useful to visualize how the molecules of DNA
can function to transmit heredity. Innumerable words, sentences,
and messages can all be represented by different combinations of the
twenty-six letters of the alphabet, as they can also be conveyed by
the two "letters" of the Morse code—a dot and a dash. The genetic
alphabet consists of only four letters—the four nucleotide bases,
A, G, C, and T. Four letters are nevertheless capable of specifying
the differences between countless genes. The number of possible
permutations of four letters in a word consisting of $n$ letters is $4^n$.
Even with two letters this makes sixteen possible words, as follows:

| | | | |
|---|---|---|---|
| AA | GG | CC | TT |
| AG | GC | CT | TA |
| AC | GT | CA | TG |
| AT | GA | CG | TC |

Suppose now that a gene is a section of the double helix of the polynucleotide chains containing ten base pairs. The number of possible permutations of four letters is then $4^{10}$, or 1,048,576. If the action of the gene depends upon the sequence of the base pairs, more than a million genes are possible. It is, of course, improbable that any kind of sequence of the bases will always make a functional gene, just as many letter combinations are nonsense combinations and not meaningful words. However, even if a majority of the theoretically possible sequences are nonsense combinations, practically an infinity of gene structures may arise if a gene is a section of the helix containing hundreds or thousands of nucleotides.

Some interesting, though of course entirely hypothetical, calculations made by Muller (1958) may be mentioned here. The amount of DNA in the nucleus of a human spermatozoon is close to four cubic microns, and the weight is a mere $4 \times 10^{-12}g$ (0.000,000,000,-004 of a gram). The weight of a single nucleotide pair being about $10^{-21}g$, there must be some $4 \times 10^9$, or four billion, nucleotide pairs in the chromosome complement in a human sex cell. Muller assumes, first, that the entire DNA in the sex cell is contained in the genes; second, that a substitution, loss, or addition of even a single nucleotide pair anywhere in the sex cell makes a new gene complement; and, third, that any combination of the nucleotides may exist (there are no "nonsense combinations"). Granting these (admittedly unproven and even improbable) assumptions, it follows that the number of possible genetic endowments is $10^{2,400,000,000}$. This is a very impressive number, at least until one realizes how completely fantastic it is. The number of atomic particles in the whole universe is believed to be a mere $10^{76}$. Let us then say simply that an infinite number of gene patterns is potentially possible and only an infinitesimal fraction of them can ever be realized.

## Gene Action

At the beginning of this chapter we mentioned Montaigne's belief that he inherited gallstones from his father. We now know that Montaigne was mistaken: he did not inherit stones, but he may have inherited a gene or genes that made their development likely. Geneticists often speak or write as follows: Person X has inherited from his ancestor Y a gene for brown eye color (or for his blood type, his musical ability, or such-and-such disease). Now what is a gene "for" an eye color like? Is it a granule of some pigment? Is a gene "for" musical ability some chemical that somehow

lubricates the auditory apparatus to make it keenly sensitive to
nuances of sound? Nobody really thinks so, and yet notions about
as crude as these are implicit in our language.

Genes do not resemble pigments, or substances which differenti-
ate the blood types or occur in a body afflicted with a certain disease. We now think of genes as sections of the molecular chains of
DNA, which contain genetic messages coded in particular sequences
of nucleotide bases. As Pontecorvo (1958) put it:

> The analogy of the genetic material with a written message is
> a useful commonplace. The important change is that we now
> think of the message as being in handwritten English rather
> than in Chinese. The words are no longer units of structure,
> of function, and of copying, like the ideographic Chinese
> characters, but only units of function emerging from charac-
> teristic groupings of linearly arranged letters.

The genetic code is stored in the deoxyribose nucleic acids; how
it is translated into messages that direct the development of the
organism is not yet understood. Several suggested explanations may
prove useful as working hypotheses. It is possible that the section
of the polynucleotide chain of DNA that acts as a gene serves as a
template for the synthesis of enzymes and other proteins, which in
turn direct the metabolic processes in the living cells. There are
some reasons to believe that the DNA does not act as a template for
the proteins directly but first transfers its "messages" to the ribonu-
cleic acids (RNA). These substances occur only in small amounts
in the chromosomes, but they are important constituents of the
cell cytoplasm, particularly of certain cytoplasmic granules in
which, or on the surface of which, protein synthesis actually takes
place.

One may then speculate that the arrangement of groups of "letters" in DNA and RNA nucleic acids (the four nucleotide bases)
may define the positions, in the molecular chains of the proteins,
of each of about twenty kinds of amino acids of which proteins are
built. Up till now the arrangement of the amino acids is fully
known in only a few proteins, among them insulin, an important
substance produced in animals by the pancreas gland. Sanger
showed that a molecule of insulin contains fifty-one amino acids of
fifteen different kinds. These are arranged in two separate chains,
which are joined together at two fixed places by bonds between
atoms of sulphur. Furthermore, the insulin molecules found in

different animals (cattle, sheep, pigs) differ slightly but significantly by the substitution of one or two amino acids in a strictly defined position in the molecule. How important such substitutions may be has been shown by Ingram in another protein, the red blood pigment hemoglobin. The hemoglobin of healthy persons differs from that of victims of sickle-cell anemia by the substitution of a single amino acid—out of the 300 or so of which hemoglobin is composed.

This last case is particularly interesting because sickle-cell anemia is known to be produced by a single gene (see p. 150). The working of heredity may, then, be visualized in the following manner. A certain sex cell differs from others in a single gene (this means, perhaps, a difference in one or in a few nucleotides in a single molecule in one chromosome) and if this sex cell functions in fertilization, this one molecule may start a snowballing series of consequences. When the gene-molecule causes one wrong amino acid to be inserted in the hemoglobin molecules produced in the body, the red blood cells with this sort of hemoglobin do not behave normally and, if all the hemoglobin is of the wrong kind (if the person is homozygous for the wrong gene), the individual develops a severe anemia and dies, usually before adolescence. This individual did not, strictly speaking, inherit anemia from his parents (both of whom were healthy), but he did inherit one wrong molecule, or one wrong part of one molecule, from each parent.

### Genotype and Phenotype

The biological inheritance of every person consists of genes received from his parents. The totality of the genes is the "genotype." The concept of the genotype framed by Johannsen (1909, 1911) is now extended beyond its initial usage: the genotype subsumes all self-reproducing bodily constituents regardless of their localization—the genes in the chromosomes as well as the plasmogenes in the cell cytoplasm.

The function of the genotype, or at least one of its functions, is to make more of itself: genes induce synthesis of their own copies. Some of the shorthand language used by biologists is grossly misleading if its metaphorical character is not understood. For example, what is the meaning of the often made statement that the genotype of a person does not change in his lifetime? Since the amount of deoxyribonucleic acids in the cell nucleus is doubled between the end of one cell division and the beginning of the next,

I obviously no longer have the genes which I had as an infant or as a fertilized egg cell; what I do have, instead, are true copies of these genes. It is even less accurate to say that I carry the genes of my remote ancestors, because I possess copies of only some of their genes. My genes do not change, but solely in the sense that they make new genes just like themselves.

It is an interesting speculation, but nothing more, that the development of the body is a by-product of the self-copying of the genes. The genes reproduce themselves by converting the materials taken up from their surroundings in the cell into their replicas. But cells and organisms, any organisms whatever, grow and reproduce by assimilation of food, in other words by intake of suitable materials from the environment. However, not all cell components give rise to their replicas, as genes do; for example, muscle and nerve fibers and various secretions are not present in the sex cells but are formed by, or from, other cell constituents, ultimately by or from genes.

A long, complex, and little known sequence of processes intervene between the genotype which was present in the egg cell at fertilization and the organism as we observe it. These processes are subsumed under the name "development." Development is neither completed in the womb nor concluded at birth. Although the embryonic, or fetal, development is the period when changes are rapid and spectacular, development goes on throughout life—infancy, childhood, adolescence, maturity, senility, and inevitable dissolution. Life is unceasing development, although some organisms, such as seeds and spores of plants, may remain quiescent for more or less long periods. However that may be, the organism can be observed and studied at any stage of the eternally recurrent metamorphosis of life. To designate the sum total of the observable characteristics of the organism, Johannsen has proposed the term "phenotype."

The phenotype changes throughout time. The changes in the phenotype of a person may be shown by, for example, a series of photographs taken at different ages, but it should be stressed that the phenotype includes more than the external appearance of a person: his physiology, metabolism, gross and microscopic anatomy, bodily chemical processes, even the appearance of the chromosomes in his cells—all are aspects of the phenotype, as are his behavior, thinking processes, and adjustment or maladjustment to society. In short, the phenotype is the total of everything that can be observed or inferred about an individual, excepting only his genes. The phenotype obviously cannot be inherited; it can only develop as life goes on. As stated above, only the genes are inherited or, more precisely still, only the genes in the sex cells, of which the genes that an individual possesses are true copies.

The genes interact with the environment, and the outcome is the process of development, or aging. Development results in an orderly succession of phenotypes. The genotype determines the reactions and responses of the developing, or aging, organism to the environment: it determines the norm of reaction. My phenotype at this moment has been determined by the norm of reaction of my genotype to the succession of environments that I have met in my lifetime; my phenotype tomorrow, or a year hence, will be determined by its present state, as modified by my responses to the environments that I shall have encountered in the meantime.

All the traits, characters, or features of the phenotype are, of necessity, determined by the genotype and by the sequence of environments with which the genotype interacts. There is no organism without a genotype and no genotype can exist outside a spatio-temporal continuum, an environment.

## Which Characteristics Are Hereditary and Which Environmental?

The man in the street believes that some traits are hereditary and others environmental. Belief in a sharp dichotomy between hereditary and environmental traits almost invariably goes hand in hand with a misunderstanding of the roles of social conditions and medicine and education: an hereditary disease is supposedly incurable, a disease contracted by exposure to some noxious environment may perhaps be cured; if the IQ of a child depends on his schooling, then it cannot be hereditary.

The dichotomy of hereditary and environmental traits is, however, untenable: in principle any trait is modifiable by changes in the genes and by manipulation of the environment. Contrary to the above-quoted opinion of Adler (p. 14), recognition of the genotypic component in human personality need not hinder the educator nor deprive him of confidence. Education is a form of management of the human environment, and except for a pathological minority, all human genotypes respond to some extent to this management. But the educator had better recognize that not all genotypes respond uniformly and different genotypes may profit most by different forms of management.

At this point, illustrations of what is meant by the statement that all characters or traits are both genotypic and environmental are in order. It is generally agreed that at least some forms of the disease known as diabetes mellitus are genetically conditioned, although it is still uncertain whether the disease behaves as a Mendelian recessive or dominant or whether there are several varieties of the disease with different genetic causations (see Chapter 5). Physiologically, the disease is due to a failure of certain cells in the pancreas to secrete enough of the hormone insulin, needed for normal utilization of blood sugars. This leads to the excretion of sugar in the urine, accumulation of fatty acids in the blood stream and blood vessels, and susceptibility to infections and other complications which may result in death. When diabetes is discovered, a reduction of sugars and starches in the diet is prescribed and in mild cases this treatment may suffice to remove the symptoms. In more severe cases regular injections of insulin are necessary to maintain health. Thus, diabetes can be "cured" by manipulation of the environment.

Most certainly neither the dietary rules nor the insulin injections change the "diabetic genes" and make the pancreas manufacture its own insulin, although they do relieve the morbid symptoms of the disease: health or disease is surely a condition of the phenotype, i.e., the well-being of persons with a certain genotype requires a sugar-free but insulin-rich environment. One may even speculate that a mankind consisting entirely of persons with diabetic genotypes could be reasonably well off in an environment where factories maintained a regular supply of synthetic insulin. Diabetes would then be an environmental disease caused by insulin deficiency, like the once-dreaded but now fortunately preventable scurvy, which is caused by a deficiency of vitamin C.

Conversely, malaria, syphilis, and influenza are environmental diseases: they arise because of infection with specific microorganisms, and persons who live in environments free of the infecting agents are free of the diseases. And yet the microorganisms infect only possessors of certain genotypes—particularly human genotypes. (Very few other animals that can be infected with the human forms of these diseases are known, and it is surely not accidental that susceptibility to syphilis, for example, is restricted to man's closest relatives among the primates.) Furthermore, not all human beings are easily infected with malaria or influenza, and there are good reasons to think that a part of the variation in susceptibility is genetic. It has long been believed that people of European origin are more likely to contract malaria and to have a severe form of the disease than natives of many tropical lands. Swellengrebel (1940) found such a situation in parts of Guiana: the human population and the malarial parasite had reached a sort of mutual accommodation, with most of the potential hosts infected but the disease rarely lethal. The discovery of Allison (1954a,b, 1955) that persons heterozygous for the sickle-cell gene are relatively immune to infection with quartan malaria is an even better example. Although this situation will be discussed in more detail later, we should here consider a population in which some persons carry the gene for sickle-cells and others do not. If such a population lived in a tropical lowland where quartan malaria was pandemic, the infection or noninfection with malaria might conceivably be a matter of heredity rather than environment.

## Hereditary and Environmental Differences

I certainly do not maintain that the nature–nurture problem is meaningless and that all human variation is always due as much to heredity as to environment. But to make the distinction between genetic and environmental effects on the phenotype meaningful, the problem must be stated with greater care than it often is.

It is easy to observe that some people have dark and others light skins; some enjoy robust health and others are handicapped in various ways; some are bright and others dull; some have kindly and others irascible dispositions. Skin pigmentation, health, intelligence, and temperament are all, like life itself, necessarily determined by the interaction of the genotypes with their environments. A question may, however, be validly posed: To what extent are the *differences* observed between persons due to genotypic or to environmental causes (Figure 2)? Or to put it another way: What part of the observed variance in a given trait in a given population is due to the diversity of the genotypes and what part to the diversity of the environments?

With the problem so stated, two things become apparent. First, the contribution of the genetic and environmental variables may be quite different for different characteristics: to which blood group a person belongs is decided, as far as is known, entirely by the genotype and not at all by the environment; which language a person speaks is decided entirely by environment and not at all by genotype, except that some low-grade mental defectives may be

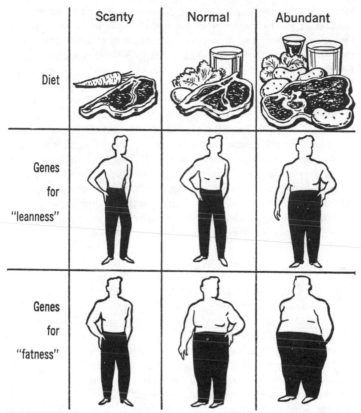

*Figure* 2. Gene-environment interaction. A person who has a gene for "fatness" may actually weigh less than a person with a gene for "leanness," if the former lives on a scanty and the latter on an overabundant diet.

unable to learn any language and the defect may be genetic. Second, the relative weights of the genetic and the environmental variables are not constant: they change in space and time.

Take human stature as an example. It has been known for a long time that children of tall parents are on the average taller than those of short parents, but by itself this proves nothing, since a parent–offspring correlation may be due to common genes or common environments. Studies of twins have shown, however, that monozygotic twins, when reared together or apart, resemble each other in stature more than do dizygotic twins. There is, then, a strong genetic component in the determination of stature. (The statures of the twins described in the classical work of Newman, Freeman, and Holzinger, 1937, were correlated rather more closely than in the newer study of Osborn and DeGeorge, 1959, see p. 82.) On the other hand, children of Japanese immigrants born in the United States are taller than their parents born in Japan. The environment is clearly responsible for a part of the variance in stature. If environment becomes homogeneous, owing to more uniform diet and child care, people will differ in stature mostly because of the differences in their genes and, conversely, in genetically homogeneous populations the environmental differences will account for a relatively greater part of the variance in stature than in genetically heterogeneous ones. There is clearly no single solution to the nature–nurture problem, and the matter must be studied separately for each character. Even then the results may have validity only for a population studied at a certain time and place.

### Heredity and Mutation

We have seen above that heredity is basically self-copying of the genes. Heredity is, therefore, a conservative force; if it were perfect, there could be no evolution. But the mechanism of heredity has a built-in feature, or, if you prefer, an inherent flaw, that occasionally makes a gene produce an imperfect copy. This is mutation.

No satisfactory theory of mutation has yet emerged. Taking the Watson–Crick hypothesis (p. 36) to be substantially correct, mutational changes in the gene might be envisaged as substitutions, deletions, or rearrangements of one or more nucleotide pairs in the chromosomal DNA chains. Other, so-called structural mutations have also been known in genetics for decades—multiplications, deletions, and rearrangements of chromosome sections, whole chromosomes, and chromosome sets.

It would be out of place in this book to review the present state of mutation studies (such reviews can be found in any modern textbook of genetics), but it must be pointed out that mutation is the ultimate source of evolutionary changes and also a source of much human misery, since most mutants that arise produce hereditary diseases, malformations, and weaknesses of various sorts. Mutation is one of the principal determinants of the evolutionary status of mankind. As pointed out before, the number of kinds of genes in a human sex cell is not known but is conjectured, on very insecure evidence, to be in the tens of thousands. Thus, even if each gene were able to mutate in just one way, tens of thousands of different mutations would be possible. Actually, many and perhaps all genes can mutate in many ways and mutation possibilities are, therefore, innumerable.

Persons, even brothers and sisters, usually differ in many genes (identical twins excepted); races presumably differ in more; species and genera in many more still. All these differences arose by sorting out the genetic raw materials provided by mutations in our close, remote, and very remote ancestors. No single mutation can, however, transform one human race into another or transform man into a different species or vice versa. This is so because genes as a rule mutate separately from each other. The probability that all the genes in a sex cell will simultaneously mutate to the states in which they were in our Pleistocene or Tertiary ancestors, or in which they will be in our descendants a million years hence, is infinitesimal and can safely be neglected.

Mutations are said to be random and undirected, and the meaning of these statements must be understood correctly. Mutations arise regardless of whether they are useful to the organism when and where they arise, or ever. If we place a population in a colder environment than that in which its ancestors lived, mutations conferring resistance to cold will presumably be no more frequent than they were before. If large body size is advantageous, mutation stimulating or inhibiting growth will be no more or less frequent than in a population which might profit by a reduced body size. If a gene mutates to a form producing an increased body size, this does not make further mutations of the same kind more probable than they were before. Evolutionary trends are directed by natural selection, and not by directed mutation. And what kinds of mutations are and are not possible in our species is determined by the historically established composition of our genotype. Thus the chemical changes that occur in a gene when it mutates are not random, but their effects on the adaptedness of the organism are.

## Frequency of Mutations

Mutations are rare or ubiquitous events, depending upon which way you choose to look at them. A given kind of mutational alteration of a given gene is rare; in other words, genes usually reproduce themselves accurately. But since the sex cells probably carry tens of thousands of genes, many of them contain one or more mutant genes which were not present in the parents who produced them (see Chapter 11).

Information concerning the frequency of mutations is indispensable for understanding human evolution. Unfortunately such information is hard to come by. It takes an enormous amount of labor to estimate the mutation rates of human genes even under the most favorable circumstances, namely for dominant changes which cause easily observable and fully penetrant alterations. The mutation yielding achondroplastic dwarfism in man is an example of such an alteration. The Danish geneticist Mørch found eight achondroplasts among some ninety-four thousand infants born in families in which neither parent was an achondroplast (see p. 114). This gives only a very rough estimate of the rate of this mutation of $4.2 \times 10^{-5}$ per generation, i.e., about forty-two sex cells per million produced by a normal (nonachondroplastic) person have a newly arisen mutant gene for achondroplasia.

It is not easy to accumulate such large numbers of observations. The difficulties increase still further under a variety of conditions: if the mutation is not fully penetrant, because a parent who seems to be free of a certain gene may actually carry it; if there are two or more genes producing superficially similar mutations, because the estimate of the mutation rate is then the sum of the rates for two or more genes which may be unequal; if the characteristics of the mutation resemble those produced by environmental changes, which might lead to overestimation of the mutation frequencies; and if the mutation is recessive, since the estimates for recessives require certain unverified and possibly wrong assumptions. These difficulties are discussed with utmost care by Neel and Schull (1954), who summarize their own data and those of other investigators as shown in Table 1.

The mutant genes listed in Table 1 cause mostly serious hereditary diseases or abnormalities (see Chapter 5). A majority of the mutation rates calculated lie between $10^{-5}$ (one mutation per 100,-000 sex cells per generation) and $10^{-4}$ (one mutation in 10,000 sex cells). It may be no more than an interesting coincidence that the estimate of the average mutation rates per generation for genes producing lethal or semilethal effects (i.e., hereditary diseases) in several species of Drosophila flies are also of the order of $10^{-5}$. To be sure, since human life is measured in years instead of days, as is the life of Drosophila, this means that, counting per unit time,

human genes are much more stable than those of Drosophila (Dobzhansky and Spassky 1954).

It is not suggested that $10^{-5}$ is the mutation rate of all human
genes or even the average mutation rate of human genes. In Drosophila and in other organisms well known in this respect, some
genes mutate more often than others. It is quite possible that the

TABLE 1

A review of the available estimates of the mutation rates in human genes
*(after Neel and Schull 1954)*

| Genes | Mutations per 1,000,000 sex cells |
|---|---|
| DOMINANTS | |
| Epiloia | 8–12 |
| Achondroplasia | 42–70 |
| Pelger's anomaly | 80 |
| Aniridia | 5 |
| Retinoblastoma | 14–23 |
| Waardenburg's syndrome | 3.7 |
| RECESSIVES | |
| Microphthalmos and anophthalmos | 10–20 |
| Albinism | 28 |
| Total color blindness | 28 |
| Infantile amaurotic idiocy | 11 |
| Ichthyosis congenita | 11 |
| Epidermolysis bullosa | 50 |
| Amyotonia congenita | 20 |
| Microcephaly | 30 |
| SEX-LINKED | |
| Hemophilia | 32 |
| Pseudohypertrophic muscular dystrophy | 100 |

human genes listed in Table 1 are more mutable than the average,
simply because it is easier to accumulate data on frequent than on
rare mutations. On the other hand, these genes are also selected
because the mutants in question are sharp and clear-cut: it is relatively easy to recognize an albino, an hemophiliac, or an achondroplastic dwarf. But not all mutations are so distinctive and many
cause slight and not easily detectable alterations. Moreover, the
evidence from organisms other than man, notably again from Dro-

sophila, shows that these small mutations are actually the most frequent type of mutational changes.

Muller (1950, 1954) surmises that small mutations are about five times as frequent as drastic ones which produce fatal hereditary diseases and spectacular malformations. The average mutation rate per gene is probably more than $10^{-5}$ rather than less. Leaning over backward, suppose that the two sex cells with which the life of every human begins contain only 20,000, or $2 \times 10^4$, genes. It will then be a conservative estimate that $2 \times 10^4 \times 10^{-5}$, or close to 20 per cent of all people, will carry one or more newly arisen mutant genes. Mutants are evidently not at all rare in human populations, nor are they rare in other organisms. This is a very important fact, the consequences of which will be discussed in Chapters 6, 11, and elsewhere.

# 3. Environmentalist Thesis and Hereditarian Antithesis

L'éducation de l'homme commence à sa naissance.
ROUSSEAU

When a child is trained completely,
his education is just as strong as his nature.
CONFUCIUS

DE TOCQUEVILLE wrote that democracy cannot endure without a religion and a philosophy. The philosophy of modern democracies, of the Western as well as the Eastern varieties, is the doctrine of equality, natural goodness, and the limitless perfectibility of man. This philosophy took shape in the eighteenth century, the Age of Enlightenment.

But if man is good by nature, why is it that so many people behave so wretchedly? The answer given by the "philosophes" of the Enlightenment was that man's good nature is subverted by bad environment, wrong upbringing, and corrupt political and social institutions. Change these institutions in accord with the demands of Reason and the inborn goodness will reassert itself. The French revolution, and more recently the Russian revolution, was believed by some to offer the requisite opportunities. But harmony and happiness have been slow in coming.

Apart from the statement of Confucius quoted above, the most ancient explicit assertion of the thesis, "All men are created alike by nature in all respects, both barbarians and Greeks," is that of Antiphon, a pre-Socratic philosopher of the late fifth century B.C. (quoted in Hadas, 1959). A little later, Isocrates thought that Athens "has made the name of Hellas distinctive no longer of race but of intellect, and the title of Hellene a badge of education rather than of common descent" (Hadas l.c.). Cicero, the Roman statesman, felt that "Nihil est unum uni tam simile, tam par, quam omnes inter nosmet ipsos sumus" (Nothing is so similar and so like another thing as we humans are among ourselves). The hereditarian antithesis was also stated early. Aristotle (384–322 B.C.) was sure that some people are free and others slaves by nature, i.e., while Greeks are naturally free, barbarians are just as naturally slaves, and that "those who are sprung from better ancestors are likely to be better men, for nobility is excellence of race."

Christ's parable of the camel passing through the eye of a needle is too explicit to be easily interpreted away, and for almost two millennia it has brought discomfort and a feeling of guilt to the affluent and powerful. Flagrant discrepancies between one's way of life and one's professed convictions are apt to make people unhappy. To assuage their consciences, the Creator is blamed for having made some people nobles and others commoners, some wise and others improvident, some talented and others incompetent. Different people are thus born to occupy different stations in life. Such, allegedly, is God's will, and to go against it is to sin.

### Nature and Nurture

Ashley Montagu (1955a), a very able modern exponent of the theory of the innate goodness of man, has stated:

> It is not evil babies who grow up into evil human beings, but an evil society which turns good babies into disordered adults, and it does so on a regimen of frustration. Babies are born good, and desirous of continuing to be good.

But if human nature is really good, why does it not resist the disordering influences of evil social environments? This is a fair question, because the human body does possess physiological mechanisms which combat and neutralize many bad influences of the physical environment. Some philosophes who were perhaps bothered by questions of this sort concluded that human nature is, to begin with, actually a void, an untenanted territory. The "tabula rasa" theory was apparently first stated clearly by John Locke (1632–1704). The mind of a newborn infant is, Locke thought, a blank page; the tale to be written there will be authored by the environment, by the conditions and experiences of living.

This point of view was and continues to be alluring to many, partly because it fits so nicely with another maxim also bequeathed to us by the Age of Enlightenment, namely that all men are born equal. Here one must guard against confusion, because the principle of equality and the tabula rasa notion refer to entirely different matters: equality is purely an ethical, a juridical, tenet (see pp. 13–15), and people do not need to be biologically (genotypically or phenotypically) alike to be equal before God and the Law. But undeniably, if you want to prove the principle of equality to a doubter, identity at birth will be a weighty argument, even though this be an equality of identical blankness.

Such ideas naturally did not appeal to believers in God-given inequality, but they felt their belief had to be made scientifically respectable, too, especially with the advent of the Age of Science in the nineteenth century. This was done brilliantly by Gobineau, an historian rather than a biologist, in his *Essay on the Inequality of Human Races* (1855). Gobineau argued that all mankind's achievements must be credited to small, creative minorities, who conquered, subdued, and put to work the much more numerous but intellectually inert common herd. Although these minorities always belonged to the Nordic race of northern Europe, they somehow appeared in all kinds of remote places—Greece, Egypt, the Near East, India, and even, according to Gobineau's recent imitators, in China and Japan. Unfortunately they knew how to govern others better than themselves: they did not refrain from miscegenation, which somewhat ennobled the subject races but debased the Nordics, whereupon their cultures declined.

The best that can be said about Gobineau's theory is that it appears to give a scientific basis to both race and class prejudice. But it convinces only those who have already made the same discoveries all by themselves. A scion of the French nobility, Count de Gobineau sadly watched the bourgeoisie capture the seats of the mighty and prognosticated the doom of civilization. (See Barzun 1937 for an historico–cultural analysis of Gobineau's philosophy.) Darwin's theory of evolution, appearing soon after Gobineau's *Essay,* failed to impress him, and he quipped, "We have not descended from the apes, but we are rapidly getting there."

Francis Galton (1822–1911), Darwin's relative and younger contemporary and one of the outstanding biologists of the nineteenth century, was, like Gobineau, a firm believer in the supremacy of heredity over environment, or of nature over nurture, as he called it. He declared that "the instincts and faculties of different men and races differ in a variety of ways almost as profoundly as those of animals in different cages of the Zoological Gardens . . . ." However, Galton was not nearly so pessimistic as Gobineau: he was the founder of the eugenical movement, obviously predicated on the belief that things may still be set right, provided only that man wakes up to his biological responsibilities and controls his own gene pool at least as carefully as he controls the genes of his domestic animals and cultivated plants. A Marxist might point out, with good reason, that Galton belonged to the opulent stratum of British society, which, during the Victorian era, had no fears of approaching eclipse.

Environmentalists and hereditarians still hotly debate the nature–nurture issue, and extreme opinions are held by both sides. A variant of the blank page theory is accepted dogma in the Soviet Union (if we think biological differences may have something to do with what people are and what they can accomplish, we are accused of debasing men to the level of beasts), and Gobineau's views, duly vulgarized, were state philosophy under Hitler and still have convinced and often passionate adherents all the way from South Africa to New York City.

White (1949), an eminent anthropologist, believes:

> From a biological standpoint, the differences among men appear to be insignificant indeed when compared with their similarities. From the standpoint of human behavior, too, all evidence points to an utter insignificance of biological factors as compared with culture in any consideration of behavior variations. As a matter of fact, it cannot be shown that any variation of human behavior is due to variation of a biological nature. . . . In a consideration of the differences of behavior between people, therefore, we may regard man as a constant, culture as a variable.

Darlington (1953), an outstanding biologist, is equally emphatic in stating the contrary view:

> Owing to inborn characters we live in different worlds even though we live side by side. We see the world through different eyes, even the part of it that we see in common. . . . The materials of heredity contained in the chromosomes are the solid stuff which ultimately determines the course of history.

Pastore (1949) compared the sociopolitical views of twenty-four psychologists, biologists, and sociologists with their opinions concerning the nature–nurture problem. Among the twelve classified as "liberals or radicals," eleven were environmentalists and one an hereditarian; among the twelve "conservatives," eleven were hereditarians and one an environmentalist. This is disconcerting! If the solution of a scientific problem can be twisted to fit one's biases and predilections, the field of science concerned must be in a most unsatisfactory state. But the nature–nurture issue need not remain intractable forever: evidence that will permit evaluation of the relative roles of heredity and environment in human variability can be obtained, and there is no reason why it should be any less conclusive in man than in, for example, field corn or Drosophila flies. This is a goal to be striven for, however. In the pages that follow, a critical evaluation will be undertaken of the inadequate evidence now available.

## Characters, Traits, and Differences

It has been shown in Chapter 2 that only genes are inherited, in the sense of being physically transferred from parents to offspring via the sex cells. Neither psychic traits, such as intelligence or personality, nor physical ones, such as skin color or blood type, are inherited in this sense. Sex cells have no skin, no blood, no intelligence, no personality. The problem must be stated differently to be meaningful. What we want to know is what causes the differences we observe among people.

In everyday life we take it for granted that no two persons are completely alike. We identify people by their appearance, particularly by their facial features, but they also differ in the state of their health and in their behavior, manners, abilities, attitudes, tastes, preferences, idiosyncrasies, etc. Much less widely known are the innumerable and multifarious variations in anatomy, such as the shape of the stomach and heart valves and the patterning of the convolutions and fissures of the brain, and in physiological and biochemical traits, even among "normal," healthy people. (The latter variations have been reviewed by the eminent biochemist Williams 1953, 1956, and also by Penfield and Roberts 1959. An excellent review of variations in human behavior in people of different cultures may be found in Kluckhohn 1954.)

Now the differences we observe among people are obviously phenotypic differences, which may be caused by genetic or environmental variables or by the interaction of the two, not necessarily by only one or the other. And yet, again and again a genetic or environmental bias has let an author assume that one variation is genetic (or environmental) because another is known to be. (A genetic bias, for example, is evident in the two otherwise valuable books by Williams referred to above.) But analogies are simply not enough—the variations in some traits (e.g., blood types) appear to be entirely genetic, in others (e.g., the language a person speaks) entirely environmental, and in still others (e.g., stature, intelligence) partly genetic and partly environmental. Nothing less than conclusive evidence for each and every trait considered is satisfactory.

As shown in Chapter 2, the old-fashioned nature–nurture debates were meaningless. The dichotomy of environmental vs. genetic traits is invalid; what we really want to know are the relative magnitudes of the genetic and environmental components in the variance observed in a given trait, a certain population, at a particular time. The problem is thus transferred to a more sophisticated level, that of quantification or measurement.

### Specific and Ordinal Traits

But, one may ask, if certain traits are necessarily present in every human being—it would seem that man, by his "nature," must have two eyes but only one mouth, an "instinct" to obtain milk from his mother's breast, and a sexual drive—are they not inborn or hereditary? Such a question is trivial, because without genes and environment, there would be no eyes, no mouth, no sucking instinct, and no sexual drive. These traits are products of the development patterns found in all vertebrates—they are specific, ordinal, or class traits.

Another meaningless question, often enough solemnly discussed, is how many traits or characters there are in man. But "trait" or "character" is simply an abstraction, a semantic device, which an observer uses when he thinks, talks, or writes about an object, and there are as many traits as we see fit to make. Although variations of the trait "stature" do, obviously, make some people tall and others short, we may analyze stature as the size of the head, trunk, and extremities, the number and arrangement of the cells in different parts, the metabolic processes which result in growth, etc. Traits are expressions, or aspects, of the organism's developmental process, which, starting with a fertilized egg cell, gradually produces a body that reaches a certain size at a certain time, forms a mouth, and evolves a sucking instinct, a sexual drive, and much else that we may choose to notice, study, and describe. Now, it is legitimate to inquire how much genes and how much environment contribute to the observed aspects of the developmental process, but one must always keep in mind that the genes govern not the aspects but the process itself. (For more discussion of this point, see Dobzhansky 1956.)

It should not be supposed that specific and other group traits are not subject to environmental and genetic variation for they certainly are. Malformed fetuses are occasionally observed with only one eye (cyclopic monsters) or no eyes at all (anencephaly), and although I am not aware of recorded instances of otherwise viable infants born without a sucking instinct, sexual behavior (the overt manifestation of the sex drive), on the other hand, varies a great deal even within a single culture, as shown by the extensive, though perhaps not reliably quantitative, data of Kinsey and his collaborators (1948, 1953). (For cross-cultural comparisons of sexual behavior, see Kluckhohn 1954.)

The question to what extent the variations in specific and ordinal traits are due to environmental and to what extent to genetic modifications may be asked as validly as in the case of intraspecific individual differences. For example, there is some information to show that anencephaly occurs among children of older mothers more often than among children of younger mothers. This would seem to indicate that something in the intra-uterine environment of older women encourages this developmental accident. On the other hand, while the frequency of anencephaly in the general population is 0.2 per cent, a woman who has given birth to an anencephalic child has a 2.1 per cent chance of having her next child similarly malformed (Neel and Schull 1954). This may or may not indicate that only carriers of certain genotypes are prone to the developmental accidents that produce anencephaly. Although the causes of the variations in sexual behavior recorded by Kinsey et al. are mostly obscure, they are certainly amenable to analysis, and these investigators have noted some correlations between forms of behavior and social and educational backgrounds. One might also inquire whether the sexual behavior of identical twins tends to be more similar than that of fraternal twins, thus testing the hypothesis that some genetic conditioning may be involved (see Chapter 4).

## Human Culture and Socialization

Anaximander of Miletos (ca. 611–547 B.C.) fancied that all creatures living on the earth, with the exception of man, arose from mud warmed by sun rays; man alone arose by transformation from some other animal. It is questionable whether Anaximander is entitled to be regarded as the first evolutionist, but his reason for ascribing to man a mode of origin different from other forms of life is interesting: "whereas all other animals are speedily able to find nourishment for themselves, man alone requires a long period of suckling; and if he had been at the beginning such as he is now, he would not have survived."

Infancy in man lasts about sixteen months, childhood generally extends to the end of the ninth year, and puberty comes, on the average, during the fourteenth year in females and a year or so later in males. Sexual maturity in anthropoid apes is attained at about the age of nine, thus making the prereproductive period in man about twice what it is in apes (Table 2). Although a prolonged

TABLE 2

Growth stages in higher primates

| Species | Pregnancy (weeks) | First menstruation (years) | Complete growth (years) | Life span (years) |
|---|---|---|---|---|
| Gibbon | 30 | ? | 9 | 30 |
| Orang-Utang | 39 | ? | 11 | 30 |
| Chimpanzee | 33 | 8.8 | 11 | 35 |
| Gorilla | ? | 9 | 11 | ? |
| Man | 38 | 13.7 | 20 | 75 |

period of juvenile helplessness and dependency would, by itself, be disadvantageous to a species because it endangers the young and handicaps their parents, it is a help to man because the slow development provides time for learning and training, which are far more extensive and important in man than in any other animal. (Darwin's enthusiastic American follower, Fiske, 1909, has stressed this point.)

Man is an out-and-out social animal, not a solitary one. The human environment is before all else the society to which a person belongs, and a society is a complex of individuals bound by cooperative interactions that serve to maintain a common life. There are, of course, many social animals besides man, and certain insect species possess social organizations in some respects more elaborate than man's. But genetically stereotyped, instinctive behavior dominates insect societies (although some conditioning may also operate), while human ones are uniquely founded on culture, which individuals learn rather than inherit through their genes (Kluckhohn 1949).

There is a surfeit of definitions of culture, from which I have selected three. To Kluckhohn and Kelly (1945) culture is "a historically derived system of explicit and implicit designs for living, which tends to be shared by all or specially designated members of a group." To Coon (1954) culture is "the sum total of things that people do as a result of having been so taught," and to Linton (1955), "an organized group of learned responses characteristic of a particular society." Since culture is acquired by training, people are not born but learn to be Americans, Chinese, or Hottentots; peasants, soldiers, or aristocrats; scientists, mechanics, or artists; saints, reprobates, or virtuous mediocrities.

The above statement does not, of course, exclude the possibility that the possessors of some genes may find it easier or more attractive to become reprobates than virtuous mediocrities, or vice versa (see Chapter 4). But it is indisputable that nobody can become any kind of person unless he belongs to a society in which he learns certain "designs for living." Learning to become a member of a given human society is called socialization or enculturation. According to Hallowell (1953):

> The maintenance of any particular form of human social organization not only requires provision for the addition of new individuals by reproduction but ways and means of structuralizing the psychological field of the individual in a manner that will induce him to act in certain predictable ways.

## Disruption of the Socialization Process

It is reported that Emperor Akbar of India (1542–1602) ordered that a group of children be brought up without learning any language, thus testing the belief that such children would eventually converse in Hebrew, the language of God. Akbar's sound scientific approach, performing an experiment to test the hypothesis that language is inborn rather than acquired, produced a negative result: the children brought up by deaf-mute nurses spoke no language but communicated by gestures (see Kroeber 1917–1952).

One may suppose that if socializing influences were withdrawn from a child's environment and yet the child survived and grew up, his behavior would have little resemblance to that of any normal human. A literature, more extensive than reliable, has accumulated describing so-called wild children, allegedly brought up by animals, or under other aberrant circumstances (summarized in

Singh and Zingg 1942, Ashley Montagu 1955, and Anastasi 1958). Most sensational is the case of the two "wolf-children of Midnapore," reportedly brought up by wolves until they were captured in 1920 at about the ages of two and eight. Their locomotion was quadrupedal, their preferred diet consisted of raw meat and entrails, they were entirely without speech and howled like wolves, etc. The authenticity of the whole story has, however, been challenged on several grounds (see Ogburn and Bose 1959).

Davis (1940, 1947) has described the child of a feeble-minded mother who was kept under conditions of extreme isolation until she was six years old. When rescued the child could not speak, did not react when spoken to, was unable to walk, did not play with toys, did not cry, and smiled only when coaxed. Before she died some five years later she learned to walk and even to run, to play with toys and with other children, and, finally, to develop intelligible speech. But this case is weak too, because the child might have been feeble-minded and consequently abnormal even if exposed to socializing influences in her early years.

## Development and Maturation

The life cycle of any organism is a sequence of stages succeeding each other in a definite order. The order is there because the developmental events at a given age or stage are brought about by the preceding events. A baby learns to walk when it has achieved a certain degree of muscular control; reproduction can only occur after the hormonal system has attained some degree of maturity. Zoologists, anthropologists, and psychologists have prepared time tables showing the advent of the various stages of development under conditions regarded as normal for a given species or population. What interests us is how rigid the sequence and timing of the developmental events really are, particularly in the development of human behavior. Suppose that some developmental events are hastened or delayed by environmental or genetic causes; will the organism be able to compensate for this disturbance and revert to the developmental path it would have traversed if the disturbance had not occurred? Or will the whole subsequent pattern be altered? As experimental biology shows, there are no generally valid answers to these questions. Developmental regulations do often occur, but permanent modifications are not rare either (Waddington 1957). Reliable evidence for human development is hard to come by.

A most interesting experiment, dealing with a pair of presumably identical twin girls, has been described by Gesell and Thompson (1941). When the twins were between forty-six and fifty-six weeks old, one of them was "subjected to hundreds of hours of preferred and specialized training designed to improve her motor coordination, her neatness, her constructiveness, her span of attention, her vocabulary." This training, while it lasted, placed the twin so trained appreciably ahead of her "control" cotwin. When, however, both twins began again to receive similar treatment, the control cotwin progressed at a faster rate, until she equaled the other.

An even more drastic experiment was claimed by Dennis (1938). Starting at the age of one month, a pair of twin girls were supposedly reared for seven months under conditions of minimal social stimulation—they were only taken from their cribs for feeding, bathing, cleaning, and dressing, and the nurses did not speak or smile, reward or punish them, gave them no toys, did not fondle them, and kept them separated by an opaque screen in a sparely furnished nursery. Nevertheless, one twin was not retarded at all, and the other only slightly, in the attainment of the stages of smiling, babbling, laughing, sitting up, creeping, standing, walking, etc. The author concluded that "the infant within the first year will 'grow up' of his own accord." An independent confirmation of these results would be desirable.

Valuable data can also be obtained by observing prematurely born children and instrumentally delivered vs. spontaneously born babies (Wile and Davis 1949). There is some evidence, perhaps not statistically valid, that the prematures tend to show a higher incidence of certain infections and to develop some behavior problems. Infants delivered by Caesarean section do not seem to develop very differently from normally born ones. (This fact is hardly compatible with theories of "birth trauma" (see p. 65), since Caesarean babies should be free of such traumas or else suffer traumas of a different kind!) When Gesell and Amatruda (1941) compared the behavioral development of babies born about a month prematurely with that of normal ones, they found that all reached similar developmental stages at the same age, counting from conception rather than birth. Now, premature babies have the "advantage" of being exposed longer to socializing influences, but such influences evidently have to come at a certain stage of the bodily development to be fully effective. An impressive demonstration of the validity of this conclusion comes from experiments on the behavior of certain animals.

## Imprinting

The classic studies of Lorenz, described in a most engaging popular book (1952) as well as in more technical publications (Lorenz 1943, and others), concern a remarkably rapid and efficacious form of conditioning, which has been termed "imprinting" (see also Tinbergen 1951, 1953). In some birds, such as geese and ducks, the newly hatched chicks normally follow their mother when she moves, but if goslings hatched in an incubator see a man before they see an individual of their own species, they may follow him and run away from geese.

In the experiments of Hess and collaborators (summary in Hess 1959), mallard ducklings hatched in an incubator were placed in a circular runway where a male mallard duck dummy, emitting a recorded human voice, was moved about. The ducklings thus imprinted were later offered a male dummy with a human voice and a female dummy with a real female duck call. Four kinds of tests were made: (1) both dummies stationary and silent, (2) both stationary and calling, (3) the male dummy stationary and silent and the female calling, and (4) the male stationary and silent and the female moving and calling. If the ducklings were 13–16 hours old at the time of the imprinting (this is the critical age for imprinting), most of them preferred the male dummy and the human voice to the female dummy and the voice of a real duck. In a further test, the ducklings imprinted in the experimental apparatus were placed in a pond together with the various dummies and real female ducks with their young. The imprinted ducklings chose the dummies and avoided the females.

Hess (l.c.) and Klopfer (1959) further discovered that some individual ducklings are more easily imprinted than others, a variability that is in part genetic, and the progeny of the "imprinters" is more easily imprinted than that of the "nonimprinters." Differences exist also between different species of ducks and other birds. Thus, wild mallards show an excellent, and wood ducks a poor, imprintability. Klopfer (1959) discovered that visual stimuli are more important in some duck species, and auditory stimuli are more important in others. This difference seems to be related to the mode of life that is characteristic of the species in its natural habitat. Klopfer also suggests that some of the behavioral variations within a species are maintained by the advantages of heterozygotes (see balanced polymorphism, p. 150).

## Psychoanalysis

One of the impressive developments of our century is the growth of the branch of psychology known as psychoanalytic theory, or depth psychology, or Freudian psychology, from the name of its original founder, Sigmund Freud (1856–1939). According to Hall and Lindzey (1954), many thoughtful people believe that "Freudian thought is one of the main currents in the intellectual stream of modern life. There is scarcely any aspect of the contemporary scene that has not felt the impact of Freud's thought." Because of the intellectual acumen and versatility of Freud and some of his followers and successors, psychoanalysis has been related to many broad problems of sociology, history, anthropology, and philosophy. In recent decades it has fired the imagination of a part of the general public, especially in the United States, and become, perhaps, the most fashionable and talked about branch of scientific lore, with consequences that are not altogether wholesome, either for the public or scientific psychoanalysis.

I shall here attempt (following chiefly Hall and Lindzey 1954) to indicate the broad lines of the psychoanalytic approach to the study of human psychic development, insofar as it bears on the problem of environmental and genetic personality determinants. Perhaps Freud's most basic postulate is that many, in fact a majority, of the mental processes, both in normal and abnormal persons, are unconscious, so that the person in whom they occur is unaware, or only dimly aware, of them. The psychic apparatus is said to be composed of three layers or tiers, called the id, the ego, and the superego.

The id consists of drives or instinct-like basic needs which produce tension that can only be released by action directed toward their gratification. Freud assumed, as some other psychoanalysts did not, that the sexual drive is by far the most important component of the id, although in his later years he added another basic drive, the aggressive. Parts of the id are the only components of the psychic apparatus present at birth. In infants the sex drive is manifested in the oral region. A stage of anal eroticism follows, lasting until about the third year, when the genital or phallic stage begins. The ego develops later in childhood, before the tenth year of life.

The ego is concerned with the adjustment of the person to his environment. It is normally directed toward satisfaction of the drives of the id, but it also acts as an arbiter of the often conflicting desires engendered by the drives when they emerge on the conscious level. The ego acts through control of the musculature and use of the sense organs, memory, and language. The desires rejected by the ego are "suppressed," and "energy" supposed to be associated with those desires is pushed down into the unconscious or "sublimated" by being turned into something else. Thus the sex drive may be sublimated in artistic creation, learning, sport, or other activity. The superego contains a person's notions of right and wrong and his opinions and ideas about things, in short his moral code and his—partly subconscious—value system, what in everyday language is described as conscience or feelings of rectitude, propriety, and morality. In a "well-adjusted" person the ego and the superego act harmoniously. Drives frustrated by the ego or superego may, under some conditions, result in neurosis.

An infant, born with only some drives of the id, becomes truly human owing to a gradual development of the ego and superego in the socialization process, which directs this development along lines acceptable to or demanded by a given culture. The ego and superego come, accordingly, from the environment. Freud apparently regarded the drives of the id as a genetically determined species of group traits, of the kind discussed on page 56. He wrote, for example, that "in all that follows I take up the standpoint that the tendency to aggression is an innate, independent, instinctual disposition of man" (Freud 1930). However, his attitudes toward genetics were decidedly ambivalent. Being a perspicacious physician, he could not fail to recognize that some mental illnesses run in families, but, on the other hand, he believed in Lamarckian inheritance ("If nothing is acquired nothing can be inherited") and felt that genetic determination might frustrate his hopes of helping his patients. It is fair to say that he simply did not give much thought to the problem of heredity, an attitude perhaps excusable in a discoverer of a whole new field of knowledge (see Jones 1955–1957).

Psychoanalytic or depth psychology and genetics are not necessarily incompatible despite the fact that the contrary opinion is rather widespread in psychoanalytic circles. This opinion stems from the same old fallacy, that a trait or a function must be either environmental or genetic, while in fact it is usually both. The drives of the id may be subject to genetic variation, in intensity and perhaps in quality, and the same may easily be true of the components of the ego and the superego, in the sense that some persons may develop them readily and others only against resistance. Psycho-analytic theory would enhance its usefulness if it clarified the manner in which the personality develops in relation to genetically varying backgrounds, and discovered the methods by which these developmental processes could be controlled for individually and socially desirable goals.

## Drives, Symbols, and Birth Traumas

Freud's view of the id, antithetic to the belief in the innate goodness of man so eloquently proclaimed by the Age of Enlightenment, follows the Judeo–Christian tradition, which asserts that man's nature is corrupt because he has inherited Original Sin. The various schools of psychoanalysis and depth psychology are not, however, in agreement concerning the contents of the id with which man is born. As pointed out above, Freud held the sexual drive to be primary and the aggressive or destructive drive next in importance, but his erstwhile follower and later opponent Adler believed that aggression and the will-to-power were the primary drives. As Adler viewed the sexual drive, it was itself an outlet for the will to conquer and dominate. Frustration of this will results in the formation of "inferiority complexes"—an expression which has certainly become a part of the vocabulary of all would-be intellectuals.

Jung and his followers also have their theories; the school of Fromm and other schools do too. Jung believes members of the human species possess a "collective unconscious" which "contains all the patterns of life and behavior inherited from our ancestors, so that every human child, prior to consciousness, is possessed of a potential system of adapted psychic functioning" (Jung 1933). According to Fromm (1951), "we are not only less reasonable and less decent in our dreams but we are also more intelligent, wiser, and capable of better judgment when we are asleep than when we are awake." But he warned that this primordial wisdom, a "forgotten language" of archetypal symbols which directed the life of primitive men, is in danger of being lost by modern men. However, Fromm says, "Jung explains this phenomenon with the assumption of a source of revelation transcending us, while I believe that what we think in our sleep is our thinking, and that . . . the influences we are submitted to in our waking life have in many respects a stultifying effect on our intellectual and moral accomplishments."

Finally, Rank (1952) believed that the normal process of birth, the passage of the infant through the birth canal, deals the infant such a tremendous blow that his whole life becomes an effort to recover from the terrible "birth trauma." Intra-uterine fetal life is, on the contrary, so blissful that it is firmly, though subconsciously, "remembered," and a drive is set up which makes the goal of life nothing less than a return to the supremely comfortable quarters of the mother's womb. Man's culture is a tolerably successful contrivance to overcome the birth trauma, but when it fails the result is a neurosis which can be overcome only by a psychoanalytic "birth therapy." But how can a process biologically so indispensable as childbirth result in the traumatization of the whole species? Granted that the painfulness of childbirth is one of the biological disharmonies of human nature (see Chapter 12), would not a species saddled in addition with birth traumas have become extinct long ago?

Such theories are frankly puzzling to biologists (and to many psychologists, as well), but their mutual incongruity is not the sole reason for the puzzlement. Theoretical conflict is perhaps what one should expect in a new field groping for orientation. The more one becomes acquainted with the literature on psychoanalysis the clearer it becomes that the basic difficulty is a lack, or at least a relative scarcity, of reliable procedures for testing and verifying its theories. Indeed, there is a wide gap between what is said by patients on psychoanalytic couches and what is inferred by psychoanalysts concerning the dynamics of psychic development. (See the symposium edited by Hook, 1959, for a discussion of this situation.) And yet, it would be shallow to reject the whole matter as "unscientific." Psychoanalysis started as a therapeutic technique, and its ability to bring relief to victims of certain neurotic disorders must be taken as a measure of its validity. What light the psychoanalytic approach will eventually shed on the nature–nurture problem remains to be seen; despite the frankly environmentalist bias of many of its exponents, the discoveries of Freud and his successors are probably amenable to interpretation in agreement with concepts of modern genetics.

## Oedipus Complex and Hypothesis of Psychic Unity of Mankind

Among the people whom Mahomet's Koran permitted to see women's faces were "male servants who have no desire for women [i.e., eunuchs], or children who distinguish not the nakedness of women." Freud had a different point of view: children do notice the nakedness of women, particularly that of their mothers, and feel jealousy and hate for their fathers. How does this "Oedipus complex" arise? Very ingeniously Freud derived it from another, and virtually universal, human trait—the abhorrence of incest. Almost all cultures, including primitive ones, outlaw incest, and there have been repeated attempts to explain the prohibition as a consequence of the undoubtedly valid fear of inbred, biologically inferior, degenerate offspring. But this explanation ascribes a scarcely credible degree of biological discernment to a generality of people. It takes carefully collected data and the application of refined statistical methods to demonstrate a causal connection between impaired health and inbreeding (see Sutter 1958).

In his famous work *Totem and Taboo,* first published in 1913 (see Freud 1931), Freud composed an engaging myth describing our early human, or prehuman, condition. Our ancestors, so the story runs, lived in small bands, each dominated by a powerful male, the father, who arrogated to himself all available females, including his own daughters, and drove away all weaker males, including his sons. But the sons joined forces and slew and ate their father. Later they repented their deed, worshipped the dead father, swore to have no sexual commerce with their female relatives, seeking mates in other bands or tribes. This pact, renouncing incest and establishing the rule of exogamy (marriage outside the tribe), was inherited by all mankind. To Freud, a believer in the inheritance of acquired traits (see above), this may have been a credible assumption. Furthermore, together with biologists his contemporaries, Freud believed that the evolutionary history of the species is repeated, in an abbreviated form, in the development of every individual. Therefore, every human child passes through an "Oedipal phase" (see also Jones 1955–1957).

While most biologists paid no attention to Freud's speculations, most anthropologists at first took a rather dim view of them. Even if the events so skillfully depicted by Freud could be shown to have taken place in human evolution (and this was most doubtful), it would not begin to explain the great variety of incest taboos and systems of kinship that exist among different people (see Murdock 1949 and Levi-Strauss 1960). A change in attitude probably dates from the studies by Malinowski (1927a, b) of the natives of the Trobriand Islands (off New Guinea). The Trobrianders have a matriarchal society in which the Oedipus complex takes a form quite different from that discovered by Freud in his native Austria: the incestuous wishes are more likely to exist between brothers and sisters than between children and parents, and the boy feels repressed hostility toward his maternal uncle, not toward his father.

Do we still need to assume that genetic endowment influences in any way our receptivity for the culture in which we have been born and reared, or to which we have been exposed as a result of migration? Many anthropologists answer this question in the negative. The so-called hypothesis of the psychic unity of mankind (see Chapter 1) is stated by Mead (1953): "There are no known differences among races of men which either interfere with or facilitate the learning of cultural forms." Yet in the very next paragraph the hypothesis is severely restricted: "There are wide individual differences among human beings which must be taken into account; these may be grouped with varying degrees of probable correctness as attributable to sex, temperament, constitutional type, or other repetitive genetic factors." Now, these two paragraphs can both be true only if the following subsidiary assumption is made: the incidence of different temperaments, constitutional types, and other "repetitive genetic factors" is alike in all races of men. We may join Howells (1955) in querying

> whether an infant Nilotic Negro could in fact become a "complete" representative of Eskimo culture, and vice versa, or whether he would die trying. And have these two culture-environments put a really extreme pressure on the adaptation potential of the human species of recent times, and on rates of evolution through genetic segregation of existing material, or have actual mutations provided new adaptations?

## Mediating Variables

A school of thought that has acquired some degree of acceptance, particularly in the United States, assumes that the decisive influences which mold human personality are to be found in the environment of the child, particularly in his emotional relationships with parents and siblings. This view has been ably popularized, particularly by Ruth Benedict, Margaret Mead, and others. In the words of Benedict (1949), "identifications, securities and frustrations are built up in the child by the way in which he is traditionally handled, the early discipline he receives, and the sanctions used by his parents."

The amount of what popular psychologists call "tender loving care" that the baby receives during his first three years decides whether he grows up to be extroverted or introverted, self-confident and optimistic or timid and pessimistic, aggressive or submissive. The imprints of these early experiences are believed to be more permanent and less easily reversed than those resulting from the experiences acquired during childhood and adolescence. The personality structure, once established, becomes resistant to modification (Hallowell 1953). It is, indeed, a common disillusionment of those who try to reform, change, or educate their mates or their friends that people stubbornly relapse into their old ways.

Adorno, Frenkel-Brunswik, Levinson, and Sanford give vent to feelings shared by not a few anthropologists, psychologists, and sociologists when they write that "the conception of personality structure is the best safeguard against the inclination to attribute persistent trends in the individual to something 'innate' or 'basic' or 'racial' in him" (quoted after Hallowell 1953). But this terribly subversive "inclination" can be exorcized only by showing how different forms of "tender loving care" and of its deprivation determine different personality structures. Evidence bearing on this problem is virtually nonexistent, except in the field of national character studies, where attempts to identify the "mediating variables" have had, at best, only indifferent success. (See the review in Inkeles and Levinson 1954 and Kluckhohn 1954.)

The "swaddling hypothesis" of Gorer (Gorer and Rickman 1950) has achieved widest dissemination, though not acceptance. The practice of swaddling infants during a part or the whole of their first year has been for centuries an accepted folk custom in much of Europe and among some American Indians and others (Greenacre 1949). The infant is bound in long strips of cloth that usually hold the legs straight and the arms down by the side of the body and severely restrict freedom of movement. Gorer finds this habit induces in Russian infants an intense and destructive rage and a "feeling of complete loneliness and helplessness." The only outlet remaining for the infant's emotions are his eyes, and for this reason the eyes of adult Russians are particularly expressive and are considered "the mirror of the soul." Swaddling, Gorer claims, is "one of the devices which Russian adults employ to communicate with the child in its first year of life, to lay the foundation for those habits and attitudes which will subsequently be strengthened by all the major institutions in Great Russian society," and therefore "it would be psychologically intolerable for Great Russians to live for any length of time without an idealized Leader." On the other hand, since the infant is, at frequent intervals, unswaddled, cleaned, fed, and petted, he maintains that "what Russians value are not minimum gratifications—enough to get along with—but maximum total gratifications—orgiastic feasts, prolonged drinking bouts, high frequency of copulation, and so on."

The swaddling that has the above influences on the Russian national character is, however, the custom of many other people, and Benedict (1949) and Gorer and Rickman (1950) find that its effects differ depending upon exactly how it is practiced. Thus, "the Polish version of swaddling is quite different from the Russian," and, to a Pole, the "defense of his honor in his later life is the great approved means of unburdening himself of resentments and turning them into personal glory." Jews also use swaddling, but the way they do it gives different results: "Among the Jews, a child's obligation to his parents is discharged by acting toward his own children, when he is grown, as his parents acted toward him. His aged parents are cared for, not by a son in his role as a son, but in his role of a wealthy man contributing to the poor" (Benedict 1949).

The mediating variable, or "clue," to the American national character has been found by Gorer (1948) in the child's rejection of the father, craving for affection, and fear of loneliness. The Japanese character has to do, it would seem, with the toilet training of Japanese infants (Benedict 1946), and that of high caste Hindus to "desertion" of the 1–2 year old infants by their mothers (Carstairs 1958). These hypotheses of mediating variables have been sharply criticized by many writers, but defended by Mead (1953, 1954) and some others. Mead assures us that the statement, "Swaddling them as infants makes Russians incapable of freedom" is a caricature; it should be instead, "The prolonged and very tight swaddling to which infants are subjected in Russian child-rearing practice is one of the means by which Russians communicate to their infants a feeling that a strong authority is necessary." But what is the evidence on which even this more "modest" claim is based? The "swaddling hypothesis" was suggested by Gorer by the gestures and body movements of some adult Russians whom he observed (Gorer and Rickman 1950, p. 211).

Acquaintance with the literature on "mediating variables" and "clues" to national characters makes it obvious that what goes for evidence and for verification of hypotheses in this field is simply not up to the standards regarded as necessary in other scientific disciplines. Hypotheses which make the handling of infants responsible for the kind of adult personality that emerges have been useful in stimulating anthropologists to collect data on the upbringing of children in various cultures. However, they have failed, to date, to throw much light on the sources of variation in human personality traits. Kluckhohn (1954) is not being unduly severe when he writes that "work in this field, however, has suffered as a consequence of its being fashionable for the last decade or two. It would be conceded generally by anthropologists today that many publications have been hasty, overly schematic, and indeed naive."

## Language as a Molder of Thought

Man's possession of symbolic language is one of the most important, if not the most important, trait differentiating him from animals (see Chapters 1 and 8). In the words of Cassirer (1944), "Man has, as it were, discovered a new method of adapting himself to his environment. Between the receptor system and the effector system, which are to be found in all animal species, we find in man a third link which we may describe as the symbolic system." Now, although the capacity to learn any language is conditioned genetically (idiocy, some forms of which are genetic, is, in fact, defined as inability to talk or to understand language), the particular language which we learn is bestowed upon us by the culture in which we grow up. The reader of this book could as well speak Chinese or Swahili if he were brought up in Peking or in Zanzibar. Linguistic diversity is a fair example of diversity due to the environment (see, however, Lenneberg 1960).

Much interesting research and speculation has been stimulated in modern linguistics by a hypothesis that Sapir (1921) suggested and Whorf (1956) then advanced. They postulated that the language we speak is not only a vehicle but also a molder of our thought: "Far from being simply a technique of communication, [language] is itself a way of directing the perception of its speakers and it provides for them habitual modes of analysing experience into significant categories."

If the Sapir–Whorf hypothesis is valid, language may be one of the channels through which the cultural environment exerts its formative influence on human personality. This is exactly the inference drawn by Lee (1949): "People of other cultures than our own not only act differently, but they have a different basis for their behavior. They act upon different premises; they perceive reality differently, and codify it differently. In this codification, language is largely instrumental." For example, the language of the Trobriand Islanders lacks comparatives, and for the Trobrianders "being is evaluated discretely, in terms of itself alone, not in comparison with others." Instead of "my head aches," a Wintu Indian says "I head ache," and the English "my hands are hot" is rendered in Wintu, "I hands am hot." According to Lee (1956), the basis of Wintu thinking "is that reality—ultimate truth—exists irrespective of man. Man's experience actualizes this reality, but does not otherwise affect its being."

Linguists do not agree how far the Sapir–Whorf hypothesis can be pushed to account for the different modes of thought in different people. (See the symposium edited by Hoijer 1954.) The most successful applications of this hypothesis have been in comparing SAE (Standard Average European) languages with languages remote from them. Even there the hypothesis does not always fare well; thus, Hockett (1954), comparing English and Chinese, finds that "the most precisely definable differences between languages are also the most trivial from the Whorfian point of view. The more important and ostensible the difference is from this point of view, the harder it is to pin down."

Comparing some SAE languages with each other, it has been argued, for example, that since the English and Russian languages manage the tenses of their verbs differently, the speakers of English and Russian have different conceptions of time, duration, and becoming. This seems doubtful, to say the least: there is no idea or thought that can be expressed in one SAE language but not in another, although it may require a circumlocution. This is not to deny the fact, well known to any translator, that the apparently corresponding words in different languages often cover different ranges of meaning, and that a language may have curious lacunae for some concepts. Thus, Russian has no word for the English "efficiency," while English has no word quite corresponding to the Russian "ooiut" or the German "Gemut" ("coziness" and "snugness" come nearest but do not quite do it). However, it would be naive to conclude that speakers of Russian cannot understand efficiency, or that speakers of English do not appreciate ooiut or Gemut.

Another possibility that should not be dismissed out of hand is that the genetically conditioned differences between the modes of thought of different groups of people may come to be reflected in their languages. A third possibility has been suggested by Darlington in an amusing hypothesis (1953). He noticed the coincidence that, in Europe, people speaking languages having the *th* phone tend to have a higher incidence of the O blood type than do people whose languages lack this phone. Since no European population consists entirely of carriers of O blood and none lacks this blood type, Darlington argues that the *th* phone is simply more congenial to carriers of O blood and less so to carriers of other blood types. The majority, as it were, imposes upon the minority a common phonetics of the kind most agreeable to it. This hypothesis is perhaps more interesting as an example of the effervescence of a brilliant scientific mind than as a description of observable reality.

## Culturology

No culture, at least no culture that endures, can be simply an aggregate of independent learned traditions; it is rather "a historically derived system of explicit and implicit designs for living" (Kluckhohn and Kelly 1945, and p. 59 above). Now, even though biological phenomena are specialized patterns of chemical and physical ones, biology is not simply a branch of chemistry or physics; biological laws and regularities must be studied as such, they cannot be deduced from chemistry and physics. The systematic and organized character of culture makes it legitimate, even necessary, to discover the regularities and laws that may exist in its structure and development. It does not follow, however, that biology is irrelevant to the understanding of culture, even as chemistry is not irrelevant to biology. Yet this is precisely the point of view adopted by some students of culture (see Chapter 1). Its ablest exponent in the United States is Leslie A. White, who has proposed the name "culturology" for a study based on the premise that culture may "be considered as a self-contained, self-determined process; one that can be explained only in terms of itself." Therefore, "to introduce the human organism into a consideration of cultural variations is therefore not only irrelevant but wrong; it involves a premise that is false. Culture must be explained in terms of culture" (White 1949, 1959).

That behavior and personality are shaped by the culture in which a person is brought up is evident. But this does not exclude the participation of genetic variations as conditioning factors. The following argument of White is, therefore, not compelling:

> The biological factor may conceivably contribute something to the variation of behavior, but this contribution is so small in comparison with the influence of the cultural factor that it may be regarded as negligible. In short, the differences of behavior from one people to another are culturally, not biologically, determined. In a consideration of behavioral differences among people therefore we may regard the biological factor as a constant, and hence eliminate it from our calculations. [See another quotation from White on p. 54.]

What is, however, the basis of the assertion that the "biological" (genetic) factor is negligible? White is not quite an adherent of the blank page theory, since he admits at least that the differences between an idiot and a person of superior intelligence may be "biological." And yet he assures us that "human nature, biologically defined, is virtually constant—it has undergone no appreciable change in the last 30,000 years at least," although he concedes, a bit grudgingly, that the "native intelligence of the Java man might have been lower than that of modern man." It is argued that participation of genetic variables must be excluded because a person's behavior resembles that of other people in his culture more than that of his parents or others in their culture. This is the hoary misconception that "hereditary" traits are not modifiable by the environment, and that traits so modifiable are independent of the genotype.

White notes that different kinds of music were composed and enjoyed by the Viennese of 1798, the black people of Harlem of 1940, the English before 1066, the Italians of the time of Palestrina, and the Nigerians, Bantus, etc. Furthermore, musical styles may be adopted by people who did not invent them. Although this is good evidence that the musical tastes are not like blood types, set irreversibly by their genes, it does not contradict the possibilities that (1) the capacity to produce and enjoy music varies among individuals within a population, (2) the incidence of musical ability varies between populations, and (3) the kind of music that one prefers may in part be conditioned genetically.

With admirable consistency, White draws from his premise the conclusion "that all of the great discoveries or inventions that have ever occurred could have been achieved without a single 'genius,'

i.e., without the aid of anyone above the present average of intelligence." To produce a great discovery, he says, you "take a person of
average intelligence, give him excellent technical training, put him
in a well-equipped laboratory, and assuming some interest and enthusiasm on his part, how could he help but make some significant
discovery?" Interest and enthusiasm—there's the rub! Not all persons of average intelligence working in well-equipped laboratories
show interest and enthusiasm; not all of them have either the wish
or the capacity to acquire excellent technical training. Some people
of genius are really desirable to increase the probability that a significant discovery will be made, and such people may be the carriers
of not quite average genetic equipments.

Culture arose and developed in the human evolutionary sequence hand in hand with the genetic basis which made it possible.
That this genetic basis has not changed for 30,000 years, or since
Java man, is most unlikely; that it is completely uniform in all
human populations is improbable; that it varies from person to person within populations is certain. To exclude in advance any consideration of the genetic basis from the study of culture is contrary
to elementary rules of scientific procedure.

# 4. Equal but Dissimilar

My idea of society is that while we are born
equal, meaning that we have a right to equal
opportunity, all have not the same capacity.
MAHATMA GANDHI

"I HAVE MADE the four winds that every man might breathe thereof like his brother during his time. I have made every man like his brother, and I have forbidden that they do evil; it was their hearts which undid that which I had said." This utterance, ascribed to the Egyptian god Re, antedates by some four and a half thousand years the Declaration of Independence, which states: "We hold these truths to be self-evident, that all men are created equal." But, surely, Re as well as Thomas Jefferson knew that brothers very often look and act unlike. Brothers, though dissimilar, are yet equal in their rights to share in the patrimony of their fathers.

A newborn infant is not a blank page; however, his genes do not seal his fate. His reactions to the world around him will differ in many ways from those of other infants, including his brothers. My genes have indeed determined what I am, but only in the sense that, given the succession of environments and experiences that were mine, a carrier of a different set of genes might have become unlike myself.

It is sometimes said that the genes determine the limits up to which, but not beyond which, a person's development may advance. This only confuses the issue. There is no way to predict all the phenotypes that a given genotype might yield in every one of the infinity of possible environments. Environments are infinitely diversified, and in the future there will exist environments that do not exist now. The infant now promenading in his perambulator under my window may become many things. To be sure, he is not likely to grow eight feet tall, but we do not know how to obtain the evidence needed to determine how tall he may grow in some environments that may be contrived to stimulate growth. It is an illusion that there is something fundamental or intrinsic about limits, particularly upper limits. Every statistician knows that limits are elusive and hard to determine, most of all when the environmental conditions are not specified.

Even at the risk of belaboring the obvious, let it be repeated that heredity cannot be called the "dice of destiny." Variations in body build, in physiology, and in mental traits are in part genetically conditioned, but this does not make education and social improvements any less necessary, or the hopes of benefits to be derived from these improvements any less well founded. What genetic conditioning does mean is that there is no single human nature, only human natures with different requirements for optimal growth and self-realization. The evidence of genetic conditioning of human traits, especially mental traits, must be examined with the greatest care.

## Family Resemblances

Heredity is said to cause the resemblance between children and their parents. This definition is good as far as it goes, but it does not go far enough. Mendel found that some of the progeny of two dominant heterozygous parents will differ from them because of homozygosis for recessive genes. Heredity may thus make children different from their parents. Hence heredity is better described as the transmission of self-reproducing entities, genes (Chapter 2). The oldest and simplest method of studying heredity is, nevertheless, to observe resemblances and differences within and between families. Galton was the pioneer of systematic studies of this sort.

In *Hereditary Genius* Galton (1869) studied 300 families which produced one or more eminent men, the eminence being defined as attainment of a position of influence or renown, such as was achieved by about one person in 4,000, or 0.025 per cent, in the Eng-

TABLE 3

Numbers of eminent male relatives per 100 eminent men in 19th-century England *(after Galton)*

| Relation | Number eminent | Relation | Number eminent |
|----------|---------------|----------|---------------|
| Father | 31 | Grandson | 14 |
| Brother | 41 | First cousin | 13 |
| Son | 48 | Great grandfather | 3 |
| Uncle | 18 | Great uncle | 5 |
| Nephew | 22 | Great grandson | 3 |
| Grandfather | 17 | Great nephew | 10 |

lish population. Galton's eminent men were statesmen, judges, military commanders, church dignitaries, and famous writers and scientists. Table 3 shows that the incidence of eminence is higher in relatives of eminent men than in the general population, and that close relatives of eminent men are more likely to achieve eminence than more remote relatives.

Clearly, eminence "runs in families." But does it follow that possession of a certain genetic endowment is necessary or sufficient to attain eminence? Surely having influential relatives is helpful, even in societies with class barriers less rigid than those of nineteenth-century England. Galton was not oblivious of this possibility. But he dismissed it because he defined the genetic endowment of eminent men as that which, "when left to itself, will, urged by an inherent stimulus, climb the path that leads to eminence, and has strength to reach the summit—one which, if hindered or thwarted will fret and strive until the hindrance is overcome, and it is again free to follow its labor-loving instinct."

This sounds perilously close to circular reasoning. Galton's clinching argument seems whimsical at present, but it was taken seriously a century ago. Class barriers are less rigid in the United States than in England; it should be easier to achieve eminence in the former than in the latter country; one might accordingly expect that the United States will produce more men of genius than England; in point of fact, the opposite is true; therefore, according to Galton, to become eminent one must inherit genes that are more frequent in the English than in the American population.

His observations, though not his conclusions, have been repeatedly confirmed in different countries by investigators studying the pedigrees and descendants of persons of varying degrees of eminence, from the indisputable eminence of geniuses such as Darwin or J. S. Bach to the relatively puny eminence of the persons "starred" in *American Men of Science* or included in various "Who's Who" directories. (The works of Juda 1953 and Bloomfield 1955, as well as the critical review by Anastasi 1958 are recommended as guides to the rather voluminous and scattered literature.)

Although it has been found nearly everywhere that eminence runs in families, it is just at this point that one must proceed with the greatest caution. The environmental bias in the data is patent —other things being equal, a son may find his way smoothest if he follows the calling in which his father excelled. But to reject the data as throwing no light at all on genetic conditioning is unreasonable: notable development of certain special abilities does occur in persons who are possessors of special genetic endowments. The data on inheritance of musical talent are particularly abundant and convincing.

Among the fifty-four known male ancestors, relatives, and descendants of J. S. Bach, forty-six were professional musicians, and among these seventeen were composers of varying degrees of distinction. Granted that in many parts of the world it is customary for members of a family to seek their livelihood in the same profession; granted also that growing up in a family of musicians is propitious for becoming a musician; it is still quite unlikely that the genetic equipment of the Bachs had nothing to do with their musicianship. The recurrence of marked musical ability among the relatives of great musicians is so general a rule that exceptions are worthy of notice. No musical talent is known among the 136 ancestors and relatives of Schumann. Although the composer was married to a virtuoso pianist, none of their eight children possessed great musical ability (Verschuer 1957). Such exceptions do not disprove that musicianship is genetically conditioned; they only show that its genetic basis is complex.

## Correlations

Galton's student and follower Pearson endeavored to show that family resemblances in what he called "mental and moral characters" follow the same rules as those in physical traits, which in turn behave like known heritable traits in animals and plants (Pearson and Lee 1903, Pearson 1904). His study of the inheritance of human stature is a classic. The stature of a group of 1,078 men was observed to vary from about 60 to 79 inches, and among fathers of these men from about 59 to 75 inches, tall fathers having on the average taller sons. The correlation coefficient was found to be 0.51 (a coefficient of zero would indicate complete independence, and unity a perfect correspondence of the statures of fathers and sons).

The meaning of such correlation coefficients is unfortunately equivocal. Since a child inherits half of his genes from each parent and siblings have half of their genes in common and half different, a parent–offspring and sibling correlation of 0.5 would therefore be expected if (a) the trait studied were determined by several identical genes with additive effects (i.e., if each of the genes increased or decreased the stature by a certain amount, regardless of what other genes were present) and (b) if the trait in question were uninfluenced by environmental variations, or if the environment were uniform for the whole population. If the environment is not uniform and the trait is sensitive to environmental variations, any degree of correlation may, theoretically, be observed regardless of genetic conditioning. Correlation studies are nevertheless useful if the environmental conditions are controlled or analyzed.

A most thoughtful study of Conrad and Jones (1940) may be used as an illustration. Intelligence tests were given to 997 persons belonging to 269 families representative of rural populations of central New England. All were native born; variations in the economic status and educational opportunities were believed to be small compared to urban communities, and the cultural tradition in the region fairly uniform and stable. Different tests were given to children, adolescents, and adults, suitable for their respective ages. The correlations observed are shown in Table 4.

TABLE 4

Correlation between intelligence test performance of members of families in rural populations of New England *(after Conrad and Jones)*

| Relatives | Correlation | Persons studied |
|---|---|---|
| Like-sex siblings | +0.45 | 475 |
| Unlike-sex siblings | +0.54 | 439 |
| Parent—offspring | +0.49 | 501 |

All the correlations were positive, and most of them were close to 0.5. Moreover, the correlations between like-sex siblings (i.e., sister–sister and brother–brother) were no larger than between unlike-sex siblings (brother–sister), although similarity of sex should have made the environments of like-sex siblings on the average more similar than those of unlike-sex siblings. The correlations between siblings were not much higher than those between parents and their children, and yet, on an environmentalist hypothesis, one would have expected a greater similarity of nurture among siblings than among parents and offspring, which should lead to higher correlations between siblings than between parents and their children. The mother–son, mother–daughter, father–son, and father–daughter correlations were about equal; the belief that the mother has a greater influence than the father on the intelligence of the children finds no support in the data.

## Heredity and Environment,
### Operational Approach in Nonhuman Material

Studies on family resemblances, though suggestive, cannot be said to have rigorously proved anything. Relatives share common genes, but they also tend to share common environments. It is useful at this point to see how the nature–nurture problem can be approached with organisms that are more amenable to experiment than man.

It is well known that representatives of many species of plants differ in appearance when grown at sea level or in the high mountains. How does one go about finding the relative contributions of heredity and environment to these differences? There was at one time as much confusion among botanists about this matter as there is now among students of human variation. In the beautiful experiments of Turesson (1922) and Clausen, Keck, and Hiesey (1940, 1948, 1951), plants found growing in different locations were cut, each individual in three or more parts (barring mutation, the cuttings obtained from a single individual have similar genotypes), and the parts replanted in different environments: one at sea level, another at an intermediate elevation, and still another in the alpine zone of a mountain range.

The plants native at sea level often proved entirely unable to live in the alpine zone, where the warm growing season was too short for them to flower and bear seed. The plants native in the alpine zone grew taller at the mid-altitude and sea-level stations than at home, and yet nowhere near as tall as the plants native to these habitats. The conclusion is, then, that the differences observed between plants native at different elevations are in part genetic and in part environmental. Each plant has its own norm of reaction, and this determines how it will grow and what it will look like in a given environment.

Compared to a student of plants, a student of man works under a handicap: men cannot be cut into genetically identical pieces and made to live in deliberately chosen environments. Fortunately, however, nature has provided an opportunity for making observations on humans of about the kind that one would have wished to make had deliberately controlled experiments been possible: multiple births—twins, triplets, etc. It was again Galton (1876, 1883) who saw the opportunity and began using it. (The voluminous literature on genetic twin studies has been summarized by Newman

1940, Kallman 1953, Verschuer 1954, Osborn and DeGeorge 1959, and others.)

## Identical and Fraternal Twins

Twins are of two kinds. Fraternal (dizygotic, binovular, or two-egg) twins come from two eggs fertilized by two different spermatozoa. They are simply siblings who are born simultaneously, and they may be either of the same sex or of opposite sexes, and their genotypes are, on the average, as different as those of brothers and sisters who are not twins. Identical (monozygotic, monovular, or one-egg) twins come from a single fertilized ovum which happened to divide into two separate individuals. They are of the same sex and have, provided no mutations occur, identical genotypes. Just what causes multiple births of either the fraternal or the identical kind is not well known. There is some evidence that the tendency to twinning is genetically conditioned; the frequency of multiple pregnancies is about 1:70 in American Negroes and in some Europeans, and about 1:45 among the Japanese, while even higher rates have been reported in Southern Rhodesia, and lower ones in Vietnam (see Neel and Schull 1954 for references). However, these racial variations are due mainly to different frequencies of fraternal twins, the frequencies of identicals being more nearly uniform. In the American white population fraternal twins are about twice as numerous as identical ones (74 fraternals vs. 39 identicals per 10,000 births).

Identical twins, having the same genes, are comparable to the experimental cuttings made from the same plant in the experiments referred to above. Ignoring the possibility of mutation, all differences observed between identical twins are presumed to be environmental, and if their environments were exactly alike, they would be "identical" in phenotype. Of course, the environment is never precisely the same for two individuals, either of the human species or of any other.

Some identical twins are, as the name implies, impressively, indeed dramatically, similar not only in their facial features but also in the diseases they suffer, and in their behavior, habits, and careers —in short, in their whole lives. Does this mean that "the environment takes a back seat to heredity" in the determination of human variations? Such a conclusion does not follow from the facts. (See, however, Cook 1951 for an opposing view.) In the first place, instances of real or fictional near-identity of people attract more attention than do twins the similarity of whom is not so complete. It is necessary to study a fair sample of twins, not twin pairs hand-picked because they are very similar.

Critical evidence comes from comparing the *average* differences of a given trait as observed in identical and fraternal twin pairs. If the variations of a trait were rigidly genetic, as with the blood types, identical twins would always be alike, while fraternal ones would often be different. With a purely environmental trait, the average difference between members of identical twin pairs will be as great as that between the fraternal ones. And if a trait varies both genetically and environmentally, identical twins will be more alike on the average than fraternal ones.

Technical statistical considerations make it advantageous to express the intrapair differences in terms of variances (sums of squared deviations from the mean for the pair) divided by the number of pairs. One may then calculate ratios of the variances observed in fraternal twins $(V_F)$ and in identical $(V_I)$ twins. The greater the $V_F/V_I$ ratio for a given trait, the greater the relative importance of the genetic conditioning in the observed differences in this trait. Another technique is to compute the correlation coefficients between the measurements of a trait observed in members of the identical $(r_I)$ and fraternal twin pairs $(r_F)$. Higher correlations for the identicals are indicative of strong genetic conditioning. One may also calculate a coefficient of the heritability of the trait $h$, according to the formulae:

$$h=(V_F-V_I) \, / \, V_F, \text{ or } h=(r_I-r_F) \, / \, (1-r_F).$$

The value of $h = 0$ indicates that the variations are purely environmental, $h = 1$ that they are purely genetic, while intermediate values may be used as estimates of the relative contributions of the heredity and the environment in the group of persons studied.

## The Physique of Twins

Data concerning the physical characteristics of twins may be considered as a paradigm. This implies no belief that physical and behavioral traits must behave alike with respect to their genetic causation. The purpose is rather to illustrate some uses and limitations of the twin study method. Table 5 summarizes some heritability estimates obtained from the data of Osborn and DeGeorge (1959) on 59 pairs of identical twins and 53 pairs of fraternal twins.

TABLE 5

Heritability (contribution of genetic relative to environmental causes) of the observed variation in certain traits *(after Osborn and DeGeorge)*

| Trait | Males | Females |
|-------|-------|---------|
| Head breadth | 0.95 | 0.76 |
| Cephalic index | 0.90 | 0.70 |
| Sitting height | 0.85 | 0.85 |
| Foot length | 0.84 | 0.82 |
| Arm length | 0.80 | 0.87 |
| Stature | 0.79 | 0.92 |
| Waist width | 0.79 | 0.63 |
| Leg length | 0.77 | 0.92 |
| Upper face height | 0.71 | 0.72 |
| Upper arm muscularity | 0.68 | 0.53 |
| Thigh length | 0.65 | 0.68 |
| Head circumference | 0.63 | 0.70 |
| Chest breadth | 0.54 | 0.55 |
| Mouth width | 0.46 | 0.64 |
| Chest depth | 0.45 | 0.17 |
| Weight | 0.05 | 0.42 |
| Bizygomatic breadth | 0 | 0.68 |
| Head length | 0 | 0.53 |

Traits such as head breadth, cephalic index (the ratio head breadth : head length), stature, and arm, leg, and foot lengths show high heritability (i.e., in these traits identical twins are much more similar than fraternal ones); weight, bizygomatic breadth (width of the face), and head length in males show ostensibly no heritability (i.e., the identicals are about as variable in these traits as the fraternals). Now, the coefficients of heritability are sometimes higher in one sex and sometimes in the other. This may be simply a matter of sampling error, and the sex difference may disappear if more twin pairs are studied. On the other hand, it is quite possible that the gene differences (which are generally the same in both sexes) manifest themselves more clearly in the phenotype of one sex than in that of the other. Thus, the head shape (measured by the cephalic index) may be more widely variable in men (heritability o.90) than in women (o.70).

Compare now the heritability estimates obtained by Osborn and DeGeorge (Table 5) with those given by Newman and his colleagues (Table 6). The two sets of data agree well enough on stature, sitting height, and the cephalic index. But while Osborn and DeGeorge find little heritability of weight, especially in males,

## TABLE 6

Correlation coefficients (r) and heritability for certain traits in identical and fraternal twins *(after Newman, Freeman, and Holzinger)*

| Trait | Fraternal | Identical reared together | Identical reared apart | Heritability |
|---|---|---|---|---|
| 1. Stature | 0.64 | 0.93 | 0.97 | 0.81 |
| 2. Sitting height | 0.50 | 0.88 | 0.96 | 0.76 |
| 3. Weight | 0.63 | 0.92 | 0.89 | 0.78 |
| 4. Cephalic index | 0.58 | 0.90 | — | 0.75 |
| 5. Binet mental age | 0.60 | 0.86 | 0.64 | 0.65 |
| 6. Binet IQ | 0.63 | 0.88 | 0.67 | 0.68 |
| 7. Otis IQ | 0.62 | 0.92 | 0.73 | 0.80 |
| 8. Word meaning | 0.56 | 0.86 | — | 0.68 |
| 9. Arithmetic computation | 0.69 | 0.73 | — | 0.12 |
| 10. Nature study and science | 0.65 | 0.77 | — | 0.34 |
| 11. History and literature | 0.67 | 0.82 | — | 0.45 |
| 12. Spelling | 0.73 | 0.87 | — | 0.53 |
| 13. Woodworth–Mathews | 0.37 | 0.56 | 0.58 | 0.30 |
| 14. Tapping speed | 0.38 | 0.69 | — | 0.50 |

Newman et al. find a sizable heritability coefficient—0.78. Are these findings contradictory? Will more careful studies establish some fixed heritability coefficient? Not necessarily; it is possible that the investigators have obtained accurate enough estimates of the heritability of body weight in the persons studied. But it happens that the twins examined by Osborn and DeGeorge were mostly adults, while Newman et al. dealt with many growing children and adolescents, and it may be that the rate of growth at some ages is rather strongly heritable, while the adult weight may be more highly variable because of differences in nutrition, health, and other factors. Here is an interesting problem that would repay further study. However, the situation does illustrate an important principle—what is inherited is not the body weight as such, but the trend of the development of the body, which may result in different weights in different circumstances.

### Intelligence in Twins

Intelligence is, ostensibly at least, the most esteemed of human qualities. What makes some people bright and others dull? Practically everybody agrees that good upbringing and education sharpen the wits, while neglect leaves them undeveloped. But many people recoil from the idea that genes are in any way involved with intelligence, and this attitude almost invariably goes with a misunderstanding of what genes are and what they do. "Inheritance of intelligence" does not mean that one's wits are decided and fixed at conception or at birth; it only means that with uniform upbringing and education people's wits would continue to be variable. Many attempts have been made to disentangle and evaluate the environmental and genetic factors which affect intelligence. Studies in this field are beset with difficulties, and while some are more reliable than others, all have been subjected to criticisms, some justified and others captious to a ridiculous degree. (Excellent recent reviews can be found in Anastasi 1958 and Fuller and Thompson 1960.) In brief, the matter stands as follows.

To measure "intelligence" is not easy. Intelligence testing was started in 1905 by Binet and Simon in France, and developed in 1916 by Terman in America (the "Stanford–Binet" test). The tests for school children and adults consist of problems, mostly verbal, contrived to estimate, primarily, the ability to handle symbols, abstractions, and logical thinking. The tests for younger children are different, estimating instead the rates of maturation of sensory and motor coordination.

To "standardize" the test, it is administered to a sample of persons who are as representative as possible of the population for which it was designed. The "intelligence quotient," or IQ, is a score showing how the person tested compares with the average score in the standardization sample. IQs in the range of 90–80 are said to indicate dullness, and 80–70 is described as "borderline," 70–50 "feebleminded," 50–20 imbecile, while scores below 20 indicate idiocy. What IQ makes one a "genius" is not well agreed upon; some psychologists are lenient enough to consider an IQ above 125 as characteristic of a gifted child or even a genius, while others exact a minimum of 180.

The work of Newman, Freeman, and Holzinger (1937) is still a classic in its field. They studied fifty pairs of identical and fifty pairs of like-sexed fraternal twins, in which the cotwins lived together and usually with their parents. Most valuable are the additional nineteen pairs of identical twins, in which the cotwins had been separated, most before they were a year old, and reared apart in different families and often in different towns. Here, then, is the nearest approach possible with human materials to the division–transplantation experiments with plants referred to above. Table 6 summarizes the salient points of the results.

For all traits studied, the identical twins were more similar than the fraternal ones, as shown by the higher correlation coefficients. Note, however, that for the physical traits studied (Nos. 1–4) the correlations for the identicals are so high that the heritability estimates (computed as shown on p. 83) turn out to be 0.75–0.81. The identical twins reared apart are about as similar in these traits as those reared together; in fact, some of the correlation coefficients happen, by chance, to be even slightly higher for the pairs reared apart. The IQs of the identical twins (traits Nos. 5–7) are, likewise, more nearly similar than those for fraternal ones; the mean differences between identical cotwins amounts to 5.9 IQ points, and between fraternal cotwins to 9.9 points. Although some authorities find this conclusion debatable, the most reasonable interpretation of the data still is that, at least among the twins investigated by Newman, Freeman, and Holzinger, the performance on the intelligence tests was in part conditioned by the genotype. The coefficients of heritability turn out to be between 0.65 and 0.80; in other words, roughly two-thirds to four-fifths of the variance observed in the fraternal cotwins reared together may tentatively be ascribed to genetic conditioning, and the remainder to environmental differences.

The intelligence tests of the twins reared apart tell another part of the story. The correlations between the IQs of the identical twins reared apart are intermediate between those for the identical and the fraternal twins reared together. The mean difference between the twins reared apart was, on the Binet test, 8.2 IQ points, i.e., less than the 9.9 points for the fraternals but greater than 5.9 for the identicals reared together. What does this mean? The most reasonable inference would seem to be that the environmental differences to which these particular identical twins reared apart were subjected produced about half as much differentiation as was caused by the genetic heterogeneity among siblings.

The investigators rated the environments of the twins reared apart as relatively superior or inferior, according to the numbers of years of schooling the twins had, and the physical, social, and educational advantages they enjoyed. As could be expected, the twin superior in IQ was usually the one who had grown up in an environment superior to that of his cotwin, and vice versa.

The twins reared together were also given the Stanford Achievement Test, designed to estimate the degree of success in learning certain subjects taught in schools. With the different components of this test (Nos. 8–12 in Table 6) the heritability estimates turned out to be lowest for achievement in arithmetic computation and highest for word meaning and spelling. These results may perhaps be used as an illustration of what heredity does and does not mean. Surely, nobody is born with knowledge of the meaning and spelling of English or any other words. But some persons learn these things more easily than others, and the variation in the learning propensities has an appreciable genetic component. Speed and accuracy of arithmetic computation (which is, by the way, not at all the same thing as mathematical ability) is, on the other hand, something that, in the material studied by Newman, Freeman, and Holzinger, depends on practice and exercise much more than on innate predisposition.

### Man as a Part of His Own Environment

We have seen that comparison of the IQs of identical and fraternal twins studied by Newman, Freeman, and Holzinger suggests that the kind of "intelligence" measured by these tests is conditioned in part genetically and in part environmentally. Wingfield (1928), Hirsch (1930), Cattell, Blewett, and Beloff (1955), Cattell, Stice, and Kristy (1957), and other investigators have obtained data on twins that led them to the same conclusion. The factual evidence in this field of study is really not in dispute, but its evaluation is. Darlington (1953) believes that twin studies have "proved to be one of the foundations of genetics"; Neel and Schull (1954) judge that "the twin method has not vindicated the time spent in the collection of such data."

The results obtained from studies on twins have been subjected to captious and farfetched criticisms, especially by some psychologists who lean toward the views of the behaviorist school (see p. 96). That the twin study method has serious limitations is true enough. These limitations should be kept in mind, but they do not warrant summary rejection of the inferences concerning the heritability of psychic traits drawn from the data on twins. For example, it has been pointed out that most of the twins studied by Newman, Freeman, and Holzinger lived in middle-class American homes. If one could find and study cotwins brought up separately in different countries, in different cultures, or in very disparate economic circumstances, one would probably obtain lower estimates of the heritabilities of some traits, particularly intelligence. Conversely, a greater equality of opportunity and a greater uniformity of schooling and economic conditions would result in higher heritability estimates. These estimates should not be construed as measures of the "intrinsic," as contrasted with the "acquired," intelligence.

Other critics contended that, since the environments of identical twins are more nearly similar than those of fraternals, the greater resemblances among the former need not be genetic. (See Anastasi 1958 for references.) For example, because identical cotwins tend to be strikingly alike, parents, playmates, teachers, etc. treat them more similarly than they would be likely to treat fraternal cotwins.

The issue at stake here is what we mean by the environment of human beings. Not all environment is like weather, to which we are exposed but which we cannot change. Even lower animals move where the conditions "please" them. Men choose, control, and to some extent create their environments. How subtle may be the consequences of such acts may perhaps be exemplified by data on the excretion of amino acids in the urine of identical and fraternal twins (Gartler, Dobzhansky, and Berry, 1955). Among the small number of twin pairs covered by this study, some of the identical and fraternal cotwins lived and took their meals usually together, while others lived and ate apart. Now, the excretion patterns of the identical twins who lived apart were only slightly more varied than the patterns of those who lived together. On the contrary, the fraternal cotwins who lived together tended to be much more similar than those who lived apart. The explanation suggested is that identical twins tend to choose the same foods even when they live apart, while fraternal twins are more likely to make different choices.

Man is a part of his own environment: he influences his environment, as well as being influenced by it. The organism and the environment are really parts of an interacting system. It is true that identical twins are treated, on the average, more similarly than fraternal twins. Considered superficially this may seem to be a serious objection to the conclusion that the traits in which identical twins resemble each other more than do fraternal twins are to some extent genetically conditioned. But this objection is due to a complete misunderstanding. Indeed, why do parents treat identical twins more similarly than fraternal ones? Surely not because of any conscious decision to do so. In fact it takes careful study to diagnose twins as identical or fraternal, and parents do not usually know for sure to which of these classes their twin children belong. Identical twins are treated similarly because of their similarity in ap-

pearance, and also because they react similarly to their surroundings, which include parents and other people. In short, they are
treated similarly *because* they are genetically similar. After all, fraternal cotwins are as often as not different in sex; sex is a genetic
trait; and at least in our society nobody expects a boy and a girl
to be treated quite alike in every respect. (That the treatment may
be more or less similar in some other real or imaginary societies is
beside the point.) Other genetic differences may have effects analogous, though perhaps less radical, than the sex difference.

### Intelligence of Foster Children and Parents

Next to twin studies, studies on foster children have yielded most
valuable data bearing on the genetic and environmental conditioning of intelligence. If a child's IQ is determined entirely by his
environment, there should be no correlation between the IQs of
foster children and their biological parents, but a positive correlation with the foster parents. Conversely, a rigid genetic determination would give a positive correlation with the biological but not
with the foster parents.

When the pertinent evidence was critically reviewed by Woodworth (1941) and Anastasi (1958), this salient fact emerged: the
IQs of foster children were less positively correlated with those of
their foster parents than they were in a "control group," composed
of children and their biological parents, matched for age and other
characteristics with those in the "foster group." Data on the IQs of
foster children and their biological parents are hard to come by, for
obvious reasons, but the scanty observations available suggest that
these IQs are positively correlated.

At least some genetic conditioning seems evident. The conclusion has, however, been questioned on several grounds. Probably
the most serious difficulty is that, at least in the United States, the
adoption agencies endeavor to "fit the child to the home," i.e., to
match as far as possible the backgrounds of the biological and the
foster parents. Furthermore, it is important that children be
placed in foster homes as early as possible, in order to minimize
the influence of the original home. Finally, it would be desirable
to study the effects of foster homes with diversified environments,
but in reality children are rarely given for adoption in poor homes.
Despite these strictures, the evidence as it stands certainly favors
the view that both the genotype and the environment are important
variables in the determination of a person's intelligence.

## Primary Mental Abilities and Personality Traits

The notion that the IQ is a general measure of a person's "intrinsic" intellectual powers is naive. Definitions of intelligence have been numerous (see Goddard 1946), but none has proved satisfactory, except for the quaint one that intelligence is what is measured by the intelligence tests. The IQs are useful because they permit fairly reliable prediction of the probable success in school of the persons tested. What the tests measure is essentially scholastic aptitude; the most widely used tests are weighed in favor of verbal ability, comprehension and manipulation of symbols and abstractions, and to some extent mathematical ability. Persons who rate high in such tests will usually be regarded, in our culture, as "bright." Remarkable competence in the performance of some tasks may, however, be unaccompanied by commensurate ability in other fields. Rife and Snyder (1931) located thirty-three "idiot savants" in institutions for mental defectives in the United States. Among these, eight were capable of astonishing feats in calculations, eight were musicians, seven painters, and ten had other gifts (see also Anastasi and Levee, 1959).

In recent years much active research has been based on a hypothesis that people vary with respect to several or even many partly independent "primary mental abilities," or group factors. Just what these abilities and factors are, and how they are to be measured, is still not generally agreed upon. Cattell and his collaborators (Cattell et al. 1955, 1957) have made an interesting attempt to explore the heritability of the "primary personality factors," for descriptions of which the reader is referred to the original papers. The list is as follows:

1. Tender-mindedness vs. tough-mindedness
2. Nervous tension vs. autonomic relaxation
3. General neuroticism vs. ego strength
4. Will control
5. Impatient dominance, immaturity vs. sthenic emotionality
6. Cyclothymia vs. schizothymia
7. Adventurous cyclothymia vs. withdrawn schizothymia
8. Socialized morale vs. boorishness
9. Dominance or independence vs. submissiveness
10. Energetic conformity vs. quiet eccentricity
11. Surgency (i.e., cheerful optimism) vs. desurgency
12. General intelligence

Tests designed to measure these factors were given to 104 pairs of identical and 30 pairs of fraternal twins living together, 104 siblings living together, and 60 siblings living apart. A fairly complex mathematical technique was developed to obtain heritability estimates from such data. For the time being the authors consider their conclusions tentative. The indications are, however, that the variance observed in their materials in the factors 6, 7, and 12 is mainly genetic, in factors 5, 8, 9, and 10 the genetic and the environmental components are roughly equal, and in factors 1, 2, 3, 4, and 11 the environmental variance predominates. An exploratory study of "primary mental abilities," analyzed by methods developed chiefly by Thurstone, has been made for identical and fraternal twins. The results have been published in summary form only (Thurstone, Thurstone, and Strandskov 1953, Strandskov 1954, Vandenberg 1956), but strong heritability of some of the primary mental abilities seems indicated.

Variations in personality and temperament are about as noticeable as variations in intelligence, but the former are even more difficult to study. Personality tests and "inventories," methods for the description of attitudes and interests, and various "projective" techniques have been evolved by psychologists, but their application to genetic studies is largely a matter for the future. One of the pioneer studies in this field is that of Carter (1935), using the so-called Bernreuter Personality Inventory. Some of the results are summarized in Table 7.

TABLE 7

Correlations in identical and fraternal twins in their scores on the Bernreuter Personality Inventory *(after Carter)*

| Twin pairs studied | Identical (N=55) | Fraternal, like sex (N=44) | Fraternal, unlike sex (N=34) |
|---|---|---|---|
| Neuroticism | 0.63 | 0.32 | 0.18 |
| Self-sufficiency | 0.44 | −0.14 | 0.12 |
| Introversion | 0.50 | 0.40 | 0.18 |
| Dominance | 0.71 | 0.34 | 0.18 |
| Self-confidence | 0.58 | 0.20 | 0.07 |
| Sociability | 0.57 | 0.41 | 0.39 |

The results are suggestive though not conclusive, perhaps because of the limited number of twin pairs studied. Most or all of the traits listed in Table 7 seem to have perceptible genetic components, although none show a strong heritability. Experiences of living make people acquire or lose self-sufficiency and self-confidence, and yet genetic predispositions toward these characteristics seem to be discernible. Very little has been done toward genetic analysis of the various responses of people to standardized inkblots (Rorschach's test); the results so far are in part contradictory and inconclusive. (See Fuller and Thompson 1960.)

## Somatotypes and Body Types

"Academic taxonomy," wrote Kant in 1775,

> deals with classes; it merely arranges according to similarities; while a natural taxonomy arranges according to kinships determined by generation. The former supplies a school-system for the sake of memorizing; the latter a natural system for the comprehension; the former has for its purpose only to bring creatures under a system of labellings; but the latter seeks to bring them under a system of laws [quoted after Count 1950].

Attempts to distinguish "apoplectic" (short and fat) and "phthisic" (tall and slender) types of men go back to Hippocrates of Cos (460–375 B.C.); nevertheless neither a "natural" nor an "academic" taxonomy, neither a satisfactory labeling nor comprehension of human variation, have emerged.

The taxonomy proposed several decades ago by the German psychiatrist Kretschmer (one of the latest editions in 1951) is still in vogue, especially in Europe. Kretschmer and his predecessors and followers distinguish three "constitutional types," namely the pyknic (short, fat, rounded), the athletic (muscular, angular, wide-shouldered), and the leptosome or asthenic (tall, slender, narrow-chested). Each body build was associated with a certain type of personality, and with proneness to certain kinds of psychic disorders. Kretschmer's system shares the fatal shortcomings of all typological schemes in biology—extreme or "pure" types are established arbitrarily; they occur very rarely among real people; the generality of men enjoy the dubious honor of being regarded as intermediate, mixed, or even discordant (displastic) specimens. The idea implicit in most typological schemes, that the "pure types" were once upon a time the only existing ones and the intermediates arose from them by miscegenation, has no foundation. It is like supposing that all human dwellings came by mixing the Empire State Building with an Eskimo igloo.

To escape from the above pitfalls, Sheldon and his collaborators (Sheldon et al. 1940, 1942, 1949, 1954) recognize that the gradations between the pyknic, athletic, and leptosome extremes are continuous. They assume instead that people vary with respect to three "components" of their physique—endomorphy, mesomorphy, and ectomorphy—which they believed represent the relative develop-

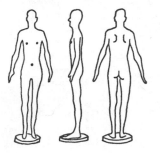 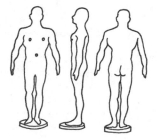

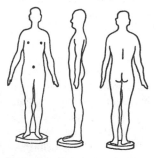 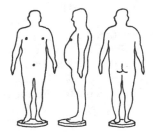

*Figure 3.* An extreme linear, or ectomorphic, somatotype *(upper left);* extreme muscular, or mesomorphic *(upper right);* balanced *(lower left);* and extreme visceral, or endormorphic *(lower right).* (After Sheldon, redrawn.)

ment of the endodermal (digestive, visceral), mesodermal (muscular, skeletal), and ectodermal (body surface, sense organs, nervous system) structures (Figure 3). The components are estimated visually, by inspecting standardized nude photographs from three aspects —front, side, and rear. Values from 1 (minimal) to 7 (maximal) are assigned for the degree of development of each component in each person. Only 88 of the possible permutations of the component ratings have been found among the 46,000 male subjects examined.

Each of the 88 "somatotypes" is described by three numerals, such as 352, which stand for the ratings of the endomorphic, mesomorphic, and ectomorphic components respectively.

Very bold claims have been made for association between the somatotypes (i.e., classes of body build) and temperaments, personality structures, and mental disorders. Thus, predominantly endomorphic physique goes together with "viscerotonia," i.e., love of comfort and good eating, sociability, lack of inhibition, and proneness to manic-depressive disorders; mesomorphic physique is linked with energy, assertiveness, love of physical exertion, domination of others, lack of compassion, and paranoid psychoses; and ectomorphy is connected with introversion, love of cerebration, privacy, paucity of energy and drive, and predisposition to schizophrenic psychoses. Going still farther afield, Sheldon and his followers find certain somatotypes characteristic of delinquent boys, generals, business leaders, people showing Christian renunciation, people who do or do not attend college, etc. The possessors of each somatotype are given descriptions in the following style: "rather unremarkable, moderately frail little fellows who seem never to be very well fed, or well loved, or even much attended to."

The entire somatotype story is disputed ground. Obviously, bodily form changes with age; it changes also with the state of nutrition, health, and disease, and with physical exercise or lack of it. (See Parnell 1954 and Hunt and Barton 1959 for further references.) Can the somatotype, the supposedly permanent and enduring base of the bodily form and of the mental frame, be discerned despite the changes and modifications? Sheldon maintains that it can be done by trained and experienced observers; the critics are not convinced. Indeed, Sheldon defines the somatotype "as a trajectory or pathway through which the living organism will travel under standard conditions of nutrition and in the absence of grossly disturbing pathology." The somatotype is, then, manifested as a series of phenotypes which result from a given genotype ("morphogenotype," according to Sheldon). Since the genotype does not change during an individual's life, neither should the somatotype. But since the only operational approach to the somatotype is through observation of the phenotype, which is admittedly subject to change, other methods are required to penetrate beyond the phenotype; Sheldon's claimed ability to do so is questionable, or at least not easily communicable.

The validity of the three components has also been challenged.

Why three, and not two, or four? Howells (1952) and Hammond (1957a, b) subjected this matter to most careful study, with the aid of a statistical technique known as factor analysis. The results are compatible with the view that ectomorphy and endomorphy are not independent components but form a single continuum—elongation and scarcity of fat, or roundness and adiposity. The second component is, then, greater or lesser development of muscularity.

Data of crucial importance for evaluation of the somatotype hypothesis have been obtained by Osborn and DeGeorge (1959). Their series of twins (see above) have been somatotyped by Sheldon. The heritability of the "components," as estimated by Osborn and DeGeorge, proved to be mostly quite low, namely:

|                     | Males | Females |
|---------------------|-------|---------|
| Total somatotype    | 0.36  | 0.61    |
| Endomorphy          | 0.45  | 0.45    |
| Mesomorphy          | 0.32  | 0.26    |
| Ectomorphy          | 0.19  | 0.74    |

From these figures it seems questionable whether the somatotype, as estimated by the techniques now used, is as significant a biological constant as it is claimed to be. And yet in the balance it still looks as if there are important biological constants underlying the observed variations of the human physique and temperament. The urgent task in this field is to discover methods of detection and quantification of these constants. In this respect, Osborn and DeGeorge's estimates of masculinity and femininity, as expressed in an individual's physique, are of interest. These are rated by recording the conformation of different parts of the body (arms and trunk proportions, waist measure, shape of the abdomen, buttocks, trochanteric pads and hip lines, thighs and lower legs). The composite score thus arrived at has shown, in the twins studied by Osborn and DeGeorge, a rather impressive heritability, namely 0.78 in males and 0.85 in females. It would appear that a meaningful measure of some biological constant is here available.

## Nature and Nurture in Condominium

In 1924, with nature-versus-nurture polemics close to their peak, J. B. Watson, the leader of the school of behaviorism in psychology and one of the staunchest partisans of the nurture hypothesis, wrote the following fighting lines:

> Give me a dozen healthy infants, well formed, and my own special world to bring them up in, and I'll guarantee to take any one at random and train him to become any type of specialist I might select—doctor, lawyer, artist, merchant-chief, and yes, even beggar and thief, regardless of his talents, penchants, tendencies, abilities, vocations, and race of his ancestors.

Watson's challenge was pure rhetoric—nobody has made an experiment according to his specifications. Now, more than a third of a century after Watson, we can deal more easily with his verbiage. Notice that the experiment would have to be done on healthy and well-formed individuals; this at once makes a considerable portion of mankind ineligible, since much poor health and malformation are plainly genetically conditioned. Is not normality here defined as developmental plasticity and educability? Notice further that Watson would have trained his normal subjects regardless of their talents, penchants, abilities, etc. But what are these things? If they are products of upbringing, they need not be mentioned in this context at all; if they have, at least in part, a genetic basis, then it is probably easier to train some persons to be doctors and others artists or merchant chiefs, etc.

Many, perhaps most, human infants could be trained, either as lawyers, or beggars, or thieves, etc., by suitably manipulating their environment. But this does not contradict the existence of genetic diversity, so that in a given environment some persons will probably become lawyers and others thieves. Or, to put it another way, different environments may be needed to make lawyers or thieves of different individuals. Or, again, those who are in fact lawyers could perhaps have become thieves, and the actual thieves could have become lawyers, if the circumstances of their lives had been different. In short, nature is not sovereign over some traits and potentialities and nurture over others; they share all traits in condominium.

The so-called inheritance of criminality is probably the best illustration of the contingent nature of determinism in human development. The pertinent facts are simple enough to ascertain. Among the inmates of prisons, convicted for all kinds of lawbreaking, there are, as in any other group of people, some individuals who have twin brothers or sisters. Attempts have been made, by several investigators working in different countries, to discover whether the cotwins of the prisoners have ever been convicted of any kind of offense. If so, the twins were recorded as "concordant" in criminality, whether their crimes were in any way similar or different; if the cotwin had no record of conviction, the twin pair was "discordant." The identical twins showed a significantly higher incidence of concordance than did the fraternal ones (only like-sexed fraternal twins are included):

|                 | Identical | | Fraternal | |
|                 | Concordant | Discordant | Concordant | Discordant |
|-----------------|-----------|-----------|-----------|-----------|
| Number of pairs | 80        | 31        | 38        | 73        |
| Percentage      | 72        | 28        | 34        | 66        |

And finally, let us consider a situation which at first sight looks merely amusing, but which has a perfectly serious bearing on the nature–nurture problem. Todd and Mason (1959) carefully recorded the smoking habits of a small collection of identical and fraternal (like-sexed) twins. Contrasting the regular smokers with nonsmokers and occasional smokers, they obtained the following results:

|                 | Identical | | Fraternal | |
|                 | Concordant | Discordant | Concordant | Discordant |
|-----------------|-----------|-----------|-----------|-----------|
| Number of pairs | 43        | 9         | 17        | 15        |
| Percentage      | 83        | 17        | 53        | 47        |

The high frequency of concordance among identical twins is statistically significant—it is too large to be ascribed to chance. Surely, this does not mean that we have discovered a gene for tobacco smoking! We do not know what makes some people smokers and others nonsmokers; many things are probably involved, including mere chance. What the data show is simply this: persons who are similar or identical in genotype are likely to react more similarly to whatever environments they may meet than persons with dissimilar genotypes. Or if you wish, the former are likely to encounter more similar chances than the latter.

The idea that a phenomenon so strictly "social" as criminality may have something to do, however indirectly, with heredity is hard for many people to accept. Ashley Montagu holds that (1959) "discordant one-egg twins ought not to be so frequent and discordant two-egg twins ought to be more frequent, according to genetic theory." What genetic theory would require these things I am at a loss to guess. If criminality were due to a gene which manifested itself regardless of the environment then discordant one-egg twins would not exist at all, but even this would not necessarily make two-egg twins discordant more often than they are. But genetic theories are far more versatile—they may even be compatible with Ashley Montagu's statement that "it is not 'criminal genes' that make criminals, but in most cases 'criminal social conditions.'" The evidence warrants only the genetic hypothesis that in certain environments some genotypes respond by criminal behavior more frequently than do other genotypes. The hypothesis does not preclude that in some other environments the former genotypes may yield law-abiding citizens, and the latter criminals.

On the other hand, no evidence warrants Darlington's (1953) dictum:

> Individuals and populations cannot be shifted from one place or occupation to another after an appropriate period of training to fit the convenience of some master planners, any more than hill farmers can be turned into deep-sea fishermen or habitual criminals can be turned into good citizens.

Experiments, some on a very grand scale, prove that such shifts are possible. Industrial revolutions have turned, and are turning before our eyes, millions of "timeless peasants" into factory workers, pastoral nomads into settled agriculturists, aristocrats into salesmen, proletarians into engineers, petty officials into intellectuals. All of which does not exclude, on the other side, the possibility that there may be some genetic differentiation between social and professional groups (see Chapters 9 and 10).

# 5. Heredity of Health and Disease

> But he who begets unprofitable
> children—what shall we say that
> he hath sown, but trouble for him-
> self, and much triumph for his foes?
>
> SOPHOCLES, ANTIGONE

IT IS CUSTOMARY in books and articles on human genetics to begin
with a description of the inheritance of characteristics transmitted
from parents to offspring according to simple Mendelian rules;
characteristics the inheritance of which is more complex are dealt
with later. This customary order has been set aside in the present
book. In the foregoing chapters situations were treated in which
the genetic conditioning was interwoven so closely with environmental modifications that the very existence of one or the other
variable was sometimes in doubt. This inversion of the usual order
was intended to emphasize a fact of cardinal importance for understanding the biological basis of human personality: whatever may
be the genetic potentialities of an individual, they are realized
through the lifelong interplay of his genotype and his environment:
nature and nurture. The genotype does not operate by gradual
superimposition of independent traits or characters, each transmitted in a neat package labeled "the gene for good behavior" or "the
gene for criminality" or the like. To be sure, there is no way known
to change the genotype with which one is born. But the manifestations of a genotype are, in principle, alterable. Although our ability to control the developmental patterns of human beings is severely limited at present, we may have confidence that medicine,
education, and social engineering are making steady headway.

## Simple and Complex Traits

There is also another reason for putting the complex ahead of
the simple in our presentation. Many of the clear-cut Mendelian
traits in man are hereditary defects, diseases, and malformations,
which are not the main concern of this book. To be sure, some

"normal" traits, such as blood types, taste blindnesses, etc., are inherited in a simple manner, but their existence is not realized by most people since rather intricate methods must be used for their detection. Differences easily observable among "normal" people, such as facial features, eye and skin color, hair color and form, stature, intelligence, personality traits, etc., are not only complex in inheritance but most of them are also environmentally labile (variable in expressivity). Thus, one's weight depends to some extent on the state of one's health and nutrition.

Why this should be so is not as strange as it may seem. When a gene changes by mutation, it alters or disrupts some physiological process in the development of the organism. If the alteration is slight or the process rather unimportant, the resulting phenotype will as a rule differ little from what it was before the mutation. Furthermore, the phenotype may be modified by environmental influences and the gene effects submerged on the phenotypic level by the environmental modifications. Such genes are called incompletely penetrant.

To illustrate: suppose person A has a gene which, in a given environment, would make his skin slightly darker than that of individual B. But if A lives indoors and B is sun-tanned, B may be more heavily pigmented than A. In order to study the inheritance of skin pigmentation, we might record the skin color of parents, siblings, and descendants of A and B, but because of environmental modifications the data obtained might be quite misleading. The inheritance of slight differences in skin pigmentation is hard to disentangle, although we are fairly sure that such heritable differences do exist.

On the other hand, consider a gene mutation which causes a strong or drastic alteration of some developmental process. This makes a phenotypic change fully penetrant, i.e., easily perceptible and much greater than any possible environmental modifications. An achondroplastic dwarf is as a rule easily distinguishable from nondwarfs, and the inheritance of achondroplasia is relatively well known: it behaves as a Mendelian trait dominant over normal growth. A sharp alteration of the developmental pattern of the organism is, however, more likely to be injurious than neutral or useful. As pointed out by Fisher (1930), there may even be an inverse relation between the magnitude of the alteration and the probability of its being harmless or useful. Thus it comes about that hereditary diseases and malformations supply many of the diagrammatically clear examples of Mendelian inheritance in man.

The facility with which a genetic change is detected in the phenotype may also be a matter of technical refinement. Modern serology (immunology) has developed methods delicate enough to detect unambiguously the presence in the red blood cells of the chemical substances that characterize the different blood types in the human species. The inheritance of blood type is known at present better than that of any other trait. Yet persons with different blood types are otherwise so much alike that the possible influences of the types on the fitness of their possessors was discovered only recently. (See the reviews in Roberts 1957, 1959a,b, Allison 1959, Sheppard 1959.) By contrast, the physiological basis of so important a disease as schizophrenia is still uncertain (Kety 1959), and the mode of its inheritance obscure.

## Skin Color

Studies on genetically simple and fully penetrant traits occupied the attention of geneticists for, roughly, the first third of the twentieth century, when genetics came into existence as a separate science. This was the right policy to follow, since the basic rules of inheritance had to be discovered before much progress in other directions could be expected. But an unfortunate by-product of this policy was the rather widespread misconception that persons who inherit a certain gene will necessarily display a certain characteristic in their phenotype, and that most heritable traits are freakish deformities in Drosophila flies and diseases or malformations in man.

Yet geneticists were always aware of the existence of traits of a different sort. Breeders who work to improve agricultural animals and plants have to deal with quantitative traits, such as the yield of grain, meat, or milk, and greater or smaller body size, proportions, or fecundity. How are quantitative traits inherited? The inheritance of skin color in the descendants of Negro and white matings is the classical example, although it has never been completely analyzed (Figure 4). First-generation Mulattoes have a skin color intermediate between the parents, as if the parental heredities were blended in the offspring. Second-generation Mulattoes continue to be intermediate, but only on the average—the variability of the skin color is much greater in the second than in the first generation. In fact, some individuals of the second generation may be as dark as pure Negroes or as pallid as pure whites. ("Pure"

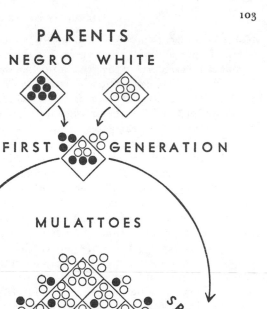

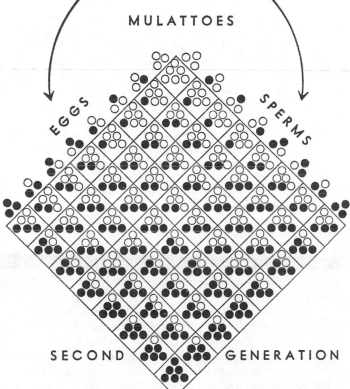

*Figure 4.* A scheme of the inheritance of the skin color difference between Negroes and whites, on the assumption that this difference is due to three pairs of genes. Black—genes producing more pigment; white—producing less pigment.

means, of course, Negroes without known white or whites without known Negro ancestry.) This great variability is evidence that Mendelian segregation of the genes for pigmentation has occurred.

Marriages of first-generation Mulattoes to Negroes or to whites (back-crosses) result in new blends, said to have three-quarters Negro or white "blood." The skin color in the offspring of the back-crosses is again intermediate on the average between Mulatto and Negro, and Mulatto and white respectively. Nevertheless the situation has thus far defied exact analysis in terms of the number of genes responsible for the skin color difference between Negroes and whites. Davenport, a pioneer student of human genetics, believed (1913) that the situation may be accounted for by the assumption of two pairs of pigment genes without dominance. On this hypothesis, Negroes would have four pigment genes, first-generation Mulattoes two, and whites none. This is certainly an oversimplification; a re-analysis of the data by Stern (1953, 1960) sets the probable number of major pigment genes between four and six pairs. But even this view does not account fully for the situation observed. Some of the variations in skin color within each race are doubtless genetic, and there exist perhaps numerous minor pigment genes that make some persons of either race relatively more swarthy or pallid. Such genes, with phenotypically minor effects, are sometimes referred to as modifying genes, or modifiers. The modifiers segregate in interracial crosses together with the major genes, the effects of which they modify. This makes the genetic analysis extremely difficult.

## Polygenes

Early geneticists regarded "blending inheritance" as fundamentally different from Mendelian inheritance. Perhaps, they thought, "qualitative" traits, such as the differences between normal and white-eyed or vestigial-winged Drosophila flies, are inherited through Mendel's genes, while "quantitative" ones, such as the differences in human skin color or stature or weight, are transmitted through "blood." Pearson and his followers (see p. 79) insistently urged such a view. Much painstaking experimental work was required to prove that Mendelian inheritance accounts for the transmission of quantitative as well as qualitative traits. The pioneer studies were those of Nilsson-Ehle (1909) on cereals, Emerson and East (1913) on corn, East (1916) on tobacco, Philipchenko (1934) on wheat, and others.

The skin color differences between Negroes and whites, or the differences between large and small varieties of rabbits, or the greater or smaller milk yield in different breeds of cattle, are due to the joint action of several or many genes. Each of these genes would, by itself, change the pigmentation or body size or milk yield by only a small amount, smaller than the variations due to the common run of environmental influences. Mather (1943) has called the genes with such individually small effects "polygenes."

Polygenes as a rule show neither dominance nor recessivity. Hybrids between large and small breeds of cattle or horses or pigs or rabbits, and presumably between tall and short races of men, may have half as many genes for large size as did the purebred large parent and half as many for small size as the small parent. They are, accordingly, intermediate in size or stature. If heredity were transmitted by "blood," there would be no reason to expect the second and the following generations of hybrids to be different from the first. With gene heredity, segregation and recombination of genes is expected in the second and following generations, and this produces an increased variability. Increased variability is what is actually observed; segregation products as large as the large and as small as the small parental race appear, if sufficiently numerous progenies are examined.

In extreme cases it may eventuate that segregants will arise which are larger than the large or smaller than the small race. The explanation of this at-first-sight peculiar behavior is simple—the large parental race might have carried some polygenes for small size and the small race some alternative (allelic) genes for large size. Indeed, if the action of the polygenes in development is additive, each contributing its share irrespective of what others do, the size will depend simply on how many genes for large or small size are present. This is the reason a breeder can select a large or small, or a high or low yielding, variety among the segregants in crosses between parents that were not very dissimilar. This is also the reason a child may grow to be taller or shorter, more round-headed or more long-headed, more intelligent or less intelligent than either of his parents.

Let us consider an illustration to make this point clear. Suppose that each of the gene alleles $A_1, B_1, C_1, D_1$, tends to increase stature (or intelligence) by a certain amount, while the alleles $A_2, B_2, C_2, D_2$ tend to decrease it. Individuals (or populations) of the genotypes $A_1A_1B_1B_1C_2C_2D_2D_2$ and $A_2A_2B_2B_2C_1C_1D_1D_1$

each have four genes for "high" stature (or intelligence) and four genes for "low" stature, and so will their first-generation progeny, $A_1A_2B_1B_2C_1C_2D_1D_2$. But in the second and later generations there will arise segregation products having from eight genes for high stature $A_1A_1B_1B_1C_1C_1D_1D_1$ to none at all, $A_2A_2B_2B_2C_2C_2D_2D_2$, and every number in between. Phenotypically identical individuals (or populations) may thus be genetically different; and if they are genetically different, then many, perhaps very many, different genotypes and phenotypes may appear in the offspring.

Polygenes are not a distinct category of genes. When a gene is altered by mutation, the change in the phenotype of the organism may be large or intermediate or small. The same gene may act as a "major" gene (oligogene) by producing a strongly different mutant allele, or as a polygene by undergoing a slight alteration (isoallele). The reason for distinguishing polygenes and major genes is a practical one. The classical method devised by Mendel for studying major genes is to cross strains differing in clear-cut characteristics (such as purple vs. white flowers in peas) and count the proportions of individuals in the hybrid progenies showing this or that character. The variant of this method used in human genetics is to follow the distribution of a trait in family pedigrees. This is not possible with polygene-based traits that appear to blend in hybrid progenies. For example, the skin colors in Mulattoes range all the way from very dark to very light; any division in color classes can only be arbitrary.

The study of polygenic inheritance requires the use of different tools, shaped by mathematical statistics. These tools are being fashioned by Lerner (1950, 1958), Mather (1951), Kempthorne (1957), Falconer (1960), and by many other investigators. From the standpoint of a classical geneticist, who would have wanted to count the genes segregating in hybrid progenies and study their effects one by one, the results are not imposing. We have seen that even with the skin color differences of Negroes and whites, which would seem to be a relatively simple polygenic situation, the number of genes and their action are uncertain. With more complex polygenic traits the number of genes concerned is quite unknown. What is solidly substantiated is that polygenes, like other genes, are carried in chromosomes. This is important enough, because it makes applicable to polygenes the fundamental rules of inheritance established with genes more amenable to study. The greatest difficulty with polygenes is perhaps didactic—their study is too abstruse a matter for a nonspecialist, particularly where human heredity is concerned.

## Hereditary Diseases and Malformations

### TABLE 8

Inherited diseases, disorders, and malformations in man. D=dominant; R= recessive to the normal condition; v=incomplete penetrance and/or variable expressivity; sl=sex-linked *(after Kallmann 1953, Sorsby 1953, Neel and Schull 1954, Hsia 1959, Montagu 1959, Stern 1960, and other sources)*

#### METABOLIC DISORDERS

| *Condition* | *Inheritance* |
|---|---|
| Albinism—little or no pigment in skin, hair, or eyes | R |
| Alkaptonuria—homogentisic acid excreted in urine, arthritis | R?, D? |
| Amaurotic idiocy, infantile (Tay–Sachs)—blindness, motor and mental impairment, death in infancy or childhood | R |
| Amaurotic idiocy, juvenile (Spielmeyer–Vogt)—like the above, but death in childhood or adolescence | R |
| Amyloidosis, primary systemic—deposition of amyloid in tissues | D |
| Cystinuria—excretion of cystine in urine, urinary calculi | R, v |
| Diabetes insipidus (nephrogenic type)—excessive urine excretion | R, sl? |
| Diabetes mellitus—low glucose tolerance | R, v |
| Galactosemia—galactose not converted to glucose | R |
| Gargoylism—gross skeletal defects, mental deficiency, slow cartilage growth, vacuolated cells in liver and spleen with deposits of as yet unidentified chemical substances | R, sl? |
| Gaucher's disease—accumulation of lipids, bronze skin, enlarged spleen, storage of cerebrosides in certain cells | R |
| Glycogen storage disease—glycogen deposits in liver, kidneys, etc. | R? |
| Gout—abnormal uric acid metabolism | D, v |
| Hypercholesteremia (primary)—extremely elevated cholesterol level, xantomas | D |
| Hyperlipemia (idiopathic)—yellow nodules on skin, abdominal pain, early myocardial infarction | R |
| Hypoglycemia—low blood sugar, mental retardation | R, v |
| Niemann–Pick disease—strong accumulation of lipoids, neurological deterioration, early death | R? |
| Phenylketonuria—phenylpyruvic acid in urine, feeble-mindedness | R |
| Porphyria—blistering and easy abrasion of exposed skin, excretion of porphyrin in feces and urine, sensitivity to barbituates | D |
| Renal glycosuria—excretion of glucose in urine, normal blood sugar | D |
| Wilson's disease—ceruloplasmin deficiency, degeneration of basal ganglia, cirrhosis of the liver | R |

*Condition*                                                          *Inheritance*

## SKIN

| | |
|---|---|
| Anidrotic ectodermal defect—sweat glands and teeth absent or rudimentary | R, sl? |
| Darier's disease—follicular papules on skin | D |
| Epidermolysis bullosa—blistering of skin following minor trauma | D, v? |
| Epiloia—abnormal growths in skin, heart, kidneys; mental defect | D, v |
| Ichthyosis congenita—leathery skin with deep fissures | R |
| Ichthyosis erythroderma—milder form of the above | R, D? |
| Ichthyosis vulgaris—"fish skin" | D, R, sl? |
| Monilethrix—beaded hair | D, v |
| Neurofibromatosis, Recklinghausen disease—nerve tumors in skin | D, v |
| Piebaldness—unpigmented spotting on body | D |
| Pili torti—short, twisted, fragile hair | D, v |
| Psoriasis—red-brown scaly papules on skin | R?, D? |
| Telangiectasia, hemorrhagic—scattered clusters of thin-walled blood vessels | D |
| Tylosis—thickened skin on palms and soles | D |
| Xeroderma pigmentosum—strong freckling, skin cancers | R, sl |

## SKELETAL SYSTEM

| | |
|---|---|
| Achondroplasia or chondrodystrophy—dwarfism of short limb type | D |
| Acroosteolysis—bone shrinkage in extremities | D, v |
| Ankylosing spondylitis—calcification of paravertebral ligaments, rigidity of spine | D, v |
| Apert's syndrome—high skull vault, eyes far apart, fusion of fingers and toes, extra fingers, etc. | D?, R? |
| Arachnodactyly—very long fingers | D, v |
| Brachydactyly—short fingers and toes | D |
| Camptodactyly—permanent flexure of fingers | D, sl? |
| Congenital amputation of arms and/or legs | D, v |
| Congenital club foot | D, v |
| Congenital dislocation of hip | D, v |
| Congenital flat feet | D |
| Craniofacial dysostosis (Crouzon)—premature closure of cranial sutures, prominent forehead, beaklike nose, protuding eyes | D, v |
| Diaphysal aclasis—exostoses on long bones | D, v |
| Funnel chest—congenital depression of chest, sinking sternum | D |
| Hallux rigidus—stiff big toe | D? |
| Hallux valgus—extreme adduction of proximal phalanx of big toe | D, v |
| Hammer toe—abnormal flexion of the second toe | D |
| Hyperphalangy of thumb—extra phalange in thumb | D |
| Osteitis deformans or Paget's disease—progressive thickening and rarefaction of bones | D, v |
| Osteochondrodystrophy or Morquio's disease—widespread skeletal abnormalities | R, sl? |

| Condition | Inheritance |
|---|---|
| Osteogenesis imperfecta—fragile bones, blue sclerae in eyes | D |
| Oxycephaly or acrocephaly—high, pointed, deformed skull | D?, R? |
| Polydactyly—extra fingers and/or toes | D, v |
| Rickets, vitamin resistant | D, sl? |
| Spina bifida—cleft spinal column | D, v |
| Sprengel's deformity—elevated shoulder blades | D?, R? |
| Split or lobster hand—severe skeletal defects in hands and feet | D |
| Syndactyly—some digits fused | D, v |

## TEETH AND MOUTH

| Condition | Inheritance |
|---|---|
| Cleft palate without harelip | D, v |
| Enamel hypoplasia—thin and discolored enamel | D? |
| Gingival hyperplasia—thickening of gums, delayed tooth eruption | D |
| Hapsburg jaw—protruding chin, lower jaw excessively long | D |
| Harelip, with or without cleft palate | R?, D? |
| Hypodontia—absence of lateral incisors or of molars | D?, R? |
| Opalescent dentine—small, soft, discolored teeth | D? |

## ALIMENTARY SYSTEM

| Condition | Inheritance |
|---|---|
| Cystic fibrosis of pancreas—pancreatic insufficiency, intestinal obstruction, disturbance of sweat and salivary excretion | R |
| Hirschsprung's disease—dilation of the colon | D?, R? |
| Multiple polyposis—polyps in rectum and colon | D |
| Peutz's syndrome—polyposis of small intestine, pigmentation of the mouth mucosa | D |
| Pyloric stenosis, familial—constriction of pyloric opening of stomach | R? |

## BLOOD AND VASCULAR SYSTEM

| Condition | Inheritance |
|---|---|
| Acholuric or hemolytic jaundice—spherocytic erythrocytes | D |
| Afibrinogenemia—deficiency of fibrinogen in blood plasma | R |
| Agammaglobulinemia—failure to develop antibodies | R, sl |
| Hemophilia—bleeder's disease, excessive and prolonged bleeding | R, sl |
| Hypochromic or microcytic anemia—various abnormalities of the erythrocytes | R, sl |
| Methemoglobinemia—a part of hemoglobin converted to methemoglobin | R |
| Ovalocytosis—elliptic erythrocytes, hemolysis | R |
| Pelger's anomaly—abnormal nuclei in white blood cells | D |
| Pernicious anemia—abnormal blood cells, achlorhydria | R, v |
| Polycythemia vera—high red blood cell count | D?, R? |
| Spherocytosis—spherocytes in the peripheral blood | D |
| Sickle-cell anemia—sickling of red blood cells when deprived of oxygen, fatal anemia | R |
| Thalassemia or Mediterranean anemia—abnormal shapes of red blood cells when deprived of oxygen, fatal anemia | R |

| Condition | Inheritance |
|---|---|
| Thrombocytopenic purpura—hemorrhagic spots in skin, scarcity of blood platelets | D, v |

### UROGENITAL SYSTEM

| | |
|---|---|
| Hypospadia—abnormal urethral opening on the penis | R, v |
| Polycystic disease of kidneys—cysts and renal insufficiency | R?, D? |

### EYES

| | |
|---|---|
| Aniridia—iris rudimentary or absent | D |
| Anophthalmia—small eyeballs | R, sl? |
| Cataract—cloudiness of the lens | D, v |
| Coloboma, macular—abnormality of the choroid | D |
| Choroideremia—degeneration of the choroid | R, sl |
| Choroidal sclerosis—hardening of the choroid | D & R |
| Color blindness—failure to distinguish red and green | R, sl |
| Corneal abnormalities—dystrophies and variations in size, shape, and curvature | D & R |
| Fundus dystrophy—degeneration of the back of the eyeball | D |
| Glaucoma—heightened intraocular pressure | D?, R?, v |
| Microphthalmos—eyes abnormally small | D?, R?, v |
| Myopia—nearsightedness | R & sl |
| Night blindness—congenital and stationary | D |
| Nystagmus—quivering of eyeballs | D & R, sl |
| Ophthalmoplegia—paralysis of ocular muscles | D |
| Optic atrophy—atrophy of the optic nerve | D |
| Retinitis pigmentosa—progressive degeneration of the retina with deposition of a pigment | R, sl? |
| Retinoblastoma—tumor of the retina | D, v |
| Subluxation of the lens—lens dislocation | D & R |

### EARS

| | |
|---|---|
| Auricular appendages—soft tumors of external ear | R?, D? |
| Cat's ear—small auricles, cup-shaped | D |
| Deaf-mutism, congenital—total deafness | R?, v |
| Labyrinthine deafness—decrease in upper tone limit | D |
| Otosclerosis—spongy osseous tissue in labyrinthine capsule | D, v |

### NERVOUS SYSTEM AND MUSCULATURE

| | |
|---|---|
| Alzheimer disease—progressive presenile degeneration of brain | D |
| Ataxia, spinal, or Friedreich's disease—incoordination of muscles, 'loss of tendon reflexes, increased curvature of arch of foot, begins early in life | R, v? |
| Ataxia, cerebellar, or Marie's disease—incoordination of muscles, atrophy of optic nerve, beginning later in life | D?, R? |
| Charcot–Marie–tooth disease—peroneal muscle atrophy, slow onset and progressive weakening of certain muscle groups | D, sl? |

| *Condition* | *Inheritance* |
|---|---|
| Dyslexia—congenital word blindness | D |
| Epilepsy, idiopathic—convulsive seizures, electro-encephalogram changes | R?, v |
| Huntington's chorea—progressive muscular spasm, disturbance of speech, dementia | D |
| Leber disease—optic nerve atrophy | R?, D?, sl? |
| Muscular dystrophy, facio–scapulo–humeral type—progressive wasting of pectoral girdle muscles in youth or adulthood | D |
| Muscular dystrophy, pelvic girdle type—progressive wasting of pelvic girdle muscles in childhood | R, sl? |
| Myotonia congenita or Thomsen's disease—hypertrophy of facial and ocular muscles | D |
| Myotonia dystrophica—myotonia and progressive dystrophy of muscles, the most severe myotonia | D, v |
| Myotonia, paramyotonia—mild myotonia after exposure of muscles to cold | D |
| Parkinsonism, shaking palsy—progressive muscular tremor and rigidity | D, v |
| Pelizaeus–Merzbacher disease—progressive paralysis and mental deterioration | R, sl?, D? |
| Pick's disease—progressive presenile or senile degeneration of the brain | D |
| Polyneuritis, progressive, hypertrophic—pain, weakness, hypertrophy of the peripheral nerves | D? |

A very incomplete list of known or suspected hereditary diseases and deviations is given, with greatest reluctance, in Table 8. Most readers expect to see some such list, and yet a list is liable to be misleading if its limitations are overlooked. Let us reiterate once more that the dichotomy of genetic and environmental traits is invalid. Inclusion and noninclusion of a trait in the list is to some extent arbitrary. Thus myopia, nearsightedness, is included, because in some pedigrees it behaves as a Mendelian recessive, although the extent of myopia may depend upon a person's home environment, reading habits, etc. Presbyopia, farsightedness, is not included, because it is so usual an accompaniment of the process of aging, notwithstanding the fact that premature presbyopia has been claimed to represent a dominant trait. Nontoxic and exophthalmic goiters are not included, although predispositions to them appear to be recessive traits, but the two forms of diabetes (insipidus and mellitus) are listed, although their manifestations are very labile.

The symbol *v* in Table 8 means that the malformation named

may or may not appear in persons carrying a given gene (incomplete penetrance), or that the extent of the malformation in such persons is notably inconstant (variable expressivity). Variations in penetrance and expressivity make the study of the inheritance of the traits marked $v$ quite difficult, and the difficulty is exacerbated by some environmental conditions producing "phenocopies," i.e., traits which resemble those produced in other conditions by abnormal genes. For example, both high and low blood pressure can be induced by certain drugs, and perhaps by some living conditions, and yet it is probable that essential hypertension and hypotension may appear in persons of certain genotypes, even if they are living under conditions in which other persons are free of these difficulties. The environmental hypertension is, then, a phenocopy of the genetic (idiopathic) one. Epilepsy may be provoked by brain injuries, or it may come without such injuries in persons genetically predisposed to this malady. Since it is not easy to distinguish the environmental phenocopy from the "genetic" epilepsy, the mode of inheritance of epilepsy still remains obscure, and the same can be said of a number of other diseases that occur in genetic and nongenetic forms.

Several conditions listed in Table 8 have been recorded to follow the dominant mode of inheritance in some pedigrees and the recessive mode in others (symbols D and R together). Such ostensibly contradictory behavior may be explained by error of observation or inference from insufficient evidence (which doubtless occurs), but there may also be other explanations. One possibility is that we are dealing with two (or more) different but clinically or structurally indistinguishable diseases or malformations caused by different genes, one of which may happen to be dominant and the other recessive to the normal, i.e., healthy, condition. This is not a fancy ad hoc hypothesis; "mimics," i.e., phenotypically indistinguishable but genetically distinct mutants, are not infrequent among Drosophila flies and elsewhere. But in Drosophila there are ways to ascertain whether two mutants are mimics or repeated changes of the same gene: the suspected mimics are crossed, and the one-gene or two-gene segregations observed in the offspring give evidence for or against the hypothesis of mimic resemblance or true allelism. Such deliberately planned crosses are, of course, out of the question with human beings.

It is also possible that the same gene may act as a dominant in some families and as a recessive in others. This likewise has ample precedent in experiments with nonhuman materials. The dominance or recessivity, as well as the degree of penetrance and expressivity, of a gene may depend on other genes (polygenes, modifiers) present in the strains crossed. Remember that every person is heterozygous for many genes; consequently many genes are segregating in any family we observe, not just the one the effects of which we wish to record. Our observations always pertain to whole genotypes, even though we may choose to study separate gene effects. Dominant and recessive glaucoma may, then, be either two different diseases that we do not know how to distinguish or one disease produced by an abnormal gene which behaves differently on different genetic backgrounds.

More dominant than recessive traits are recorded in Table 8, but it does not necessarily follow that hereditary diseases and malformations are more often dominant than recessive. The reverse may be the case; recessive mutants are distinctly more numerous than dominants in Drosophila. The effects of dominant genes, especially if they are fully penetrant, are, however, more easily studied in human pedigrees than those of recessives. A dominant trait present in a child must (if it does not arise afresh by mutation, see below) be present in at least one of the parents, one of the grandparents, and so on in more remote ancestors. This is not so with a recessive; a recessive trait appearing in a child in homozygous condition might well have been carried hidden in a heterozygous state in both parents and, in fact, might not have been manifested at all in the child's known ancestry. It is, consequently, much easier to ascertain the genetic nature of a dominant trait than a recessive one. Many recessive traits in man are probably overlooked and not recognized as genetic at all.

The list of diseases and malformations in Table 8 gives an idea of how great is the variety of human afflictions due to defective heredity. A book at least as large as this one would be needed to describe these afflictions adequately and to summarize the evidence, so often disappointingly meager and contradictory, as to the mode of their inheritance. And yet, since the load of defective heredity which human populations carry is an important factor in their evolution, it is opportune at this point to consider somewhat more thoroughly two examples of relatively simple genetic defects. We choose for this purpose achondroplastic dwarfism and diabetes mellitus, traits already referred to above. More complex, probably polygenic, situations will be taken up later.

### Achondroplastic or Chondrodystrophic Dwarfs

Achondroplastic dwarfs are characterized by short arms and legs with stubby fingers and toes, contrasting with a normal-sized head and trunk. These dwarfs apparently occur in all races of man; the god Bes in ancient Egypt and the son and servant of the Hindu god Shiva were both represented as achondroplasts, proving the antiquity of this condition. Achondroplasts are represented also in the Olmec sculptures (fourth century B.C.) of the New World. Analogous dwarf variants exist in several species of animals (Pekingese dogs, some cattle, mice, rabbits, fowls, etc.). The developmental basis of achondroplasia seems to be abnormal ossification of skeletal cartilage, especially in the epiphyses of the long bones of the arms and legs.

Achondroplastic dwarfs in man are heterozygous for a dominant gene with complete penetrance. Marriages in which one parent is a dwarf and the other normal should produce dwarf and normal children in about equal numbers. In the pedigree of a large family from Utah described by Stephens (1943), such marriages have yielded, in three generations, 40 dwarfs and 52 normals. The deviation from the ideal 46:46 ratio may be due to chance or a greater mortality of achondroplastic infants. Some investigators, observing the birth of an occasional achondroplastic child from two normal parents, have claimed that the achondroplasia was produced by homozygosis for a recessive gene. Such exceptional births, however, can be shown to be due to mutation, not to recessivity, since the individuals concerned transmit the trait to about half of their children.

A most valuable study of achondroplasia was made by Mørch (1941) in Denmark. He found that infants with achondroplasia are subject to rather high mortality, while adults may enjoy fairly normal health. However, 108 dwarfs studied by Mørch produced only 27 children, half of whom were dwarfs. This compares with 582 children produced by the 451 normal siblings, brothers and sisters of the dwarfs. The low reproductive rate of the dwarfs has several causes. Parturition in achondroplastic mothers frequently requires Cesarean section, which was a dangerous operation until recently. Also, many dwarfs remain unmarried, perhaps because their appearance varies so much from the ideals of beauty prevalent in our culture. Here, then, is an example of culture influencing the fate of a gene! Finally, it is possible that some achondroplastic dwarfs do not wish to have children who may inherit their physical defect.

However that may be, the number of children per dwarf parent is $27:108=0.25$ and per normal sibling of the dwarfs $582:457=1.27$. Achondroplasts are, then, much less efficient transmitters of their genes to the following generations than are their nondwarf siblings (see Popham 1953). Since this is so, will the gene for achondroplasia become less and less frequent from generation to generation, and is it bound eventually to disappear? This would happen if it were not for the fact that the supply of achondroplastic genes in human population is constantly replenished by mutation. Mørch has estimated the frequency of this mutation. Among 94,075 children born at a certain hospital in Denmark, 10 were achondroplasts. Among these, 2 were children one of whose parents was an achondroplast; they, consequently, inherited their abnormalities from the dwarf parent. The other 8 were born in families in which neither parent was an achondroplast; the gene for achondroplasia here arose by mutation. The 94,075 children came from 188,150 sex cells; the frequency of mutation in the gene for achondroplasia is, then, $8:188,150=0.000,042$ approximately, or 42 per million sex cells, or $4.2 \times 10^{-5}$. We shall consider this matter further in the following chapter (p. 137).

## Diabetes Mellitus

Sugar is an important source of energy for vital processes in the body tissues. Human blood always contains sugar in solution, and the level of blood sugar is remarkably constant. When it tends to decrease, as during starvation, some sugar is discharged from the liver, which has a store of it; when sugar is taken with food, it is used up or stored in tissues and the liver. Only if so much sugar is eaten that the utilization and storage cannot keep pace with the intake will the excess be removed through the kidneys in the urine. Now, metabolizing sugar for energy is facilitated by the hormone insulin, the source of which is the pancreas, a gland located under the stomach. More or less sugar is burned depending upon the amount of insulin in the blood. In some persons the production of insulin is impaired, which leads to disruption of the utilization of sugar. While sugars are ingested with food in amounts easily handled by the normal body, the blood sugar level in the insulin-deficient organism rises until it reaches the point where sugar has to be jettisoned in the urine. This disturbance of the metabolism is called diabetes mellitus; it may set in motion a whole series of other derangements.

It has been known for at least three centuries that diabetes mellitus "runs in families." Numerous investigators have accumulated a large collection of pedigrees in which diabetes occurs, but the difficulties in the way of analysis are so serious that a fully satisfactory theory has yet to emerge (Harris 1950, 1959, Steinberg and Wilder 1952, Siniscalco et al. 1953). The greatest obstacle is that diabetes may strike at any time from childhood to advanced senility, although it most often does so between 45 and 65. In the jargon of genetics, the diabetic genotype is incompletely penetrant, since some persons who are its carriers live through their quota of years without manifest disease symptoms. The genotype has also variable expressivity—the disease may be severe or fatal, but it may also be so mild that the person concerned is unaware of having it at all.

The question that naturally presents itself is whether the different varieties of diabetes are manifestations (1) of the same genotype or (2) of two or more different genotypes having in common the disruption of sugar metabolism. Both hypotheses have found adherents. On the one hand, it is believed that severe diabetes appearing early in life results from homozygosis for a recessive gene, while milder forms with onset in senescent persons derive from the same gene in heterozygous condition or from a different dominant gene. Another theory holds that all diabetes is caused by a recessive gene in homozygous state. Now if the gene were completely penetrant and dominant, every diabetic child would have, barring mutation, at least one diabetic parent. If it were completely penetrant and recessive, marriage of two diabetics would yield only diabetic children. These tests are inapplicable to incompletely penetrant genes, and the clinching evidence for incomplete penetrance of diabetes is that only 62 per cent of the identical twins one of which is diabetic are concordant (compared to only 12 per cent concordance for fraternal twins).

An interesting attempt to obviate the difficulty was made by Siniscalco et al. (1953). They studied 47 families in which at least two siblings had reached the age of 60 or above, one or more with clinically diagnosable diabetes. This minimizes but does not eliminate the chance that persons recorded as free of diabetes will develop the disease later. Their data are as follows:

 27 families, neither parent diabetic—167 children, 43 diabetics
 14 families, one diabetic parent — 82 children, 34 diabetics
  8 families, two diabetic parents — 59 children, 18 diabetics

The authors favor the hypothesis of a single recessive gene with incomplete penetrance. The variations in the time of onset and in the gravity of the disease would then be accounted for partly by environmental fluctuations and partly by the presence of modifying genes which produce no diabetes by themselves but assume importance in diabetic persons. In families in which two or more children are diabetic, the brothers and sisters show greater similarity in the character of the disease than do unrelated persons, which is strong, though not conclusive, evidence of the existence of such modifiers.

The incomplete penetrance makes unreliable statistics on the frequency of genes for diabetes. Diabetes is more common than most people realize. Among persons aged 60 and over, frequencies as high as 20 per thousand (in Denmark) and even 51 per thousand (in a town in New England) have been recorded (see Sorsby 1953, p. 530). Assuming that the gene for diabetes is recessive, this would mean that a considerable proportion of the sex cells in human populations carry this gene (cf. p. 141).

## Muscular Dystrophy

The genetic study of muscular dystrophy faces a still different situation and a different set of problems from those in the study of achondroplastic dwarfism or diabetes. Muscular dystrophy is a chronic and progressive weakening and wasting of the musculature. It gradually affects most muscles of the body and makes its victim unable to walk, eventually confining him to bed. The number of persons in the United States affected by this disorder is estimated as high as 200,000, nearly two-thirds of the victims being preadolescent children. The Muscular Dystrophy Association of America was organized in 1950 to promote research and better understanding of the disease and the needs of its victims. No fully effective treatment for muscular dystrophy has so far been found.

It has been known for some time that muscular dystrophy is another one of the familial diseases. However, all attempts to determine its mode of inheritance have met with indifferent success, some pedigrees suggesting dominant, others recessive, and still others sex-linked inheritance (in the last type the gene is located in the X-chromosome, which is present in duplicate in females and singly in males). The work of Chung and Morton (1959) and Morton and Chung (1959b) brought the long-awaited break-through in the assault on the problem. These authors used the mathematical method of discriminant function analysis; without going into highly tech-

nical details, the essence of this method consists in identifying constellations of symptoms of the disease. Although each of the symptoms may be variable, the probability that all the different symptoms of disease A would occur by chance in a victim of disease B
is small, and it becomes smaller as more symptoms are studied.
The investigators were able to show that "muscular dystrophy" is
a name applied commonly to at least three different diseases which
they were able to distinguish clearly and to a relatively small residual group of diseases for which the information is insufficient for
analysis. Abbreviated quotations of the characteristics of the three
diseases are as follows.

The *facio–scapulo–humeral* form is caused by a dominant, not
sex-linked gene, affecting both sexes about equally. The disease
starts most often in adolescence, and the muscles of the face and
shoulder (scapulohumeral) are usually the first to be affected. The
progress of the disease is slow, with periods of apparent arrest, and
most patients survive and remain active, the age of death not being
hastened. Fertility is nearly normal. The gene arises by mutation
at an estimated rate of about $5 \times 10^{-7}$ (5 in 10 million sex cells).

The *limb–girdle* form is due to a recessive, not sex-linked gene,
affecting both sexes. The disease usually begins in childhood but
sometimes in middle age (up to 45 years), the muscles of the pelvis,
or less frequently of the shoulder, being affected first, often with a
temporary hypertrophy of the muscles of the calves. The progression of the disease is variable, but severe states with inability to
walk are usually reached 20 to 30 years after the onset; death may
occur at any age but the mean longevity is between 30 and 40
years. The victims sometimes marry and beget children, but their
fitness (see Chapter 6) is only about one-quarter of normal. About
16 persons per 1,000 are carriers of this gene, mostly in heterozygous
condition and therefore healthy. About 38 per million are homozygous and develop the disease if they live long enough. The mutation rate is about $3.1 \times 10^{-6}$ (or 31 in 10 million sex cells).

The *Duchenne* form is due to a sex-linked, recessive gene and
manifests itself mostly in males, usually before 5 years of age but
occasionally as late as the third decade. Pelvis muscles are affected
first, then the shoulder muscles; inability to walk is usually reached
within 10 years of the onset but sometimes much later. Apparent
hypertrophy of calf muscles is frequent; so is progressive deformity
with muscular contractures and skeletal distortions. Death occurs
usually in the second decade but sometimes much later. The vic-

tims rarely reproduce, their fitness being only about 4 per cent of normal. The estimated mutation rate is about $9 \times 10^{-6}$ (9 per million sex cells).

It is probable that when other diseases are studied as thoroughly as muscular dystrophy they will also be shown to be caused by several different genetic mechanisms. A preliminary analysis by Chung, Robinson, and Morton (1959) of the accumulated data on deaf-mutism suggests that several different recessive and dominant genes may be involved. The recessives seem to be completely penetrant, but the dominants are only partially so.

## Mental Diseases

No maladies are more mysterious and awesome to man than the disorders of his psyche. In fact, the recognition of these afflictions as diseases, and not signs of possession by evil spirits, has been painfully slow. And despite all the advances of modern medicine, the causation of the most widespread and hence most important psychic disorders remains unsolved. To be sure, the organic bases of several relatively rare kinds of mental impairments have been discovered (a metabolic disturbance in phenylketonuria, brain lesions in some neurogenic disorders; see Table 8). We do not know nearly enough to give even a partial explanation of the cause of so widespread and serious a suffering as schizophrenia. A whole medley of biochemical and physiological disturbances have been reported in schizophrenics, but as Kety (1959) shows in his thoughtful review, it is uncertain whether any of these disturbances are causes rather than consequences of the illness.

For want of known physiological or anatomical lesions or symptoms, a psychiatrist is obliged to base his diagnoses of his patients' mental illnesses on observable abnormalities in their behavior and speech. But human behavior, healthy or pathological, is infinitely variable, and it is, therefore, more difficult to recognize disease entities in mental disorders than in other types of ill health. Three groups of mental disorders are currently recognized by most authorities—schizophrenia and manic depressive and involutional psychoses. Schizophrenia is characterized by "split personality," withdrawal from other people and from reality, indifference to one's surroundings, hallucinations, etc. Manic depressive or cyclophrenic psychosis shows oscillations between extremes of excitement and profound depression. Involutional psychosis occurs mostly in presenile and senile persons, bringing forth states of agitated anxiety, depression, and delusional ideas.

Luxenburger in Germany, Essen-Möller and Böök in Sweden, Slater in England, Kallmann and others in the United States, have produced an impressive amount of evidence for the recognition of genetic predisposition as a primary agent in at least some variants of schizophrenia. Kallmann (1953) located in mental hospitals in New York 953 patients whose condition was diagnosed as schizophrenia and who had twin brothers or sisters. Of these, 268 were identical and 685 fraternal twins. Kallmann and his colleagues then investigated the families from which these "twin index cases" came, with results shown in Table 9.

TABLE 9

Incidence of schizophrenia among relatives of schizophrenics
*(after Kallmann)*

| Relationship | Per cent schizophrenics |
|---|---|
| General population (unrelated) | 0.7—0.9 |
| Step-siblings (unrelated) | 1.8 |
| Half-siblings | 7.1 |
| Full-siblings | 14.2 |
| Parents | 9.3 |
| Fraternal cotwins | 14.5 |
| Identical cotwins | 86.2 |
| Identical cotwins reared together | 91.5 |

It may be noted that investigators other than Kallmann obtained somewhat lower rates of concordance among schizophrenic twin pairs, but the concordance among identical twins was always higher than among fraternal ones, as can be seen in Table 10.

TABLE 10

Percent concordance in schizophrenia among identical and fraternal twins
*(after Kallmann)*

| Investigator | NUMBER OF PAIRS | | PERCENT CONCORDANCE | |
|---|---|---|---|---|
| | Fraternal | Identical | Fraternal | Identical |
| Luxenburger | 60 | 21 | 3.3 | 66.6 |
| Rosanoff | 101 | 41 | 10.0 | 67.0 |
| Essen–Möller | 24 | 7 | 16.7 | 71.4 |
| Slater | 115 | 41 | 14.0 | 76.0 |
| Kallmann | 685 | 268 | 14.5 | 86.2 |

While the incidence of schizophrenia in the general population is somewhat less than one per cent, Kallmann finds that in marriages where one parent is a schizophrenic and the other is not, the expectancy of schizophrenia among children is about 16.4 per cent. In families in which both parents are schizophrenics, 68.1 per cent of the children suffer the same fate. Kallmann's working hypothesis is that predisposition or vulnerability to schizophrenic psychosis is caused by homozygosis for a single recessive gene. Persons who carry this gene in heterozygous condition do not develop clinical schizophrenia, but they have a "schizoid" personality with some mild symptoms, such as introversion, rigidity, compulsiveness, and oversensitivity. Such persons are by no means uncommon—they should constitute between 10 and 20 per cent of the "normal" population. Some of them are inclined to develop involutional psychosis in old age.

Kallmann's hypothesis of a single recessive gene for schizophrenia may or may not be an oversimplification (Sjögren 1957). In any case, two facts stand out equally clearly—certain genotypes give rise to the hazard of schizophrenic breakdown, and this breakdown may or may not occur depending on environmental good or bad luck. It is clear that schizophrenic genotypes are incompletely penetrant because concordance in identical twins is always short of 100 per cent. On Kallmann's recessivity hypothesis this also follows from the fact that only 68 per cent, not 100 per cent, of the children of two schizophrenic parents develop schizophrenia.

This makes rather pointless the polemic concerning the genetic and the "psychodynamic" origin of schizophrenia. It is surely legitimate to search the life histories of schizophrenics for circumstances that may have hastened or retarded the disease, or made it more or less acute. Kallmann himself found that robust physique and good nutrition tend to mollify the disease, and ectomorphic physique and loss of weight to aggravate it. On the other hand, Mark (1953) compared the child-rearing practices of mothers of schizophrenics with a control group. The former tended to display excessive devotion and to be more restrictive in managing their children than did the latter. But it surely does not follow that excesses of maternal devotion and strict regulation can induce schizophrenia in every child regardless of his genetic makeup. Is it not possible that an inclination to such behavior is likely to occur in mothers who are themselves schizoid personalities? Nor does it follow that a child with a schizophrenic genotype is fated to suffer a breakdown and end his life in a mental hospital; he may be regarded a peculiar fellow by his neighbors, and a schizoid by psychologists, but with good fortune and sheltered existence he may go through life without seeing a psychiatrist. Collection of more reliable data, rather than more speculation, is what is needed to secure a satisfactory solution of the problem of the roles of genetic and environmental variables in causation of schizophrenia.

The incidence of manic depressive psychosis in the American population is about 0.4 per cent (Kallmann 1953). Concordance between relatives in this disease is 16.7 per cent in the half-siblings and 22.7 per cent in the full siblings of Kallmann's twin index cases and 25.5 per cent in fraternal cotwins and 100 per cent in identical ones. Kallmann believes that "the recurring potentiality for exceeding the normal range of emotional responses with extreme but self-limited mood alterations" may depend upon a single dominant gene with incomplete penetrance. Whether the carriers of this gene become psychotic or remain merely "cycloid personalities" depends upon the circumstances of their lives and perhaps on modifying genes. The assumption of a single dominant gene can hardly be considered anything more than a highly tentative working hypothesis; the existence of some genetic basis for manic depressive psychosis is, however, rather well substantiated.

## Homosexuality

Sexual play among individuals of the same sex occurs in many higher and in some lower animals. It is particularly common among males when females are absent or in short supply, but it may also occur when females are available. It is, however, in man alone that some persons of either sex find homosexual relations equally attractive as or more attractive than heterosexual ones.

Homosexuality has been tolerated in some societies and regarded a heinous crime in others (Kluckhohn 1954). "Socratic love" was an occupation highly fitting for a gentleman in ancient Greece (Brinton 1959), "berdaches" (transvestites) are accepted members of some American Indian tribes, but in Hitler's Germany homosexuals risked being consigned to gas chambers. Tolerated or persecuted, homosexuals are probably not entirely absent in any society. Kinsey et al. (1948) have shocked paladins of morality in America by divulging the open secret that various forms of homosexual behavior (of which they distinguish six degrees, from predominantly heterosexual to exclusively homosexual) are by no means rare, amounting to some 37 per cent of the males they interviewed.

The preservation of the species evidently depends upon heterosexual unions, which alone result in reproduction. Predominantly or exclusively homosexual preferences are therefore a biological puzzle. Starting with Freud himself, psychoanalytically oriented investigators have sought to solve it by searching for clues in childhood experiences. Many factors conspire to make the sexual development of humans uncommonly liable to disruption, and among these are prolonged childhood with sexual immaturity and dependence upon the ministrations of the parents and other adults; appearance of the sexual drive long before the possibility of its biologically meaningful satisfaction; urgency and persistence of the sexual drive during most of life and without seasonal remissions as in other animals; and severe and rigid channeling of sexual conduct by the customs and moral codes prevalent in a given society. The consequent privations, frustrations, and conflicts lead to the crises, tragedies, comedies, rebellions, and surrenders which all the world literatures, even more than scientists, never weary to describe. Now, it does seem to be established that many of the parents of homosexuals are in various ways notably inadequate in their treatment of their children, causing in the latter regressions and fixations on immature levels of sexuality, inversive anxieties, submission to the father, or eroticized identification with the mother (Hoch and Zubin 1949, Henry 1955).

A quite different causation is indicated by the work of Kallmann (1952, 1953). His evidence comes again from a study of twins. Among 44 homosexual male twins who had identical twin brothers all were concordant, i.e., both cotwins showed overt homosexual behavior after adolescence. Among 51 pairs of fraternal twins one of whom was homosexual, only 13 were concordant. More than that, among the identical twins there was a large measure of concordance even in the degree of deviation, as measured by the Kinsey scale. This was not the case with fraternal twins. Kallmann was unable to ascertain that homosexual behavior is more frequent among the fathers and siblings of his homosexual patients than it is in the general population. This is perhaps not surprising in view of the enormous difficulties confronting the study of this complex and elusive problem.

The psychodynamic and genetic theories of the origin of homosexuality are often regarded as contradictory and incompatible.

The truth is, of course, otherwise. Without questioning the value of the account offered by depth psychologists, it may still be doubted that it is as full and satisfactory as they believe it to be. Let us suppose that all persons who exhibit deviant sexual behavior as adults are found to have had certain kinds of experience in their childhood, particularly in their relations to their parents. But does it follow that such experiences induce sexual deviations in every-body who had them in his biography? Or does this happen only to the carriers of certain genetic endowments, which are apparently not rare in human populations?

Hutchinson (1959) proposes the very interesting hypothesis that these genetic endowments "operate primarily on the rates and extent of development of the neuro-psychological mechanisms un-derlying the identification process and other aspects of object rela-tionships in infancy." Such genotypes may be favorable for emo-tional and intellectual development in some circumstances but lead to sexual deviations and consequent maladjustment in others. Human sexual behavior is so obviously plastic, so dependent on the mores of the milieu and on health and occupation, that a rigid ge-netic determination would produce many more social misfits than exist in reality. But it certainly does not follow that genetic pre-disposition plays no role in a person's behavior, or that all respond alike to their childhood experiences, their upbringing, or the sexual mores of the company in which they find themselves.

### Longevity

One absolute certainty about human life is that it will end in death. Just when the ultimate disaster will come is as a rule merci-fully hidden from each man. Statistics disclose very little. "Natural" death is relatively probable in infancy, less so during childhood, least so during youth; the probability then increases, at first slowly and finally rapidly, toward old age. Several decades ago, Pearl (1922) showed that survivorship curves, plotted as logarithms of the numbers of survivors against age may be remarkably similar for quite diverse organisms. The curve for man happens to resemble that for Drosophila flies, man's age in years being roughly equated to a fly's age in days.

Some of the infant mortality is due to infectious diseases, poor nutrition, and neglect. This kind of mortality has, little by little, been minimized in technologically advanced countries; one hopes that this will be done globally. Infant death due to elimination of lethal and semilethal mutant genes may however continue to occur as a sort of irreducible minimum mortality. The probability of natural death would then increase as a function of age, especially after the close of the reproductive period. Biologically this makes sense. It will be shown in the following chapter that the genetic fitness of a genotype, and by extension of an individual, is measured by the contribution it makes, relative to other genotypes or individuals, to the gene pool of the succeeding generations. The fittest is the parent of the greatest number of surviving children. (This is actually an oversimplification, but it will do for the present.) Now, the probable number of children that an individual will produce if he remains alive is evidently greater for a young person than for an old. The genotypes that foster the well-being of the young will accordingly have, other things being equal, greater selective value than those that favor the old. Selection will not act directly to promote health or survival during postreproductive ages, unless in so doing it confers some advantage on the reproductive ages as well. This is, very briefly stated, the evolutionary background of the phenomenon of senility (Comfort 1956, Williams 1957).

Longevity is plainly susceptible to environmental modification. It generally increases as the living standards in a country become higher and the medical care more adequate. In the United States the life expectancy at birth was 41.5 years in 1868, 62.3 years in 1941, and 68.3 years in 1958 (data of the Institute of Life Insurance). Surely this change is environmental, not genetic. There is, however, good evidence showing that, in the same environment, the carriers of some genotypes tend to live longer than those of others. Kallmann and his collaborators (Kallmann 1953, 1957, Jarvik et al. 1957, 1960, also Verschuer 1954) undertook a longitudinal study of 1,492 senescent twin "index cases." For the twins who survived beyond 60 the mean age difference at the time of death was as shown in Table 11, in which only like-sexed fraternal twin pairs

TABLE 11

Average differences in the life span (in months) of cotwins surviving to ages between 60 and 70 years *(after Jarvik et al.)*

| Twins | Male | Female |
|-------|------|--------|
| Identical | 50.0 | 114.0 |
| Fraternal | 75.0 | 127.5 |

are included. Male identical twins die, on the average, within four years of each other, while for fraternal twins the difference is about six years. No less impressive are the data for the rates of senile decline, as measured by a battery of psychological tests (vocabulary, digit symbol, block design, tapping, etc.). Aging progresses rather uniformly in identical twins, while fraternal twins frequently show faster or slower deterioration than their cotwins.

## The Adaptive Norm

Hamlet's "thousand natural shocks that flesh is heir to" was an underestimate; the shocks are innumerable. The examples given in the foregoing pages of diseases and malformations for which a genetic basis has been apprehended or surmised give only an inkling of how complex and varied this field of study really is. And the reader must be reminded again that the distinction between genetic and nongenetic diseases is neither clear-cut nor rigid. Degenerative diseases of old age are not ordinarily classed as hereditary, and yet the faculty of contracting them must be within the norms of reaction of some human genotypes. Moreover, there is much evidence that the carriers of different genotypes are prone to suffer from different degenerative diseases and at different ages. It is neither an accident nor wholly a matter of environmental fortuities whether one's life will be ended by a cardiovascular disease, nephritis, cancer, diabetes, or a general debilitation which makes one succumb to an infection which the organism would have taken in its stride at a younger age.

We nevertheless speak of good or normal health and ill health, of genetically handicapped people and those free from such handicaps, and finally of normal and abnormal people. The use of the word "normal" poses a semantic problem. No end of misconception and lax thinking is caused by the belief in something called "normal man" or "normal human nature." This phantom is imagined by some to be full of good intentions waiting only for propitious circumstances to manifest themselves and by others a nasty brute bent only on mischief and evil (see Chapters 2 and 3). But trouble is in store whichever preconception is espoused, for either makes you expect people to act alike, whereas they are plainly diverse in their behavior.

A kind of "normal man" idea exists in biology in the classical theory of population structure, which we shall consider further in Chapter 11. The essence of this theory is that normal people carry mostly normal genes, and for most of these genes they are homozygous. Only a minority of the genes are represented in human populations by two or more alleles each, and then one of the alleles is normal and the others abnormal. The adaptive norm of the human species would, according to this view, consist of those who carry mostly or only normal genes, while the unfortunate ones who happen to carry abnormal genes will need the attention of medicine to help them and of eugenics to eliminate them.

According to the balance theory of population structure things may not be so simple (see Chapter 11). This supposes that some genes are represented in populations by two, several, or many alleles. For such genes, no allele is necessarily normal, and good health and high fitness occur mainly in heterozygotes for pairs of different alleles. The homozygotes would usually be less fit. The upshot is, then, that there are not only many but also many kinds of normal, healthy, and highly fit people. The adaptive norm is a great array of genotypes, not just one or a few genetic complexes. Medicine had better be versatile, for not all patients will respond alike to its ministrations. Eugenics must still be more dexterous, for instead of making everybody alike, possessing some one optimal genotype, it will have to engineer a gene pool of the human population that would maximize the frequency of the fit and minimize that of the unfit.

We need not commit ourselves at this stage to a choice between the classical and the balance theories. They have in common the recognition that the boundary between the adaptive norm and the genetically handicapped sector of the population is not sharp. As the standards of fitness are made more rigid, this latter sector seems to expand. One possible definition of the adaptive norm might exclude only those persons who, because of their genetic defects, must be permanently hospitalized or cared for in special institutions; another definition would exclude even those whose genetic handicaps require medical attention or special regimens at any time in their lives.

The concept of the adaptive norm is useful despite the arbitrariness of its delimitation. Rules of sanitation and hygiene, techniques of instruction and education, social services, legislation, and the whole body of custom and usage are tailored to fit the adaptive norm, broadly or narrowly conceived. The evolutionary origin of the adaptive norm and the deviations from it is a major problem which the science of man has to face.

# 6. Natural Selection and Survival of the Fit

Zeus feared that the race would be exterminated,
and so he sent Hermes to them, bearing reverence
and justice to be the ordering principles of cities
and the bonds of friendship and conciliation.

PLATO, PROTAGORAS

IN ONE of the few rhetorical passages in *On the Origin of Species,*
Darwin described the action of natural selection as follows:

> It may be said that natural selection is daily and hourly scru-
> tinizing, throughout the world, every variation, even the
> slightest; rejecting that which is bad, preserving and adding
> up all that is good; silently and insensibly working, whenever
> and wherever opportunity offers, at the improvement of each
> organic being in relation to its organic and inorganic condi-
> tions of life.

Natural selection is, however, a blind, mechanical, automatic,
impersonal process. Its ironclad necessity was clearly expounded by
Darwin in an argument that can be reduced to a few sentences. Any
organism needs food and other resources in order to live; the resources are always limited; the number of individuals of any species
is therefore also limited. Any species is capable of increasing in
number in a geometric progression; sooner or later the state will
be reached when only a part of the progeny will be able to survive.
The statistical probability of survival or elimination, despite accidents, will depend on the degree of the adaptedness of individuals
and groups to the environment in which they live. This degree of
adaptedness is in part conditioned by the genetic endowment.
Therefore, carriers of some genotypes will survive, or will be eliminated, more or less frequently than will the carriers of other genotypes, and the succeeding generations will not be descended equally
from all the genotypes in the preceding generations, but relatively
more from the better adapted ones. Therefore, the incidence of
better adapted forms will tend to increase and the incidence of the
less well adapted ones to decrease.

## Some Necessary Semantics

Unintended and confusing meanings are liable to adhere to words borrowed from everyday language to construct scientific terminology. We have seen in Chapter 1 that the theory of evolution is plagued with such confusion. Darwin said that evolution is brought about by natural selection, which is in turn the outcome of the survival of the fittest in the struggle for life. One of the meanings of "natural" is the state of affairs preceding or excluding man-made changes. Since man's environments are largely man-made, this definition would render natural selection in man impossible. But "natural" in "natural selection" only means that the selective process does not arise from human choice.

"Struggle" suggests strife, contention, competition. Darwin himself wrote that "from the war of nature, from famine and death, the most exalted object we are capable of conceiving, the higher animal, directly follows." Although we cannot close our eyes to competition, war, famine, and death in nature, natural selection does not ineluctably depend on any of these things. Birch (1957) defines competition thus: "Competition occurs when a number of animals (of the same or different species) utilize common resources the supply of which is short; or if the resources are not in short supply, competition occurs when the animals seeking these resources nevertheless harm each other in the process." Natural selection may also take place, as shown by Birch and others, when resources are not limiting, if the carriers of some genes possess greater reproductive potentials than the carriers of other genes. Finally, a genetic endowment which is superior under competition may be inferior in the absence of competition, or vice versa.

And who is the "fittest"? Does natural selection make us fit for life in the society of other men, or for wisdom, or for endurance, or for longevity? Natural selection has, indeed, developed all these qualities in human evolution, but it does not necessarily ordain any of them. Darwinian fitness is measurable only in terms of reproductive proficiency. Its guiding principle is "be fruitful, and multiply, and replenish the earth."*

---

*Muller (1959) has scant patience for this view. He writes: "A favorite cliché with those who do not understand this situation is the statement that, by definition, natural selection must always be acting and must always be favoring the fitter." It is indispensable to distinguish clearly Darwinian fitness from "fitness" as excellence in human evaluation. The two not only are not identical but are sometimes in opposition.

By and large, high Darwinian fitness does go together with the maintenance or advancement of harmony between the organism and its environments. Indeed, this is what enabled life on earth to endure and even to prosper. Natural selection is not, however, a benevolent spirit guiding evolution toward sure success. The high fitness of a population is often attained at the expense of some poorly adapted, unhealthy, or downright inviable individuals (balanced polymorphism, see below). Paradoxically, high Darwinian fitness may even arise from a kind of subversion of the reproductive processes of the organism, which may lead to extinction of the species (Wallace 1948, in Drosophila; Dunn 1957a,b, in mice). It is man and man alone who can probe, scrutinize, and question the wisdom of the evolutionary process which brought him into being, and who can devise improvements that, in his judgment, will be better than those nature hath wrought.

## Natural Selection, Darwinian and Pre-Darwinian

Owing to the splendid simplicity and deductive character of the idea of natural selection, it is not surprising that it was anticipated in various ways. Darwin certainly had predecessors. The Greek Empedocles and the Roman Lucretius fancied that animals arose first as disjointed body parts—heads, trunks, extremities. These proceeded to combine at random, but only some combinations were viable and the rest died out. Whether or not these two philosophers really anticipated Darwin is for the reader to judge. There is, however, no question at all that Maupertuis, Buffon, Erasmus Darwin, Blyth, Chambers, and others did so during the eighteenth and the first half of the nineteenth century. (Among numerous recent works on the history of the idea of evolution, see Eiseley 1958, Darlington 1959, Greene 1959a,b, and Wilkie 1959.) The idea of evolution by natural selection was certainly "in the air" when Darwin and Wallace published their celebrated essays in 1858.

Darwin himself acknowledged that the idea of natural selection was suggested to him by reading Malthus' work, which maintained that uncontrolled growth of human populations was the cause of poverty, hunger, and war (1798 and later editions). Wallace acknowledged the same source. A bizarre consequence of this was to discredit Darwin in the Soviet Union, where Malthus is an evil word and guilt by association is ground for conviction. Yet Darwin may well have been mistaken in this acknowledgment, as shown by Eiseley's startling discovery of the forgotten writings of Edward

Blyth. Between 1835 and 1837 this remarkable man published several articles in one of the principal biological periodicals of his time (republished in Eiseley 1959). These articles contain all the essentials for a theory of natural selection, stated with a clarity second only to Darwin's. But Blyth argued that natural selection (a term he did not use) was an agent that kept the species constant, not one that changed them! At present we know that selection can do both—stabilizing or normalizing selection removes the deviants, while directional selection brings about transformation of species (see below).

Darwin was probably familiar with Blyth's ideas, although he did not acknowledge it. Some writers contend that Darwin in general was too cavalier in the treatment of his predecessors. To Darlington (1959),

> it seems incredible that the apostle of evolution should have been so deficient in historical sense; so much so that, although deeply interested in his own priority, he never realized that his own ideas were secondhand. He thought he had worked them out himself, even when he had only sorted them out.

This is uncharitable. Darwin's one great preoccupation was to discover whether evolution had occurred and what brought it about. He did little to facilitate the task of future historians. It is not certain that he could have easily done so had he wished. One incontrovertible discovery of depth psychology (not exactly unsuspected even long before) is that man is conscious of only a part of his thinking processes: the nature of the creative thought in the mind of a scientist or poet is a mystery to the creator himself, perhaps more than to his biographers. Wallace has stated that the idea of natural selection took shape in his mind during an access of malarial fever! In any case, Wilkie (1959) is right to feel

> very strongly that the theory of evolution must be considered as a scientific theory, a theory, that is, proposed to explain or systematize a set of facts, and that no one has any claim to be considered as a serious rival to Darwin in the "discovery" of this theory who did not conduct his evolutionary studies upon a reasonably wide basis of facts. To have ideas, aperçus, is not enough, and it is the overvaluation of such clever but uncontrolled guesses which is apt to produce the ludicrous . . . fallacy of combination, in which fragments of the final theory are

collected from widely scattered sources and are combined in such a way as to impugn the originality of him who was the first to see how such a synthesis was possible.

## Natural Selection, Post-Darwinian

Really great discoveries transcend the limits of the science in which they are made. They may impair or destroy established popular beliefs and require acceptance of new ones. Or they may bolster beliefs, sometimes conferring upon them an aura of allegedly unchangeable "scientifically proven" truth. Scientists often have a naive faith that if only they could discover enough facts about a problem, these facts would somehow arrange themselves in a compelling and true solution. The relation between scientific discovery and popular belief is not, however, a one-way street. Marxists are more right than wrong when they argue that the problems scientists take up, the ways they go about solving them, and even the solutions they are inclined to accept, are conditioned by the intellectual, social, and economic environments in which they live and work. The acceptance and the subsequent development of Darwinism illustrate this.

Evolution theory, especially that of the evolutionary origin of man, met with the determined opposition of religious traditionalists. The celebrated debate between T. H. Huxley and Bishop Wilberforce in 1860 showed, however, which was the winning side. Huxley's quick repartee sufficed for the bishop's discomfiture. It is less generally realized how quick and eager was the acceptance of evolution elsewhere, even in quarters that otherwise had few sympathies in common. The radical Left welcomed evolution with open arms. Karl Marx was so delighted that he wanted to dedicate the second volume of *Das Kapital* to Darwin, an honor Darwin declined. (An uncut copy of Marx's classic still lies in the library of Darwin's mansion at Down.) In Russia, the liberal intelligentsia saw in evolution a weapon to combat traditional religion, eliciting Dostoevsky's angry remark that Russians take for unshakable truths what elsewhere are mere hypotheses.

The conservative Right was no less pleased, though for different reasons, and, as befits conservatives, after a bit of delay. The mild and judicious Bagehot (1873), whose *Physics and Politics* is still readable despite its anachronistic title (by "physics" he meant natural science, particularly biology), declared that competition and conquest between tribes and nations was nothing less than Darwinian struggle for existence and evolution by natural selection. Now, even casual reading of Darwin shows that his "struggle for existence" was a metaphor and did not necessarily imply combat (see Chapter 1).

But this was not what political conservatives wanted Darwinism to mean, so they set up a theory of social Darwinism without bothering to include in it more of Darwin than his name. (See reviews in Barzun 1941, Hofstadter 1955, and Brinton 1959.) To social Darwinists,

> the most popular catchwords of Darwinian "struggle for existence" and "survival of the fittest," when applied to the life of man in society, suggested that nature would provide that the best competitors in a competitive situation would win, and that this process would lead to continuing improvement. ... They suggested that all attempts to reform social processes were efforts to remedy the irremediable, that they interfered with the wisdom of nature, that they could lead only to degeneration" [Hofstadter, l. c.].

Since Nature is "red in tooth and claw," it would be a big mistake to let our sentiments interfere with Nature's intentions by helping the poor, the weak, and the generally unfit to the point where they will be as comfortable as the rich, the strong, and the fit. In the long run, letting Nature reign will bring the greatest benefits. "Pervading all Nature we may see at work a stern discipline which is a little cruel that it may be very kind," wrote Herbert Spencer.

The slogan "survival of the fittest" was coined by Spencer and accepted by Darwin not without hesitation. The superlative in it deftly suggested that the struggle for life was so inexorable that eventually all but the one fittest must fall by the wayside. From there it was only a step to Nietzsche's superman. Although Nietzsche had only contempt for Darwin as a mere "English shopkeeper," his own great book *Thus Spake Zarathustra* has in it, as Brinton (1959) justly remarks, much more of Darwin than of Zoroaster. And from Nietzsche (1844–1900), the pedigree of ideas sends a branch to Hitler, with his one master leader of one master race.

### From Kropotkin to Johannsen

Efforts were made, of course, to rescue Darwin, or at any rate the theory of evolution, from social Darwinists. Living beings may struggle for existence by fighting each other or by helping each other. Darwin was not oblivious of this fact, but it remained for Kropotkin (1902) to give it due emphasis. Those who repeat the dictum that men behave like wolves do not make it too clear whether they mean the behavior of wolves to sheep or wolves to wolves. Wolves, after all, live in packs. And a female spider may intend to use her husband for a meal, but in fact he usually makes good his escape. A really solitary animal is a rare phenomenon. Individuals of the same and of different species are interdependent in various degrees, and their relations range all the way from cut-throat competition, to tolerance, to adventitious or obligatory cooperation. Nature's stern discipline enjoins mutual help at least as often as warfare. The fittest may also be the gentlest.

Kropotkin's arguments made only a ripple on the evolutionary thought of his day, partly because scientific vindication of callousness was more desired than that of compassion, and partly because of the uncritical character of some of the evidence with which he, a dilettante in biology, tried to bolster his case. Moreover, at the turn of the century and later the thinking of evolutionists was going in a different and, as we see now, a wrong direction.

Darwin claimed that natural selection is inferable from all that is known about life; he did not claim to have observed it in operation. He thought it was too slow to make its effects noticeable within a human lifetime, but that artificial selection served as a good model. Darwin's followers were eminently successful in proving evolution as an historical event, that evolution did actually occur. But not much progress was made in clarifying its mechanisms. In fact, there was some retrogression; the Larmarckian inheritance of acquired characters was admitted by Darwin as an aid to natural selection, but by others it was considered a substitute for natural selection. Weismann (1834–1914), proving as convincingly as one can prove a negative that such inheritance does not exist, inaugurated a purely selectionist Neo-Darwinism. But it was again selection inferred and not observed.

Moreover, while Weismann was successful with other evolutionary problems, he was unable to explain the source of the genetic variation with which selection operates. At the turn of the century de Vries propounded his mutation theory but failed to see that it explained genetic variety. On the contrary, to him it was not mutation and selection but mutation instead of selection that was significant. Biologists as well as popularizers gravely discussed whether

"Darwin's theory" was or was not disproved. Neo-Darwinists had to suppose that selection itself somehow creates materials for more selection. In other words, if you select, for example, for a greater extent of white spotting in a race of laboratory rats there will arise by mutation whiter and whiter variants; if you select for less spotting there will appear mutations for new, genetically darker variants.

This idea was tested by Johannsen in extremely simple and beautiful experiments. He used a species of beans which, like Mendel's peas, reproduced mostly by self-fertilization, i.e., by union of female and male elements produced by the same plant. Starting with a commercial "variety" and keeping the progenies of individual plants separate, Johannsen obtained relatively large-seeded and small-seeded lines. Thus, the selection was effective. But then Johannsen selected larger and smaller seeds from the same "pure line," the progeny of a single self-fertilized individual. This time the selection did not work, and the offspring of the large and small beans were identical on the average. To be successful, selection needs pre-existing genetic variation to operate with, and it cannot generate this variation.

The repute of the theory of natural selection reached an all-time low during approximately the first quarter of the current century. Yet during this time discoveries that upheld its validity were made. The work of T. H. Morgan and his school showed that the mutation process is the source of the raw materials of evolution with which selection operates.

### From Jenkin to Chetverikov

Many weighty objections raised against Darwin's theories by biological pundits of his day were adequately answered by Darwin or his followers. But one objection, made by the engineer Fleming Jenkin in 1867, was really difficult. Suppose, he wrote, that a very fit variant arises in some population, for example, a white-skinned person in a black population (let us not wrangle with Jenkin as to why this example should be very fit); will the whole population soon become white? Not at all; the white mutant (in our modern terminology) will marry a black, his Mulatto offspring will again marry blacks, and in a few generations the white variant will disappear as completely as a drop of ink in a sea of water. It is not a bad guess that Darwin grasped at the reed of Lamarckism because he saw no way out of Jenkin's objection.

Yet the answer would have been available, had only Darwin known about Mendel's work published in 1865. Jenkin assumed, as did Darwin and all contemporaries but Mendel, that the hereditary "bloods" of the parents inextricably blended in the progeny. Genes do not, however, blend; they segregate. The genes for white skin do not disappear, although, this being a polygenic trait, they do become scattered in many individuals. What seems to us, having the advantage of hindsight, very simple, took many years and much insight to discover. Even after the rediscovery of Mendel's work in 1900, Hardy and Weinberg did not prove their theorem of the constancy of gene frequencies until 1908. And only in 1926 did Chetverikov finally lay the ghost of Jenkin's objection. Among other conclusions, he stated:

> Every mutation which arises is absorbed by the species in a heterozygous condition, and, provided that selection is absent, remains indefinitely conserving its frequency. . . . Selection selects not only a gene which determines the character under selection, but it affects the whole genotype (the genotypic milieu), leads to an intensification of the trait selected, and in this participates actively in the evolutionary process.

Chetverikov's work was published in Russian and remained less well known than it deserved (an English translation Chetverikov 1961). But the problem was now ripe for solution. The great trio of Fisher (main work in 1930), Wright (1931), and Haldane (1932 and earlier), largely independently of each other and of Chetverikov, worked out the mathematical theory of population genetics that became the basis of the biological theory of evolution.

### Mutation and Fitness

We have seen above that mutations occur in man, as they do in other organisms. In point of fact, mutations are not at all rare; perhaps as much as 20 per cent of the population carry mutants newly arisen in their parents (see p. 294). The supply of genetic raw materials with which natural selection will operate is therefore ample.

Yet we have to face a peculiar fact, one so peculiar that in the opinion of some people it makes nonsense of the whole biological theory of evolution: although the biological theory calls for incorporation of beneficial genetic variants in the living populations, a vast majority of the mutants observed in any organism are detrimental to its welfare. Some are lethal, causing incurable diseases or fetal deaths; others are sublethal, killing off or incapacitating most of the carriers but allowing some to escape; still others are subvital, damaging health, resistance, or vigor in a variety of ways. Among the genes listed on Table 8, retinoblastoma and infantile amaurotic idiocy are examples of lethals (except that some children with retinoblastoma can be saved by timely surgery), epiloia and hemophilia are semilethals, and achondroplasia, albinism, and color blindness are perhaps subvital.

The situation is not so clear with small mutants, polygenic changes, which are not exemplified in Table 8 because their detection is inordinately difficult. But there is no question, at least in Drosophila, that minute changes, usually affecting the viability of their carriers adversely, not only occur but are in fact several times more frequent than the large changes. We observe variations among "normal" people, in part undoubtedly genetic, in such traits as stature; hairiness of the body; shape of the head, face, nose, or lips; hair color; voice, etc. These genetic variations could have arisen only by mutations, and they probably continue to arise now. Are such mutations neutral, neither assisting nor hampering survival and reproduction? This matter is not so simple as it may seem and in fact belongs to much disputed ground (see p. 295). It can be argued that neutral mutations do not exist, since neutrality is merely a zero point on a continuous scale of fitness; any genetic change is, then, either helpful or harmful on the average. This is valid enough logic, but it overlooks the fact that the effects of a genetic variation on fitness depend on the environment, which is never absolutely constant. However, a mutation may still be to all intents and purposes neutral, oscillating up and down from the zero point on the fitness scale. A little more or less hair on your chest, or a slightly greater or lesser prominence of your nose, would probably make no difference to your success in life, unless, perhaps, you were a Hollywood star.

The evolutionary perspective of a species would still be unpromising if the best it could produce were neutral mutations. Useful mutants do arise, and their occurrence is solidly substantiated by experimental evidence, obtained, however, chiefly in organisms remote from man. I shall here attempt to indicate only the broad lines of the pertinent findings. The crucial point is that one can speak meaningfully of the usefulness or harmfulness (of the positive or negative effects) of a genetic variation on fitness (on the probability of survival and of the production of a greater or smaller progeny) only in and with respect to a certain environment. "Environment" must here be understood in the broadest sense. It comprises physical environment—temperature, humidity, climate, soil; biotic environment—associated organisms which serve as food or act as predators or parasites or competitors; social or cultural environment—obviously most important in human welfare; and finally genetic environment—a changed gene may be useful when associated with some genes and harmful when associated with others.

A genotype that suffers in one environment may flourish in another. Striking illustrations of this are the insecticide-resistant mutants in insects and the drug- or antibiotic-resistant mutants in bacteria. Are the mutations that confer on house flies resistance to DDT insecticides useful or harmful? They are certainly useful when a fly population faces a DDT spray; they are neutral or harmful in the absence of DDT. Some antibiotic-resistant mutants in bacteria are, wonderful to relate, unable to live without the antibiotic in their food medium, and yet the antibiotic kills "normal" bacteria. In man, being heterozygous for the sickle-cell gene makes one at least relatively immune to certain forms of malaria; this is quite useful if one lives in a country where malarial infection may occur, but not useful where malaria is absent.

### Useful Mutation—a Needle in a Haystack

The effects of mutations on fitness are thus contingent on the environment. Persons homozygous for the recessive gene causing diabetes mellitus were much worse off before than after the discovery of insulin therapy. It is conceivable that achondroplastic dwarfs might be less handicapped in finding mates in some cultures than in others. A black skin is a more serious disadvantage in the Transvaal or Alabama than in New York or London or Rio de Janeiro, and in the latter places more serious than in Madras, Sudan, or Ghana. But all this is very far from saying that environments may be discovered making all or even many mutants useful, or at least neutral. Although a hereditary disease is not necessarily incurable (see Chapter 2), acquaintance with genetically conditioned diseases and malformations in man, such as those mentioned in Table 8, should make anyone wary of pushing this argument too far.

Even though some mutations may be useful under some circumstances, and more may be neutral, most are unconditionally deleterious in all existing environments. Considered from the point of view of human welfare, mutation in man can only be regarded as undesirable on the whole. Any increase in mutation rates is certain to increase the store of human misery due to defective heredity (see Chapter 11). Reduction of mutation would redound to mankind's benefit. This is not inconsistent with the recognition that useful mutants did occur in the evolutionary line which produced man, for otherwise, obviously, mankind would not be here. The apparent paradox is resolved if one considers that adaptive evolution does not come from mutation alone but from the interaction of mutation and selection.

An analogy may help to make the situation clear. Consistently useful mutants are like needles in a haystack of harmful ones. A needle in a haystack is hard to find, even though one may be sure it is there. But if the needle is valuable, the task of finding it is facilitated by setting the haystack on fire and looking for the needle among the ashes. The role of the fire in this parable is played in biological evolution by natural selection. Selection fails to perpetuate harmful mutants, even though these are many; it perpetuates the neutral ones in proportion to their frequency; and it multiplies the useful ones, even though these are few. Many bad mutations could hardly be accepted in man for the sake of the few good ones, even if we could rely on selection to further the spread of those which are "good" in our human estimation. This would mean using human suffering to fertilize the soil in which posterity would grow, an ethically unacceptable procedure. The ethical problem is not, however, acute, since natural selection is no substitute for human knowledge and judgment (see Chapters 11 and 12). The biological "fire" has done wondrously well in the past, making the genetic endowment of mankind adapted to the environments in which men live. But in the future man will have to replace it with a gentler agent.

Why the populations of most species are genetically variable, containing some better and some less well adapted variants, Darwin did not know. He ascertained that genetic variation was a fact, and he had no choice but to take it for granted. This was the Achilles' heel of his theory, of which he was fully aware. He essayed, especially in his later years, to appeal to the Lamarckian principle of the inheritance of acquired traits, but this was a false lead. The answer had to wait for the development of genetics in the twentieth century. The answer is—mutation. The process of mutation supplies the genetic raw materials with which natural selection can operate.

## Gene Frequency

To understand the operation of natural selection, the matter must be considered quantitatively. For more than half a century, evolutionists talked about natural selection; more recently they have begun to try to measure the selection. Readers who will be dismayed to see in the following pages some "mathematics" may at least be assured that this mathematics will not go beyond first-year algebra.

In 1908, Hardy and Weinberg independently propounded a theorem that is the basis of population genetics. Suppose that among the inhabitants of some lonely island, which neither loses emigrants nor gains immigrants, there are persons with blood group O and others with blood group A. The difference in the blood groups is inherited very simply—the O condition being recessive and the A dominant. Let us denote the gene for O blood group by the symbol $i$ and for A by the symbol $I$. People belonging to O and A blood groups intermarry at random, since there is neither preference nor avoidance of marrying a partner of like or unlike blood group, and most people do not know their blood group anyway. Suppose also that the gene $I$ does not mutate to $i$ or vice versa, and that the blood groups make no difference to the number of children a family can raise.

Now, granting the above assumptions, let us inquire how frequent persons with O and A bloods will be in the next generation or in several generations hence. Will, for example, the dominant gene become more and the recessive less frequent, as beginners in genetics are prone to believe? Or will the genes $I$ and $i$ somehow mix and produce some intermediate blood type, as biologists would have been likely to suppose before the discovery and rediscovery of Mendel's laws? For convenience of analysis, let us suppose that each person in the population contributes an equal number of sex cells to a common pool; the next generation comes from random union of female and male sex cells from this *gene pool*. The fraction $p$ of the sex cells will carry the gene $I$, and the fraction $q$ the gene $i$; $p$ and $q$ are *gene frequencies*, and $p + q = 1$.

Since the sex cells with $i$ and $I$ unite at random (because marrying is random with respect to the blood groups), the chance of the union of an egg and a spermatozoon with $I$ is $p \times p = p^2$; of two sex cells with the gene $i$, $q \times q = q^2$; and of an egg with $I$ and a spermatozoon with $i$, or an $i$ egg with an $I$ spermatozoon $2 \times p \times q = 2pq$. Hence the proportions of the three genotypes in the population will be:

$$P^2II \text{ (A blood)} + 2pqIi \text{ (A blood)} + q^2ii \text{ (O blood)} = 1$$

Individuals $II$ are homozygotes and $Ii$ heterozygotes, but because of the dominance of $I$ over $i$ they will all belong to A blood group. The crux of the matter is that the gene pool of the next generation will have the same frequencies of the two genes as before, namely:

$$I = p^2 + pq = p\,(p + q) = p$$
$$i = pq + q = q\,(p + q) = q$$

The frequencies, $p$ and $q$, of the genes $I$ and $i$ and the incidence of persons belonging to A and O blood groups in the population will remain constant from generation to generation. Suppose, for example, that 50 per cent (fraction 0.5) of the population has A blood and the remainder O blood (this is close to reality in the Blackfeet Indian tribe of Montana and the adjacent part of Canada.) The incidence of the gene $i$ in the gene pool of this tribe is $q = \sqrt{0.5} = 0.71$ approximately. The frequency of $I$ is $p = 1 - 0.71 = 0.29$. Among the persons with A blood $p^2 = 0.29^2 = 0.084$ will be homozygotes $II$, and $2pq = 2 \times 0.71 \times 0.29 = 0.412$ heterozygotes $Ii$. If a population contains 90 per cent of O persons and 10 per cent of A persons, the gene frequencies are $q = \sqrt{0.9} = 0.95$ and $p = 1 - 0.95 = 0.05$. Homozygotes $II$ will then be rare, $p^2 = 0.05^2 = 0.0025$, or one-quarter of one per cent, and most persons of A blood group will be heterozygous $Ii$.

The incidence of A blood group in human populations remains unaffected even if these populations move from one country to another (provided, of course, that there is little or no intermarriage with the new neighbors). This makes the study of the blood groups a valuable tool for tracing the history of human migrations (Mourant 1954).

## Elementary Evolutionary Events

Suppose we take a culture of colon bacteria, *Escherichia coli*, growing in a nutrient broth in a test tube, and add an amount of streptomycin sufficient to kill all "normal" bacteria and permit only the streptomycin-resistant genotypes to survive. The outcome of the experiment will depend on whether some resistant mutants were present in the culture before the streptomycin was added. This will, in turn, depend on how many bacterial cells the culture contains. If the mutation from nonresistant to resistant arises at a rate of about $10^{-8}$ per bacterial generation (cell division), a culture of a million cells ($10^6$) derived from a single normal progenitor will in about 99 out of 100 cases not include a mutant; but a single culture of a billion cells ($10^9$) will probably contain several mutant individuals, and these will divide and multiply. When the broth is plated on the surface of a jellied nutrient medium in a flat plate, spotlike colonies of resistant cells will grow on it, and from them new cultures consisting of resistant bacteria can be derived. An environmental agent, streptomycin, has selected a variant genotype, a resistant line. This is the directional form of selection. The selection is artificial if the experiment is made as described. It is natural when antibiotic-resistant infections develop in the body of a patient treated with an antibiotic drug. The essence of the evolutionary event is identical in both cases—interaction of mutation and selection.

Streptomycin-resistant mutants arise in bacterial cultures regardless of whether or not streptomycin is added—to put it simplemindedly, the bacteria do not "know" whether they will have to struggle for life in a streptomycin environment. Now, if some of the resistant mutants are neutral and neither harm nor help their carriers in the absence of streptomycin, they will very slowly accumulate in the cultures. Theoretically, the normal genotype will eventually mutate itself out of existence and be replaced by the resistant one. Actually this is unlikely to happen: first, it would take billions of generations, a long time even for bacteria; second, the gene for resistance may mutate back to normal, and this reverse mutation will become important when the resistant genotype becomes frequent; and third, most resistant genotypes are at some disadvantage in the absence of antibiotics, and natural selection will oppose them.

Some resistant mutants are, in fact, unable to live without streptomycin, which they now need as a nutrient. Natural selection will then wipe out such mutants soon after they arise in cultures without streptomycin (the mutant cells probably linger for some time but do not reproduce successfully). We can say that in this case natural selection purges the ill-adapted mutants from the population. This is what Schmalhausen (1949) calls the "stabilizing" and Waddington (1957) the "normalizing" form of natural selection.

### Selection against Dominant Detrimental Mutation

Bacteria reproduce mostly asexually, by simple fission. In higher organisms sexual biparental reproduction is the rule. An individual is diploid, receiving a set of chromosomes with a full complement of genes from his mother and another full set from his father. The evolutionary events in sexual diploids are more complex than in asexual bacteria, and since man happens to belong to the former we must consider them in more detail.

An example of a dominant mutation in man is achondroplastic dwarfism, which was discussed in the preceding chapter. Let us denote the gene for this dwarfism as $D$ and the gene for normal growth as $d$. The gene $d$ mutates to $D$ at a rate $u$, which in this case is about 42 per million sex cells, or $u = 4.2 \times 10^{-5}$. Suppose that a population contains originally no achondroplastic dwarfs. Since it is highly improbable that the mutation will be present in both the female and male cells from which an individual arises (the chance is about $2 \times 10^{-9}$, which is negligible in man), the dwarfs will all be heterozygotes, $Dd$. We have also seen (p. 114) that, in Denmark, the number of children per dwarf parent $(Dd)$ is 0.25, and per normal parent $(dd)$ is 1.27. The dwarfs transmit their genes to the next generation at a rate of only $0.25 : 1.27 = 0.20$, or 20 per cent as efficiently as do normals. We shall call this efficiency the *fitness* (or *adaptive value*, or *selective value*) of the genotype, and denote it by the symbol $W$. Taking the fitness of normals, $dd$, to be 1, the fitness of the heterozygous, $Dd$, achondroplasts will be $W = 0.2$. We may also say that the achondroplastic condition is opposed by natural selection of $s = 1 - 0.2 = 0.8$. This value, $s$, is called the *selection coefficient*.

In the following generation the population will contain two kinds of $D$ genes for achondroplasia, those newly arisen by mutation and those transmitted by the achondroplastic parents from the previous generation. In the gene pool of the population, a fraction $u$ will be the newly arisen $D$ genes, and a fraction $0.2u$ the $D$ genes retained in the population, a total $p = 1.2u$. In the next generation there will be $u$ new $D$ genes and $1.2u \times 0.2 = 0.24u$ retained ones, a total $p = 1.24\,u$. Eventually the new mutations will just make up for the loss of the $D$ genes because of the low fitness of their carriers; the frequency, $p$, of these genes will then become constant. This condition is known as the *genetic equilibrium*. It will be reached when the frequency of the gene for the achondroplasia is:

$$p = u/s,$$
or $p = u/0.8 = 1.25u = 1.25 \times 4.2 \times 10^{-5}$, or 525 per 10 million sex cells.

Using the Hardy–Weinberg theorem (see above) we find that the population equilibrium will be as follows:

| Phenotype | normal | achondroplast | inviable? |
|---|---|---|---|
| Genotype | $dd$ | $Dd$ | $DD$ |
| Frequency | $q^2 = 0.999,895$ | $2pq = 0.000,105$ | $p^2 = 0.000,000,003$ |
| Fitness $(W)$ | 1 | 0.2 | 0? |

There will be roughly one achondroplastic dwarf per 10,000 persons in the population (105 per million, with a large probable error); only about 3 per billion homozygotes for the gene $D$ are likely to be formed, and it is suspected that they will be inviable; most persons will, of course, be normal, $dd$. Thus, the detrimental dominant mutants will not accumulate in the population to any great extent—the frequency of achondroplasts is only slightly greater than double the mutation rate. If the fitness of the mutant were close to normal, the accumulation would be greater. For example, if mutant individuals produce 90 per cent as many children as do normals, $s = 0.1$, the gene frequency of the mutant in the gene pool will be $p = u/0.1 = 10u$, or ten times the mutation rate. Deleterious recessive mutants will accumulate to a greater extent.

## Selection against Recessive Detrimental Mutation

Infantile amaurotic idiocy is a fatal disease of infants and children, due to homozygosis for a recessive lethal gene, which we may symbolize as $am$ (the normal condition of this gene is, then, $Am$). In Table 1 we find the estimate of the mutation rate from $Am$ to $am$, made by Neel and his collaborators, is 11 mutations per million sex cells or $u = 0.000,011$. How frequent will this gene be in human populations?

Here we are forced to make an assumption, namely that the persons who are heterozygous carriers of this gene, $Am\ am$, are no different from the normal noncarriers, $Am\ Am$, i.e., are neither harmed nor strengthened by being heterozygotes. The assumption may not be warranted because a slight gain or loss of fitness, let us say of one per cent, would probably go undetected. Now, the mutation, so long as it is rare, will exist almost entirely in heterozygous condition, $Am\ am$, and natural selection will neither encourage nor discourage its spread. A recessive gene, even one which causes fatal disease when homozygous, is said to be sheltered from natural selection in heterozygous condition.

As more and more mutant genes, *am*, are added to the gene pool of the population, the frequency, *q*, of this gene will gradually rise. Obviously this cannot go on indefinitely, since the heterozygotes *Am am* will eventually become so frequent that marriages in which both parties are, unknown to themselves, heterozygotes will occur. In such a marriage, *Am am* $\times$ *Am am*, one-quarter of the children born should be homozygous *am am*, amaurotic idiots, and they will die in infancy. The death of one amaurotic idiot removes two *am* genes from the population. So, the population will gain some *am* genes by mutation and lose some others owing to their elimination by selection in every generation. When the loss balances the gain, the population will have reached a genetic equilibrium.

How frequent will the gene *am* be in the gene pool at equilibrium? This is not hard to find. According to Hardy–Weinberg, if the frequency of the gene in the gene pool is *q*, the frequency of individuals homozygous for it, in the present instance of amaurotic idiots, will be $q^2$. To reach an equilibrium, this must be equal to the frequency of the mutations produced, *u*. Therefore,

$$q^2 = u, \text{ and } q = \sqrt{u}.$$

If $u = 0.000,011$, the equilibrium frequency will be $q = 0.0033$, in other words 33 sex cells per 10,000 will carry this gene, or the frequency of the gene will be 300 times greater than the mutation frequency! Its heterozygous carriers in the population will be $2pq = 2 \times 0.9967 \times 0.0033$, or 0.66 per cent approximately.

Recessive mutants accumulate in populations much more than do dominants with equally strong detrimental effects. This is true even of genes that are lethal when homozygous, i.e., have fitness $W = 0$, and are opposed by a selection $s = 1$. If the fitness is not so low, the accumulation will be much greater still. The formula for equilibrium frequency of detrimental recessive mutants in the gene pool is:

$$q = \sqrt{u/s},$$

of which the formula given above for recessive lethals is a special case, when $s = 1$.

As an illustration, assume that a relatively mild recessive defect, such as albinism, arises by mutation with a frequency $u = 0.000,028$ (see Table 12), and that it decreases the fitness of its carriers by only 20 per cent $(s = 0.2)$. The frequency of the gene for albinism in the gene pool at equilibrium will then be:

$$q = \sqrt{u/s} = \sqrt{0.000,028 : 0.2} = \sqrt{0.000,14} = 0.0118$$

In other words, about one per cent of the sex cells will carry the gene for albinism, although the frequency of the albinos in the population will be only some 14 per 100,000 persons. Designating the gene for normal pigmentation as $A$ and for albinism as $a$, we shall have the following situation:

| Phenotype | normal | normal | albino |
|---|---|---|---|
| Genotype | $AA$ | $Aa$ | $aa$ |
| Frequency | $p^2 = 0.9765$ | $2pq = 0.0233$ | $q^2 = 0.000,14$ |
| Fitness $(W)$ | 1 | 1 | 0.8 |

Note that the heterozygous carriers of albinism, in whom the recessive gene is sheltered from natural selection, are expected to be some 166 times more frequent than the homozygotes in whom the effects of this gene are exposed to the judgment of the environment.

## The Genetic Load in Drosophila

A rough, tentative, makeshift estimate of the average mutation rate given above is $10^{-5}$ per gene per generation, in man, as well as in Drosophila. In other words, about 1 sex cell in 100,000 carries a newly arisen mutant in a given gene in each generation. A human sex cell carries probably no fewer than 10,000 $(10^4)$ genes; a fertilized egg contains, then, at least 20,000 genes. Therefore, about $2 \times 10^4 \times 10^{-5}$, or 20 per cent, of persons carry one or more newly arisen mutants in every generation (see Chapter 2). This is a lot of mutations.

The critical problem is what happens to the mutants after they arise and enter the gene pool of a population. We know that a great majority of mutants are harmful. Natural selection counteracts the spread of harmful genes. It does so more efficiently with dominant mutants, less efficiently with recessive hereditary diseases, malformations, and weaknesses. This is because a recessive gene exerts its full detrimental effect only when homozygous; in heterozygous condition it is protected, sheltered, from natural selection by the normal dominant allele.

Looked at from a slightly different angle, there is a constant inflow into the gene pool of a population of detrimental mutant genes. Natural selection cannot eliminate all these genes at once, in the generation in which they appear. They persist in the population for some generations—more or fewer depending on the degree of harm they produce and on whether they act as dominants or recessives. The population carries therefore a *genetic load*, consisting of deleterious or potentially deleterious genes, accumulated because of mutation over a series of generations.

How large, or "heavy," are the genetic loads? This can be studied more easily in populations of Drosophila than in human populations. Such studies were pioneered in 1927 by Chetverikov and since developed by many investigators in about ten species of Drosophila flies. The results are, very briefly, as follows. Suppose that we collect a sample of some hundreds or thousands of specimens of some species of Drosophila in their natural habitats (fermenting fruit, tree sap, etc.). Examined under a microscope, these flies will usually appear to be rather uniform and "normal." Rather less variety is noticed among flies than among a similar number of people met with on a city street, perhaps because our eyes are better trained to perceive differences among people than among flies.

An enormous amount of genetic variability is, however, hidden behind the façade of external uniformity. To reveal this variability the flies are taken to a laboratory and a series of crossing experiments are arranged. For a description of the experimental techniques see, for example, Sinnott, Dunn, and Dobzhansky (1958, pp. 222, 249). The essence of this technique is to obtain flies that carry in duplicate (are homozygous for) certain chromosomes which were present in a single dose in wild flies collected in nature. If a chromosome contains one or more mutant genes which have different effects when homozygous than when heterozygous, their effects will now be manifest in homozygous flies. The genetic loads thus revealed in fly populations are enormous. *Drosophila pseudoobscura* is a species having five pairs of chromosomes. The following are the percentages of second chromosomes (one of the five pairs), in populations from California and Texas, which show certain effects in homozygous conditions (Spassky et al. 1960):

| | |
|---|---|
| Lethal | 17% |
| Semilethal | 7% |
| Subvital | 78% |
| Female sterility | 11% |
| Male sterility | 8% |

Lethal chromosomes in double dose kill the individual before it reaches the adult stage (i.e., death occurs during the egg, larval, or pupal stages). In terms we usually apply to humans, these are fatal hereditary diseases. Semilethals cause death of fewer than 100 per cent but of more than 50 per cent of the homozygotes, while subvital chromosomes cause still milder diseases, with less than 50 per cent mortality. Sterility means inability to reproduce; only complete sterility, not a diminished fertility, was recorded in these experiments.

Every fly contains, of course, two second chromosomes, one received from the female and the other from the male parent. It is easy to compute (see p. 141 for the method) that the following percentages of the flies contained two, one, or no chromosomes of a given kind.

|                  | Two    | One    | None   |
|------------------|--------|--------|--------|
| Lethal           | 3.0%   | 28.0%  | 69.0%  |
| Semilethal       | 0.5%   | 13.0%  | 86.5%  |
| Subvital         | 61.0%  | 34.0%  | 5.0%   |
| Female sterility | 1.0%   | 20.0%  | 79.0%  |
| Male sterility   | 0.5%   | 15.0%  | 84.5%  |

Nor is this all. The fly species concerned has other chromosomes which accumulate genetic loads only slightly smaller than the second chromosomes just considered. Taking this into account, one may estimate that approximately the following percentages of the flies in nature are *free* from the respective varieties of detrimental chromosomes:

| Free from lethal chromosomes | 35%  |
|------------------------------|------|
| "      "    semilethal    "  | 75%  |
| "      "    subvital      "  | 1.5% |
| "      "    female sterility | 75%  |
| "      "    male         "   | 80%  |

### The Genetic Load in Man

Now, has all this any bearing on man? Man is not just an overgrown Drosophila. Some laws of biology apply, however, to men as well as to flies. Necessary and sufficient conditions for the accumulation of a genetic load are: (a) occurrence of mutation, (b) at least some mutations being detrimental, and (c) at least some mutations being recessive, or, if dominant, then not completely lethal. Man fulfills these conditions. Although we cannot estimate the magnitude of the genetic load in man as accurately as in Drosophila, there is good evidence that such a load exists. This evidence comes from observations on inbreeding, i.e., on marriages of relatives.

When the spouses are relatives, close or remote, the chances are increased, if only slightly, that some of the progeny will be homozygous for one or more chromosomes derived from the common ancestor. A part of the genetic load which was carried in that common ancestor may thus be uncovered in the descendants. Although marriage of very close relatives is interdicted in all human societies, less close relatives, such as cousins, are permitted to marry; this furnishes the opportunity of making in man observations somewhat analogous to those described above in Drosophila. The increase of the incidence of hereditary diseases in the offspring of marriages between relatives (cousins, uncle and niece or aunt and nephew, second cousins, etc.) over that in marriages between persons not known to be related is slight—so slight that geneticists hesitate to declare such marriages disgenic. And yet, statistical data show that the progeny of relatives do suffer some loss of average fitness. Sutter (1958) in France, Neel (1958a) and Schull (1958) in Japan, and others have made careful observations on the offspring of marriages between relatives. Table 12 gives an example of the data obtained.

TABLE 12

Death, per 1,000 children born, in progenies of parents known and not known to be related, in three districts in France *(after Sutter 1958)*

| District | Parents | Stillborn | Neonatal | 2–12 months | 1 year or over |
|---|---|---|---|---|---|
| Morbihan | Unrelated | 21 | 23 | 29 | 55 |
| | Related | 50 | 41 | 38 | 96 |
| Finistere | Unrelated | 21 | 13 | 25 | 70 |
| | Related | 28 | 31 | 50 | 96 |
| Loire-et-Cher | Unrelated | 19 | 21 | 19 | 39 |
| | Related | 26 | 30 | 24 | 56 |

It should be understood clearly that only a part of the deaths recorded in Table 12 can be ascribed to genetic causes. Most of these deaths (and we cannot determine accurately just what proportion of them) are due to diseases and to environmental accidents of various sorts. Yet it is a fact that the mortality is greater among children whose parents are relatives. It would seem that such children are on the average less resistant to all kinds of environmental hazards than are descendants of unrelated parents.

Making certain simplifying assumptions and using an extremely ingenious mathematical method, Morton, Crow, and Muller (1956) deduced from comparisons of mortalities in the offspring of related and unrelated parents that the average genetic load in human population amounts to about 4 lethal equivalents per person. A "lethal equivalent" is not the same thing as the lethal chromosome which we detect in experiments with Drosophila. It is rather an increment of the genetic load sufficient, if permitted to manifest itself, to reduce the Darwinian fitness of an individual to zero. A lethal equivalent may, of course, be a result of summation of several deleterious mutants, each causing only a slight loss of fitness.

### Hybrid Vigor and Balanced Polymorphism

We have seen that most mutations are detrimental to the organism. The normalizing, or stabilizing, form of natural selection tends to eliminate detrimental mutations. Natural selection is not however perfectly efficient; some generations elapse between the origin and the elimination of a detrimental mutant. The yet uneliminated deleterious mutants compose a part of the genetic load. Another part of the genetic load, the balanced load, comes from the operation of the *balancing form* of natural selection.

The discussion thus far has been concerned with the interaction of mutation and selection for dominant and for recessive traits. Dominance is, however, not an all-or-nothing phenomenon. A heterozygote may resemble one of the homozygotes, or may be in any degree intermediate between the homozygotes. There are many known cases of incomplete dominance or incomplete recessiveness, and of absence of dominance when the heterozygote is exactly midway between the homozygotes.

More interesting is the situation when a gene causes hybrid vigor or heterosis, making the heterozygote more fit than either homozygote. (This is sometimes referred to as "overdominance," but the precise meaning of this term is not firmly agreed upon.) A good, though perhaps rather special, case of a heterotic mutant in man is the gene for sickle-cell disease (Figure 5), brilliantly analyzed by Allison (1954a,b, 1955). The essence of this story is that a recessive gene, *si*, produces in double dose *(si si)* a severe anemia which makes the homozygotes die, usually before adolescence. The gene is, thus, an almost complete lethal when homozygous. But the heterozygotes,

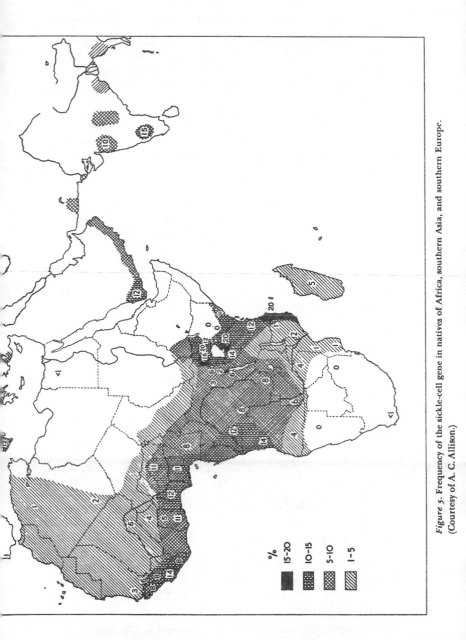

*Figure 5.* Frequency of the sickle-cell gene in natives of Africa, southern Asia, and southern Europe. (Courtesy of A. C. Allison.)

having one normal and one mutant gene, $Si\ si$, enjoy nearly normal health, although they may be diagnosed by an examination of their red blood cells, which contain some abnormal hemoglobin.

The work of Allison (1954a,b, 1955, 1959) and others has made it seem probable (although some people are still unconvinced) that the heterozygotes are more resistant to certain virulent forms of malarial fevers (falciparum malaria) than the normal homozygotes, $Si\ Si$, who do not carry the mutant gene at all (Figure 6). The heterozygous carriers of the gene for the sickle-cell disease will therefore possess the highest fitness in a population living in a country where falciparum malaria is prevalent. The homozygous $si\ si$ die of anemia and many homozygous "normals" die of malaria. Another gene, which produces when homozygous a condition known as Mediterranean anemia or thalassemia, probably also confers some immunity to malaria on its heterozygous carriers. It is suggestive that the combined distribution regions of the sickle-cell and the thalassemia genes in the tropics of the Old World (Figures 5 and 7) resemble that of the falciparum malaria (Figure 6). The fitness of the three genotypes may be represented thus:

| Phenotype | Not anemic, malaria-susceptible | Not anemic, malaria-resistant | Anemic, dies early |
|---|---|---|---|
| Genotype | $Si\ Si$ | $Si\ si$ | $si\ si$ |
| Fitness | $1 - s_1$ | $1$ | $1 - s_2$ |

The symbols $s_1$ and $s_2$ stand for the selection coefficients, which measure the deficiency of fitness in the homozygotes compared to the heterozygotes. Since the anemic homozygotes usually die before they reproduce, $s_2$ is close to unity, and their fitness is close to zero. The value of $s_1$, the disadvantage of the normal homozygotes, will depend on the environment. It is zero where malaria is absent, but it may be perhaps as high as 0.5 where the infection is very common.

What will natural selection do in such a situation? With no falciparum malaria the gene $si$, which causes a lethal hereditary disease when homozygous, will be rare. But where the heterozygote has an advantage, however small (i.e., $s$ is greater than zero), selection will establish an equilibrium with both $Si$ and $si$ persisting in the population indefinitely. The frequencies of both genes are predictable according to simple formulae:

$$Si \text{ gene, } p = s_2/(s_1 + s_2); \qquad si \text{ gene, } q = s_1/(s_1 + s_2).$$

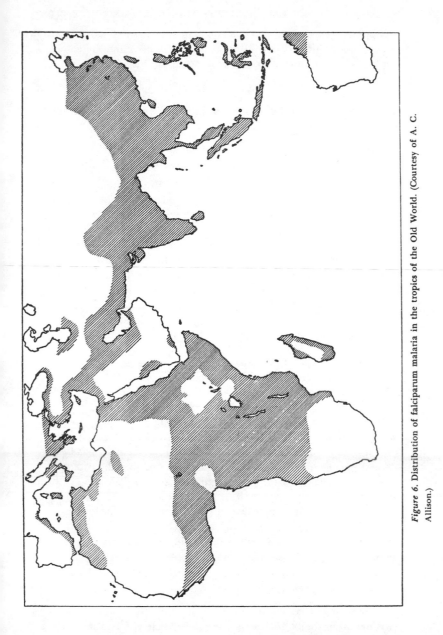

*Figure 6*. Distribution of falciparum malaria in the tropics of the Old World. (Courtesy of A. C. Allison.)

Suppose, for example, that the homozygotes $Si\ Si$ suffer from malaria to the extent of diminishing their reproductive rate by 20 per cent ($s_1 = 0.2$) compared to the heterozygotes. Therefore,

$$p = 1/(1 + 0.2) = 0.83; \qquad q = 0.2/(1 + 0.2) = 0.17.$$

When the population reaches an equilibrium, among the children there will be:

| $Si\ Si$, malaria susceptible | $Si\ si$, malaria resistant | $si\ si$, anemic |
|---|---|---|
| $p^2 = 0.83^2 = 0.69$ | $2pq = 2 \times 0.83 \times 0.17 = 0.28$ | $q^2 = 0.17^2 = 0.03$ |

As many as 3 per cent of the children will die of anemia before maturity in every generation. This would seem to be a very strange result of natural selection—survival of the fit and continuous production of some very unfit. But do not forget that the population contains also 28 per cent of the "fittest" malaria-resistant and nonanemic persons. A calculation would show that the average fitness of the population is maximized when the genes $Si$ and $si$ have reached their equilibrium levels. Anthropomorphically, we are tempted to say that this high fitness is "paid for" by sacrificing some innocents to an early death, an ethically unacceptable procedure. Social Darwinists may even be tempted to recall "nature red in tooth and claw."

An important point to note is that with the heterozygote being the fittest genotype, the population will be polymorphic, i.e., will consist of two or more genetically distinct types of individuals (susceptible-resistant, anemic-nonanemic). Polymorphism maintained by hybrid vigor in heterozygotes is one of the forms of *balanced polymorphism*. How widespread this phenomenon is in human populations is a problem on which no agreement has been reached (see p. 295). At this point it may be noted that the intensity of the balancing selection (the magnitudes of the selection coefficients) which are observed with balanced polymorphisms, as studied in Drosophila and elsewhere, are much greater than biologists a generation ago thought likely. This had made natural selection not merely probable but also observable experimentally. More about this in Chapter 9.

### *Directional Selection*

Normalizing selection opposes the spread in the populations of detrimental mutants. Its role is essentially negative; it protects the

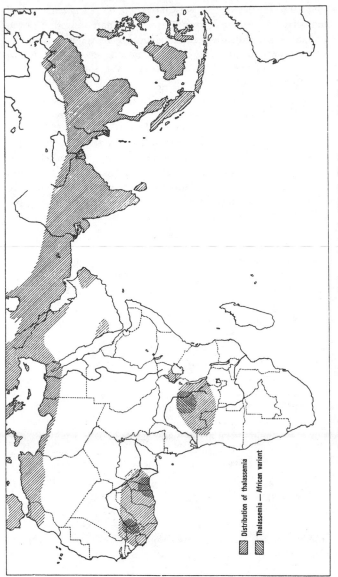

*Figure 7.* Distribution of Mediterranean anemia (thalassemia) in the Old World. (Courtesy of A. C. Allison.)

Distribution of thalassemia

Thalassemia — African variant

average characteristics of the population; it is, really, survival of the mediocre. It is obviously important in human and other populations, since it prevents them from becoming arrays of freaks. The balancing and the diversifying forms of natural selection maintain the adaptedness of the population to its environments by other methods. Owing to advantages of the heterozygotes, or to advantages enjoyed by the different genotypes in different environments, the population becomes polymorphic, consisting of two or several more or less clearly distinguishable kinds of individuals.

The directional (or dynamic; Schmalhausen 1949) form of natural selection alters the genetic composition of a population in response to a changing or changed environment. It may occur also without alteration of the environment, if new and favorable mutations or gene combinations arise or are introduced into the population. Directional selection was in the center of Darwin's thinking. It is perhaps the most important agency bringing about long-term evolutionary changes.

In recent years some instances of selective change have been observed in populations in nature, in higher organisms as well as in microorganisms. The most spectacular example is the spread, during, approximately, the century after the industrial revolution, of melanic (dark-colored) mutants in several species of moths (Kettlewell 1956, 1958). In some industrial regions in England where the vegetation is blackened by soot, the melanics have replaced the original light populations almost entirely. The selective factor has been convincingly shown to be the protective coloration of the dark moths on contaminated and of light ones on uncontaminated vegetation. Even more rapid changes have recently been recorded in a species of Drosophila in California, but the environmental factors which brought them about are obscure (Dobzhansky 1958).

The mathematics of selection is complex, and interested readers are referred to the works of Lerner (1950, 1958), Li (1955), Haldane (1959), and others. Here we shall consider only some points of particular importance for the discussions that follow. Suppose that in some population a gene is represented by two variant alleles, $A$ and $a$. If the three genotypes, $AA, Aa, aa$, are alike in fitness and mutation is rare the population will, generation after generation, have these genotypes represented with frequencies (according to Hardy and Weinberg):

$$p^2\,AA + 2pq\,Aa + q^2aa.$$

Now suppose that a change in the environment occurs, such that one of the genotypes, say the recessive *aa*, produces on the average $1 - s$ surviving progeny for every survivor produced by *AA* or *Aa*. In other words, the recessive is discriminated against by a selection coefficient *s*. It can be shown that the frequency, *p*, of *A* will then increase, and *q* of *a* will diminish at the rate $\Delta q$ per generation:

$$\Delta q = -spq^2/(1 - sq^2)$$

Some interesting conclusions follow from consideration of this formula. First, the rate of change of gene frequencies can be zero (in other words, the frequencies will reach constancy) only if the selection coefficient, *s*, is zero, i.e., if there is no difference in fitness between the genotypes. Second, no matter how large or how small *s* is, the favored gene will become established $(p = 1)$ and the unfavorable one will be eliminated from the population $(q = 0)$. This disposes of the objection repeatedly raised against the theory of natural selection, that to be selected a trait must confer a great advantage on the organism, while small improvements will be of no avail. The opposite is true—given enough time even a small difference in fitness will make selection effective. Third, the speed of the selection process will depend not only on the selection coefficient but also on the frequencies of the genes selected, *p* and *q*. Selection will be most rapid when both *p* and *q* are large, and inefficient when either one is small. Table 13 brings this out clearly.

TABLE 13

Increment of change of gene frequencies per generation, when selection favors a dominant gene and discriminates against a recessive gene in the generation selected

| q | s=0.5 | s=0.2 | s=0.1 | s=0.01 |
|---|---|---|---|---|
| 0.99 | 0.0096 | 0.0024 | 0.0011 | 0.000099 |
| 0.90 | 0.0664 | 0.0193 | 0.0088 | 0.000818 |
| 0.50 | 0.0714 | 0.0263 | 0.0128 | 0.001266 |
| 0.10 | 0.0045 | 0.0018 | 0.0009 | 0.000091 |
| 0.01 | 0.00005 | 0.00002 | 0.00001 | 0.000001 |

One may see that when the recessive gene in the population is frequent (50 to 90 per cent of the gene pool), selection against it diminishes the incidence of the gene rapidly—at a rate of 6 to 7 per cent per generation with strong selection $(s = 0.5)$, and 0.1 per cent per generation even with weak selection $(s = 0.01)$. However, when the same gene becomes rare, selection is accomplishing little; with the initial frequency of the gene of 1 per cent in the gene pool (0.01) even strong selection causes only a five-thousandth of one per cent drop per generation. To state the same point with a slightly different emphasis, the number of generations needed to reduce the frequency of a deleterious recessive from 0.99 to 0.50 is much smaller (559 generations with $s = 0.01$) than that needed to go from 0.50 to 0.01 (10,259 generations with the same selection). Below 0.01 the selection is slow indeed. The same is true in principle when selection favors the recessive $(aa)$ and discriminates against the dominant genotypes $(AA$ and $Aa)$. Here selection is very slow while the favored gene is rare, speeds up as it becomes frequent, and slows again somewhat in the last stages before the dominant is eliminated entirely.

Since the length of a human generation is estimated to be at least twenty-five years on the average, it may seem that the selectional changes are far too slow to be of much significance in the foreseeable future. There are several considerations that contradict this. In the first place, we have assumed that the selective advantages and disadvantages of various genotypes remain constant indefinitely. This is most unlikely; the intensity of selection is a function of the environment, which changes very rapidly, especially in human evolution. A few generations of intense selection accomplish more than many generations of a laxer one.

Furthermore, there is a relation between the intensity of selection and the reproductive powers of the organism. Lerner (1958) compares the progress of selection in a species in which each pair of parents produce twenty offspring of which two survive, and in a form in which each couple produce only four offspring of which two survive. Selection can be more efficient in the former than in the latter case because, while the desired character is rare, a greater proportion of the parents of the successive generations can be selected to have the character in the more fecund species. This difference is important when the desired character is rare in the population, and decreases when it becomes more frequent. Selection coefficients that are low to start with may increase in later stages. This may be of consequence in human evolution, because the demands made on an individual are adjusted to what "the common man," the majority of the population, is regarded as capable of achieving.

### Are Culture and Natural Selection Compatible?

The contents of the present chapter may seem remote from human evolution. Indeed, is natural selection still operating in the human species? Have not culture, technology, and modern living made natural selection obsolete or confined it to the few surviving savages? Many writers so believe. Their arguments run about as follows. Until recently our ancestors lived the wholesome lives of wild animals. They had to struggle and fight for survival, and only the strongest, quickest, craftiest, most aggressive or those with greatest foresight survived—the rest succumbed. This "salutary" process may still be going on in the parts of the world where birth and death rates are high and more than half of the persons born die before reaching their thirtieth year, but in technologically advanced countries birth and death rates are low, necessities of life assured to almost everybody, environmental hazards and infectious diseases controlled—the unfit as well as the fit survive and reproduce. There is no natural selection.

This problem will be dealt with in more detail in Chapter 11. Here we must clarify a general point. Selection occurs whenever two or more genotypically distinct classes of individuals transmit their genes to the succeeding generations at different rates. The rate at which the carriers of one genotype propagate their genes relative to other genotypes is the measure of the *Darwinian fitness,* or *adaptive value,* or *selective value* (these terms may be used interchangeably), of these genotypes. Selection would be absent if everybody were married and every pair of parents conceived the same number of children, all of whom survived. It would also be absent if the numbers of surviving descendants were due entirely to chance and not at all to their genetic makeup. Without selection some individuals (for example, those born of younger or those of older parents) could still be healthier or "fitter" than others.

But it is at this point that one must proceed with the greatest caution. Darwinian fitness is not the same as fitness in the vernacular. Robust health and strong muscles do not necessarily go together with high Darwinian fitness. Darwinian fitness is reproductive efficiency. Health, hardiness, vigor, prowess, bravery, intelligence, foresight may or may not enhance Darwinian fitness, depending upon how they affect the reproductive potential. Obviously, one has to survive to sexual maturity in order to reproduce;

however, both in man and in the lowly Drosophila, the most fecund type is not always the most spectacularly large or powerful one.

How much opportunity is there in man for selection to occur? Crow (1958, 1961) proposes to measure this with the aid of an index $I = V/\overline{W}^2$, where $V$ is the variance (the sum of squared deviations from the mean, divided by the number of observations) of the number of children born per person, and $\overline{W}$ the mean number of these children. The greater the $I$ the greater the opportunity for selection to operate. The index $I$ is, however, the sum of two components, $I_m$ due to mortality and $I_f$ due to variations in the numbers of children born to different parents (i.e., variations in fertility). $I_m$ is the ratio of the proportions of the children who fail to survive ($p_d$) to those who do survive ($p_s$) to maturity ($I_m = p_d/p_s$). The fertility component is $I_f = V_f/\overline{x}_s^2$, where $V_f$ is the variance of the number of children born per person who survives to maturity, and $\overline{x}_s^2$ the mean number of children per survivor.

Now, the greater the mortality and the variations in fecundity, the greater is the opportunity for selection. Suppose that all children born survive to maturity (an ideal yet to be attained); there may still be plenty of opportunity for selection if $I_f$ is large. The really critical issue is whether it is high mortality or large variations in fecundity which give most opportunity for natural selection to act.

Crow (1961) and Spuhler (1961) analyzed some demographic data available in the literature and made a rather unexpected dis-

TABLE 14

$I_f$ is the index of opportunity for selection due to variations in fertility in certain populations. $\overline{W}$ is the mean number of children ever born to women who have survived to the end of their reproductive periods *(after Crow 1961)*

| Population | Children born ($\overline{W}$) | $I_f$ | Source of data |
|---|---|---|---|
| Rural Quebec, Canada | 9.9 | 0.20 | Keyfitz |
| Hutterites, U.S.A. | 9.0 | 0.17 | Eaton and Mayer |
| Gold Coast, Africa | 6.5 | 0.23 | Fortes |
| New South Wales, Australia, 1898–1902 | 6.2 | 0.42 | Powys |
| U.S.A., born in 1839 | 5.5 | 0.23 | Barber and Ross |
| U.S.A., born in 1866 | 3.0 | 0.64 | Barber and Ross |
| U.S.A., alive in 1910 | 3.9 | 0.78 | U.S. Census |
| U.S.A., alive in 1950 | 2.3 | 1.14 | U.S. Census |
| Ramah Navajo Indians | 2.1 | 1.57 | Spuhler |

covery—the index $I_f$ tends to increase as the number of children born per family decreases (Table 14). The index is actually lowest in populations in which the average number of children per family is large, as in the rural districts of the Province of Quebec, Canada (9.9 children per family, the index 0.20), or among the members of the sect of Hutterites (9.0 children per family, the index 0.17). It is highest in the least fertile populations (1.14 in the U.S. in 1950, and 1.57 among the Navajo Indians at Ramah, New Mexico). The reason for this is that the variances of the number of children per family do not grow as rapidly as do the squares of the mean number of these children, thus increasing the index $I_f$ in populations with fewer children per family.

Of course, the value $I_f$, the fertility component, does not tell the whole story. How is the index $I$, which measures the total opportunity for selection, influenced by variations in mortality and by those in fecundity? Spuhler (1961) gives the mortality and fecundity components $(I_m$ and $I_f)$ and the total index $(I)$ for a series of populations. Although the data are not all consistent, the general trend seems to be this: where fewer children are born per family but a greater proportion of them survive, the reduction of $I_m$ is usually more than compensated for by an increase in $I_f$, giving a higher total index, $I$.* With childhood mortality entirely eliminated, natural selection may continue to operate on genetic endowments which influence the probability that people will marry and that they will wish and will be able to bear children. The presumption so often made that reductions in childhood mortality destroy natural selection is not necessarily warranted.

*I am greatly obliged to J. F. Crow and J. N. Spuhler for permission to read their papers in manuscripts before publication, and to refer to the data contained therein.

# 7. The Emergence of Man

Gestaltung, Umgestaltung
Des ew'gen Sinnes ew'ge Unterhaltung
GOETHE

THE STRUCTURE OF THE HUMAN BODY resembles that of other animals, and the similarity is greatest with monkeys and apes. This was recognized quite clearly by Aristotle. In the mid-eighteenth century, Linnaeus included man in his classification of animals and considered man and the anthropoid apes species of related genera —*Homo* and *Simia*. This may seem surprising since Linnaeus upheld the doctrine of the separate creation of species, but there was no inconsistency here, since Linnaeus believed in the Great Chain of Being, an idea widely accepted during the eighteenth and a good part of the nineteenth centuries (Lovejoy 1936, Krutch 1957, Wilkie 1959). Nature was viewed as a single, linear series of increasingly perfect forms, from inanimate objects, through simple and complex organisms, to man, and to the spiritual world. Placing man and apes in the same zoological genus did not mean that one evolved from the other or that both descended from common ancestors; it meant only that they were about equal in the level of complexity and perfection of their bodies.

Lamarck, although he believed in the Great Chain of Being at least as strongly as Linnaeus, was, despite some precursors, the first consistent evolutionist and did derive man from animal ancestors (1809). Darwin (who no longer believed in the Great Chain) did the same, implicitly in *On the Origin of Species* in 1859 and explicitly in the *Descent of Man* in 1871. Huxley and Vogt in the same year, 1863, and Haeckel in 1866 and 1874 marshaled evidence from comparative anatomy and embryology that placed man squarely in the zoological order of primates, together with apes, monkeys, and lemurs. This evidence still stands, but now it is greatly augmented. Simpson (1953) makes man a separate family, *Hominidae*, next to the family *Pongidae*, which contains living and fossil apes and the fossil australopithecines, while Heberer (1956) broadens the family *Hominidae* to contain the subfamilies *Euhomininae* (living and fossil man) and *Praehomininae* (australopithecines), and retains the family *Pongidae* exclusively for the apes. But these authors would be the first to acknowledge that neither classificatory scheme changes the substance of the matter— man is a primate and a close relative of the apes and of the australopithecines.

It is an altogether separate problem to trace the stages through which the evolutionary development of man and his relatives among the primates passed during the history of the earth. Logically it is possible to conceive of a situation in which we would be certain that man has evolved but would know nothing about the actual history of his evolution. However, numerous investigators have devoted their lives to tracing the history of man's bodily frame and his cultural and spiritual developments. Human paleontology, archaeology, and history have accumulated an enormous wealth of data, and the pace of discovery has greatly accelerated in recent decades. It will nevertheless be freely admitted that many stages of man's development remain obscure, and many others are established so insecurely that future discoveries will almost certainly upset the current schemes. Yet what has been learned is of profound importance in man's eternal quest to know himself.

### Evidence of Human Evolution

Lamarck, Darwin, and their successors spared no effort to adduce proofs that man is kin to all life. They have succeeded as well as could be desired—the view that man has descended from ancestors who were not men is verified as fully as an event of the past not witnessed by observers capable of recording and transmitting their testimony can be. These proofs are now part of elementary biology, and may be dealt with quite briefly here.

*Evidence from comparative anatomy.* The human body is constructed on the same general plan as the bodies of other animals, in an order of increasing similarity with vertebrates, mammals, primates, and apes. Every bone of the human skeleton is represented by a corresponding bone in the skeletons of apes and monkeys. Some of these corresponding, homologous bones so characteristically differ in shape that the species can be diagnosed from a single bone; others are more nearly similar. For example, the long bones of the arms of man and chimpanzee are difficult to distinguish (Schultz 1950, Le Gros Clark 1959); the same is true of some other organs and organ systems. Man shares with monkeys and apes the following specialized traits, among others: stereoscopic and color vision, loss of mobility of external ears, replacement of a muzzle by a face, reduction of the sense of smell, loss of tactile hairs, occurrence of menstrual cycle, absence of breeding season, birth usually of a single offspring, great maternal care, and dominance of adult males over females and the young. Some of the traits in which monkeys, apes, and man differ are listed in Table 15.

TABLE 15

Comparison of some traits of monkey *(Cercopithecus)*, ape (chimpanzee), and man *(after Washburn and Avis)*

| Trait | Monkey | Ape | Man |
|---|---|---|---|
| Locomotion | quadrupedal | brachiating | bipedal |
| Shoulder | moderately mobile | very mobile | very mobile |
| Stretching arms | forward | to side | to side |
| Arm muscles | large extensors | large flexors | large flexors |
| Free-arm supination | 90° | 180° | 180° |
| Thumb | small but used | small, used less | large, much used |
| Viscera | adjusted to quadrupedal posture | adjusted to upright posture | adjusted to upright posture |
| Sleep | sitting | lying down | lying down |
| Growth rate | slow | slower | slowest |
| Sexual maturity | 2–4 years | 8 years | 14 years |
| Full growth in male | 7 years | 12 years | 20 years |
| Infant dependency | 1 year | 2 years | 6–8 years |
| Female receptivity | in oestrus | in oestrus | continuous |
| Canines in male | large | large | small |
| Adult male provides food | never | never | major responsibility |
| Territory | small | small | large |
| Shelter | none | temporary nest | shelters, houses, fires |

A considerable amount of ingenuity was expended in trying to find some component part or structure in the human body that was wholly absent in other primates. This would have supposedly made man "unique." These attempts did not succeed; the differences between man and apes are quantitative and not qualitative, as are the differences between one ape species and another. Yet in some ways man does differ quite appreciably from apes: the human foot differs strikingly from the human hand, while in most apes the upper and lower extremities are more nearly similar (hence the name "quadrumana," the four-handed ones, applied to apes in old literature). The origin of this human condition is understandable: human feet are adapted for walking and supporting the whole weight of the body. And the mountain gorilla, an animal that spends much of its time walking on the ground, has a foot reminiscent of the human foot. Not even the human brain, where, if anywhere, unique structures could be presumed to exist, shows any such structure. Broca's area, long supposed to occur in man alone, has been found in the brain of the monkey *Hapale* (see Rensch 1959b). This area is an important, though apparently not indispensable, center of speech (Penfield and Roberts 1959).

*Evidence from embryology.* The so-called Baer's law ("rule" would be a better name) states that the younger the embryos of different animals are, the more they resemble each other, while they become more and more distinct as they grow older. Haeckel made this the "biogenetic law," which he interpreted to mean that the development of the individual (ontogeny) is a telescoped repetition of the evolutionary development of the group (phylogeny). So stated the biogenetic law is certainly wrong, because embryos of one animal do not resemble adult forms of other animals, only their embryos. There is, in any case, no necessary recapitulation of the evolutionary changes that happened in their ancestors in the development of the descendants. Embryos as well as adults undergo changes that adapt them to their environments and, therefore, tend to make them successful in the performance of their biological functions.

Yet making all allowances for overstatements and exaggerations, it remains true that many features of human ontogeny make no sense at all except on the assumption that they are retentions of the developmental patterns of remote ancestors. The celebrated gill arches, which are formed in human embryos and in those of other land-dwelling vertebrates, are also present in embryos of fishes, but in the latter they eventually become the supports of functioning gills. Can one avoid the inference that our ancestors had gills that were used as such? The arteries issuing from the heart of a human or any other mammalian embryo have at first an unmistakable resemblance to the arteries of fishes, then to the arteries of amphibians (frogs, toads, and salamanders), only to be completely rebuilt as they later develop. The human embryo at a certain stage has a tail formed like those of mammalian embryos that have tails as adults. Does this not suggest that our ancestors had tails?

*Evidence from vestiges.* All the numerous muscles of which the musculature of the human body is composed are represented by corresponding muscles in the anthropoid apes. One of the muscles *(peroneus tertius)* of the human foot supposed to be absent in apes was found in 5 per cent of the chimpanzee and 18 per cent of the gorilla specimens studied, and it is absent in some humans (Le Gros Clark 1959). However, some of these muscles, like those of the external ear in man, are mere vestiges apparently devoid of function. So is the vermiform appendix, corresponding to a capacious portion of the intestines of some herbivorous mammals. It is only reasonable to conclude that these are remains of structures that were much more developed in man's ancestors.

To be sure, this argument can be inverted—why have useless organs not disappeared entirely in evolution? But consider what a traceless disappearance of the coccyx, for example, would necessitate. The tail in the embryo is a part of the axial skeleton, which includes also the vertebral column and the skull, and formation of the axial skeleton is an integral part of the basic developmental pattern in all vertebrate animals. Assuming that man might get along just as well without his vestigial tail (the coccyx) as with it, and this is an assumption very difficult to demonstrate conclusively, what advantage would there be in reconstructing the development of the axial skeleton so that its posterior end would be suppressed from the beginning? If there existed a gene which alone took care of the development of the coccyx and nothing else, this gene might well be lost. But the genes do not act in so crude a fashion. The component processes of development are, rather, interdependent, and the basic plan of the development tends to be retained for long periods in evolution. This is probably the basis of Baer's rule and of similar generalizations. (See Dobzhansky 1956 for further discussion.)

*Evidence from physiology, genetics, and serology.* Body functions which are identical or similar in different animals are no less suggestive of common evolutionary descent than are resemblances in body structures. Not only do most diverse animals respire, digest food, excrete metabolic waste products, and reproduce, but they also perform these functions in much the same way. Most impressive is the fact that many enzymes and complex enzyme systems, such as those involved in the Krebs cycle of cellular respiration, have been discovered in organisms otherwise utterly different. Some enzymes in human cells are found also in yeast cells!

The basic mechanisms of reproduction and transmission of heredity are universal. Genes and chromosomes occur in man, in all animals and plants, and in microorganisms down to bacteria and bacteriophages. Simple viruses have been rightly called "naked genes." All sexually reproducing organisms show processes of chromosome pairing and reduction (meiosis). People ignorant of biology find it hard to believe that an analysis of the heredity of pea plants or Drosophila flies can tell us anything about human heredity. The basic mechanisms of heredity discovered by Mendel and his successors are, however, universal in the living world. Of course these basic mechanisms imply only a unity in variety, and detailed study discloses almost infinite variations, some of which occasionally border on the bizarre (as in some species of the flies *Sciaridae* and *Cecidomyidae*, which display certain features of chromosome behavior found nowhere else).

But by far the most impressive demonstration of the unity of life is given by the discovery that the "genetic code" throughout the living world is composed of only four "letters" of the "genetic alphabet" (Chapter 2). All biological evolution, extending over a period of some two billion years, has occurred on the level of genetic "words" and "sentences," no new "letters" having been added or, as far as known, lost. The simplest interpretation of this is either that life arose only once and all living things stem from this one event, or that the existing "genetic alphabet" proved to be more efficient than the others and is the only one which endured.

While the above similarities between man and other organisms cannot reasonably be interpreted except as the consequences of a community of descent, they are hard to measure and express quantitatively. The bones and muscles of the human body are more similar to those of other primates than to those of, say, carnivores or rodents or birds, but one cannot say that they are twice or ten times more similar. An approach to such quantification is possible with the immunity reactions of blood sera, first explored by Nuttal more than half a century ago. The serum (the liquid part of the blood) of species A is repeatedly injected into the blood stream of species B—B is thus immunized against A. When the immune serum of B is mixed in a test tube with a serum of A, a precipitate is formed, and the amount of the precipitate can be measured. Now, if the serum of B immunized against A is mixed with a serum of a third species, C, a precipitate may or may not be formed. If it is formed, the amount is generally greater if the species A and C look similar than if they look different. So measured, man proves to be most similar to the chimpanzee and less to the orangutan, the gibbon, the Old World monkeys, and the New World monkeys in that order (Mollison 1941).

## Living Primates

Man's ancestry extends back through the ages to primordial life. All that lives is our kin. In this book we have to restrict ourselves, however, to only a small period of man's past, during which time the hominid stock became separated from the nonhuman branches. Even this relatively recent history is shot through with uncertainties; authorities are often at odds, both about fundamentals and about details.

A brief account of the living primates will serve as background for discussion. All primates other than man are tropical animals. The great apes, family *Pongidae,* are the chimpanzee *(Pan)* and the gorilla *(Gorilla)* in Africa and the orangutan *(Pongo)* and the two gibbons *(Hylobates* and *Symphalangus)* in southeastern Asia. Apes are specialized for life in the trees of tropical forests; they, particularly the gibbons, are efficient "brachiators," swinging by their arms from branch to branch. Their arms are longer than their legs, and both their hands and feet have opposable thumbs and big toes and serve as grasping organs. The tail is always absent; the body is larger (gorilla) or smaller (gibbons) than man.

Monkeys of the Old World, family *Cercopithecidae,* and of the New World, *Cebidae,* are smaller than apes or men. Many of them have long tails, some prehensile ones, and most are tree-dwelling animals (baboons may, however, live in treeless country). Their gait is quadrupedal. The prosimians, now confined mostly to the island of Madagascar, have movable and unusually large ears, elongated snouts rather than "faces," long and often bushy but not prehensile tails. They are nocturnal in habit; their eyes are directed sideways and are incapable of binocular or color vision.

An animal famous among zoologists is the tarsier *(Tarsius,* family *Tarsiidae).* It is a rare forest-dwelling animal of the Philippines and Indonesia that seems to combine the characteristics of the prosimians with those of the monkeys and apes and even some from a lower order of mammals, the insectivores. It has some features of specialization of its own—enormous eyes, fusion of some and elongation of other bones in the legs, etc. Nevertheless, it is the sort of creature that may be a remote but relatively unmodified descendant of a primitive group of ancient primates which gave rise to lemurs, monkeys, apes, and man.

Which of these animals did the ancestors of man resemble most closely? As stated before, it is obvious nonsense to ask which ape or monkey now living was the remote ancestor of man or of any existing species other than itself, because apes and monkeys have themselves developed from something else. But it may be asked whether there was a common ancestor of man and apes, or of man and monkeys, and if so what this ancestor was like.

A variety of hypothetical answers to this question have been offered. Man's ancestor was pictured as a brachiating ape who abandoned his life in the trees, descended to the ground, and lost the long, grasping arms specialized for brachiation. A far-fetched hypothesis stated that man sprang from a tarsierlike animal and developed parallel to but quite independently of those lines which led to monkeys and apes. Since man so obviously resembles apes and monkeys more than he does the little tarsier, this would mean that all these resemblances were acquired independently, by parallel evolution. Other hypotheses derive man and apes from a common ancestor that had not yet acquired the brachiating habit, or from a still more remote ancestor common to both apes and monkeys (Straus 1949, Heberer 1959).

## Irreversibility of Evolution

We shall not at this point try to adjudicate between the above hypotheses but try merely to understand the chief source of doubt and uncertainty. Can an evolutionary specialization once acquired be lost without trace, and the primitive condition restored ("primitive" being the ancestral one)? For example, every organism is specialized for something—man for culture, apes for brachiation, tarsier for nocturnal life in tropical rainforests. If man's ancestor were a brachiator, should we not find some trace of this condition in his organization? The absence of such traces poses a still more fundamental question—is evolution reversible? Can evolution double back on itself and return to the ancestral status?

Evolution at the lowest level, that of mutation, is reversible. Resistance to antibiotics in bacteria arises by mutation, but resistant strains produce some mutants which lose the resistance. Note that the reversal to nonresistance is not necessarily due to back-mutation in the same gene that once mutated to resistance. It may be, instead, a mutation in a different gene which suppresses the effects of the first mutation. The "new" nonresistant strain will then differ from the original one actually in two genes.

The effects of natural selection are in principle also reversible so long as they are concerned with *microevolutionary* changes which involve alterations of only a few genetic elements. But as evolution proceeds more and more genes are altered, and more and more of them pass through several or many consecutive mutational alterations. *Mesoevolution,* formation of races, species, and perhaps genera, and even more *macroevolution,* changes on generic, familial, ordinal, and higher levels, involve gene alterations so numerous that the probability of retracing all the genetic steps in reverse becomes negligible. The principle of irreversibility of evolution, well established in paleontology and comparative morphology (see Simpson 1953, Rensch 1959a) is borne out also by genetics. Evolution becomes more and more irreversible as it goes on.

Suppose, however, that the environment in which a species lives undergoes a cyclic change, for example growing colder and then warmer again. As the climate grows colder, the species may undergo genetic changes adaptive to cold; can it re-adapt itself to warmth? The re-adaptation to warmth need not be any more difficult than the adaptation to cold was—both will depend on the availability of genetic raw materials on which natural selection can act. But the re-adaptation may occur in two ways.

First, if the old genes, adaptive to warmth, were not completely eliminated from the population during the cold phase, they may now be selected and the gene pool may revert to its old state. This is actually observed in some species of Drosophila in California. These flies produce several generations per year, and since some genetic variations are more favorable in spring than in summer and autumn, a microevolutionary change occurs every year and is undone as the season changes.

On the other hand, the return of the old environment may find the species so greatly altered genetically that it is no longer the same organism which returns to the old environment. The re-adaptation will then be constructed from new genetic materials, and a new form will result. For example, there are good reasons to think that mammals and other land vertebrates developed from fishlike ancestors who lived in water. Whales, porpoises, and seals, however, returned to live in the water again. Their bodies re-acquired fish-like shapes which were adapted to movements in water, but they did not become fishes on that account. Instead they retained mammalian structures that they had inherited from their land-dwelling ancestors.

There is nothing inherently improbable in the hypothesis that man is a descendant of an apelike animal who was a brachiator but came to live on the ground and forfeited the brachiating habit. To test this hypothesis, the anatomist looks for structures in human bodies that would suggest retention of ancestral traits indicative of brachiation. If he does not find such structures he must reject the hypothesis, unless the supposition that these traits may have faded away without trace and been replaced by other adaptations would seem acceptable. It is this supposition that must be judged. The diverse opinions can only be reconciled by the discovery of fossil remains of the inhabitants of the past (Straus 1949). Yet even if we find among fossils some of the real, rather than the theoretically reconstructed, ancestors of our species, the characteristics of fossils are subject to the same evaluation as those of living animals, and, consequently, the division of opinion may not be eliminated.

## Fossil Nonhuman Primates

Man is understandably more interested in the evolutionary antecedents of his own species than those of any other. Fossil remains of creatures that may have been our very distant ancestors or cousins attract more attention than those of other animals. This is a boon and a bane. Persistent search for human and primate fossils is being repaid by numerous finds, and the rate of discovery is steadily increasing. (Even so, the material available to human paleontologists is nowhere near as extensive as that for some other groups, e.g., for the horse tribe.) On the other hand, investigators often submit to the temptation of speculating on the basis of scanty bone fragments (and, it goes without saying, virtually all finds are fragmentary). A minor but rather annoying difficulty for a biologist is the habit human paleontologists have of flattering their egos by naming each find a new species, if not a new genus. This causes not only a needless cluttering of the nomenclature but is seriously mis-

leading because treating as a species what is *not* a species beclouds
some important issues (see p. 183).

In addition to the original papers on individual finds, excellent
reviews of human and primate paleontology have been published
by Weidenreich (1946), Heberer (1951, 1956, 1959a,b), Patterson
(1954), Breitinger (1955), Le Gros Clark (1955), Boule and Vallois
(1957), Piveteau (1957), and Gieseler (1959). These do not include
the more popular accounts which are too numerous to mention.
The picture of primate evolution which emerges is, however, a
very tentative one, almost certain to be changed by future discoveries.

The subdivisions of geological time, the Tertiary and post-Terti-
ary periods, which come under consideration in connection with
the evolution of the primate order are shown in Table 16. Tarsioids

TABLE 16

Tentative chronology of some human and prehuman fossils
*(compiled from Gieseler, Howell, Colbert, and other sources)*

| Period | Epoch | Stage | Beginning, thousands of years ago | Primates (H=Homo) |
|---|---|---|---|---|
| Quaternary | Recent | Postglacial | 10 | modern mankind |
| | | Würm glaciation | 120 | H. sapiens sapiens (Cro-Magnon) / H. sapiens neanderthalensis |
| | Pleisto-cene | 3rd interglacial / Riss glaciation | 240 | H. sapiens soloensis / H. sapiens presapiens |
| | | 2nd interglacial / Mindel glaciation | 480 | H. erectus pekinensis / H. erectus erectus |
| | | 1st interglacial | 600 | H. erectus heidelbergensis (?) / H. erectus modjokertensis / Australopithecus sp. (?) |
| | | Günz glaciation | | |
| | | Villafranchian | 1,000 | Australopithecus sp. (?) |
| Tertiary | Pliocene | Astian / Pontian | 12,000 | ? / Dryopithecus, Oreopithecus |
| | Miocene | Vindobonian / Burdigalian | 29,000 | Dryopithecus / Proconsul, Pliopithecus |
| | Oligocene | | 39,000 | Parapithecus, Propliopithecus |
| | Eocene | | 58,000 | Prosimians, Tarsioids |
| | Paleocene | | 73,000 | |

and prosimians are the only primates that have left rather numerous fossils in Paleocene and Eocene strata. Thereafter they disappear from the fossil record, perhaps because they gave rise to and were supplanted by higher primates. The living *Tarsius* and other prosimians, relics of once widespread groups of animals, now remain only in tropical refuges, like the island of Madagascar and Indonesia. An important fossil, *Parapithecus,* was found in lower Oligocene strata in Egypt. Though unfortunately represented only by a single mandible (lower jaw) with teeth, it seems to bridge the gap between the tarsioids and Old World monkeys; *Parapithecus* may even be "broadly ancestral" to the hominid stock (Patterson 1954). In the same strata as *Parapithecus* there was found a fragmentary mandible of another primate, *Propliopithecus,* which may be regarded as a primitive ape related to the now living gibbons. Evolutionary changes were happening fast among the primates in these mid-Tertiary times.

Another interesting animal is the *Proconsul,* represented by remains of an estimated 450 individuals. Mostly bone fragments but also one rather incomplete and deformed skull were recovered from lower Miocene deposits on an island in Lake Victoria, in equatorial Africa. According to the structure of its teeth and skull, this animal (or animals, since three rather dubious species have been made) belonged to the family *Pongidae,* apes, but had some primitive features resembling Old World monkeys. The bones of the legs show, however, several traits which are interpreted to mean that *Proconsul* had not yet developed the brachiating specializations of the apes now living. Instead, it was probably walking on all fours, like some ground-dwelling monkeys.

*Proconsul* may stand close to the common ancestor of both the pongid and the hominid stocks. He is unlikely, however, to be that ancestor himself because in Miocene and Pliocene periods there existed already a subfamily, *Dryopithecinae,* of the anthropoid ape family, *Pongidae.* Numerous but mostly very fragmentary remains of *Dryopithecinae* have been found in places ranging from Europe (France, Germany, Spain) to India (famous deposits rich in fossils in the Siwalik Hills, foothills of the Himalayas), and Africa (Kenya). No surprise is caused by finding remains of apes in Europe, since that continent, together with North America, enjoyed warm temperate to tropical climates during the Tertiary period. Numerous genera and species of *Dryopithecinae* have been named, mostly on the basis of bone fragments, particularly teeth. What emerges

from this jumble of names is that during the second half of the
Tertiary period the hominid primates, particularly the pongid ape
stock, were undergoing rapid evolutionary development and diversification. The dryopithecines were certainly not identical with
modern apes, and their leg bones indicate that at least some of them
had not yet acquired the specializations that go with the brachiating
habit.

The most interesting but also controversial *Oreopithecus,* found
as far back as 1856 in Tuscany, Italy, in strata variously dated as
upper Miocene or lower Pliocene, was originally believed to have
been a kind of cercopithecine monkey. Hürzeler (1958), who dug
up several new specimens and restudied the old ones, judges, however, that its dentition and its arm bones (ulna) have so many
humanlike characteristics that the animal must be classed a representative of a subfamily *Oreopithecinae,* belonging not to the ape
family *(Pongidae)* but the human family *(Hominidae).* Hürzeler's
view is supported by several authorities, including Heberer (1959a,
b). If borne out by further studies, this would mean that a representative of the human family perhaps existed as far back as late
Miocene times, and that the evolutionary line which eventually
produced man separated from that which produced apes very long
ago—no less than 11 million years (see Table 16). At present this
is only an unconfirmed working hypothesis (see Straus and Schön
1960).

### The Man-Apes, Australopithecinae

Easily the most important fossils bearing on the early stages of
human evolution have been discovered from 1924 on in the southern half of the African continent, chiefly in South Africa, by
Broom, Dart, Robinson, Leakey, and others. They belong to a
subfamily *Australopithecinae.* Simpson (1945) places this subfamily
in his family *Pongidae* and Heberer (1959a,b) places it in the
family *Hominidae,* but as pointed out above their opinions are less
divergent than they may seem on the surface. Nineteenth-century
evolutionists liked to speculate about the "missing link" between
man and his animal forbears. The australopithecines are one of
such "links," no longer missing. This remains true even if, as some
authorities contend, they are still not the direct ancestors but a
collateral branch of the human stock .

By 1954 remains of at least 65 and possibly as many as 100 australopithecines had been discovered in South Africa alone (Robin-

son 1954). The geological age of the australopithecines is not yet certain, and this is the weakest part of the story. They most probably date from the Villafranchian stage, i.e., the oldest part of the Pleistocene epoch at the boundary of the Pliocene epoch of the Tertiary period (Table 16). As the late Pliocene and early Pleistocene epochs have yielded no other hominid fossils (Howell 1959), the australopithecines would in part fill this gap—if their dating is correct—and would have to be considered candidates for the honor of being man's ancestors. If on the other hand, their age proves to be more recent, say toward the middle of the Pleistocene epoch, they will have to be regarded as contemporaneous with other hominids. This latter contingency would not rob them of interest, since they may still be regarded relatively unchanged descendants of man's ancestors, surviving at a time when a more advanced human species was also in existence.

The bones of the australopithecines show several exciting attributes. The shape of their pelvis, particularly of the iliac bone, is definitely hominid and not pongid. These creatures must have walked erect, which is borne out further by the conformation of the femur bone and of a bone of the foot. The dentition is likewise more manlike than apelike (this is, however, challenged by Zuckerman 1954). Yet their brain was small (see p. 200), and the shape of the skull, though certainly unlike that in any modern ape, was definitely not human.

Because of the small brain size and on the whole a more pongidlike than hominidlike skull, the australopithecines were at first regarded as peculiar apes. The discovery of their bipedal stance convinced most (though not all) authorities that the australopithecines were more manlike than any known ape. The recent and momentous discovery (Oakley 1957, Leakey 1959, 1960, Kurth 1960a) that at least some sites containing australopithecine bones contain also some very primitive stone tools, pebble tools, suggests that they were close to crossing "the Rubicon" between animality and humanity. Since these pebble tools were made of a kind of stone which is not found in the rock shelters where the bones were found, they must have been deliberately collected and altered. Australopithecines were, then, not only tool-users but also the first known toolmakers. Pebble tools occur in different parts of Africa south of the Sahara, though not in Europe or Asia, in sites of the Villafranchian stage (Howell 1959, Washburn and Howell 1960). Africa may prove to have been the cradle of humanity.

Though a whole swarm of generic and specific names have been given to australopithecine bones, there is no compelling evidence that there ever existed more than three species of a single genus— *Australopithecus*. It is also very important to note that these man-apes lived in a very large territory. The richest collecting sites were, as stated above, discovered in South Africa, but Leakey (1959, 1960) found australopithecine remains accompanied by pebble tools farther north, in Tanganyika. A fragment of a mandible with three teeth found by Koenigswald in Java and given the resounding name of *Paranthropus (Meganthropus) palaeojavanicus,* may represent another australopithecine. If true, this would mean not only that these supposed ancestors of ours traveled far, but also that they continued to exist for a long time, since the Java find is dated as post-Villafranchian. (Note added in proof: The Tanganyika remains are now supposed to be very ancient—some 1,750,000 years old. If this astonishing date is confirmed it would follow that toolmakers existed for a much longer time than anybody hitherto dared to suppose.)

Only a bare mention need be made of the so-called "giant problem." The teeth of the supposed Javanese australopithecine are remarkably large, and the mandible in which they are anchored remarkably thick. Even much larger teeth of some primate were found on sale in a Chinese drug store in Hongkong. Weidenreich (1946) considered them to have some hominid characteristics and surmised that our ancestors may have been much larger animals than we are. This surmise finds little favor with other authorities. The Hongkong teeth may have belonged to a fossil ape related to the living orangutan *(Pongo)*, and large teeth do not necessarily indicate a proportionally large body.

## Homo Erectus *and His Relatives*

The most ancient, undoubtedly human remains have been found in eastern Asia, in Java, and in northern China. They are entitled to share with us the genus *Homo,* although they were not yet members of our species, *sapiens*. The Java man, described as *Pithecanthropus erectus, P. robustus,* and *P. modjokertensis,* will be referred to as the species *Homo erectus,* race *erectus*. The Peking man, named *Sinanthropus pekinensis,* is a northern race of the same species as Java man and will be called *Homo erectus pekinensis*. The geological ages of the strata in which the remains of *Homo erectus* were found are difficult to correlate with the standard European

sequence (Table 16). These remains are tentatively assigned to
Mid-Pleistocene (Mindel glaciation or the Mindel–Riss interglacial). The Peking race is probably somewhat younger; it is contemporaneous perhaps with the second (Mindel–Riss) interglacial
or the third (Riss) glacial in Europe. Peking man is represented by
relatively abundant material, at least forty individuals, mostly
fragments of course but together they give a reasonably complete
picture of the whole skeleton. The material on Java man is much
smaller, but still sufficient to establish the critically important
points.

*Homo erectus* undoubtedly walked erect; the femur of his leg
is indistinguishable from modern human femur. His brain capacity
was larger than that of the australopithecines—710 to 1,000 cc in
the Java race and 900 to 1,200 cc in the *pekinensis* race. The shape
of the skull, especially in the Java race, is definitely not like that
in modern man: the skull cap is long and flat and the frontal bone
forms a continuous ridge over the eyes (supraorbital torus), resembling that in the chimpanzee and in the gibbons. The lower jaw,
unlike that in modern man, has no chin; the dentition shows a
mixture of human and ape characteristics.

No implements were found together with the bones of Java
man, but this does not prove that he did not possess them. Peking
man made stone artifacts, rough flakes and crude stone choppers,
which show relatively little progress over the industry of the australopithecines. However, remains of hearths are abundant in the
caves in which Peking man lived; he was, consequently, acquainted
with the use of fire (Oakley 1956a,b, 1958). (The original Promethe-
us seems to have resided near the present capital of China.)

How wide the geographic distribution of *Homo erectus* was, is
an open question. Arambourg has described three lower jaws and
a parietal bone from Ternifine, Algeria, which were found in deposits believed to be contemporary with the second (Mindel) Glaciation in Europe, or with the Second Interglacial. These bones
(given the name *Atlanthropus mauritanicus*) resemble most those
of Java and Peking men and may represent a race of *Homo erectus*.
The same may be true of the mandible found at Mauer, near Heidelberg, Germany, in a stratum of the first interglacial (Günz–
Mindel) age. The possessor of this jaw, named *Homo heidelbergen-
sis*, would be, then, an estimated 530,000 years old—the most ancient European hominid (Gieseler 1959). The most dubious member of the *Homo erectus* group is *Telanthropus capensis*, repre-

sented by a mandible with five teeth and a fragment of another mandible, found in South Africa, allegedly in the deposit that contained bones of *Australopithecus*. If *Telanthropus capensis* is accepted at face value, it would follow that two different hominid species were living for a time side by side in South Africa. However, *Telanthropus* may actually be a younger form.

## The Pre-Sapiens and the Pre-Neanderthalians

We do not know nearly enough to give a satisfactory account of the appearance of modern man, *Homo sapiens*. During the last Ice Age (Würm), Europe was inhabited by a peculiar race of men, the Neanderthalians. They were long regarded a separate species, *Homo neanderthalensis*, intermediate between modern man and his apelike ancestors. Yet before Europe was inhabited by the Neanderthalians, there apparently existed a race of men more like ourselves than the Neanderthalians were, and the Neanderthalians ended by being replaced, rather abruptly, by a race of *Homo sapiens* whose bones were much like our own. So it looks as if *Homo sapiens* appeared, disappeared, and reappeared again.

Remains of the early precursors of *Homo sapiens* have been found at Ehringsdorf and at Steinheim in Germany, at Swanscombe near London, at Fontechevade in central France, and at Saccopastore near Rome (the Saccopastore remains may have belonged to a person of the Neanderthal race). Most of these finds belong to the last interglacial (Riss–Würm) age and most are accompanied by stone implements of a primitive kind. Swanscombe man possibly knew fire (Oakley 1956b). All are more or less fragmentary. It is nevertheless probable that with these remains the stage of modern man, *Homo sapiens*, has been approached. The brain volume of the Ehringsdorf skull is estimated to be 1,450 cc, Saccopastore 1,200–1,300 cc, Steinheim 1,100–1,200 cc, and Fontechevade 1,450 cc, and these values are within range of the brain volumes in modern man, *Homo sapiens sapiens*. The general shape of the braincase, the position of the occipital foramen, and the shape of the mandible were all in varying degrees closer to modern men than to the Neanderthalians who during the last glaciation (Würm) followed this early race in Europe. Just how much they resembled ourselves in their facial structure and in other characteristics remains questionable. New finds are greatly to be desired.

It should also be noted that these early Europeans were by no means all alike. In fact, Ehringsdorf, Steinheim, and Saccopastore are somewhat more Neanderthallike and are styled "pre-Neanderthalians," while Fontechevade and Swanscombe are "pre-*sapiens*" (Boule and Vallois 1957). What kind of humans or prehumans were living at this time, so strategic in human evolution, on continents other than Europe, is insufficiently known. In Java, not far from the place where *Homo erectus* was found but in a geologically younger stratum, there came to light five fairly well preserved skulls and six more fragmentary ones which can be designated as *Homo sapiens,* race *soloensis.* With a braincase capacity of about 1,300 cc and an unmistakably human conformation of the skull, the *soloensis* race has a series of traits still reminiscent of *Homo erectus.* This naturally suggests the hypothesis that *Homo erectus erectus* became transformed in Java into *Homo sapiens soloensis,* and that the latter was further transformed into the now living Australian aborigines (Weidenreich). We shall return to this hypothesis below.

Two skulls found far apart in Africa, one in Northern Rhodesia and the other near Capetown, represent another distinctive race, *Homo sapiens rhodesiensis,* studied by Singer (1954). With a skull capacity of 1,200–1,280 cc, it shows resemblances to the European Neanderthal and to the Javanese *soloensis,* without being identical with either. The geological age of the *rhodesiensis* race is not entirely certain, but it seems to belong to the end of the Pleistocene. Whether it has or has not contributed any of its genes to the gene pool of the now living mankind is unknown.

## The Neanderthal Race

Severe climatic conditions prevailed in Europe during the last (Würm) glaciation. Starting from a source in Scandinavia, a continental ice sheet extended down to northern Germany, south-central Russia, and northern England. Not only the Alps but also lesser European mountain ranges were heavily glaciated. Tundralike country extended along the margins of the ice. It is probably in response to the rigors of the environment of this time that a race, *Homo sapiens neanderthalensis,* was formed, the remains of which were discovered in 1856 at Neanderthal, near Düsseldorf, Germany. Other remains were subsequently found in France, Belgium, Spain, Italy, Czechoslovakia, Yugoslavia, Palestine, Crimea, Persia (Kurth 1960b), and southern Turkestan. It is probably the best known form of fossil man, other than the full-fledged *Homo sapiens sapiens.*

Neanderthal man was short and squat, with massive bones, large head, a brain capacity of about 1,450 cc on the average, a facial region strongly developed in comparison with the braincase, a receding forehead, strong brow ridges, a strong and chinless mandible, and large teeth. He is usually supposed to have had a very stooping posture, but this has been denied by at least one recent authority. He lived chiefly in cave shelters but perhaps also in the open, was well acquainted with the use of fire, and manufactured rough stone tools of the so-called Mousterian culture type. He was a hunter, a meat eater, a dresser of animal skins which he probably used for clothing, and a possessor of a rudimentary spirituality (see Chapter 8).

## *Where Did* Homo Sapiens *Come From?*

Some 35,000 to 40,000 years ago, while the Würm glaciation was still at its height, the Neanderthal race was replaced in Europe, apparently rather suddenly, by men whose bones were structurally like our own. These men were invaders from outside Europe, since they brought with them a culture quite different from that of the Neanderthalians. They were again physically far from uniform. The Cro-Magnon people who left their remains in central France were tall (some almost 6 feet) and of athletic physique. They have been matched, as far as the measurements of their bones are concerned, with people now living as far apart as those in southern Sweden, the Basques in northern Spain, and the Kabyles in Algeria. The fossil Grimaldi people in southern France were like some Negroids now living in Africa, and the fossil Chancelade race in France has been matched with Eskimos (Boule and Vallois 1957). Of course this does not necessarily mean that these fossil men were actually like Swedes, Negroes, or Eskimos in every trait. What is important is that mankind was always variable, never uniform.

Modern man, *Homo sapiens sapiens*, was from the beginning a wanderer and a colonizer. No precise dates can be given, but toward the end of the Pleistocene he is already a cosmopolite who appeared in eastern Asia, Australia, Africa, and America. A tantalizing question which naturally presents itself is where, when, and from what source he arose. We do not know nearly enough to give even a partial answer, and this complex and elusive problem is further obscured by the imprecision of its formulation. What, indeed, do we mean by the place of origin of a species? Since species differ in numerous genes, a new species cannot arise by mutation in a single individual, born on a certain date in a certain place (we ignore here so-called allopolyploid species which have no relevance to the human case). Instead, species arise gradually by the accumulation of gene differences, ultimately by summation of many mutational steps which may have taken place in different countries and at different times. And species arise not as single individuals but as diverging populations, breeding communities, and races which do not reside at a geometric point but occupy more or less extensive territories. Races are incipient species, in the sense that they may diverge and become species, not in the sense that every race is bound to become eventually a separate and distinct species.

The evolution of the animal kingdom, or the vertebrate phylum or the class of mammals, is usually represented as a branching tree. The base of the tree is the, often hypothetical, common ancestor, the branches the diverging and ramifying descendants, and the twigs the species or groups of species. The tree thus symbolizes the *cladogenesis* (Rensch 1959a), i.e., the adaptive radiation, the tendency of the evolutionary stream to become subdivided into numerous branches, only to have most of them become extinct because of failures to keep adjusted to changing environments.

It is usually assumed, by a sort of long-established tradition, that the evolution of the hominids must also be portrayed as a branching tree. This leads, however, to a predicament. The several australopithecines, and the Java, Peking, Ternifine, Heidelberg, Solo, Rhodesia, Neanderthal men, and other forms duly provided with generic and specific names in Latin, are placed on the branches or twigs of the human evolutionary pedigree. But almost every one of these fossils exhibits some peculiarities and specializations absent in modern man and in other fossils. Now, because of an exaggerated reverence for the principle of irreversibility of evolution (see p. 169), it is difficult to regard any form a direct ancestor of any other. Despite its many branches, the trunk of the pedigree would remain hypothetical. This interpretation would make man have many fossil collateral relatives but no progenitors. The derivation of *Homo sapiens*, then, becomes a puzzle. He must have originated in some country in which no fossils have been discovered—an easily defensible hypothesis since human fossils have been found in only a few places.

A candelabra is another, less orthodox, way of portraying evolutionary descent. The common ancestor is pushed into the dim past (for hominids as far back as the little *Tarsius*), and the different evolutionary lineages are assumed to have undergone parallel changes and to have acquired similar characteristics quite independently of one another. The modified descendants of different lineages may then come to resemble each other more than they resemble their own ancestors. Applied to human descent, this view has been pushed to patent absurdity. About half a century ago a German professor by the name of Klaatsch solemnly proclaimed that the white race came from a chimpanzeelike ancestor, the black race from a gorillalike one, and the yellow race from an oranglike one. Something about equally far-fetched has been urged by Gates (1948).

Exaggeration of the importance of evolutionary parallelisms almost invariably goes hand in hand with beliefs in autogenesis (see p. 15) as the prime mover of evolution. Different branches of the hominids, or the primates, or the mammals, or even of the living world as a whole, were predestined from the beginning to develop in the direction of humanity, and they did the best they could to reach this foreordained goal. A belief in autogenesis was pivotal to Weidenreich (1946), one of the most discerning students of human evolution. (However, he combined this view with the hypothesis of specific unity of the hominid stock, thereby making his conception very different from those of other adherents of autogenesis). To Weidenreich, Java man and Neanderthal man were not only fossil hominids found in certain localities but also necessary stages through which the evolutionary development of any hominid had to pass, either simultaneously or at different times. Thus he recognized that Java man *(Pithecanthropus)* and Peking man *(Sinanthropus)* were only races of the same species but supposed that the former gave rise, through Solo man and Keilor man, to the now living Australian aborigines, while the latter developed into the Mongoloid branch of mankind. Similar developments occurred in Europe, giving rise to the white race, and in Africa, producing the black race. Mankind as it now exists is, then, a product of the parallel development of several lines.

Evolutionary trends, parallel changes in different lineages taking place either synchronously or at different times, are well known in paleontology. One of the clearest and most widespread trends in animal evolution is gradual increase in body size; animals, both vertebrate and invertebrate, tend to get bigger than their ancestors. Simpson (1944, 1953) and Rensch (1947, 1959a) have shown particularly clearly that such trends are best understood as the outcome of orthoselection, a long-continued process of natural selection favoring a certain quality or feature. Being large is often advantageous, for defense, offense, or for other reasons, hence animals tend to grow larger more often than smaller. But there is no inexorable law that all animals must become larger, and in some evolutionary lines they remain constant in size or even grow smaller. Or else, in the same line, periods of increasing size may alternate with periods of constancy or decrease.

## What Is a Species?

Mankind, *Homo sapiens,* is a single biological species. It could not have arisen by the coalescence of two or several ancestral species, no matter how much parallel development these may have undergone.\* Here a brief discussion of the biological species concept is in order. Can we define species? If we require that a definition of species always enable a biologist to decide whether the forms he observes are distinct species or merely races of one species, then nobody has invented a definition. It may, moreover, be doubted that such a definition will ever be invented. Strangely enough, such a "success" would come close to overthrowing the theory of evolution. The core of Darwin's argument was that species arise from races by a process of gradual divergence. Unless evolution had stopped (see Goudge 1957 for a discussion of this possibility), there must be found instances of incipient species, i.e., forms that will be too distinct to be regarded races of one species but not distinct enough to be counted species. To classify them either as races or as species, is, then, arbitrary.

It does not, however, follow that the distinction between species and races is always arbitrary. A more adequate discussion of race is reserved for Chapter 10. At this point it is sufficient to state that in sexually reproducing organisms contemporaneous races are genetically open systems, while species are genetically closed systems. What is the evidence that mankind is a single species differentiated into races and not several species? It is that race hybridization,

\*Such a statement would not be valid for all species. Some species, especially in plants, arise by hybridization of two pre-existing species, followed by doubling of the chromosome complement (allopolyploidy). And in some fairly well authenticated cases, again in plants, species arose from recombination products formed by hybridization of other species. Although few notions are too far-fetched for somebody not to apply them to human evolution, nobody to this writer's knowledge has seriously contended that man is a product of hybridization of two or several apes or monkeys.

miscegenation or intermarriage, have occurred wherever human races lived side by side for any length of time. Races are capable of exchanging genes and do exchange genes. Perhaps there is no recorded instance of intermarriage between some races, say of Eskimos with Papuans, but Eskimos as well as Papuans do interbreed with other races; channels, however tortuous, for gene exchange exist between all human races.

*Genetically effective* interbreeding is absent between species. Contemporaneous species do not exchange genes, or do so but rarely. There is, for example, no living species with which man could interbreed. Although the horse and donkey species are hybridized on a large scale to produce mules, mules are wholly, or almost wholly, sterile, so that no gene interchange results. Lions and tigers are also species, and although fertile hybrids between them can be obtained in captivity, the species differ so much in their habitats and habits that they do not occur together and do not hybridize in nature.

### Reproductive Isolation

Any genetic agencies that decrease or prevent gene exchange between species are called reproductive isolating mechanisms. Many such mechanisms are known. They range from differences in preferred habitats, behavior, courtship rituals, and breeding seasons, to difficulties of fertilization and inviability or sterility of the hybrids. No one of these isolating mechanisms occurs universally between all species: not all species are "intersterile"; not all lack sexual attraction for each other; not all differ in habitat preferences or in mating seasons. Any one isolating mechanism may be strong enough to isolate a species, but the separation of species is usually accomplished by a combination of several mutually reinforcing mechanisms.

Species in sexual organisms are, then, closed breeding communities, i.e., systems of populations having access to a common gene pool but reproductively isolated from other populations with separate gene pools. Biologists have been talking and writing about species for at least two centuries. The definition just given is couched in the idiom of modern biology and particularly genetics. There has been some divergence of opinion as to whether species should be defined this way. The controversy need not concern us here, since what really matters for our present purpose is the fact that there is a stage in the evolutionary divergence of populations when genetically open systems (races) become genetically closed systems (which we may call species, or else invent a different name).

The evolutionary importance of this stage cannot be overstressed. The development of reproductive isolation, the closure of the genetic system, makes the evolutionary divergence irreversible. So long as populations can exchange genes, the genetic differences between them are subject to swamping and dissolution by hybridization. The races of man furnish some of the clearest illustrations of this—history records many examples of race fusion and of emergence of new hybrid races (see Chapter 10). It is possible at least to imagine a fusion of all human races into a single, greatly variable population. By contrast, the genetic differences between man and chimpanzee or man and gorilla or chimpanzee and gorilla can no longer be swamped. Although this has not been demonstrated by rigorous experiments, it can hardly be doubted that the reproductive isolation between species as distinct as these is complete. One or more of these species may become extinct, but they cannot merge into a single species.

To state the same point with a different emphasis, a species is an evolutionary unit. A favorable mutation or a gene combination arising in any human race on any continent may, propelled by natural selection, find its way into all populations of the human species and become a universal property of the latter. But a mutation arising in a chimpanzee cannot benefit the species of man, or vice versa. Species when fully formed have the genetic links between them severed and embark on separate evolutionary careers.

Species differentiation is obviously of two kinds. Man, chimpanzee, and gorilla are contemporaneous, reproductively isolated species. But their common ancestor, whatever he may have been and wherever he may have lived, belonged to a species assuredly different from all of them. It is meaningless to speak of reproductive isolation of species whose periods of existence did not overlap. The common ancestor would have to be placed in a separate species because he must have differed from the living species which are his descendants. This matter has been admirably analyzed by Mayr (1942), Simpson (1945, 1953, and elsewhere), and others. Temporal races, subspecies, and species are established by analogy with contemporaneous ones. Living species are reproductively isolated, and living races are not; noncontemporaneous forms that differ in appearance (as far as this can be judged from fossil specimens) about as much as living races do are described as races, and those that differ about as much as do living species are designated species. Since evolution is a continuous process we would not find gaps anywhere, if we could know all the links between the common ancestor and the now living species; cutting the continuum into species or races would then be arbitrary. The incompleteness of the fossil record is here, strange to say, a help—the "missing links" are convenient breaks which are used to draw race or species boundaries.

## Races and Species of Fossil Man

An attempt to classify the fossil hominids is shown in Table 17. The tentative character of this attempt cannot be overemphasized; new discoveries will not only add new forms but will probably change the interpretation of the old ones. We recognize two genera —*Homo* and *Australopithecus*. The generic category of classification is biologically arbitrary, it is merely a matter of classificatory

TABLE 17

A tentative classification of species and subspecies of fossil hominids

| Genus | Species | Race (subspecies) | Geographic distribution |
|---|---|---|---|
| *Australopithecus* | *africanus* | *africanus* | South Africa (Taungs) |
| " | " | *transvaalensis* | South Africa (Sterkfontein, Makapan) |
| " | *robustus* | *robustus* | South Africa (Kromdraai) |
| " | " | *crassidens* | South Africa (Swartkrans) |
| " | " | *boisei* | East Africa (Tanganyika) |
| " | *palaeojavanicus* | *palaeojavanicus* (?) | Java (Sangiran) |
| *Homo* | *erectus* | *erectus* | Java (Trinil, Sangiran) |
| " | " | *modjokertensis* | Java (Modjokerto, Sangiran) |
| " | " | *pekinensis* | China (Peking) |
| " | " | *heidelbergensis* (?) | Europe (Germany) |
| " | " | *mauritanicus* (?) | North Africa (Algeria) |
| " | " | *capensis* (?) | South Africa (Swartkrans) |
| " | *sapiens* | *sapiens* | cosmopolite |
| " | " | *presapiens* | Europe (Germany, England, France, Italy) |
| " | " | *rhodesiensis* (?) | South Africa and Rhodesia |
| " | " | *soloensis* | Java (Ngandong) |
| " | " | *neanderthalensis* | Europe, western and central Asia |

convenience how many genera (or subfamilies or families) one chooses to make, while species, as stated above, are objective biological phenomena as well as devices of classification. Our interpretation of human evolution will vary depending on how many contemporaneous, sympatric, and reproductively isolated species we find.

Following Weidenreich (see above), Dobzhansky (1944a) and Mayr (1950) entertained the hypothesis that only one human or prehuman species existed in any one territory at any one time level in evolutionary history. In view of Robinson's (1954) fairly convincing demonstration that two species of australopithecines may have lived in South Africa within a relatively short period of time, if not simultaneously, this hypothesis remains now probable only for the representatives of the genus *Homo*.

The path of evolution leading to the emergence of mankind may, in the light of the above hypothesis, be sketched as follows. One of the species of *Australopithecus* (if, indeed, there were several contemporaneous ones) became dependent for survival on tool-making and tool-using. It adopted, thereby, a way of life that no other animal species ever led. The new way of life created a challenge to which the species responded by becoming even more dependent on the invention of better tools that could be used in new ways. The successful response to the challenge, via natural selection, accelerated the tempo of the evolutionary change. The species became classifiable as *Homo*, no longer as *Australopithecus*.

The evidence required to decide where and when the transformation of *Australopithecus* to *Homo* took place is lacking. We know that both the Sterkfontein and the Tanganyika australopithecines *(Australopithecus africanus transvaalensis* and *A. robustus boisei)* were tool users, and this may mean that attempts to adopt the new way of life occurred in more than one species. As to time, the Villafranchian stage of the Pleistocene period seems most probable. (Since the Villafranchian stage is estimated to have lasted for some 500,000 years, this is no precise dating anyway!) However it may have been, the form that was most successful in the new way of life probably increased and spread to new countries. The species *Homo erectus* lived, at some time during the Middle Pleistocene, apparently in a tremendous territory extending from Java and China to Europe and North Africa (and, if the race *capensis* really belongs to the same species, cf. Table 17, to South Africa). *Homo erectus* may well have met in some parts of this territory a species of

*Australopithecus* other than that from which it itself arose (and fossil remains of the *Australopithecus* ancestral to *Homo* may well not have been preserved or not yet discovered).

As *Homo erectus* spread to new countries and resided there for some time, it differentiated into races (Table 17 lists six such races). But if our interpretation that these were indeed races of the same species is correct, then no two of these races would be expected to have lived simultaneously in the same territory. In fact, two of them *(erectus erectus* and *erectus modjokertensis)* did live in the same country (Java), but the first named is more recent than the second. Weidenreich (1946) and Koenigswald (1958) quite logically conclude that *modjokertensis* is the ancestor of *erectus,* and *erectus* is ancestral to *Homo sapiens soloensis* (Table 17).

### Monophyletic or Polyphyletic Origins

Whether living mankind is descended from a single ancestral form (monophyletically) or from several forms (polyphyletically) has long been inconclusively disputed. Extravagant notions which appealed particularly to race bigots because they claimed that the different human races arose from distinct *species* of apes, have been mentioned above. The problem appears in a different light when it is asked whether our species arose from only a small sector or from a large array of populations of the ancestral species.

Only one species of *Australopithecus* could have been our ancestor. Other species of *Australopithecus* contemporaneous with that ancestor became extinct without issue. This is so because there is only one hominid species now living, and it cannot be derived from two or more reproductively isolated species. But we cannot lightly dismiss the possibility that the now-living human species carries in its gene pool genetic elements derived from most or from all the fossil races of *Homo erectus* and *Homo sapiens,* though in very unequal proportions. On the other hand, we may be descended from only one ancient race, all others having petered out.

The evolution of races will be discussed in Chapter 10; suffice it here to be reminded that races are genetically open, and species genetically closed systems. A new mutation which arose in a species of *Australopithecus* could not penetrate into the gene pool of another contemporaneous species. Suppose, however, that a favorable mutation or an important invention such as the use of fire appeared in or was made by *Homo erectus pekinensis* somewhere in China. It probably would have conferred an adaptive advantage on the clan, tribe, or race in which it arose, and these favored populations, increased in number, probably overflowed into the territories of neighboring populations. They did not necessarily keep their genes or their inventions for themselves alone because populations of the same species usually mate when they meet. This is true even when one group conquers another; many of the conquered are slain and perhaps used for meals, but some, particularly women, may be spared and infuse their genes into the gene pool of the conquerors.

Some 35,000 to 40,000 years ago men whose bones were much like our own and who are therefore classified as *Homo sapiens sapiens,* appeared in Europe. It seems that by at least 24,000 years ago modern man was living in North America; his camp sites have been found in Nevada (Willey 1960). When modern man populated the American and Australian continents, his geographic distribution became nearly world-wide. Ideally, we would like to trace the components of the gene pool of the modern *Homo sapiens* to those of the various ancestral populations. Given the present state of our knowledge this is not possible, but we may consider two examples of evidence, both fragmentary and inconclusive, which show how the problem may be approached.

Some of the tools that early man made and used were of stone. Since man's stone tools are much less perishable than his bones, these artifacts have been found in many more places all over the world than have skeletal remains. Now, the technology of stone tool-making underwent an evolution of its own, and the sequence of stone tool styles has been worked out by archaeologists in more detail than the sequence of changes in the bones of the skeleton. There is, of course, no necessary relation between the physical features of a man and the kind of tools he is using. However, as people move from one territory to another they habitually take their tools or ways of manufacture with them, and the distribution of the tool styles in space and in time is, therefore, an indication of the distribution of their owners.

Two fairly distinct stone tool technologies persisted for millennia during the middle of the Pleistocene epoch. One, the Abbevillian and Acheulean tradition, made use of so-called hand axes, stone cleavers, and various stone flakes. Such tools have been found over an immense territory, embracing Europe, Africa, and western Asia, including most of India. The second tradition characteristically employs crude stone choppers and chopping tools, usually made of stone pebbles. This second tradition dominated eastern Asia, from Burma to China and Java (Movius 1948, 1953). It was the Western tradition which developed more successfully and in late Pleistocene yielded superior stone-working techniques, which eventually dominated the world. It may turn out that the distribution of the Western and the Eastern stone tool traditions was connected with the distribution of the Western (relatively little known) and the Eastern (relatively better known) races of *Homo erectus* (see above). To some authors this suggests that modern man is descended from one or more of the Western and not at all from the Eastern races of *Homo erectus*. This does not necessarily follow from the evidence. Although the possession of a superior stone technology probably benefited the descendants of the ancient Westerners when they eventually invaded eastern Asia, the Eastern races may have contributed some genes to the modern races of that part of the world or to mankind as a whole. In fact, Weidenreich (1946 and earlier) was convinced that the present Mongolian race shows some features derived from the *pekinensis* race of *Homo erectus*.

It is anatomical rather than archaeological evidence that connects the Neanderthal race with other races of *Homo sapiens*. As more and more remains of Neanderthal man were discovered in more and more widely spaced places, it became clear that this race varied greatly both in time and space. The accumulated evidence has been admirably analyzed by Howell (1951, 1957, 1958); another somewhat different hypothesis has been developed by Weckler (1954). The "classic Neanderthalians" were a very distinctive variety of humanity. They were fairly short and powerfully built people with large brains and elongated but low braincases, strong supraorbital tori (a kind of bony shelf above the orbits and root of the nose), broad chests, and generally rugged bones. But people of this "classic" type lived only during the early phase of the last (Würm) glaciation and only in western Europe—Rhine valley of Germany, Belgium, France, Spain, and Italy. The inhabitants of east-central Europe, Russia, southwestern Asia, Iran (Shanidar), and Turkestan did not show as strong a development of all of the above traits as did the western Europeans. Nor did the more ancient inhabitants of western Europe; remains found at Fontechevade and Montmaurin in France and at Saccopastore in Italy may be regarded as intermediate between the "classic" race *neanderthalensis* and the more ancient race *presapiens*.

A most interesting series of fossils found in Palestine has been studied in detail by McCown and Keith (1939), McCown (1950), and Howell (1958). A remarkably variable population, broadly contemporaneous with the "classic" Neanderthalians of western Europe, bridges the gap between that race and modern men. This has been interpreted in a variety of ways—that the population was "in the throes of evolutionary change" from *neanderthalensis* to *sapiens,* that it came from hybridization of these two races, or that it was in transition between *presapiens* and *neanderthalensis* (see also Stewart 1960).

The divergence between these interpretations is, however, more apparent than real, if it be clearly understood that we are dealing here with evolutionary processes within a single species, not with transitions between competing, reproductively isolated species. Not very far from Palestine, in the valley of the Nile, one can observe today a not too different situation, namely intergradation between the white and black races of *Homo sapiens.* Surely this does not mean that the white race is here emerging from the black, or the black from the white; nor does it mean that every inhabitant of Upper Egypt or the Sudan has one black and one white parent. Where the geographic distribution areas of two races (subspecies) come in contact, gene diffusion takes place and intermediate populations are formed. These intermediates may be very ancient and may resemble to some extent the ancestral populations from which the races sprang (primary intergradation), or they may be formed owing to migration or to shifting of race boundaries (secondary intergradation; see Mayr 1942). When the time dimension is added, the opportunities for intergradation are enhanced further.

There is every reason to think that the "classic" Neanderthalians of western Europe were "a stabilized variety only during the initial phase of the last Glacial, due to isolation and perhaps in response to the imposed rigors of a harsh subarctic climate imposing severe selective pressures" (Howell 1957). Regardless of whether there may have been sporadic survivals of the Neanderthalians even toward the end of the Pleistocene period (Zeuner 1958), the Neanderthal race was an evolutionary development within the genetic system of the species *Homo sapiens.*

# 8. Human Mental Faculties and their Antecedents

Omnia, quamvis diversis
gradibus, animata sunt.
SPINOZA

ALL MEN belong to the same species. Mankind is a biologically meaningful entity, just as it is an entity culturally, sociologically, and philosophically. The old question, whether the human species is monophyletic or polyphyletic in origin has, as shown in the foregoing chapter, no longer the same meaning it once had. The sort of biological species man is could hardly have arisen through the coalescence of two or more ancestral species. It arose by transformation of an ancestral species, though probably not equally from the different geographic races of which that species was composed.

Leibnitz once remarked that "the present is saturated with the past and pregnant with the future." For a man of the seventeenth century this was a noteworthy discernment: the other minds of that century were dominated by the idea of a static world of created species. Leibnitz's utterance epitomizes, rather, the point of view of modern evolutionism. In the foregoing chapter we have reviewed the information bearing on the historical antecedents of man and his relatives. Woefully incomplete though this information is, it still permits some inferences concerning the causes which led to the emergence of the salient characteristics of *Homo sapiens*, a most extraordinary biological species.

### Upright Stance and Tool Use

"Owing to the development of an upright posture, man has acquired free and skillful hands, implements for the finest operations, and persistent groping for new and clear ideas . . . With language begins his intellect and his culture" (quoted after Rensch 1959b). This astonishingly modern idea was expressed by the German philosopher Herder, some eighty years before it was argued by Darwin in *The Descent of Man* and some 170 years before our day! Our present views concerning the interrelationships between human physical evolution and the evolution of his tools are due mainly to the brilliant work of Washburn (1950, 1959), Bartholomew and Birdsell (1953), Oakley (1954, 1957, 1958), Washburn and Avis (1958), Washburn and Howell (1960), and others. The basic thesis is that the physical and genetic endowments of the human species now living have evolved as a result of and hand in hand with the development of culture. That is to say biological evolution and cultural evolution are interdependent. Washburn states the thesis in these words: "Much of what we think of as human evolved long after the use of tools. It is probably more correct to think of much of our structure as the result of culture than it is to think of men anatomically like ourselves slowly developing culture."

Probably the most serious gap in the fossil record of hominoid primates is the absence of known fossils in Upper Pliocene strata (see Table 16). The Villafranchian stage is represented only by the South-African australopithecines. These are, however, tremendously significant because originally even so expert an anatomist as Weidenreich regarded the australopithecines as peculiar apes. The conformation of their pelvis, particularly of the ilium bone, one of the most distinctive bones in which human and ape skeletons differ, showed, however, that the australopithecines walked erect (see, however, Zuckerman 1954). Another important trait is the size of the canine teeth. In monkeys as well as in apes, particularly in the males, the canines are large and project above other teeth, and the animals use them for defense and for offense. In man the canines are smaller and are not used as weapons. In the australopithecines the canines are more like those in man than those in apes. This fact led Bartholomew and Birdsell (1953) to infer that the australopithecines were tool-users. The inference has been borne out splendidly by the discovery of stone tools in at least two australopithecine sites (see p. 187).

The australopithecines have acquired two manlike traits—upright stance and tool-making—which are, in combination, of commanding importance. Has man become a tool-user because his hands were freed from walking duties and became available for handling tools? Or have his hands developed because he was a tool-user? It is unprofitable to speculate which of the two came first; this would be akin, most likely, to asking whether the chicken or the egg came first. The two traits probably developed together, reinforcing each other and conferring progressively higher adaptive advantage on their possessors. However, bipedal locomotion arose from quadrupedal locomotion in several groups of animals but it did not always lead to the employment of the anterior extremities for tool-using or tool-making. For example the large Australian kangaroos move by leaping on their hind paws but their small front legs are used relatively little.

Conversely, tool-use has evolved in several animals lacking a pair of hands or upright posture. One of Darwin's finches of the Galapagos Islands utilizes cactus spines, which it holds in its beak, to pry out insects from bark fissures (Lack 1947). The California sea otter uses stones to crack open the mollusk shells on which it feeds. There are well authenticated cases of tool-use even among insects: a paralyzing wasp, *Ammophila,* uses a pebble as a "hammer" to press down the soil around the opening of its burrow; the ants *Polyrachis* and *Oecophylla* fasten together leaves with silken threads produced by their own larvae, whom the adult ants wield in their mandibles like tubes of glue. To be sure, all men not merely use tools but make tools, and so apparently did at least some of the australopithecines. Tool-use may be a purely instinctual activity, as in the insects mentioned above; tool-making is a performance on a psychologically higher level.

Bartholomew and Birdsell (1953) reconstruct the mode of life of the australopithecines as follows. They subsisted both on vegetable and on animal foods—berries, fruits, nuts, buds and shoots, shallow-growing roots and tubers, reptiles, mollusks, crustaceans, insects, eggs, nesting birds, and smaller mammals up to and including baboons. Remains of some larger mammals, giraffes and antelopes, found together with the australopithecines, more likely came from scavenging from kills made by large carnivores (such as lions) than from their own hunting. The absence of strong canine teeth implies the use of implements such as sticks and clubs for killing and butchering the game. The use of fire is considered unlikely (although this was claimed by Dart, one of the original discoverers of the australopithecine remains). It is possible though not certain that some of the australopithecines hunted not singly but in bands, and such hunting encouraged or even necessitated cooperation and communication among the hunters.

### Man's Similarity to Simian Fetus

Among many attempts to fathom the mainsprings of human origins, that of Bolk (1926) has been in vogue with some anthropologists (Keith 1949 and earlier writings, Tappen 1953, Ashley Montagu 1955b, Hallowell 1960, and others). A not uncommon type of evolutionary change in some groups of animals is that called fetalization, pedomorphosis, neoteny, or proterogenesis (see Rensch 1959a). In this change the developmental processes of the organism are so retarded that adulthood and sexual maturity are reached at a stage of bodily development that would correspond to the juvenile or even fetal stage in other related animals. Man is supposed to be fetalized as compared with the apes, since in the adult man the size of the head and the relative proportions of its parts resemble those in juvenile apes more than those in adult apes. Bolk speculated that fetalization may have been caused by changes in the hormone balance in the body, especially by a decrease in the production of the anterior pituitary hormone.

The fact that it takes man about twice as long as the apes to reach complete body growth has already been referred to (see Table 2). Although the duration of pregnancy in apes (253–275 days) is of the same order as in man, only some 23 per cent of adult brain volume is achieved in man by the time he is born (and only some 55 per cent at the end of the first year) compared to more than 50 per cent at birth in the apes. The milk teeth develop in man between 7.6 and 28 months after birth and in the chimpanzee between 2.7 and 12.3 months after birth; the permanent dentition appears between 6.2 and 19.9 years in man and between 2.9 and 10.2 years in the chimpanzee (Krogh 1959).

It is really no disparagement of the fetalization theory to say that it falls short of providing a causal explanation of human evolution. Why has human evolution shown a trend toward fetalization? We cannot suppose that human evolution was predestined to show this or any other trend. This would imply a belief in autogenesis (see p. 16). An important step toward a satisfactory theory could only be an elucidation of the biological meaning of the fetalization process, i.e., of the function it served in the organisms in which it occurred. Moreover, human development is not simply ape development slowed down (Portmann 1944, Schultz 1950, 1956). The average increase in weight in the human fetus is 12.5

g per day, while in the orangutan it is only 5.7 g per day. However, this rapid growth continues in man for the whole first year of infancy, slowing down thereafter; in the apes weight increases more uniformly, and after three years of age the apes overtake man in body mass.

There is no question that these peculiarities of the human growth pattern were important in human evolution. Human infants are born quite helpless compared to ape or monkey infants, not to speak of colts, calves, or lambs who can run after their mothers almost immediately. This necessitates in man a kind of parental care more assiduous and prolonged than in any ape, a fact which served as the point of departure for Freud and other depth psychologists (see Chapter 3, also Roheim 1950 and LaBarre 1954). And yet it is this helplessness and prolonged dependence on the ministrations of the parents and other persons that favors in man the socialization and learning process on which the transmission of culture wholly depends. This may have been an overwhelming advantage of the human growth pattern in the process of evolution. That this pattern suggests a fetalization is an interesting fact, but by itself it throws little light on the natural selective processes that must have operated in human evolution.

The idea, stemming apparently from Fischer (1914; quoted in Reche and Lehmann 1959), that the peculiarities of human evolution are due to man being a domesticated or, rather, a self-domesticated animal, has also made some impact on the thinking of anthropologists and biologists. Now, this theory obviously depends on the meaning one may give to "domestication." The evolution of domesticated animals and plants differs from that of wild forms chiefly because artificial selection partially replaces natural selection. The selection pressure is shifted from traits that favor the survival and reproduction of the population in the wild to those useful to the owner and the breeder (Herre 1959). However, natural selection continues to operate in man even in environments created by his culture, and in any case it is not yet replaced by artificial selection. Hence we cannot speak of "domesticated" man as we can of domesticated animals or plants. In fact, "domestication" of man is too vague an idea to be scientifically productive. The conjecture, it should be added, that domestication enhances the mutation rate of genes is unconfirmed for animals and gratuitous for man.

## Family Integration

Man may or may not be "pre-eminently a sexual animal," as claimed by Freedman and Roe (1958). However, his reproductive biology is a rather unusual one among mammals, and this has unquestionably exerted a profound influence on the evolutionary pattern of the human species. The normal, in the sense of being most frequently met with, mammalian sexual pattern makes the female receptive to the advances of the male only at a certain more or less limited stage of her estrus (hormonal) cycle. This stage of female receptivity (heat, rut, mating season) corresponds to the time when fertilization and subsequent pregnancy are most likely. In most mammals this stage coincides with some particular season of the year. However, in some mammals, including most if not all species of monkeys and apes, the estrus cycles in different females are not synchronized, so that at any time some females are sexually receptive. And, finally, the human female remains between the times of menarche (first menstruation) and of menopause more or less uninterruptedly receptive. This, as will be shown below, favors the development of the monogamous family.

It is a rule, which applies not only to mammals but to diverse other animals, that males tend to be sexually aggressive and indiscriminately eager to mate with any and all receptive females, while the females are generally more choosy and demure, or less easily excitable. This rule breaks down with species in which copulation takes place once in a lifetime and with strictly monogamous species where mates are paired permanently. As suggested by Bateman (1948), the same mechanism probably underlies both the rule and the exceptions. Nature is prodigal with male sex cells, parsimonious with female ones. For example, although only one spermatozoon fertilizes an egg cell, in man a single ejaculation contains on the average some 200 million sperms. Excepting some marine organisms, females, on the other hand, produce relatively few eggs. The number of the surviving progeny of a male is, then, likely to be proportional to the number of females he has inseminated; even if some copulations result in no progeny, the supply of spermatozoa will probably remain ample. And it is the amount of the surviving progeny that mainly counts under natural selection (see Chapter 6).

Other things being equal, sexually aggressive males of polygamous species are favored by natural selection. The size of the progeny of a female is limited not only by the number of eggs she produces but, in mammals, by the length of pregnancy and maternal care. A female must economize her resources. Accepting a wrong male (a male of another species, or a sterile, diseased, or genetically inferior male) may diminish or eliminate her progeny. Natural selection favors, then, discriminative passivity in females.

Despite numerous and careful studies, the social organization and sexual habits of monkeys and apes are insufficiently known. (See Carpenter 1942, 1954, Yerkes 1943, and Nissen 1951 for further references.) These things vary from species to species, but most often one or a small number of strong, adult, and active males assemble a "harem" of females with whom they mate whenever the females are receptive. Adolescent, weak, and old males are driven out of the band and forced to live singly or in small groups on the peripheries of the territories defended by the active males; the outcasts, however, remain ever eager to break in and supplant the dominant males.

The energies of a nonhuman primate male are, then, consumed by keeping out competitors and protecting the band from external enemies. Primate males help little in the business of raising children—this is left to the females; nor do they give food to females or the young. In fact, there is an hierarchy of precedence (dominance) established within a band so that the strongest male has the first choice in feeding, while individuals low in the hierarchy accept ungrudgingly or perforce their subordinate position. The hierarchy is, however, a fluid one. Yerkes (1939) made the important observation that a female chimpanzee in a sexually receptive state not only rises in the hierarchy above nonreceptive females but is even deferred to by males.

In the absence of evidence to the contrary, it is reasonable to suppose that our prehominid ancestors had a social organization not unlike that in modern apes. As pointed out particularly by Etkin (1954) and LaBarre (1954), this organization must have crumbled under the impact of an altered diet and of tool-use. A primate female is either pregnant or carrying an infant or a child during most of her adult life. She is able to provide food for herself and her baby so long as that food consists of fruits or other vegetable products gathered from the tropical forest. With the transition to upright posture, ground living, omnivorous or carnivorous habits, and a hunting and food-gathering economy, a different sort of division of labor must have been favored by natural selection.

Continuous sexual receptivity of the female made monogamous family life possible and thus freed the male from the constant necessity of warding off interlopers. He could now specialize in hunting and food gathering away from home, while the female could remain more nearly stationary, tending her offspring, gathering food in the near vicinity of her abode, and doing the domestic chores that accumulated with the growth of technology and, particularly, with the use of fire. As the male was now able to relax his aggressiveness and dominance, particularly over his mate, domination could change to cooperation and in the long run even to chivalry. If man is "pre-eminently a sexual animal," he has at least managed to make his sexual urges less acutely competitive than they were in his remote ancestors. Cooperation between mates made possible the extended family (individuals of several generations with their respective mates living together) and eventually clans, tribes, and nations. Different males now could cooperate to provide for the families and this permitted stalking, cornering, and killing big game that was inaccessible to the lone hunter until he was equipped with powerful weapons. Cooperation, in turn, made communication a necessity and stimulated the development of language. Thus a series of new selective pressures were set up, of a kind which did not exist on the prehuman level.

The question may again be raised as to whether upright stance, tools, constant sexual receptivity of females, symbolic language, monogamous family, change in food habits, or relaxation of male aggressiveness came first. Obviously we cannot answer with certainty, but it is most likely that these changes went together, with mutual reinforcement. What we are dealing with is the emergence of a whole new evolutionary pattern, a transition to a novel way of life which is human rather than animal. This is an example of an infrequent type of evolutionary change, which Simpson (1944, 1953) has called "quantum evolution." Evolutionary alterations in general, and especially those in quantum evolution, are unlikely to involve changes of one trait at a time. The whole genotype and the whole phenotype are reconstructed to reach a new adaptive balance.

## Brain Size

One of the striking peculiarities of the human species is its large brain. Increases both in absolute brain size and in that relative to the body size have been prominent in the line of descent leading to man. Since brains are not preserved in fossil condition, the volume of the braincase cavity (cranial capacity) is measured instead. Cranial capacity is somewhat larger than, but is correlated with, brain volume. It is on the average greater in males than in females, but variable in either sex. Krogh (1959) gives values of 230–450 cc for the female and 350–480 cc for the male chimpanzee and 356–596 cc for the female and 387–655 cc for the male gorilla. Gorillas are larger but not more intelligent than chimpanzees. With fossil skulls which almost always have to be reconstructed from fragments, measurements of the cranial capacities involve errors (see Mettler 1956). Nevertheless, the trend toward increasing brain size is unmistakable, as seen from Table 18. Between the australopithecines

TABLE 18

Cranial capacity in hominid evolution
*(after Krogh, Washburn, and others)*

|  | Capacity (in cc) |
|---|---|
| Australopithecines | 450–550 |
| *Homo erectus erectus* | 770–1,000 |
| *Homo erectus pekinensis* | 900–1,200 |
| *Homo sapiens neanderthalensis* | 1,300–1,425 |
| *Homo sapiens sapiens* (Recent) | 1,200–1,500 |

and modern man, the brain size has approximately trebled; yet the body of the former was only slightly smaller than that of the latter (the body weight of australopithecines is estimated to have been about 120 lbs.).

The importance of brain size has long been a matter of debate. Opinions have ranged from complete scepticism to a willingness to use brain size as a measure of the "innate" mental capacities of individuals and groups. There is no question that among living men brain size is not a reliable measure of the individual's capacity. Boule and Vallois (1957) give the figures of 2,012 cc for the cranial capacity of Ivan Turgenev, 1,965 cc for Bismarck, and 1,830 cc for Cuvier, but only 1,294 for Gambetta. Anatole France is also said to have possessed a small brain volume. The same authors quote the following averages for cranial capacities in the adult males of different human populations: Andamanese—1,300 cc, Australian Aborigines—1,340 cc, Parisians—1,550 cc, Auvergnese—1,585 cc.

Large cranial capacity is evidently not indispensable for high intelligence or achievement. But it is a fallacy to conclude that since brain size alone does not unalterably set the level of intelligence, the two variables are not in any way related. Such a conclusion probably again reflects the misconception that a trait is either wholly genetic or wholly environmental. The effects of brain size on mental capacity have been studied in animal materials, particularly by Rensch and his school (reviews and references in Rensch 1958, 1959a, 1960). The speed of learning and the learning capacity have been compared in pairs and groups of related species and races of contrasting body (and brain) sizes—white rats with white mice, elephants with horses, donkeys with zebras, large breeds of poultry with medium-sized and small ones, and large with small fishes. The animals were trained to discriminate between signs such as a black cross (marking a food reward) and a black square (unrewarded) on a white background, a narrowly striped pattern (rewarded) and a broadly striped one (unrewarded), and objects of different colors, etc.

The speed of learning proved to be greater sometimes in the smaller and sometimes in the larger forms, but the average number of "tasks" (patterns or colors) learned was greater in the larger ones—8 in rats, 6 in mice; 20 in elephants and in horses, 13 in donkeys, and only 10 in zebras; 7 in large fowls, 5 in medium-sized ones, and 4 to 5 in small ones; 6 in large fish (trout), 2 to 4 in small ones (guppies). The retention of the learned tasks (memory) was definitely superior in the larger animals. The "best" rat remembered all its learned tasks for 154 days, the "best" mouse for 103 days; the rat still retained one discrimination after 459 days, the mouse after 195 days. The elephant remembered 12 tasks after the lapse of one year. A horse having learned 20 tasks remembered all of them 6 months later, a donkey only 7 out of 13 after 3½ months, a zebra 10 out of 10 also after 3½ months. The large poultry breed retained 6 learned tasks after 20 days, the small breed only 3 out of 5 after the same number of days. Rensch concludes that the memory retention is about proportional to the brain size in the animals experimented with by himself and his colleagues. He cautiously suggests as a possible mechanism that larger brains contain nerve cells with more numerous branches (dendrites), which permit more numerous interconnections between the cells and, thus, a greater variety of paths of nerve impulses.

## Brain Differentiation

Mental capacities are not determined by brain poundage alone. An elephant's brain is at least thrice the size of a human brain (5,000–6,000 cc), but an animal with a very large body obviously needs a large brain to sustain even its vegetative function. At least one anthropologist has advanced the amazing contention that there may not have been any increase in the mental capacity of the human species since Java man. Though unlikely in the extreme, such a view cannot be dismissed on the basis of brain size alone. However, not only the size but also the structure of the human brain is remarkable (see Rensch 1958, 1959a,b).

A trend is discernible in the evolutionary history of vertebrate animals, from fish to man. The brain increases not only relative to body size, but the forebrain (the anterior portion of the brain) increases most of all. In fish, the forebrain houses chiefly the centers of the olfactory sense. It is much larger and more complex in reptiles, and in mammals it becomes not only the largest portion of the brain but acquires on its surface a so-called cortex which contains several layers of nerve cells. In mammals the cortex becomes complexly folded, which permits the brain to accommodate ever larger numbers of nerve cells (some ten billion in man).

The brilliant and fascinating experiments of the neurosurgeons Penfield and Roberts (1959) on their patients have done much to advance the knowledge of the localization of functions in the human brain. According to them, only man's cerebral cortex has a control mechanism for vocalization. The sounds that are emitted by other mammals are controlled in a quite different part of the brain. The near-uniqueness of the so-called Broca region of the human brain has been mentioned above (p. 165), but here it must be pointed out that "there is a very large increase in the extent of the temporoparietal cortex that becomes obvious in passing from anthropoid ape to man."

The question that logically presents itself to an evolutionist at this point is: How could centers governing new and unusual functions arise in the cortex of the human brain if they were not previously located there? The answer apparently is that the brain is astonishingly plastic. Penfield and Roberts (l.c.) testify that "the human cerebral hemispheres are never twice the same in form and in the patterning of convolutions and fissures." For example, in most people the speech area of the cortex lies asymmetrically in the left brain hemisphere, although it may occasionally lie in the right one. Moreover, a brain lesion suffered in infancy in the speech area may result in the displacement of the whole cortical speech machinery to the corresponding portion of the right hemisphere, which normally serves other functions. It is tempting to speculate that this plasticity leaves room for further evolutionary improvements (but also for degradation) of the human brain.

## Instinct

Man is not simply a very clever ape. On the contrary, he possesses some faculties that occur in other animals only as rudiments, if at all. Quantum evolution, emergence of novel adaptive designs, may involve breaks in the evolutionary continuity when the differences between the ancestors and the descendants increase so rapidly that they are perceived as differences in kind. Antecedents of the new designs may, nevertheless, be detected in the old ones. We must equally resist the temptation to regard man either as something completely unlike any animal or as something devoid of all novelty (see, however, Portman 1944 and White 1949, 1959, who succumb to the first view, and Harlow 1958, who gives in to the second). For example, legs in land-living vertebrates were new organs, since fishes from which the land vertebrates descended had no legs. Comparative anatomy shows, however, that the extremities of the land vertebrates arose from the paired fins of their fishlike ancestors.

Progressive evolution of behavior in the animal world has led to the interposing of more and more nervous processes between the stimuli arriving from the environment and the organism's responses to them. The "forced" movements (taxes) of unicellular organisms in response to light, gravity, temperature, or food substances are mostly genetically determined, immediate, and relatively invariant. The same is true of unconditioned reflexes, although here the external stimulus is first transmitted from the periphery of the organism to the central nervous system where it is switched onto a "motor" nerve fiber or fibers which lead to the reacting organ. The reactions of a newborn infant, sucking, swallowing, urinating, crying, etc., are mostly unconditioned reflexes. So are such adult reactions as the contraction or dilation of the pupil with light, muscular twitches and jerks in response to sudden or painful stimuli, etc.

Instincts are more complex forms of behavior which may be interpreted as concatenations of unconditional reflexes released by certain stimuli. Instinctual behavior is particularly important in insects, where it may reach astonishing intricacy and marvelous perfection. A bee, an ant, a hunting wasp, or a caddis fly are born fully able to execute many and complex operations used in obtaining food, providing for offspring, or building and maintaining the nest. What is most remarkable is that this instinctual behavior is highly adapted, and in this sense purposeful, to the environments in which the species normally lives, but it is liable to become disoriented, incoherent, and injurious to the actor in new and unaccustomed environments.

The nature of instinctual behavior is insufficiently understood (see Lorenz 1943, 1952, Tinbergen 1951, 1953, 1959, Thorpe 1956). Definitions of instinct have been so many and varied that for a time psychologists preferred to avoid the term altogether. But the phenomena subsumed under this name have to be labeled somehow, and in recent years the term has been vindicated. Stone (1951) defines instinct as the "unlearned patterns of behavior, occurring alike in all members of a species and serviceably complete on the occasion of their first appearance." Another definition is given by Kubie: Instinct is "the direct and indirect expression of biochemical body processes, through inherited yet modifiable networks of neuronal synaptic patterns which are molded in turn by superimposed, compulsive and phobic mechanisms" (cited in Freedman and Roe 1958).

Stone's definition is objectionable to an evolutionist, because species could not evolve if some of their traits were not subject to variation. Lehrman (1953, 1955) and Schneirla (1955) rightly pointed out that behavior, which is part and parcel of the development pattern of the organism, is subject to environmental modification, including modification by learning. They went too far, however, when they argued that instinctive behavior is not inborn or inherited. Since behavior is a part of the organism's phenotype, its modifiability does not preclude genetic conditioning. The environmental stability or plasticity of a trait is itself genetically controlled. The genetic architecture of the species renders certain that some developmental processes will occur in all the circumstances that an individual is likely to meet in the natural habitats of its species (Schmalhausen 1949, Waddington 1957). Some instincts are among such genetically vouchsafed traits (see p. 56), and this is the reason for their apparent rigidity. However, "the direct and indirect expression of the biochemical body processes" is hardly a useful part of a definition of instinct because no manifestation of life is believed to be anything else.

In higher animals and most of all in man instinctual behavior is intertwined with, overlaid by, and serves merely as a backdrop to learned behavior. Yet it would be rash to treat this backdrop as unimportant. Sexual behavior is a striking example of the give-and-take among instinct and learning. Beach (1948) found that male rats reared in complete isolation copulate normally when offered receptive females, and females reared in isolation react normally to the approaches of males. This is not so with the chimpanzee (Nissen 1951). Sexual behavior is quite variable in different individuals; individuals raised without an opportunity to observe the mating behavior of others do not copulate when first meeting a receptive partner. However, if left with a suitable mate for a few months they eventually do so. In man the sexual libido is obviously a part of the normal development pattern of the species, though probably varying greatly in intensity in different persons. The overt manifestations of this libido are, however, largely culturally determined and hence learned; even the consummatory sex act is not wholly instinctive.

Owing to the highly complex intermeshing of instinctive and learned behavior, no fixed list of human instincts or drives has been or probably can be given (for a discussion of the relationships between instinct and drive, see Thorpe 1956). Rensch (1959b), nevertheless, mentions sexual, maternal, social-status-seeking, hunting, collecting, and cleanliness instincts. Maslow (1954), though refusing to give a list of human drives, names the following "basic needs"— physiological and aesthetic needs, and needs for safety, belongingness, love, esteem, self-actualization, knowledge, and understanding. The two lists overlap but clearly do not coincide. They may both be valid, provided that one does not envisage an instinct, a drive, or a basic need as something isolated and independent of other instincts, drives, or needs. It may be objected that, for example, the "cleanliness instinct" seems to be conspicuously missing in many people, but this objection is not very serious. A preference for cleanliness may be frustrated by a cultural setting. It is known to have been inverted in some ascetics, who mortified the flesh by making it endure filth. This feat of asceticism is, in fact, an argument for the idea that cleanliness is some sort of a tendency of the human animal, for if it were not there would have been no merit in its self-denial.

## Learning

Pavlov (1849–1936), a great scientist who suffered the posthumous indignity of having his work become dogma in the Soviet Union, demonstrated that stimuli releasing unconditioned reflexes may be replaced by previously indifferent stimuli. Placing food into the mouth of a dog releases the flow of saliva (unconditioned reflex), but the flow of saliva may also be released by the mere sight of food or by the sound of a bell, provided that the food was shown to the dog or the bell was sounded on repeated previous occasions just before the dog was fed (conditioned reflex). Acquisition of conditioned reflexes enables animals to react to a great variety of stimuli ("signals") emanating from the external world, the environment. The sum of the conditioned reflexes was called by Pavlov the first signal system, which permits the animal to profit by experience and learning.

Thorpe (1956) defines learning "as that process which manifests itself by adaptive change in individual behavior as a result of experience." This may be unduly optimistic—learning has developed in evolution as a powerful adaptation, but one learns also useless and downright wicked things! Most animals can learn, and learning has been claimed even for unicellular organisms. But by and large the proportion of behavior that is learned increases from the lower to the higher organisms and reaches its maximum in man. Although learning has been thoroughly verified in insects (e.g., in the honey bee; Frisch 1955), insect behavior as a whole is predominantly instinctual. Man's behavior, on the contrary, is very largely a product of culture, imparted by teaching and learning, particularly during the socialization process in infancy and childhood (Chapter 3).

The surprisingly ample learning capacities of an ape have been revealed in the fascinating experiment of Hayes and Hayes (1951, 1954), which is described in a most engaging book. Vicky, a chimpanzee, was adopted as a three-day old infant by two people who brought her up in their home as though she were a human child. Vicky learned easily a number of human activities, such as eating and drinking at a table, washing herself and brushing her teeth, washing dishes and dusting furniture, opening cans and bottles, sharpening pencils, playing with mechanical toys and even with a dial telephone. She learned to obey a number of commands (for example, "close the door"), to recognize objects from their photographs, and to score on nonverbal intelligence tests at about the level of a human child of her chronological age.

At the same time Vicky developed several typical chimpanzee behavior features, such as rocking on her haunches when frightened and "bluffing" by assuming a threat posture, which she could not have learned from her human foster parents. These actions may, therefore, have been instinctual. It was in learning human language that Vicky's abilities proved decidedly limited. Her vocabulary finally consisted of three words, "mama," "papa," and "cup," which she used only when her desires expressed by gesticulations were not granted. This failure was not due to any incapacity to utter the sounds (Yerkes and Yerkes 1929) but rather resembled the condition known in humans as aphasia, failure to speak owing to injury of the speech centers in the brain (see above). Vicky's behavioral phenotype was certainly unlike anything any other chimpanzee ever had, and yet it was obviously within the norm of reaction of the chimpanzee genetic endowment.

## Insight and Generalization

Insight is apprehension of relations; generalization is derivation of a general principle from particular instances. These are predominantly and characteristically human faculties, utterly absent in the newborn and developing only gradually, usually together with the ability to speak. Their traces are, nevertheless, observable in some animals. Rensch and Dücker (1959) trained a civet cat *(Viverricula malaccensis)* to choose between a box containing food, marked on the top with two black circles of unequal size, and a box lacking a reward, marked by two equal-sized circles. Then thirty other pairs of marks were used, the unequal pair always marking a reward and the equal one always empty. The animal eventually developed an "averbal general concept" of oddity vs. equality and could choose between a box marked with nine unequal dots and one with nine equal-sized dots. It was, however, unable to extend this concept to discriminate between two similar letters or numerals and two dissimilar ones. The experiments of O. Koehler and others (see Thorpe 1956 for references) have shown that such averbal concepts of number may be developed in some birds. They can be trained to locate a reward marked by a certain number of dots of different shapes and arrangements.

The work of W. Köhler (1921) on the chimpanzee remains a classic despite manifold objections raised against some of his interpretations. In his experiments a male chimpanzee learned to get a banana, placed out of reach of his arm, by means of a bamboo pole and thus to use a tool. Then a banana was placed out of reach of the available bamboo poles. As the frustrated ape continued to play with the poles, he suddenly inserted one pole into the other and proceeded to go after the banana with the longer pole. Thorpe

(1956) suspended in a glass cylinder some seeds attached by a string to a perch. A bird could obtain the seeds only by pulling the string with its beak and holding the loops with its foot. Of the twenty-eight wild-caught birds (great tits), four succeeded after a few trials, while the rest showed no signs of progress. The survival value of such "insight learning" to the animal is evident.

### Symbol and Language

Composing formal definitions is a favorite mental calisthenic with scientists. Biologists, however, do not excel in these calisthenics: their basic concepts, life, individual, gene, species, etc., have never been defined to general satisfaction. But this imprecision does not greatly interfere with their use in the communication of ideas. Man has been variously described as the political animal, the tool-maker, the symbol-maker, the son of God, the god-maker, etc. All these definitions have their uses. Symbol-making and the use of symbolic language are the most distinctive human faculties, although they are in some degree foreshadowed below the human level.

In Cassirer's words (1944),

> Man has, as it were, discovered a new method of adapting himself to his environment. Between the receptor system and the effector system, which are to be found in all animal species, we find in man a third link which we may describe as the symbolic system. . . . Man's outstanding characteristic, his distinguishing mark, is not his metaphysical or physical nature, but his work.

Pavlov expressed the same idea much before Cassirer when he spoke of a "second signal system," consisting of word symbols, superimposed in man, and in man alone, onto the first signal system of conditioned reflexes. White (1949) goes even farther, perhaps a bit too far, when he says,

> All human behavior originates in the use of symbols. It was the symbol which transformed our anthropoid ancestors into men and made them human. . . . It is the symbol which transforms an infant of *Homo sapiens* into a human being; deaf mutes who grow up without the use of symbols are not human beings. . . . Human behavior is symbolic behavior; symbolic behavior is human behavior.

A symbol is "a thing the value or meaning of which is bestowed upon it by those who use it" (White 1949). A word is a symbol and human language is a symbolic language. There is nothing in the sound of *buch, livre, liber, kniga, biblion,* or *kitab* to indicate that they all mean the same as *book.* Vicky the chimpanzee did learn with great difficulty the use of three human words, but it was beyond her power to assign a meaning to them. A child can invent a "language." So-called animal languages are not languages in the human sense. A dog may utter and "understand" so many sounds that it "almost speaks," but it does not quite; its sounds are mostly emotional outbursts, perhaps comparable to our expletive monosyllabics, and a dog is not likely to alter their meaning arbitrarily or to transmit the alteration to its progeny (Kroeber 1917–1952).

Hockett (1959) lists the following properties as characteristic of human languages in contradistinction to animal ones: duality of patterning, which means that separate significant sounds (phonemes) are by themselves meaningless but are meaningful when functioning as constituents of words (i.e., as morphemes); productivity, which refers to the ability to compose new but nevertheless understandable utterances from words which occurred in previous communications, i.e., to the fact that a finite number of words can express an infinite number of ideas. Arbitrariness is the quality already mentioned above, that the meaning of a word is socially agreed upon and is not deducible from the component sounds. Interchangeability means that a speaker is capable of saying anything that he can understand when someone else says it. Displacement means that we can speak of objects and acts regardless of their distance in space and in time (animal calls usually refer to immediately present situations). Human languages, being a part of culture, are wholly acquired by learning and, though genetically conditioned, are not transmitted by genes; animal "languages" are so transmitted (see Lenneberg 1960 for a thoughtful discussion of this point).

The sole verified example of a symbolic "language" in a nonhuman animal (though obviously not having all the properties listed above) is found, remarkably enough, not among mammals closely related to man but among insects. The fascinating studies of Frisch have shown that a honey bee having discovered a source of food is able to impart to her hivemates the information concerning the location and the distance of this food from the hive. The bee, returning to her hive, performs a "dance" on the surface of the comb.

This dance is richly symbolic: its speed indicates the approximate distance of the food from the hive; its inclination to the vertical tells the direction of the food with respect to the position of the sun. The "dance" excites the worker bees in the neighborhood of the dancer, who begin to follow her movements and eventually fly to the food source in accordance with the information received. It goes almost without saying that the "rules" of the dances are genetically fixed and not acquired by instruction or agreement among the bees of a given hive. However, the behavior of a worker bee develops gradually, a newly hatched individual does work only inside the hive and starts foraging for food outside only later.

The "language" of bees is profoundly interesting because its existence shows that symbolic languages must have arisen in evolution at least twice, obviously independently in unrelated organisms. It arose as a learned trait in man and as an instinctual performance in the bee. To explain the benefits of communication by language would be belaboring the obvious. Human language, because it is learned, has made cumulative experience and cultural transmission possible, and adaptation by culture is vastly more potent and versatile than adaptation by genetic change. Biological genetic evolution certainly did not cease when it became supplemented by cultural evolution (see Chapter 11), yet the evolution of culture has transformed man's way of life in the last 5,000 years more than biological evolution has in at least ten times as long an interval.

There is no way of telling at what stage in the evolution of man language was acquired. Attempts to set the attainment of a certain brain volume as a precondition for the origin of language are unconvincing. Sapir (1921) was probably right to say,

> It is, indeed, in the highest degree likely that language is an instrument originally put to uses lower than the conceptual plane and that thought arises as a refined interpretation of its content. . . . The instrument makes possible the product, the product refines the instrument.

Etkin (1954) plausibly connects the acquisition of language with the constant sexual receptivity of the human female, emergence of monogamous family, division of labor between females and males, and cooperation of hunters in tracking and killing big game. If so, the beginnings of language probably antedate the emergence of the species *Homo sapiens*.

## Learned Tradition on the Subhuman Level

A lively controversy raged during the twenties when Pavlov in Russia and McDougal in America claimed that conditioned reflexes are more easily established in the progeny of conditioned animals than in the progeny of unconditioned ones. It was alleged that laboratory rats conditioned after a number of lessons to make certain choices produced offspring that required fewer lessons for a similar conditioning. Since human culture involves conditioning, this would mean that culture acquired by learning and training may become, at least in part, gene transmitted. Careful repetition of the experiments failed to bear out the early claims, and Pavlov did not press them in later years. The apparent inheritance of the conditioning was doubtless due to the trainers' unconscious selection of animals that were trained most easily. It is, indeed, probable that the facility with which an animal may be conditioned is in part genetically controlled, but this is a far cry from maintaining that the genetic basis of the conditioning is built or even strengthened directly by the conditioning of the ancestors.

Conditioning, learning, and training have to be started afresh in every generation, because culture is not transmitted by genes. However, this does not by any means rule out the existence of genetic variations which make the acquisition and perpetuation of culture more or less difficult. Inasmuch as symbolic language is the basic mechanism of the transmission of human culture, and symbolization has little precedent on the animal level, the specifically human form of culture is confined to man and to man alone. Nevertheless, learning and conditioning are not restricted to man. The behavior of some animals is in part due to conditioning by parents and other members of the flock, band, or society. Modification and social transmission of this conditioning have actually been observed. Here, then, we find the closest analogies with or antecedents of human cultural transmission.

Bird songs are in part learned. Some birds are capable of producing a great variety of vocalizations and tend to imitate the sounds that they hear other birds make, especially their parents and conspecific individuals. In different localities the populations of a species may have different "song dialects" which even the human ear can easily distinguish. It is difficult to decide to what extent such dialects are inborn or acquired but it is probable that in some instances they are at least in part learned (Mayr 1942, Thorpe

1956). Different local populations of a species may also show preferences for different foods or may follow different techniques of hunting and procuring their meals. In some birds and mammals these habits, too, are in part learned by imitation from parents or other individuals.

In a small cove on the northern coast of Marajo Island, which is just south of the equator in the Amazon estuary, I observed in 1956 a colony of the common South American scavenger vulture *Catharista atratus* that lived on fish entrails thrown overboard from the vessels of a fishing fleet. Although this bird does not normally get its food from salt water, the individuals in the colony just mentioned had learned to catch the discarded fish as they hit the water or even before they touched the water. The colony quite likely acquired the habit by imitating the few birds that first "discovered" the new feeding opportunities, perhaps accidentally. The spread, although not the discovery, of new feeding habits has been recorded in some bird species, particularly in the great tit which has learned to remove cardboard milk bottle tops and drink the milk. This habit became rather widespread in England in recent decades.

By far the best organized and most careful observations of the establishment of new habits have been made by a group of Japanese students (Imanishi 1957, 1960, Miyadi 1959; see also a review in Frisch 1959). The habits of several colonies of the monkey *Macaca fuscata* were studied. In the colony most studied, paper-wrapped caramel candies were offered to the monkeys. At first they consistently rejected the candy, and only eventually did some juvenile monkeys pick them up and unwrap and eat them when not watched by their elders, who attempted to prevent such unusual behavior. The caramel-eating habit spread first to other juveniles, then to their mothers, then to the dominant males, and last of all to the subadult males who are normally kept on the fringes of the colony. The whole sequence took at least three years, and even then some subadult males had not yet acquired the novel habit. The analogy with the food habits in different human populations is evident. What one eats or refuses to eat is determined largely by what other members of one's family and one's group regard as fit or unfit to eat. Which, again, does not rule out the occurrence of genetically conditioned idiosyncrasies in dietary matters—members of the same family or group often find different foods palatable.

The Japanese workers also observed and compared several

bands of *Macaca fuscata* and found them perceptibly different not only in food habits but also in social structure and inter-individual behavior. In one of the colonies a new food habit (eating wheat) was introduced by the dominant male leader of the band, and spread rapidly to females and juveniles. In another band the precedence of the dominant individuals was enforced by fierce fighting, and most individuals bore traces of wounds, while in still another the fighting was merely "symbolic." In some colonies the foraging for food starts from a fixed "center of operations," but other bands wander around and rarely return to the same place. Some bands have greater sexual license than others: a female who copulates with a subdominant male may be either severely punished by the dominant one or tolerated by him. Although the proof that these differences are acquired rather than genetic is not as complete as may be wished, it is most likely that the different monkey colonies have different learned "protocultures."

## Play

"The human nervous system possesses curious and profound hungers for many objects which are neither meat nor drink, neither satisfiers of oxygen need, nor of sex need, nor of maternal need, nor any other more obvious visceral demand" (Murphy 1958). Such needs are "curious" because man is a product of evolutionary development, and evolution is utilitarian. No theory of human evolution that ignores its pragmatic aspect can be valid. On the other hand, in man utility may mean something subtler than satisfaction of visceral demands.

Indeed, man lives not by bread alone. Play and aesthetics, two "hungers" which have at first glance baffling biological meanings, may be considered briefly. There exists a voluminous literature on play in humans and animals, but the concept of play is hard to define with precision (Beach 1945, Wittgenstein 1953). By and large, play is a self-rewarding activity, i.e., the performance of the action constitutes its own recompense. Play occurs chiefly, if not exclusively, in vertebrate animals, and particularly among the higher ones, mammals and birds. The behavior of invertebrates is too stereotyped to permit play. In other words, their "appetitive behavior" (such as courtship) is too rigidly tied to its satisfaction in the consummatory act (copulation). Man has been described as the most playful of all animals *(Homo ludens,* Huizinga 1955). At any rate, playing and games are among the cultural universals in all mankind (Murdock 1945).

Although this is disputed by some authorities, play is still most satisfactorily viewed as a means to an end: it facilitates learning, acquisition of skills, practice and exercise, exploration of and familiarization with the environments in which the individual lives or may live. As is to be expected from this view of play, the amount of time spent at play is greater in childhood and youth than in adulthood and senility. On the other hand, the chief compensations for the disabilities of old age are, indeed, persistent skill of hands and deftness of mind, and both are a result of the restless and ostensibly idle and pointless curiosity that is expressed in the urge to explore, to pry into the nature of things, and to enjoy forms, sounds, colors, and thoughts and ideas.

Although some forms of play (those which are chiefly muscular, for example) are basically similar in higher animals and man,

> there is, indeed, good reason for thinking that the prolonged childhood of the human species, coupled with the extreme infantile sexuality (occurring as it does so long before there is any possibility of consummatory sexual behavior), have been of prime importance in the process of freeing appetitive behavior from the primary needs. This and man's growing mastery of his environment have been the essential first steps not only for play but for all those activities which transcend mere maintenance and which underlie the mental and spiritual development of man; activities which, though originating in "play," have produced real advances in knowledge and comprehension of the scheme of things, and which may, for all we know, offer vistas of advance in the millennia to come, compared to which our present understanding will seem puny and infantile in the extreme [Thorpe 1956].

### Art and Æsthetics

Play certainly occurs in many animals, but aesthetics and art are usually regarded as exclusively human possessions. Sensitivity to beauty and making or doing things that are perceived as "beautiful" are among the traits that elevate man above the brutes. This renders the problem of the origin and biological meaning of art and aesthetics in human evolution particularly challenging.

Let it be clear at the outset that the beauty of nature refers to human feelings about certain natural objects, not to these objects themselves. It is man who is enthralled by the grandeur of a snow-clad mountain range, and it is man who admires the splendor of such butterflies as *Morpho* or *Ornithoptera* fluttering under a tropical sun or even pinned in an entomological collection. As nearly as we are able to make it out, the biological function of all this glory of form and color is pragmatic: in animals it serves as species recognition marks in sexual unions. The real and unsolved problem is why these displays seem so superb also to man. There is no reason to think that females and males of *Ornithoptera* or *Morpho* enjoy the sight of each other any more than do female and male lice and other creatures that we find repulsive.

Yet, in some situations it becomes really difficult not to impute to animals some sort of aesthetics. The performances of the bower birds, family *Ptilorhynchidae*, of which about nineteen species occur in Australia or New Guinea, are most extraordinary (Marshall 1954). At the approach of the mating season, the males build display grounds consisting of variously constructed "bowers" and "maypoles," to which they eventually entice females, and in or near which the matings take place. Nests, however, are built elsewhere. Most astonishingly, the bowers are decorated in various and often highly elaborate fashions. Some species cover an "avenue" approaching the bower with objects such as bleached animal bones, pieces of stone and metal, and silver coins if they can get them. Other species make a "meadow of moss," on which they arrange brightly colored fruits or flowers, which are there for display and are not eaten. Still others paint the walls of the bower with fruit pulp, or charcoal, or dry grass mixed with saliva. At least one species manufactures a painting tool out of a small wad of spongy bark.

Some bower birds not only select objects that seem beautiful to us but maintain them in an attractive state: they replace faded flowers and decayed fruits with fresh. They also adhere to a certain color scheme: a bird using blue flowers will throw away a yellow flower inserted by an experimenter, while a bird using yellow flowers will not tolerate blue ones. The type of bower built and the nature of its adornments are, however, species-specific. The bird "artist" does not seem to experiment with different possible decorations and choose that which he likes best. Although his actions seem to be instinctive and automatic, it is impossible to deny that a well-adorned bower may give the bird a pleasure which can only be called aesthetic.

The remarkable experiments of Rensch (1957) come closest to demonstrating the reality of such "protoaesthetic" phenomena in nonhuman mammals and birds. The experimental animals (monkeys, birds, etc.) were offered for play (i.e., without any reward) the choice of six pieces of white cardboard with black patterns of various sorts—symmetrical or asymmetrical, with or without rhythmical repetition of the constituent components, with steady or faltering lines, etc. The cardboard pieces were arranged in a circle, and the experimenter recorded which pattern the animal took first in its paw or its beak. The animals showed preferences for symmetrical and rhythmical patterns, and for those with steady rather than faltering lines. This agrees with the well known findings of psychologists who studied the elements of aesthetic preferences in human subjects (see Arnheim 1954 for further references). Morris (1961) has described some engaging experiments in which apes (particularly chimpanzees) were offered painting instruments and actually "composed" pictures, uncomfortably similar to the creations of certain "advanced" schools of modern painting.

The origin of such elementary aesthetic, or protoaesthetic, impulses has been the topic of much speculation. There is no question that some manifestations of "beauty," particularly of the human body, are related to sex; the aesthetic is, undoubtedly, affiliated with the erotic. The psychoanalytic school has done much to unravel these erotic connotations, which are often complex and devious and which frequently remain unconscious even after persistent introspection. But it may well be doubted whether psychoanalytic explanations are as complete and compelling as we have been assured they are. There may be, indeed, something more than faintly sexual in the pleasure of riding and in the admiration of horseflesh. The evidence that mountains seem beautiful because they suggest feminine breasts is far from convincing.

Many and varied attempts have been made to develop a theory that would explain the functions of art and aesthetics in the human species. As far as I know, nobody has approached this problem in a way that makes better sense to an evolutionist than Jenkins, a philosopher (1958). According to Jenkins, man's experience in relation to the world has three functional components—the aesthetic, which focuses upon the "particularity" (individuality) of things; the affective, which concentrates upon their import; and the cognitive which sees their consequences.

These components direct a person's attention toward, respectively, particular things, the self, and the environment. The integrated action of the three yields a comprehensive and coherent understanding of things. The biological function of the affective component is to keep us sensitive to our vital needs and concerns. That of the cognitive component is to focus attention upon the causes and consequences of the present occasion and on the similarities and connections of things and events. We undertake the enterprises of science, philosophy, and technology to explain things by clarifying their relations to each other.

The function of the aesthetic component "is to keep response sensitive to the actual thing or situation that we confront; it directs behavior towards clarifying the intrinsic character of occasions and events in all of their richness and concreteness." The aesthetic experience is, then, a necessary mode of our acquaintance with the world and with our own selves. Artistic expression and creation are consequences of this experience.

> Until we have achieved a coherent vision, our insights are cursory and scattered, we sense meanings that are portentous but imponderable, and our hold on particularity is neither refined nor stable. We feel this inadequacy, and are driven to repair it. So every aesthetic encounter with things points to its completion through expressive and creative activity.

Perhaps the same idea was expressed very concisely in the fourth century A.D. by Salustius, who wrote that myths are "things which never happened but always are" (quoted in Sarton 1952), and in the nineteenth century by Mallarmé, who thought that the task of poetry was "to simplify the world."

Some forms of art seem to be related to play. The development of skill, almost any skill, is likely to be a source of intense gratification, as observations of children plainly show. The physical medium with which an artist works is always a challenge to his skill. Painters strive to wrest the most from pigments, sculptors from stones or clay, musicians from sounds, poets from words, dancers from their own bodies. Successful domination of the medium is a satisfying experience not to the artist alone but to his audience as well. This latter fact makes artistic activity a source of social cohesion, and the adaptive value of cohesion in human societies can hardly be overestimated. (For a utilitarian interpretation of the role of art in human societies, see Hauser 1951.)

The hypothesis that artistic activity enhances the fitness of human populations explains the otherwise unintelligible fact that art arose early in human evolution. The almost incredible perfection of the cave paintings at Altamira in Spain and Lascaux in France shows that art already existed and perhaps had a long tradition when the Würm glaciers were retreating in Europe. For these paintings were not the product of an isolated genius who worked solely for his personal pleasure. They had a function. Their location, in deep interiors where they could only be seen by dint of special effort, and their contents, primarily representations of game animals rather than the human form, both strongly suggest that they served some ritual, probably of a magical sort.

Magic and "spirituality" certainly antedate the appearance of *Homo sapiens sapiens* in Europe. Neanderthal man had a "cult of skulls" and funeral rites of some sort (Bergounioux 1958). It has even been suggested that Peking man, *Homo erectus pekinensis*, may have engaged in a ritual cannibalism; his remains consist almost exclusively of skulls with broken occipital parts, as if for extraction of the brain for ceremonial consumption (Bergounioux, l.c.).

The origins and development of spirituality, magic, ritual, and religion have long been studied by anthropologists and sociologists. The classical work in this field is that of Durkheim (1915 and other publications). He regarded religious rituals, symbolisms, and orders as "collective representations" which function as integrative factors increasing social cohesion. Malinowski (quoted in Firth 1955) most explicitly states a similar idea: "Magic serves not only as an integrative force to the individual but also as an organizing force to the society." This suggests that the adaptive significance of aesthetic and religious experiences lies in their humanizing this unruly beast, *Homo sapiens*.

# 9. Polymorphism, Class, and Caste

PEOPLE are obviously similar to each other and, as obviously, different from each other. Most religions, from Christianity to Marxism, but with the conspicuous exception of Hinduism, hold that the similarities are more meaningful and outweigh the differences. The Christian view is that all men are sons of God, and therefore all are brothers; the corollary is that all have equal rights to life and to self-realization. Scientifically considered, however, the similarities and the differences are incommensurable. Both have to be studied; it is folly to neglect either.

Although all men now living are members of a single biological species, no two persons, except identical twins, have the same genetic endowment. Every individual is biologically unique and nonrecurrent. It would be naive to claim that the discovery of this biological uniqueness constitutes a scientific proof of every person's existential singularity, but this view is at least consistent with the fact of biological singularity.

Anyway, genetic individuality is not the whole story. Superimposed on the individual variability there is a group variability. Very few biological species are panmictic, i.e., consist of a single Mendelian population in which the chances of mating of any two adult individuals of opposite sex are equal. Such panmictic species are shrunken relics of formerly more differentiated species now on the verge of extinction. Man is certainly not such a species. Owing to geographic and social factors, mankind is divided and subdivided into a multitude of overlapping and criss-crossing mating groups, Mendelian populations subordinate to the species, the members of which are more likely to intermarry among themselves than with members of other populations. The boundaries between these populations are often, even as a rule, both blurred and shifting in time and space; and yet the gene pools of the populations

usually differ in the relative frequencies of certain genes, and sometimes also qualitatively.

The variability of the human species is not static. Populations,
tribes, communities, classes, castes, and races expand and contract,
emerge and disappear, and change in composition in various ways.
A biological species is usually in the throes of genetic change, and
man is no exception. We need not agree with Darlington's opinion,
quoted in Chapter 1, that heredity is the ultimate determinant of
the course of history. This view is too simple to be credible; no
single formula can describe so vast and varied a field as human
history. But the materials of heredity are variables implicated in
history.

### Cladogenesis and Anagenesis

Despite the separation being neither clear-cut nor rigid, it is
convenient to distinguish two kinds of biological evolution—*cladogenesis,* or branching, and *anagenesis,* or phyletic, evolution (Simpson 1953, Rensch 1959a). Any species tends to spread and to occupy
all available territory and all environments. As a consequence, the
species may split into races, races may develop reproductive isolation and become new species, these species may pursue separate
evolutionary courses and diverge to become genera, etc. Thus an
originally single evolutionary unit breaks up into several or many
independent ones. Organic diversity is thereby increased; the world
is populated with more and more distinct kinds of organisms.

On the other hand, a species may become progressively altered
genetically in the course of time. A species, an inclusive Mendelian
population (see p. 183), may change its genetic composition, either
to improve its adaptedness to an environment which remains relatively static, or because the environment changes with time. The
species remains then a single species, a single evolutionary unit, but
it becomes altered more and more, so much so that the populations
that lived at different time levels have to be classified as different
species, genera, etc.

Both cladogenetic and anagenetic changes took place in man's
ancestry, but the latter predominated. The evidence now available
(see Chapter 7) is compatible with the assumption that, at least
above the australopithecine level, there always existed only a single
prehuman and, later, human species (which evolved with time from
*Homo erectus* to *Homo sapiens*). Mankind was and is a single, inclusive Mendelian population and is endowed with a single, corpo-

rate genotype, a single gene pool. All men share biologically so many common features, all are fundamentally so similar, because an advantageous genetic change arising anywhere in the species was and still is able to diffuse from the place of its origin and to become a part of man's common genetic patrimony. Predominance of anagenesis over cladogenesis is one of the distinguishing marks of human evolution.

## Polytypism and Polymorphism

Anagenesis dominated human evolution in the sense that the human species did not break up into a cluster of derived species. But it cannot really be overstressed that mankind was and is genetically heterogeneous. And though the separation is again neither clear-cut nor rigid, two kinds of heterogeneity should be distinguished. Mankind is a *polytypic* species composed of a cluster of races, Mendelian populations with more or less different gene pools. And mankind is *polymorphic,* each population being genetically variable, containing, in fact, as many genotypes as it has individuals (identical twins excepted).

It is opportune here to be reminded of a fundamental biological principle (see Chapter 6). Organic diversity is the adaptive response of living matter to the challenge of the diversity of environments. In other words, living beings are diversified because their environments are diversified. If the world's environments were as homogeneous as those, for example, in a laboratory test tube with nutrient broth on which microbes are grown, one kind of organism, a single genotype, would conceivably be sufficient to exploit the resources of the environment. (Even then the life activity of this single kind of organism might create an environmental heterogeneity and hence a place for another kind of organism.) The real world offers, however, a great diversity of environments. How is life to cope with this diversity? No gene complement is the paragon of adaptability, superior in all environments. The only trend, direction, or, if you wish, aim, goal or purpose, discernible in life and its evolution is the production of more life. This trend manifests itself, through the instrumentalities of mutation and natural selection, in the diversity of organisms.

A question now inevitably suggests itself: Why does the adaptation to the environment sometimes take the form of cladogenesis, splitting into distinct races or species, and sometimes of polymorphism, intra-populational diversity? Some plausible speculations can be offered. Individuals of a species who live together in the same locality, *sympatrically*, may have a variety of environmental opportunities: an insect may feed on different plants, a plant may grow in different soils, people may obtain their livelihood by hunting or fishing or agriculture. It may be that one genetic endowment enables its possessor to deal equally efficiently with all these environments. If so, a genetic uniformity will prevail. But if one genotype "agrees" better with one environmental factor and another genotype with another, then a genetic diversity may be preferable. Under these conditions a population which contains several adaptive genotypes will be better off than a genetically uniform one, and natural selection will favor diversity, polymorphism, the presence of genotypes suited for different aspects (ecological niches) of the available environments.

The origin of polytypism is equally simple. Populations that live in different territories, *allopatrically*, face different environments. Different genotypes may accordingly be favored by natural selection in different territories, and a living species may respond by becoming polytypic. It becomes differentiated into more or less distinct Mendelian populations—local tribes or demes, races, or subspecies.

Splitting a single species into two or more derived ones is more complex. Intraspecific polymorphism and polytypism within a single species could have been the total extent of the organic diversity in nature if it were not for two factors—sexual reproduction and gene interaction. Suppose that there are two environments, which we may denote as $x$ and $y$, and that a genotype containing the genes $A_1$ and $B_1$ is well adapted to the environment $x$, while a high fitness in $y$ results from the gene combination $A_2B_2$. Suppose further that the intermediate gene combinations, $A_1B_2$ and $A_2B_1$, are good neither in $x$ nor in $y$. If the environments $x$ and $y$ occur in different countries, the problem of adaptation is solved rather easily: allopatric populations, geographic races, will be formed, one being $A_1B_1$ and the other $A_2B_2$.

A difficulty arises, however, if the environments $x$ and $y$ occur in neighboring territories. The races $A_1B_1$ and $A_2B_2$ are likely to meet, mate, and produce segregating hybrid progenies, which will include the ill-adapted genotypes $A_1B_2$ and $A_2B_1$. The difficulty becomes greater if the environments $x$ and $y$ occur together in the same territory (for example, different food plants growing side by side), and may be solved in two ways. The more radical way is to sacrifice sexual reproduction; the less radical but just as efficient way is to develop a reproductive isolation (see p. 184) which would prevent the interbreeding of the populations $A_1B_1$ and $A_2B_2$ and hence preclude the appearance of the inferior types $A_1B_2$ and $A_2B_1$.

Both ways have been resorted to in organic evolution, the second more often than the first. The first has led to the emergence of asexual reproduction and parthenogenesis (development without fertilization). It is relatively more common among plants than among animals. The second has led to the splitting of a single species into two or more still sexual but reproductively isolated species. Animal and plant species now living on earth number at least two million. Pairs or groups of closely related sexual species often co-exist sympatrically, without forming any hybrids and ill-adapted gene combinations. But human evolution has followed neither of the above courses. Man has remained a single, though highly polymorphic and polytypic, sexual species.

The full meaning of this fact has not been appreciated. It implies that the hybrids between human races are not frequently deficient in fitness compared to the parental races which produced them. Where miscegenation leads to no loss of fitness, there is no stimulus for natural selection to foster the development of reproductive isolation and the consequent breaking up of a single species into two or more derived ones. There may be two reasons why race hybrids in man enjoy a fitness equal to the parents. First, the genotypes $A_1B_1$, $A_1B_2$, $A_2B_1$, and $A_2B_2$ in our scheme may be adaptively equivalent in the environments in which they live. Second, when the environment is highly diversified, as it is in civilized societies, all these genotypes may find suitable opportunities. The countless occupations, callings, and pursuits that advanced human societies offer (corresponding to ecological niches on the biological level) are enough to accommodate human polymorphism.

The same argument may be stated with a slightly different emphasis. The adaptive function of the genetic variability has been altered in the human species by cultural development. Culture is an extrabiological method of adaptation. However, it is conditioned by, dependent on, and interacts with biological mechanisms (see Chapters 11 and 12). People may achieve adaptation to their environments through learned rather than inborn automatic responses, and most, though certainly not all, human genotypes can do so successfully. Knowledge and wisdom, then, may enable certain genotypes that in precultural environments would be interdicted by natural selection to survive by choosing or creating for themselves suitable environments.

The effect of civilization is to standardize some aspects of the environments in which people live and to increase enormously the variety of other aspects. Regardless of climates, people live in dwellings of more or less similar type, eat not very radically different foods, and even wear much the same clothes. Moreover, this standardization of the external, physical, material aspects of living is doubtless on the increase: one finds at least some people leading pretty similar lives in New York, Moscow, Cairo, Madras, Tokyo, and Bogota. On the other hand, a complex society needs a tremendous variety of different people—farmers and teachers, mechanics and artists, clerks and physicians, and so on almost ad infinitum. Civilization makes the occupations of people diversified, not homogeneous. It was the development of culture that prevented the human species from breaking into several species, and at the same time favored human variation and polymorphism.

## Chromosomal Polymorphism in Drosophila

At this point an illustration of the workings of polymorphism and polytypism in nonhuman populations would be useful. Populations of Drosophila flies lend themselves to experimentation more easily than human populations. *Drosophila pseudoobscura,* which occurs in the western United States and in Mexico, is one of the species which are polymorphic with respect to what may seem a curiously recondite character—the arrangement of the genes in their chromosomes. Two or more, up to seven, chromosomal forms may occur together in a single locality, and the flies that carry them interbreed freely. Every fly has five pairs of chromosomes, one in each pair derived from the mother and the other from the father. The two chromosomes of a pair may have the same gene arrangement (chromosomal homozygote) or different gene arrangements (chromosomal heterozygote). Let us designate the kinds of the chromosomes by some letters—ST, AR, CH, etc. A population will then consist of the chromosomal types ST/ST, AR/AR, CH/CH (homozygotes) and ST/AR, ST/CH, and AR/CH (heterozygotes).

The flies of different chromosomal types are identical in appearance. They can, however, be diagnosed by microscopic examination of the chromosomes in the cells of the salivary glands of their larvae. It seemed at first that it made no difference to a fly which type of chromosomes it carried—just as it seemed to make no difference to a man which type of blood he had (see p. 280). But it was discovered that in some localities in California the relative frequencies of the chromosome types undergo regular changes with the seasons. Table 19 shows that in a certain population the ST chromosomes become more frequent and the AR chromosomes less so as the season progresses; the changes must be reversed in winter when the flies hibernate. The changes are cyclic and repeat themselves year after year.

TABLE 19

Relative frequencies (in percentages) of three kinds of chromosomes, ST, AR, and CH, in the population of the fly, Drosophila pseudoobscura, at different seasons in a certain locality in the Sierra Nevada of California (after Dobzhansky 1952)

| Month | ST | AR | CH |
|-------|-----|-----|-----|
| May | 26 | 47 | 19 |
| June | 29 | 43 | 20 |
| July | 30 | 38 | 20 |
| August | 40 | 30 | 14 |
| September | 36 | 31 | 21 |

We can infer that, during the summer, flies with ST chromosomes are more fit than those with AR chromosomes, while the opposite is the case in winter. Drosophila flies breed rapidly and produce several generations per year in nature (the exact number is unknown). Natural selection acts accordingly—it increases the incidence of ST chromosomes during the summer and of AR chromosomes during the winter. This working hypothesis is, at least in part, borne out by experimental tests. Populations of Drosophila flies can be created in the laboratory in "population cages" made of wood and glass or some other material. A mixture of flies containing known proportions of the desired chromosomal types is introduced into the cage; a jar with a nutrient medium is inserted and the jar with the worked-out medium removed at suitable intervals. The flies breed freely up to the limit imposed by the amount of the food given (some 1,000–4,000 adult individuals, many more eggs and larvae). Natural selection can work in this highly "artificial" population. From time to time a sample is taken from the population, and the relative frequencies of the different chromosomes it contains are determined under the microscope.

The experimental populations show that the fitness of the flies with different chromosomal types is far from equal and that in most environments the chromosomal heterozygotes are superior to the homozygotes. (Thus, the fitness of AR/CH is higher than that of AR/AR and the latter higher than CH/CH, etc.) Now it has been shown in Chapter 6 that when a heterozygote is more fit than both homozygotes, natural selection brings the population to an equilibrium, at which the homozygous genotypes continue to occur with frequencies depending upon their relative fitness. There are good reasons to think that a similar situation obtains also with the gene for sickle-cell anemia in man; the heterozygous carriers have an advantage over noncarriers in malarial countries. In Drosophila we can go farther—the experiments permit estimation of the approximate magnitudes of the fitnesses and the selection coefficients involved. This is one of the rare occasions in biology when the study of natural selection can be put on a quantitative basis. For example, in a certain experiment the fitness, taking the heterozygote to be unity, proved to be (Dobzhansky 1948a):

| Chromosomal type | AR/CH | AR/AR | CH/CH |
|---|---|---|---|
| Darwinian fitness | 1 | 0.86 | 0.48 |
| Selection coefficient | 0 | 0.14 | 0.52 |

The figures show that the selection operating in these populations is a very powerful one: the fitness of the CH/CH homozygotes is perhaps less than half that of the AR/CH heterozygotes. In this sense the CH/CH condition may be considered a hereditary disease! And yet the polymorphism may be regarded as Drosophila's way of keeping up its adaptedness to the environments in which it lives. This polymorphism is maintained by natural selection, and it is balanced owing to the "hybrid vigor" of the heterozygotes.

It is not well understood just what the physiological properties are that make the heterozygotes highly fit. It is apparently a complex matter, including a higher fecundity, longevity, resistance to crowding, etc. What is known, however, is that the relative fitness of the chromosomal types is exquisitely sensitive to the environment. The figures given above are from experiments in which the populations were kept at a temperature of 25°C (77°F) and on a certain food. Changing the temperature or the food may alter the fitness a good deal. Thus, dropping the temperature by only 10°, to 15°C (59°F), makes the homozygotes and heterozygotes equally fit within the limit of the sensitivity of our experimental procedure.

## Chromosomal Races in Drosophila

Observations on seasonal changes in the composition of polymorphic Drosophila populations (Table 19) showed that the chromosomal types differ in fitness, not in laboratory experiments alone
but in nature as well. It is consequently reasonable to expect that
the inhabitants of localities with different environments will differ
in composition. Such differences may, in fact, be observed between
populations of localities at no great distance from each other. Populations of *Drosophila pseudoobscura* that live at different elevations
were studied in midsummer in the Sierra Nevada mountains of
California. Table 20 shows the data. The horizontal distance be-

TABLE 20

Frequencies (in percentages) of three kinds of chromosomes, ST, AR, and
CH, in populations of the fly, *Drosophila pseudoobscura,* living at different
elevations in the Sierra Nevada of California *(after Dobzhansky 1948a)*

| Elevation (feet) | ST | AR | CH |
|---|---|---|---|
| 850 | 46 | 25 | 16 |
| 3,000 | 41 | 35 | 14 |
| 4,800 | 32 | 37 | 19 |
| 6,200 | 26 | 44 | 16 |
| 8,000 | 14 | 45 | 27 |
| 8,600 | 11 | 55 | 22 |
| 9,900 | 10 | 50 | 20 |

tween the lowermost and the uppermost localities is about 60 miles.

It is evident that ST chromosomes become less and AR (and
perhaps CH) chromosomes more frequent as one ascends the slope
of the mountain range. Just what aspects of the low-altitude environments favor ST and of the high elevations promote AR is unknown. It is tempting to relate the altitudinal distribution of the
chromosomal types to their seasonal one—ST chromosomes are
encouraged at low elevations and by warm summer weather, and
AR at high elevations and during the cold season. Be that as it may,
the inhabitants of the different elevations are genetically, *racially,*
distinct. But note that the distinction is merely one of relative frequencies of the same genetic variants. Inspection of the chromosomes of an individual fly does not tell us from which part of the
mountain slope it came. One has to have a population sample of at

least a dozen, and better a hundred, flies to venture a surmise as to whether they came from a low-altitude or mid-altitude locality. This fact is illuminating: races are not individuals but Mendelian populations, and race differences are differences between populations. Races in sexually reproducing organisms are Mendelian populations which differ in the incidence of some genetic variants in their gene pools (Dobzhansky 1944b).

Or to change the emphasis somewhat, race differences are compounded of the same genetic materials in which individuals within a race, a population, may also differ. The frequency of ST chromosomes quadruples as one descends the mountain slope from an elevation of 8,000–9,000 feet to about 1,000 feet (Table 20). Nevertheless flies with ST chromosomes occur at all elevations. This illustrates an important point: in contrast to a species, which is a genetically closed system (Chapter 7), a race is a genetically open system, i.e., the genotype of an individual is not rigidly determined by the race from which he sprang.

Race differences may be of different magnitudes. The populations of *Drosophila pseudoobscura* from Colorado or Texas contain many AR chromosomes, but ST and CH chromosomes are rare. The populations from southern Mexico contain very few or none of the chromosomal types that are common in California (Tables 19 and 20) and have instead chromosomes that are found rarely or not at all in California. With only rare exceptions, one may distinguish between a single individual from the mountains near Mexico City and a single specimen from California by the chromosomes. Yet a careful study discloses that the chromosomal differences between Mexico and California populations are still quantitative rather than qualitative. The situation in man is parallel: natives of Nigeria are easily distinguished from natives of Norway by skin color and other traits, but it is not so easy to distinguish by his appearance a Norwegian from an Italian or a Spaniard, or at any rate from a German or a Russian.

### Races, Classes, and Castes as Mendelian Populations

Human variation presents a situation vastly more complex than that in the Drosophila fly discussed above. We may, however, use the latter as a paradigm to help elucidate the former. The basic distinction between variations within populations (polymorphism) and variations between populations (polytypism) must always be remembered in any inquiry into the causes of human variation. The distinction is fundamental. Since members of a population intermarry, the variants which the population contains may be members of the same family. Spouses, siblings, and parents and children are always carriers of different genotypes, but these are derived from the gene pool of a single population; it is absurd to consider brothers and sisters, or parents and children, as belonging to different races. Members of different populations do not intermarry, or do so less often than members of the same population. Race differences are differences between populations, not between individuals.

A student of human variation has to ascertain whether the group of people he plans to study are actually members of a Mendelian population and constitute a fair sample of that population. This task is incomparably more complex in anthropology than in zoology or in botany. With the exception of domesticated animals and plants, parasites, and some narrowly specialized feeders, representatives of an animal or a plant species residing in the same neighborhood may fairly be assumed to be members of one Mendelian population. This was probably also true for man in the preliterate era, but it is not true for modern man. Especially in cities but also in the country, neighbors often belong to different linguistic, religious, economic, and other groups; members of such groups may be as unlikely to intermarry as people residing thousands of miles apart.

A group of people accosted on a street of New York or Bombay or Rio de Janeiro would probably not be a meaningful sample of any population (except if these people were drawn in proportion to the relative numerical strength of the different communities, castes, and religious denominations residing in a given city; but such a sample would really be a compound of separate subsamples representative of the different communities). One may also choose to study a group of people who are heavy smokers or nonsmokers, criminals or law-abiding citizens, victims of tuberculosis or malaria or schizophrenia, or college graduates. Studies of this sort are certainly legitimate to characterize the groups chosen, but such groups should not be confused with races or social classes, because smokers, criminals, and schizophrenics are not mating groups but are, instead, drawn from many diverse mating groups. All this may seem so obvious as to be trite; and yet mistakes of the above sort have been made over and over again.

The foregoing should not be construed as denying that any human population contains different, often strikingly different, kinds or sorts or, if you wish, "types" of people. This is merely another way of saying human populations are polymorphic. So are the populations of Drosophila discussed above; we have seen that some of these populations are racially distinct because they contain different proportions of certain chromosomal forms, but it would be preposterous to call a chromosomal form a "race," because there may be as many as six such forms among a pair of parents and their progeny. Human populations often contain different proportions of certain polymorphs (such as blood groups, see below), but what is *racially* distinct is one population compared to others, not one polymorph compared to others.

The constitutional types, or somatotypes, already discussed in Chapter 4, are relevant at this point. Whether the distinctions between the somatotypes, as characterized by Sheldon and others, are as clear-cut as they claim does not concern us here. But it is an indisputable fact that in most human populations people are strikingly variable in body build; such differences occur even among members of the same family (you may be a fairly extreme ectomorph, but your brother or sister may be decidedly mesomorphic or endomorphic). To put it in other words, human populations are polymorphic for body build.

Anthropologists and human geneticists will have to discover how polymorphism in body build is best described and how it is inherited. The situation suggests that there are in human populations several variable genes with relatively large phenotypic effects, the segregation of which causes some people to be fat and others slim, some muscular and others frail. These polymorphic genes may be maintained in populations either because they produce highly fit heterozygotes (perhaps the "balanced" or intermediate somatotypes are heterozygous?) or because different somatotypes are favorable for different occupations or professions.

It is quite unnecessary to suppose, as is often done, that human polymorphism arose through race mixture. It is highly unlikely that at any time in the past there existed races in which everybody had the same body build or stature or blood type. Ancient human populations may have been less variable than modern ones but much polymorphism was doubtless always present. On the other hand, human populations may well differ in the proportion of slim and fat and muscular polymorphs they contain. The suggestion of Brues (1959) is very interesting in this connection: a light, linear body build may be favored in populations that live by hunting and pursuing game (the "spearmen"), while a heavy, muscular build is advantageous to users of blunt crushing implements and projectile weapons requiring momentary application of a large force (the "archers"); a brawny constitution is also favored in settled agriculturists who must be capable of sustained hard labor. Changes in implements and techniques of obtaining sustenance very likely demanded changes in the incidence of different body builds. This is perhaps one of the ways in which the evolution of culture influenced the evolution of human physique, and vice versa.

Mankind is a clear-cut, discrete, and closed genetic unit. There is no gene exchange between man and any other animal species. It cannot be overstressed that classes and races, Mendelian populations within the human species, are not such units. Few human populations are wholly isolated on a geographic or social island and these not for many generations. Indian castes and subcastes perhaps came closest to such a status yet failed to attain it. More usually the boundaries of human isolates are blurred; the "isolates" are not really isolated. Consider the inhabitants of any large American city. In New York, the Spanish, Italian, and Yiddish-speaking communities are predominantly endogamous, but occasionally members marry each other and those of northwest European descent. But this is not the whole story, because within each linguistic or ethnic division there are subdivisions according to wealth, education, social status, and, in some of them, religion and other grounds. No group is, however, closed enough to exclude all intermarriage with others, and some persons may belong to two or more communities. These complexities are bound to be reflected in the genetic composition of the populations. Races and classes are neither biologically nor sociologically clearly defined or discrete units. This may be irksome to an investigator who would rather have them neatly pigeonholed, but this does not make them any less real biological phenomena.

## Blood Groups

The predilection which biologists show for investigating blood groups puzzles some people, and since such investigations will be described in the present and the following chapters, an explanation is in order. In 1900 Landsteiner discovered that the red blood cells of one person agglutinate, i.e., clump together, when placed in the blood serum of certain other persons. He found that such tests enable four blood types, blood groups, to be distinguished, called O, A, B, and AB. It was found later, especially by Bernstein, that the blood groups are determined by three alleles of a gene, now called $i$, $I^A$, and $I^B$. People with O blood are homozygous $ii$, with A blood homozygous $I^A I^A$ or heterozygous $I^A i$, B blood $I^B I^B$ or $I^B i$, and AB blood $I^A I^B$. A person's blood type can be determined quickly and unambiguously by a competent technician from a small sample; a collection of samples drawn from a population permits calculation of the frequencies of the genes $i$, $I^A$, and $I^B$ in the gene pool of that population (see Chapters 6 and 10).

Using blood sera from certain persons, or animals, or even extracts from certain plants, it is possible to distinguish a number of further blood types among people. More and more types are being discovered, and the rate of discovery has accelerated in recent years. (A review, already outdated, is in Mourant 1954.) The blood types belong to several "systems," each determined by a different gene; no less than a dozen such genes are known and more will almost certainly be found. The "rhesus" (Rh) system has become familiar to the public, since it was discovered that a genetic difference in the father's and mother's Rh blood types may lead to disease in their infant (see below).

The blood type is determined by genes independently of environment, state of health, or age (after infancy). The advantages of such rigid genetic determination can hardly be overestimated. Suppose that two populations differ in the incidence of the O blood type and also in skin color and muscles. Provided the difference in the incidence of O bloods is statistically assured, the conclusion is justified that the populations in question are genetically different. But how about the other differences? One must be able to exclude the possibility that they are purely environmental, due, for example, to members of one population spending more time outdoors and doing heavier work than those of the other. To verify or to refute this possibility is often very difficult or impossible.

## Microgeographic Races in Wales

An enormous amount of work determining the frequencies of the blood types in populations of different parts of the world has been done and is being done by many investigators. The bearing of this work on the classification of human races will be discussed in

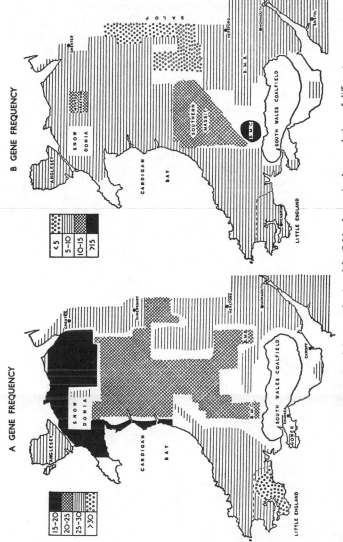

*Figure 8.* The frequencies of the genes for A and for B blood types in the populations of different parts of Wales. (After Mourant and Watkin.)

the following chapter. Here we shall consider the fascinating study of Mourant and Watkin (1952) on the blood types in different parts of Wales, which has revealed a most instructive situation.

Inhabitants of Wales, like people almost everywhere (see Chapter 10), are polymorphic for blood type: O, A, B, and AB persons are found. Figure 8 shows, however, that the distribution of the types is not uniform; significant local variations in the gene frequencies are observed. In the northern part of Wales the gene $i$ (for O blood group) is relatively frequent and the gene $I^A$ (for A blood) relatively rare; in the mountains of the southern part (especially in the Black Mountains of Carmarthenshire) the gene $I^B$ (B blood group) is more frequent than elsewhere in Wales.

Wales is a small country. Microgeographic variations in the populations studied by Mourant and Watkin remind us of those found among the Drosophila flies of the Sierra Nevada (Table 20). But there is a difference. In Drosophila, variations are brought about by the pressure of natural selection on a trait of high adaptive significance, but there is no reason to suppose that selection favors different blood types in different parts of Wales. Evidence from anthropometry (measurements of body dimensions and proportions), linguistics, history, and archaeology ably marshaled by Mourant and Watkin suggests the persistence of genes of extremely ancient western European populations. The Celtic-speaking inhabitants of the northern part of Wales, and those of parts of Scotland and Ireland, resemble in blood group frequencies certain populations of North Africa (Berbers). Mourant and Watkin speculate that the high B blood frequency in southern Wales may be a relic of even more ancient, paleolithic, inhabitants of western Europe. Persistence of a supposedly ancient genetic trait (high frequency of a certain gene) and of an ancient cultural trait (language) is found also in another remarkable European population, the Basques.

## Indian Castes

The Indian caste system is the grandest, though perhaps not deliberate, apparently unsuccessful genetic experiment ever performed on human populations. The genetic results have not been adequately studied, and the time for such a study is running out, since modern India is discontinuing the experiment. The Indian caste system is an arrangement of utmost complexity, extraordinarily difficult for a non-Indian to grasp and portray. The following account is based chiefly on the works of Riesley (1915) and Ghurye (1957, 1959) and on discussions with several Indian colleagues, among whom N. K. Bose and K. Dronamraju, of Calcutta, and P. C. Biswas, of Delhi University, were most enlightening.

Genetically the most significant caste units are the so-called sub-castes—endogamous groups into which the inhabitants of India are rigidly divided: one has to marry a person from the same subcaste in which one happens to be born. A complete catalogue of the sub-castes does not seem to exist; their number is estimated to be at least two thousand, and two hundred or more may be sympatric in the same district of the country. This arrangement does not necessarily lead to a high incidence of marriage between relatives. The chances of inbreeding are decreased because, the population of India being close to 400 million, many subcastes are large and because many of them are further divided into so-called gotras. The gotras are as a rule exogamous groups: marriage partners have to come from different gotras, although from the same subcaste. Because one belongs to the same gotra as one's father, the system does not always prevent marriage to a maternal relative, although marriage of close kin is forbidden.

Each caste has many subcastes, and the number of the former is still in the hundreds. Traditionally most castes and subcastes engaged in a particular occupation. Although the strictness with which this rule was enforced varied greatly in time, in different castes, and in different parts of India, everybody was supposed to, and usually did, take up the vocation, employment, or business which by custom belonged to his caste. Bose (1951) characterizes the situation succinctly:

> The careful way in which the tradition of close correspondence between caste and occupation was built up is clear indication of what the leaders of Hindu society had in mind. They believed in the hereditary transmissibility of Character, and thought it best to fix a man's occupation, as well as his status in life, by means of the family in which he had been born.

We may take as an example the following list of castes of Bengal as shown in the 1931 census of India, the last census in which an attempt was made to record the number of persons belonging to the different castes. (I am obliged to Indera P. Singh, of Delhi University, for a transcription of this list and to N. K. Bose for indicating the traditional caste callings.)

| Bagdi, agriculturists | 987,570 |
| Baidya, physicians | 110,739 |
| Bauri, agricultural laborers and domestic servants | 331,268 |
| Brahmin, priestcraft, teaching | 1,447,691 |
| Chamar, leather workers, tanners, cobblers | 150,458 |
| Dhobi, washermen | 229,672 |
| Dom, basket makers and agriculturists | 140,067 |
| Goala, milkmen, cattlemen | 599,283 |
| Hari, basket makers, bamboo workers | 132,401 |
| Jogi, weavers of coarse fabrics | 384,634 |
| Mumin (Jolaha), weavers, mostly Moslems | 270,292 |
| Kaibartha Chasi, agriculturists ⎱<br>Kaibartha Jalia, boatmen ⎰ | 2,733,338 |
| Kayastha, scribes, clerks | 1,558,475 |
| Kumhar, potters | 289,810 |
| Kurmi, vegetable gardeners | 194,652 |
| Namasudra, boatmen, agriculturists | 2,094,957 |
| Nai (Napit), barbers | 451,068 |
| Pod (Poundra), agriculturists | 667,731 |
| Rajbansi, boatmen, fishermen | 1,806,390 |
| Rajput, soldiers | 156,978 |
| Tanti (Tatwa), weavers of finer fabrics | 330,518 |
| Teli, oil pressers | 503,189 |

The traditional prescribing of occupations for each caste went hand in hand with the hierarchical structure of Hindu society, the rigidity and the permanence of which amazes a non-Hindu observer. The order of social precedence of the castes was largely fixed; the restrictions placed not only on intermarriage but also on other forms of social intercourse went, in the heyday of the caste system, beyond what partisans of apartheid and white supremacy dared to invent. The downtroddenness of the Untouchables was a particularly ugly affair.

The possibility of genetic divergence of the castes and subcastes, making them adapted to their respective occupations and conditions, is of greatest interest to a student of human evolution. For how many generations each caste and subcaste had the opportunity to be genetically selected for its respective adaptive specialization is impossible to determine, or at any rate it has not been determined. The number of castes has grown with time, the budding-off of new castes having been more frequent than caste fusion. The antiquity of the caste system is beyond doubt: three castes are mentioned in the *Rigveda*, composed before 1500 B.C., and the Greek Megasthenes, who came to India about the year 305 B.C., wrote:

It is not permitted to contract marriage with a person of another caste, nor to change from one profession or trade to another, nor for the same person to undertake more than one, except he is of the caste of philosophers, when permission is given on account of his dignity [quoted in Ghurye 1957].

This could have been written as well in A.D. 1905.

For how long the castes and subcastes were genetically closed Mendelian populations is uncertain. Caste revolts and insurrections appear to have been much less frequent in the history of India than were uprisings of peasants and other oppressed groups in the West. The caste system gave a certain sense of security and stability: an individual felt himself a member of a group which was in turn a part of an organized whole, a system which proved itself workable for at least two millennia. A sure place in life, even a mean one, apparently was felt to be preferable to no place at all (Bose 1951).

The amount of semilicit and illicit gene exchange between the castes is a moot point, except that there certainly was some. The *Institutes of Manu,* composed between A.D. 100 and 300, stated that "the woman is considered in law as the field, and the man as the grain; now vegetable bodies are formed by the united operation of the seed and the field." The practice of hypergamy, a man of a higher caste taking a wife from a lower caste, was repeatedly discouraged by Brahmins but recurred again and again. Concubinage was another practice regarded as socially acceptable in some places, the children of a concubine belonging usually to the caste of their mother. This means that both upward and downward gene diffusion, from the lower to the upper castes and vice versa, took place to some extent. Its effects through the ages led to a genetic convergence of the castes in at least their physical traits. The consequence is that "in general in a linguistic region the castes are physically more related to one another than to similar castes outside the region" (Ghurye 1957). Which, in biological language, means that allopatric populations of the same caste diverged genetically, while sympatric populations of different castes converged.

At least some sympatric caste populations remain nevertheless genetically distinguishable (e.g., in blood group frequencies) and, to some extent, also physically, as shown most clearly by Sanghvi (1953). Some Indians claim an ability to tell by appearance the caste to which a person in their home province belongs. The physical marks of the castes are at least in part remnants of their different racial origins and migrations. The Brahmins trace their origin to the Aryan-speaking, light-skinned peoples who invaded India from the northwest at about 1500 B.C., subjugated the dark-skinned, aboriginal populations, and instituted the caste system. Patanjali wrote in 150 B.C. that "the physical characteristics of a Brahmin were fair skin and tawny hair" (quoted in Ghurye 1957). More recent invaders and migrants (e.g., the Parsis from Iran and the Europeans) formed, in effect, castes of their own.

It is a separate problem whether the different occupations pursued by members of the castes and subcastes, in some cases doubtless for many generations, made them genetically specialized in their respective fields. Scientific integrity demands that final judgment be withheld until reliable evidence becomes available; we are here confronted with a nature-nurture problem of highest complexity (see Chapters 3 and 4). Some things are, however, unmistakable. Although many millions of Indians still cling to occupations which were traditional in their castes for centuries or even millennia, the winds of change are blowing in India and elsewhere in the "Unchanging East." The demands of living in the age of new technologies, industries, and occupations, have brought to India numerous new callings and professions, and selection by caste specialization has, at any rate, not made people unable to learn new trades, even radically different from their traditional ones. Some of the new employments tend to be monopolized by one or another of the old castes but others are not. It would be most interesting to study under properly controlled conditions the incidence of various aptitudes in different castes.

In modern India caste barriers are beginning to crumble. Caste intermarriage continues to be rare, but a Brahmin and an Untouchable sit at neighboring office desks, factory benches, and take their meals together in college dining rooms. The caste system was an experiment on a grand scale that attempted to breed varieties of men genetically specialized in the performance of different functions. To all appearances, such a specialization has not been achieved.

## Social Mobility in China

The most ancient of the existing advanced civilizations, the Chinese, evolved a socio-genetic system which was, in a sense, the converse of that of India. For some twenty-five centuries, the key ideas of Chinese civilization were those of Confucius (551–479 B.C.), who, claiming merely to have "transmitted" more ancient wisdom, said: "In education there should be no class distinctions." Yet neither Confucius nor those who shaped the destinies of the Chinese society were in any meaningful sense democrats or egalitarians. At least until the advent of Mao Tse-tung, China was a land of harsh social inequalities, resembling the feudal order of medieval Europe. But there was this all-important difference: high status and privileges were conferred upon men according to their individual merit rather than their aristocratic birth or their affluence. The principle involved was stated by the sage Mencius (371–289 B.C.):

> Some labor with their minds and some labor with their physical strength. Those who labor with their minds rule others, and those who labor with their strength are ruled by others. Those who are ruled sustain others, and those who rule are sustained by others. This is a principle universally recognized [cited after Ho 1959a].

To be sure, the splendid principle of classless education was never wholly realized in actual practice, but efforts to bring the theory and the practice together were often being made. Since at least the year A.D. 684, some members of the ruling class were recruited from the general population by means of stiff competitive examinations, and this unique civil service system endured until the revolution of 1911. Nobility and wealth of course helped to acquire the education needed to pass the examinations, but they did not guarantee a degree, which was a prerequisite of high social status. Only during the system's decadence did the government see itself forced to sell some "academic" degrees, but even then the earned degrees were more numerous than the bought ones. And strangest of all from the standpoint of Western political mores, the examinations required years of intensive study of subjects as "impractical" as Confucian classics, poetry, philosophical discussion, elegance of language, and good handwriting.

These arrangements in fact resulted in a remarkable social mobility—both upward and downward. Considerable documentary information is available for the periods of Ming and Ch'ing dynasties, lasting more than half a millennium (1368–1911), and has been studied to some extent (Chang 1955, Ho 1959a; I am obliged to Morton Fried for directing me to these references). Already under the early Ming emperors, China worked out a kind of a nation-wide scholarship system which enabled some poor but ambitious youngsters to start their "scholarly" careers. Ho (1959a) gives data on the family backgrounds of 10,463 examinees between the years 1371 and 1904. Of these, 3,217, 30.7 per cent, came from families which had held no degrees or offices for three preceding genera-tions. These may be regarded as cases of remarkable upward social mobility. And only 589, 5.6 per cent, of the examinees came from "distinguished families." The proportion of the former was high-est in the fifteenth and sixteenth centuries (Ming dynasty) and lowest during the decadent period of the nineteenth century.

Sad to relate, this remarkably enlightened system did not result in China in an appreciable diminution of the misgovernment, cor-ruption, cruelty, or oppression so prominent also in the history of Western civilization. Whether or not, as some authors believe, China possesses a more ample "evolutionary potential" than the West does (Sahlins and Service 1960) remains to be demonstrated.

## The Jews

Situations which in their genetic aspects parallel some features of the Indian caste system are not unknown elsewhere. Perhaps the most remarkable is among the Jews. Claiming descent from the Hebrews of ancient Palestine, the Jews have lived for two millennia as minority groups (dispersion, Diaspora) among various other peoples of Europe, Asia, Africa, and, recently, the whole world. Their religion and their extraordinary group cohesion acted as social isolating mechanisms which made them Mendelian popula-tions plainly delimited from other sympatric populations. Further-more, they often pre-empted certain trades and occupations, not with the rigidity or exclusiveness of Indian castes but still to an extent that might have made genetic specialization a theoretical possibility. As with the Indian castes, the occupational as well as the genetic isolation of the Jews is loosening because of the stresses and opportunities of modern living and modern ideas.

The history of the Jews, studied in painstaking detail, obviously cannot concern us here. Our problem, which has received much less attention, is to determine the extent to which the Jews in dif-ferent countries remained genetically distinct from neighboring populations and the extent allopatric Jewish populations continue to be similar to each other. Mourant (1955b) has analyzed the numerous but scattered observations on blood type frequencies in various Jewish communities. A part of the data is shown in Table 21.

TABLE 21

Frequencies (in percentages) of the A and B blood groups in the gene pool of Jewish and non-Jewish sympatric and allopatric populations *(after Mourant)*

| Country | Jews | | Non-Jews | |
|---|---|---|---|---|
| | A | B | A | B |
| **AFRICA** | | | | |
| Morocco | 22.7 | 16.4 | 19.6 | 12.9 |
| Algeria | 21.5 | 15.5 | 20.6 | 12.6 |
| Libya | 22.7 | 16.4 | 20.4 | 11.6 |
| **EUROPE** | | | | |
| Netherlands | 25.9 | 6.2 | 26.6 | 6.1 |
| Germany | 27.1 | 11.5 | 28.2 | 8.9 |
| Poland | 28.5 | 12.5 | 27.3 | 14.8 |
| Lithuania | 25.5 | 13.0 | 24.0 | 13.2 |
| Ukraine | 28.7 | 12.4 | 26.5 | 15.6 |
| Karaites (Ukraine) | 16.4 | 20.2 | 26.5 | 15.6 |
| **ASIA** | | | | |
| Yemen | 17.4 | 9.5 | 17.5 | 6.7 |
| Iraq | 30.0 | 20.3 | 21.2 | 17.4 |
| Kurdistan | 33.6 | 14.7 | 24.8 | 17.8 |
| Iran | 25.9 | 18.5 | 22.7 | 16.0 |
| Turkestan | 20.8 | 21.6 | 26.5 | 18.5 |
| Cochin (India) | 11.6 | 14.3 | 19.0 | 14.4 |

The Jews evidently are not a homogeneous or unified race. The Jewish populations which lived as castes in different countries have experienced considerable genetic divergence, and that divergence has been, unsurprisingly, usually in the direction of the non-Jewish populations among which they lived. At the same time, the Jews remained genetically distinct from their non-Jewish neighbors and to some extent preserved genetic similarities most likely attributable to a common descent. Mourant stresses particularly the uniformity of the populations of Ashkenazim (Jews of central and eastern European descent) and Sephardim (Jews of western Mediterranean descent), despite their centuries-long residence among different peoples. In agreement with this, there exist data showing that the incidence of a number of diseases differs considerably in the Jewish and in the non-Jewish populations sympatric with them. A part of these different disease susceptibilities is almost certainly genetic.

## Social Class and Equality of Opportunity

Although the genetic isolation of Indian castes was both more rigid and more prolonged than the class barriers elsewhere, evidence is lacking that they have become genetically specialized for their respective occupations. This may seem to make superfluous other inquiries into the possibility of such specialization among social classes. Lack of evidence is, however, not quite the same thing as negative evidence. It is fair to say that Indian castes have not become genetically as unpliantly specialized for their professions as, for example, the different breeds of horses which were fitted for different types of work by the conscious or semiconscious efforts of their human masters. However, the possibility of differing incidence in different castes of some aptitudes cannot at present be excluded. Furthermore, caste and class stratifications are, biologically considered, somewhat different "experiments."

As stated above, a person's caste is determined by that of his parents and by nothing else: one cannot be promoted to a higher caste or demoted to a lower one by any personal achievements or failures. A man of low caste could only hope that good behavior in his present life might let him be reincarnated in a higher caste. Class differentiation is, however, less rigid. Even the most rigid class society allows some individuals of humble birth to climb and others of privileged birth to slide down the social ladder.

Anthropologists and sociologists have described a great variety of societies which have existed at different times and places or which may be instituted in the future. Any social organization defines the basis of the genetic structure of the society concerned. The relations between social and genetic structures are insufficiently understood, at least from the point of view of modern evolutionary biology. This problem is too large and too complex to be tackled in this book, but we may explore the genetic implications of a single social variable—the degree of vertical social mobility which the structure of a society makes possible. The polar opposites are here a caste society and a society which would provide complete equality of opportunity to its members: the leaders of Hindu society thought that men neither are or should be equal; the democratic ideal, as formulated particularly during the Age of Enlightenment, is that equality of opportunity is an inherent right of every human being. The existing societies range between these extremes.

Cicero did not regard beautiful thoughts like those quoted in Chapter 3 incompatible with the existence of slavery. Neither did Alexander the Great, who is credited with having been the first to conceive the idea of universal brotherhood (Sarton 1959), nor the authors of the Constitution of the United States. Slavery did not entirely exclude social mobility. Some slaves were manumitted, and some of them achieved wealth and nobility; comely slave girls shared the beds of their masters, and their descendants occasionally succeeded to riches and even to thrones. But people were also sold into slavery, for misdeeds or for carelessness. The proudest aristocrat has in his pedigree one or more ancestors about whom nothing is known. There has always been some gene diffusion between the first families and the last families.

Equality of opportunity neither presupposes nor promotes equality of ability. It only means that every person may, without favor or hindrance, develop whatever socially useful gifts or aptitudes he has and chooses to develop. Civilization fosters a multitude of employments and functions to be filled and served—statesmen and butchers, engineers and policemen, scientists and refuse collectors, musicians and sales clerks. Equality of opportunity stimulates the division of labor rather than sets it aside; it enables, however, a person to choose any occupation for which he is qualified by his abilities and his willingness to strive.

Suppose then that the occupant of every cradle would have an opportunity to develop, if he so chooses, whatever talents or faculties he may have. He may elect to undergo the prolonged and rigorous training needed to qualify him for some specialized or responsible function; to this end he may have to postpone the satisfaction of sexual drives and desires for ease, comfort, and a family. Or rejecting such postponements, he may take up a job for which brief and simple training is sufficient and enjoy a less strenuous and more leisurely life. An equality of opportunity so complete is approached but has not been reached in any society. It is alleged to prevail under Communist regimes, but the actual situation there resembles rather that envisaged in the well-known utopia of George Orwell, where some people are more equal than others.

Genes do not decree that their carriers will be able and will choose to be musicians, scientists, wrestlers, or anything else. Much depends on the environment and, regardless of whether you do or do not believe in metaphysical freedom of the will, on individual choice. But genes bias choices, make some careers easy and others difficult, and tip the scales at critical moments. No matter how hard I tried, I could not have become a champion wrestler, sprinter, painter, or concertmaster. But I doubtless might have become many things different from what I am. Most occupations do not require very specialized aptitudes; or, to put it differently, most human genotypes qualify their carriers for a multitude of the roles human societies offer.

It should not be assumed that equality of opportunity would make genetic variation unimportant. Precisely the opposite is true. If being the son of somebody eminent in a certain profession smooths your way in that profession, you may be tempted or even forced to enter it without being either attracted or fitted to it. The drawback of the caste and rigid class systems is precisely that they induce people to take up functions for which they are incompetent; hence so many worthless kings and barons. Equality of opportunity tends to make the occupational differentiation comport with the genetic polymorphism of the population, and would be meaningless if all people were genetically identical.

Equality of opportunity, whether complete, as is only dreamed of, or partial, as exists in some societies, favors rather than hinders aggregation of genetically similarly conditioned people. It is inevitable that musicians will meet other musicians on the average more often than scientists or engineers or wrestlers or politicians, while scientists and engineers will, owing to professional necessity and to community of interests, be often in the company of other scientists and engineers respectively. The same holds for their families, even if these latter are themselves not much interested in music or science or engineering.

Proximity of potential mates increases the chance that the potentiality will be actualized. This has been shown, for example, in the careful study of Cavalli-Sforza (1958) on the marriage habits of the population in a section of northern Italy. The occupational and professional associations become also mating communities, Mendelian populations. This is one of the sources of assortative mating which prevails in most human societies. People genetically or environmentally conditioned for similar occupations have a statistically greater chance to marry each other than do people of different conditioning.

## Social Class and Natural Selection

Social Darwinists have, ever since Galton almost a century ago, urged that social classes differ in their genetic endowments and the differences have been brought about by natural selection enhancing the fitness of each group of people for their respective occupations. As envisaged by Darlington (1953),

> The genetic sequence of civilization . . . is that the genetically fixed capacities of individual men influence their beliefs and their social behavior; secondly, having done so, they in turn influence the groups in which the individuals will mate; and thirdly, the mating group selects and concentrates the genetic capacities of individual men. By this circular sequence we can now see that a differentiation of society is established on a genetic basis.

This hypothesis cannot be dismissed out of hand but it certainly requires the closest scrutiny.

Human intelligence, personality, special abilities, health, vigor, etc. are to some extent genetically, as well as environmentally, conditioned (Chapters 3–5). Human populations do contain genetic variants some of which are more and others less fit for certain specialized types of work, although most "ordinary" employments may perhaps be regarded as requiring no skills which any healthy individual cannot acquire easily. In theory, it might be possible to breed different varieties of men for different employments, in the same manner as different varieties of dogs or horses or cattle have been bred. How efficient such a breeding program might be, a geneticist would hesitate to say, since the heritability of human skills, excepting some highly specialized ones (perhaps champion wrestlers, virtuoso musicians, outstanding singers, poets, and the like), appears to be rather low. Without the benefits of genetic knowledge, selective breeding of men was recommended by some authors in their utopias, beginning with Plato's *Republic*.

I wish to stress that the genetic selective processes will operate differently depending upon the degree of social mobility a given society permits and upon how much equality of opportunity its citizens enjoy. Furthermore, social mobility will in general favor genetic progress and its absence will slow it down. Consider the genetic situation in a society with rigid class or caste barriers first.

Suppose that a class of warriors is originally formed of persons who have distinguished themselves by their military prowess, or that a class of statesmen is made up of people who have demonstrated their wisdom and their administrative abilities. Accepting for the sake of the argument that the prowess and the abilities are to some extent genetically conditioned, the caste or class might then commence with a high concentration of genes that confer competence and specialized skills on their possessors. History suggests that this may have happened at certain times and in certain places. Regardless of whether their abilities were genetically or environmentally conditioned, some aristocratic elites performed quite creditably in cultural advancement, as even Marxists grudgingly admit. Such was the small aristocracy of the golden age of ancient Greece, whose maintenance and leisure came from the labor of a mass of slaves. Material wealth and power should be only means to other and higher ends; yet history shows that want and poverty have not been propitious for cultural flowering.

Rigid caste and class systems break down genetically, however, and cease to operate as instruments of cultural advance. The genetic endowments of closed castes and classes are not long maintained. Able and talented parents often produce descendants far below their levels of excellence, because the genetic basis of many, in fact of most, variable human traits consists of groups of genes with individually small effects, polygenes (see p. 104). A person of outstanding ability may carry a constellation of genes which interact in a most favorable manner, but the gene constellations break down and the component genes are reassorted when the sex cells of the next generation are formed. We inherit genes, not genotypes, of our parents, and we transmit our genes, not our genotypes, to our children. A caste originally recruited entirely from persons of high ability will contain some less able individuals in the following generations.

To maintain the genetic excellence of a caste, it is necessary to retain the competents and to remove the incompetents, preferably in every generation. But this presupposes social mobility, which is precisely what class and caste barriers do not allow. The incompetents will probably muddle through somehow and leave their genes in the class population. Moreover, whatever semilicit or illicit gene exchange takes place between classes will most likely come through marriage with women of other and usually lower classes. Aristocrats have frequently valued pulchritude above gene quality in their mates. The selection which may operate on the founders of an aristocratic elite, selecting them for certain abilities, inevitably weakens, or is nullified or reversed, in later generations. A ruling or professional class may continue to be competent despite the genetic dilution, but if so, its competence is no longer genetic. An hereditary occupation has the advantage of permitting children to learn their familial trade from an early age.

Let us now look at the genetic consequences of equality of opportunity. Suppose that the opportunity to receive education and specialized training and to choose a career of any sort depends entirely on a youngster's aptitudes and not on the ability of his parents to pay for his education, or even to feed and care for him properly, so that his faculties may become manifest. It is possible that most carriers of genes favoring outstanding musical abilities will become musicians, possessors of mathematical abilities mathematicians, of scientific abilities scientists, etc. Because of assortative mating (see above), these aggregates of people would to some extent at least assume the character of Mendelian populations, in which the genes for certain special abilities will tend to be concentrated. Musicians, mathematicians, and scientists might perhaps form elites or guilds or unions or fraternities. Whether these elites could also be considered social classes is doubtful; they would bear little resemblance to the social classes of existing societies. Indeed, the descendants of musicians who do not inherit the abilities of their parents, or their perseverance in training, or who possess some other talents or tastes, would automatically drop out of the musicians' guild. Descendants of nonmusicians in whom the proper genetic endowments for musicianship would arise would as automatically move in.

Ironically enough, it is often assumed that recognition and appreciation of the importance of genetic conditioning of human capacities would justify the setting up of rigid class barriers and a hierarchical organization of the society. Hereditarians are often political conservatives. And conversely, predilection for equality of opportunity goes together with a democratic outlook, with stressing the importance of the environment and soft-pedaling heredity (see Chapter 3). Yet even the most elementary understanding of the principles of genetics suffices to show that it is only under uniform environments that genetic differences between individuals or populations would become clearly manifest. And vice versa, environmental heterogeneities tend to obscure and conceal genetic differences. The closer the approach to equality of opportunity in a society, the more the observed differences between its members are likely to reflect their genetic differences. Inequality of opportunity acts, on the contrary, to hide, distort, and falsify the genetic diversity.

The occupational and class differentiation in the existing societies is, contrary to Darlington's opinion, not established on a genetic basis, precisely because none of these societies now provides or has provided, as far as the historical record goes, anything approaching an equality of opportunity to its members. The greater the rigidity of the class barriers, the less the opportunity for social mobility, the more genetically meaningless is the social stratification. On the other hand, what Max Lerner (1957) has called "open-class society" does contain the possibility of forming elites which would be to some extent genetic. According to Lerner, an open-class society, at least in the form that is shaping up in America, does not

> mean an absence of rank, class, power, or prestige. More exactly it means a class system that is casteless and therefore characterized by great mobility and interpenetration between classes. ... How classless is this society? Only in the sense that the class formations in it are fluid, that mobility is the rule rather than the exception, and that class change is impressively obtainable.

### Diversifying Selection

What would be the genetic consequences of an open-class society? We do not know nearly enough to answer this question with assurance. Open-class societies in America and elsewhere are relative novelties in terms of the number of human generations they have existed, and the degree of their "openness" has varied with time. Communist societies, which are perhaps better described genetically as open-class rather than classless, are even newer. Furthermore, the form of natural selection that may be supposed to operate in open-class societies is of a rather special kind, which Mather (1955) has called disruptive, but which I prefer to call diversifying selection ("disruptive" suggests disorder or disarray, which is not what diversifying selection brings about).

Diversifying selection may occur when a Mendelian population faces two or more environments, habitats, or ways of life that favor different genetic endowments. Its outcome tends to be genetic diversification—the appearance of a variety of genotypes adapted to the respective environments. The brilliant experiments of Thoday

(1959), Thoday and Boam (1959), and Millicent and Thoday (1960) on Drosophila flies provide a model which we may use as an illustration. The experimenters selected for twenty-five generations flies that had a larger and smaller number of so-called sternopleural chaetae (bristles or hairs on a certain part of the fly's body). The selection was made in the following peculiar manner. Four lines, or families, were established, denoted A, B, C, and D. In every generation, all parents of lines A and B had the highest numbers of bristles in the populations they came from, and all parents of lines C and D had the lowest in their populations. The lines A and B are consequently called the "high" lines and C and D the "low" lines. In every generation, the female parents came from the populations they contributed to; males always came from a different population. Thus, females having the largest numbers of bristles were selected from A and B populations; the "high" A females were crossed, in alternate generations, to males from the B and D lines likewise having the largest numbers of bristles in their lines. The "high" B females were crossed in alternate generations to

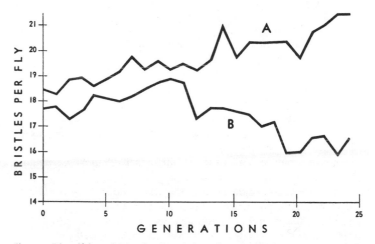

Figure 9. Diversifying selection for the number of certain bristles on the body of the fly, *Drosophila melanogaster*. In the "high" line (A), individuals with the highest number of bristles from the "high" line were mated in every generation to individuals with the highest number of bristles from the "low" line. In the "low" line (B), individuals with fewest bristles from the "low" line were mated in every generation to individuals with fewest bristles from the "high" line. The experiment showed that the "high" line became gradually more and more distinct from the "low" line in the number of bristles. (Courtesy of Professor Thoday.)

"high" males from the C and A lines. In the lines C and D, females were selected with lowest numbers of bristles. The "low" C females were crossed in alternate generations to D and B males having the lowest numbers of bristles, and the "low" D females were crossed, also in alternate generations, to A and C "low" males.

The lines A and B are, accordingly, being selected for a high and C and D for a low number of bristles. A and B receive, however, an inflow of genes from the "low" lines C and D, and C and D from the "high" lines A and B. A somewhat analogous situation is easily conceivable in man. Suppose that one class of people consists mostly of tall persons and another of short, and tall stature is preferred or favored in the first class and short stature in the second. Social mobility in such a society might take the form of the tallest individuals of the "short" class marrying into the "tall" class, and the shortest persons of the "tall" class marrying into the "short" class. The experiments of Thoday and his colleagues suggest that social mobility of this sort may not prevent the "tall" class getting taller and "short" class getting shorter. Their results, dealing of course with Drosophila, are diagrammed in Figure 9. The figure shows the mean numbers of bristles in the "high" and the "low" lines in different generations of the experiment. Though the observed course of the selection progress appears rather erratic, it is evident that the "high" lines are getting higher and the "low" ones lower in the numbers of bristles.

## Selection for Educability

Have we, then, arrived at the conclusion which social Darwinists and racists have urged all along, that the existing stratification of the social classes reflects their "native" abilities? No, the matter is much more complex and, as far as our present understanding goes, the opposite conclusion is more likely warranted.*

It is possible, and indeed probable, that occupational differences between human populations usher in some correlated genetic differences. This is a far cry from an apologia for the existing distribution of economic rewards and influence in societies with rigid class barriers, which social Darwinists and racists attempt to justify. On the contrary, we have shown above that it is equality of oppor-

---

*Having mentioned in previous writings the possibility of different incidence of some abilities in classes and races of man, I have been indicted by certain Communist authors as an ideologist of racism. This, I think, I am not; but one should not avoid discussion of scientific issues because of willful misrepresentation of one's views.

tunity that may instigate formation of genetic elites, and that inequality frustrates this process. But we should be on our guard that seeing the obvious we do not miss the significant.

Being competent in one's occupation or endeavor patently increases one's social and usually also one's Darwinian fitness. But there is a form of excellence which in human societies increases fitness even more. This is the ability to learn and to become competent in any one of several occupations or trades. To put it in other words, specialization for one vocation may make one biologically and socially fit, but educability permitting a choice of any one of several vocations would yield maximum fitness. The advantage of educability will appear even greater if a family lineage or a population, rather than an individual, is considered. Except possibly with Indian castes, an occupational specialization is not likely to endure for many generations. This is true for at least two reasons. First, as a culture evolves, new occupations and new demands in old occupations constantly arise. The rate at which new vocations emerge increases as a culture becomes more complex. Who needed airplane pilots a century ago and how many blacksmiths are needed now in technologically advanced countries? Second, a family's fortunes have often fluctuated "from shirt sleeves to shirt sleeves in three generations," and not only in the relatively open-class society of America. Genetic specialization is a dangerous method of adaptation; with the environment changing specialization may result in extinction. This danger is greatest in human societies because their environments change fastest.

Dobzhansky and Ashley Montagu (1947) pointed out that the quality most consistently favored in man by natural selection has been educability. Capacity to profit by experience, to adjust one's behavior to the requirements and expectations of one's surroundings, trainability for whatever occupations or professions the society has available—educability, in short, confers the highest Darwinian fitness on human genotypes. Culture is man's most potent means of adaptation to his environment; genetically conditioned educability is his most potent biological adaptation to his culture.

This view did not pass unchallenged. Darlington (1953) believes that

individual adaptability is indeed one of the great illusions of common-sense observation. It is an illusion responsible for some of the chief errors of political and economic administration today. Individuals and populations cannot be shifted from one place or occupation to another after an appropriate period of training to fit the convenience of some master planner, any more than hill farmers can be turned into deep-sea fishermen or habitual criminals can be turned into good citizens.

Despite all the inadequacy and uncertainty of our knowledge of human genetics, there is plenty of evidence contrary to Darlington's view, and this evidence is conclusive.

History abounds in proofs that individuals and populations can successfully be shifted from one place or occupation to another. Industrial revolutions in many countries throughout the world have amply shown this. The near ancestors of millions of industrial workers have been mostly "timeless" peasants tilling the soil. The movement from the soil to industrial cities is even now under way, and on a grand scale, in some "underdeveloped" countries. Granted that this movement may in some instances be genetically selective; it is even more often due to social causes which defy genetics. Are we to believe that millions of rustics happened to have been genetically pre-adapted to stand at factory benches and operate lathes and solve engineering problems? Does this not strain one's credulity? Pre-adapted they were, indeed; but what pre-adapted them was a process of natural selection extending for many millennia, which fostered educability, and did so in all classes and races of people, in short, in the species *Homo sapiens*.

# 10. Race

And I say unto you, that many shall come
from the east and west, and shall sit
down with Abraham, and Isaac, and Jacob,
in the kingdom of heaven.

MAT. 8:11

THE SCIENTIFIC STUDY of human races is at least two centuries old. There are nevertheless few natural phenomena, and probably no other aspect of human nature, the investigation of which has so often floundered in confusion and misunderstanding. And this is only partly due to the biases and passions engendered by race prejudices and consequent defense reactions. The situation is aptly described by Washburn (1953):

> During the last fifty years, although excellent descriptive data were added, techniques improved, and problems clarified and defined, little progress was made in understanding the process and pattern of human evolution. The strategy of physical anthropology yielded diminishing returns, and, finally, application of the traditional methods *by experts* gave contradictory results.

Birdsell (1951a) is no less emphatic: "The present methodological approaches utilized in race studies are bankrupt."

These harsh words are not to be construed as a denial of the value of the information so painstakingly collected by several generations of physical anthropologists. The body of data which they gathered will remain the basis of further work on human racial variation. It is the interpretation of these data that has proved troublesome, because they were not always collected as they should have been in the light of our present understanding. The problem that now faces the science of man is how to devise better methods for further observations that will give more meaningful results. This requires a better understanding of the biological basis of the phenomenon of race.

### Vicissitudes of the Race Concept

A detailed review of the history and the present status of human race studies would be out of place in this book. Much of the early work has been conveniently summarized in anthology form by Count (1950). Blumenbach (1752–1840), who classified human races, was a younger contemporary of Linnaeus (1707–1778), who classified all natural objects. In his dissertation of 1775, Blumenbach divided mankind into five races—Caucasian (white), Mongolian (yellow), Ethiopian (black), American (red), and Malayan (brown).

However, skin color is obviously not the only trait in which people differ. Some people have straight and others wavy or curly or frizzly or peppercorn hair; some have prominent and thin and others broad and flat noses, thin or thick or everted lips; some are tall and others short or pigmy, some have long, others intermediate, and still others round heads, etc. If the variations in all these traits paralleled each other, race classification would be strengthened. But they frequently do not: for example, some people in southern India have very dark skin but straight or wavy hair, and the Bushmen in South Africa have peppercorn hair but yellowish skin. A race classification made on basis of the hair shape would be different from that based on skin color or height or head shape.

Attempts were also made to characterize races by complexes of traits. Such peoples as the Australian aborigines, the Melanesians of New Guinea and neighboring islands, the Polynesians of the wide Pacific, the Ainus of northern Japan, and many others cannot be fitted into the fivefold Blumenbachian classification; they were made separate races. But where was the multiplication of races to stop? One author proposed to recognize more than two hundred races. Toward the end of the nineteenth and in the twentieth century the number of different race classifications proposed was almost as great as the number of classifiers. Indeed, the more you subdivide races the more difficult it becomes to delimit them, because some intermediate populations will be found.

For a time it was fashionable to divide the inhabitants of Europe into Nordic (tall, blond, long-headed), Alpine (medium height, brown-haired, round-headed), and Mediterranean (medium height, brunette, long-headed) races. This seems to make sense if one compares the inhabitants of, say, Sweden with those of Austria, Sicily, or Spain, although even here some "troublesome" individuals and families are found. Some Swedes have brown or black hair and some Spaniards are blond and blue-eyed, and yet they cannot validly be excluded from the race to which their brothers or sisters or their neighbors belong. Furthermore, if one studies, district by district, the inhabitants of Germany or France or northern and central Italy, one finds every conceivable intermediate between the Nordic, Alpine, and Mediterranean "races."

It seems not unreasonable to guess that the presence of so many intermediate and unclassifiable individuals and groups results from hybridization. History records numerous migrations of people, and in modern times mobility has become greatly accelerated and intermarriage of persons of different origins increased. Perhaps, then, neatly distinct "pure" races existed in the past, although they are at present submerged in a mass of hybrids, mixtures, or "mongrels," except, perhaps, a few that survive in some isolated places. This idea was first advanced, apparently, by Kant in the eighteenth century (see Count 1950) and has lingered ever since. That hybrid populations exist is, of course, evident. The Tartars were Mongoloids when they settled in eastern Russia, but seven centuries of occasional intermarriage with their white neighbors has made them a decidedly intermediate group. New races are emerging in tropical America (alloys of Indian, Mediterranean white, and Negro), in Hawaii (Polynesians, whites, and Mongoloids), in parts of the United States (Negroes and whites), and elsewhere. But a closer look at the theory of ancient pure races discloses fatal weaknesses.

How does one go about tracing the presumed ancestral races? One way is to choose among living people a few tribes, clans, or even individuals with a convenient combination of traits, and to declare them the original "types" and the sources of the blends observed in people elsewhere. One may, for example, select some very tall, blond, straight-haired, round-headed, straight-nosed, and thin-lipped persons and some other short, black, frizzle-haired, long-headed, broad-nosed, and thick-lipped ones to be the pure races. Everybody else, then, may be represented on paper as derived from the recombination of traits that resulted from mixtures between the chosen prototypes. Alas, there is no reason to think that mankind ever consisted of uniform races with requisite combinations of traits (or any other pure races), or that the people now living came from such a mixture.

Ancestral races have also been devised by attributing to them certain characteristics found in fossil skulls and skeletons, which are at any rate remains of people who actually lived. This can, of course, be done the more easily since one is not handicapped by any knowledge of the external characteristics (pigmentation, hair, shape of the soft parts of the face and the body) of the people whose skeletons are preserved. And living individuals whose head and body proportions agree reasonably well with those in the fossil specimens can usually be found and photographed.

## Racial Typologies

Such outstanding nineteenth- and early twentieth-century anthropologists as Broca, Topinard, and Ripley declared race to be "an abstract conception." So abstract it became that "at the present time rarely, if indeed ever, we discover a single individual corresponding to our racial type in every detail. It exists for us nevertheless" (Topinard). Obviously, under this system, every anthropologist can manufacture racial types to suit his taste. Then when biometrical techniques came into fashion, Czekanowski, Stolyhwo, and their successors in Poland, and Hooton and his pupils in America, tried to subdivide populations into racial components or "morphological types" characterized by a series of measurements. Hooton and Dupertuis (1955) examined a large sample of adult males in Ireland and divided them into the following "types":

| | | | |
|---|---|---|---|
| Pure Nordic | 55 | Dinaric | 1,728 |
| Predominantly Nordic | 649 | Nordic Mediterranean | 2,747 |
| Celtic | 2,408 | Pure Mediterranean | 33 |
| East Baltic | 105 | Nordic Alpine | 1,754 |

The fatal flaw of racial typologies is that the morphological types are arrived at by a sort of intuition, which means that they are picked out arbitrarily, even when chosen by experienced investigators. No amount of mathematical statistics can overcome this defect. (See a thoughtful critique by one of Hooton's ablest pupils, Hunt 1959.) Coon (1939), selecting his types chiefly on the basis of similarity with fossil specimens, distinguished about ten types among the populations of Europe. Coon recognized, however, that "typical" individuals are more or less rare and that the actual populations consist chiefly of intermediates. In most parts of Europe two or several of these types occur in the same population.

Race typologies draw no distinction between intra-populational variability or polymorphism, and inter-populational differences, those between Mendelian populations (see p. 219). For example, do Celts marry Celts and Dinarics marry Dinarics in Ireland? Are the Irish families in which one parent is a Celt and the other a Nordic or Mediterranean to be regarded as race crosses? It is unlikely that in Ireland or anywhere else the choice of a spouse is ordinarily made on the basis of a careful examination of the racial type. To be sure, the slight but significant differences in blood group frequencies that Fisher and Vaughan (1939) found among people with different surnames in England suggest assortative mating (see the foregoing chapter). But as long as no evidence is available of some kind of assortative mating affecting the Irish racial "types," they will have to be regarded as arbitrary slices of essentially continuous phenotypic variability.

### Distribution of Blood Group Genes in Human Populations

Race differences may be large or small. We have seen in the foregoing chapter that populations of the fly *Drosophila pseudoobscura* which live at different elevations a few miles apart in the Californian mountains differ in the relative frequencies of certain chromosomal forms (Table 20). These populations are, therefore, racially distinct, but the distinction is small and purely quantitative. Populations of the same species in California and southern Mexico, some two thousand miles apart, differ more strongly— chromosomal forms common in southern Mexico do not occur or are rare in California, or vice versa. One could seal the distinction by giving the Californian and Mexican races official names in Latin. But it has not seemed expedient to do so, since the names of the places of origin of the populations serve as labels just as well as Latin names would. Moreover, geographically intermediate populations are, by and large, intermediate in genetic composition, so that what we have is really a chain of racially distinct populations.

Human populations present a similar state of affairs. We have seen that the populations of Wales, geographically almost as close as the Drosophila populations mentioned above, show a slight but nevertheless significant diversity in the incidence of the genes responsible for the A–B–O blood groups (Figure 8). These are small, minor, or microgeographic races. Consider now the data in Table 22 which deals with the major or macrogeographic races. This Table reports the frequencies of the so-called "Rhesus" (or Rh) blood group gene which has about a dozen known variants (alleles) that, for reasons we need not enter into, are denoted by combinations of small and capital letters C, D, and E.

TABLE 22

Percentage frequencies in various populations of eight forms of the Rh blood-group gene *(after Mourant 1954)*

| Population | CDE | CDe | CdE | Cde | cDE | cdE | cDe | cde |
|---|---|---|---|---|---|---|---|---|
| | | | | | *Genes* | | | |
| **EUROPE** | | | | | | | | |
| English | 0.1 | 43.1 | 0 | 0.7 | 13.6 | 0.8 | 2.8 | 38.8 |
| Danes | 0.1 | 42.2 | 0 | 1.3 | 15.1 | 0.7 | 1.8 | 38.8 |
| Germans | 0.4 | 43.9 | 0 | 0.6 | 13.7 | 1.0 | 2.6 | 37.8 |
| Italians | 0.4 | 47.6 | 0.3 | 0.7 | 10.8 | 0.7 | 1.6 | 38.0 |
| Spaniards | 0.1 | 43.2 | 0 | 1.9 | 12.0 | 0 | 3.7 | 38.0 |
| Basques | 0 | 37.6 | 0 | 1.5 | 7.1 | 0.2 | 0.5 | 53.1 |
| **AFRICA** | | | | | | | | |
| Egyptians | 0 | 49.5 | 0 | 0 | 9.0 | 0 | 17.3 | 24.3 |
| Hutu | 0 | 8.3 | 0 | 1.6 | 5.7 | 0 | 62.9 | 21.6 |
| Kikuyu | 0 | 7.3 | 0 | 1.4 | 9.9 | 1.4 | 59.5 | 20.4 |
| Shona (S. Rhodesia) | 0 | 6.9 | 0 | 0 | 6.4 | 0 | 62.7 | 23.9 |
| Bantu (S. Africa) | 0 | 4.7 | 0 | 5.8 | 8.5 | 0 | 59.6 | 21.4 |
| Bushmen | 0 | 9.0 | 0 | 0 | 2.0 | 0 | 89.0 | 0 |
| **ASIA** | | | | | | | | |
| Yemenite Jews | 0.5 | 56.1 | 0 | 1.0 | 7.9 | 0 | 6.4 | 28.2 |
| East Pakistan | 1.6 | 63.3 | 0 | 6.5 | 7.6 | 0 | 3.9 | 17.1 |
| South Chinese | 0.5 | 75.9 | 0 | 0 | 19.5 | 0 | 4.1 | 0 |
| Japanese | 0.4 | 60.2 | 0 | 0 | 30.8 | 3.3 | 0 | 5.3 |
| **AUSTRALASIA** | | | | | | | | |
| Australian aborigines | 2.1 | 56.4 | 0 | 12.9 | 20.1 | 0 | 8.5 | 0 |
| Papuans | 1.6 | 94.4 | 0 | 0 | 2.0 | 0 | 2.0 | 0 |
| Javanese | 1.2 | 84.0 | 0 | 0 | 8.3 | 0 | 6.5 | 0 |
| Marshallese | 0 | 95.1 | 0 | 0 | 4.4 | 0 | 0.5 | 0 |
| **AMERICA** | | | | | | | | |
| Eskimos (Greenland) | 3.4 | 72.5 | 0 | 0 | 22.0 | 0 | 2.1 | 0 |
| Chippewa | 2.0 | 33.7 | 0 | 0 | 53.0 | 3.2 | 0 | 8.0 |
| Blood | 4.1 | 47.8 | 0 | 0 | 34.8 | 3.4 | 0 | 9.9 |
| Navajo | 1.3 | 43.1 | 0 | 0 | 27.7 | 0 | 28.0 | 0 |

Perhaps the most remarkable finding is that the gene cDe is far more frequent in all populations native to Africa south of the Sahara Desert than anywhere else in the world. In the populations reported in Table 22 its frequencies are close to 60 per cent, although frequencies from 48 to over 90 per cent have been recorded (Mourant 1954). In Egypt the frequency is about 17 per cent, which is much less than in sub-Saharan Africa but higher than elsewhere. This is not unexpected, since the valley of the Nile is a corridor through which the genes of the Negroid populations south of the Sahara have for millennia diffused toward the Mediterranean Sea, and vice versa. But note that the cDe gene is nevertheless present in a fraction of the gene pool almost everywhere in the world: a sample of Navajo Indians from Ramah, New Mexico, had as high as 28 per cent of these genes (though this is perhaps in need of confirmation). Does it follow that once upon a time everybody in sub-Saharan Africa was homozygous for cDe, and in the rest of the world nobody had this gene? Should Europeans, Asiatics, and Americans who carry the cDe gene be presumed to have some Negro ancestry? There is no basis whatsoever to think so. The gene cDe is almost cosmopolitan in distribution, though for some unknown reason it reaches its highest frequency in Africa.

Consider now the Papuans of New Guinea. In skin color and in facial features, these people would not be very conspicuous on a street in New York's Harlem. Do they, like Africans, have many cDe genes? On the contrary, this gene is rare in New Guinea; but the gene CDe attains there a frequency over 90 per cent, almost the highest in the world (Table 22). In Africa, except in Egypt, the CDe gene falls to its lowest frequencies anywhere, but it is common among Indonesians, Melanesians, and Australian aborigines, i.e., among the populations of places geographically nearest to New Guinea. Europeans and American Indians are generally intermediate between the Africans on one side and the Australasians on the other in the frequencies of the CDe gene.

The gene cde, the so-called Rh-negative, reaches its highest recorded frequency among the Basques, a people in the Pyrenees Mountains of northern Spain and adjacent France, who may be a relic of very ancient inhabitants of western Europe. This gene is fairly common in other Europeans (and, of course, in white Americans), less so among Africans and peoples of southwestern Asia and India, and is rare or absent elsewhere (Table 22). Here, again, it was suggested that the Rh-negative gene arose in Europe, that the ancestors of the Basques may have been homozygous for it, and that it penetrated in other populations owing to race mixture. There is a special reason why this hypothesis seemed plausible. Children from marriages in which the mother is homozygous for the Rh-negative and the father is homozygous or heterozygous for the Rh-positive gene (the four of the eight genes in Table 22 having the capital letter D) are liable to suffer from a form of jaundice. Unless there is special treatment they may die soon after birth or may even be aborted before birth. The Rh-negative gene is under a selective disadvantage in populations in which it is in a minority. It is, however, difficult to explain how a population, such as the presumed ancestors of the Basques, could have become homozygous for Rh-negative in the first place. It seems on the whole more probable that the Rh-negative genes are maintained in many human populations by some mechanism such as an advantage of the Rh-positive/Rh-negative heterozygotes. What this advantage may be is completely unknown, however.

There are at least eight other genes which determine workable immunological characters of human blood. These are the "classical" or ABO gene, M–N, Lewis, P, Kell, Lutheran, Duffy, and Kidd genes (some of these names refer to persons who produced blood sera by means of which these genes were detected). The literature dealing with the variations in the properties of human blood is enormous; it has been most ably brought together by Boyd (1939) and Mourant (1954; this work contains references to 1,716 other publications), Mourant et al. (1958) and others. Only the briefest summary can be given here.

Let us first consider the ABO system, the longest known and most extensively studied. Most populations are mixtures of persons with O, A, B, and AB bloods. American Indians living in Central and South America are exceptional in being almost uniformly O; Australian aborigines and North American Indians have O and A but no B or AB (except as introduced by miscegenation with European invaders). The B gene is most frequent in populations in the heartland of Asia and in India (over 30 per cent of the gene pool) and it becomes less frequent westward (under 10 per cent in countries facing the Atlantic and most of the Mediterranean Sea) and also eastward (Japan, Philippines, New Guinea, islands of the Pacific). The gene for A is, on the contrary, more frequent in Europe than in Asia and Africa. It is also frequent in parts of Australia and reaches its highest recorded frequencies, up to 80 per cent of the gene pool, in the Blackfoot and Blood Indians of the northwestern United States and the adjacent part of Canada.

The M blood group is most prevalent among American Indians and least frequent among Australian aborigines and Melanesians. In most of Europe, Asia, and Africa, M is somewhat more frequent than N (50–70 per cent M). The geographic distribution data for the other blood-type genes are much less abundant than for the foregoing. The gene S (the secretor gene) has frequencies close to 50 per cent in most of Europe, in Egypt, and in Japan; about 38 per cent in American Negroes; and close to 100 per cent in American Indians. The frequency of the gene P is also about 50 per cent in Europe but considerably higher among Negroes (over 80 per cent) and lower among Chinese and South American Indians.

The Kell (K) and Lutheran (Lu$^a$) genes have frequencies of 5 per cent in most European populations. K is even less frequent in Africa (except among the Bushmen), China, Malaya, and in most American Indians; Lu$^a$ seems to be absent in India and in Australia. The Duffy (Fy$^a$) and Kidd (Jk$^a$) genes promise to be very interesting but are very imperfectly known. The frequency of Fy$^a$ is about 40 per cent in Europe, except among the Lapps (55–81 per cent), but it is higher in Asia (70–90 per cent) and lower in Africa (6–8 per cent). It is high in most American Indians tested but apparently absent in one South American Indian tribe. Jk$^a$ makes up about 50 per cent of the gene pool in England and among white Americans but about 78 per cent in Negroes and 100 per cent in a tribe of Dyaks from the island of Borneo. The Diego (Di$^a$) gene seems, on the basis of exploratory studies, to be absent in whites and Negroes but present in American Indians, Chinese, and Japanese.

## Boyd's Classification of Human Races

Studies on the distribution of the blood groups in the populations of the world are progressing rapidly. It should be possible in a not too distant future to describe every human population objectively and quantitatively in terms of the composition of its gene pool with respect to its blood group genes. It should, however, be clearly understood that what is thus described and characterized are Mendelian populations, not individuals.

For example, the tests of the blood of the present writer (made through the courtesy of P. Levine) showed the following: type O, homozygous M, heterozygous for Rh genes CDe and cDE, heterozygous S/s, absence of P, K, and Lu$^a$, and presence of Fy$^a$. What inference can be made from these data concerning my race? I am unlikely to be a native of sub-Saharan Africa, since the frequency of CDe/cDE heterozygotes is only about 2 per cent there. I am also rather unlikely to be a Melanesian or an Australian aborigine, because M homozygotes are infrequent among these people. Otherwise my blood-group genotype is sufficiently nondescript that persons with a similar gene constellation may be found in many parts of the world.

Does this make the blood groups valueless for race classification? Not at all; the differences revealed by the blood-group studies promise fair to give a good basis for estimating the relationships of human populations. Boyd (1950, 1953) proposed the following fivefold race classification:

1. *European (Caucasoid)*—high frequencies of Rh cde and CDe, moderate frequencies of the other blood-group genes; M usually slightly above and N below 50 per cent

2. *African (Negroid)*—very high frequency of Rh cDe, moderate frequencies of the other blood-group genes

3. *Asiatic (Mongoloid)*—high frequency of B, few if any cde

4. *American Indian*—mostly homozygous O but sometimes high frequencies of A; absence of B, few if any cde, high M

5. *Australoid*—moderate to high A, few or no B or cde, high N

Boyd also postulated that there may have existed on the continent of Europe a sixth race, Early European, which had a very high incidence of Rh cde and probably no B, of which the Basques are the survivors. He did not utilize the data on P, K, Lu$^a$, Fy$^a$, and Jk$^a$ genes which did not exist or were too scanty when he wrote. Except for the hypothetical Early European, Boyd's classification contains no striking innovations compared to those of the classics of anthropology. Having the latter confirmed by blood group tests is, however, no mean achievement.

## Coon–Garn–Birdsell Race Classification

It has been pointed out above that the value of the blood groups for racial studies lies in the precision of their diagnosis and in the facility with which the differences observed may be expressed in terms of the gene frequencies in the populations studied. This certainly does not mean that the more easily visible differences in color, stature, hair form, etc. should be disregarded. Coon, Garn, and Birdsell (1950) and Garn (1961), paying due regard to all observable physical traits, have proposed a somewhat finer subdivision than did Boyd. Garn recognizes the following nine major "geographical races":

*Amerindian*—the pre-Columbian populations of the Americas

*Polynesian*—islands of the eastern Pacific, from New Zealand to Hawaii and Easter Island

*Micronesian*—islands of the western Pacific, from Guam to Marshall and Gilbert Islands

*Melanesian–Papuan*—islands of the western Pacific, from New Guinea to New Caledonia and Fiji

*Australian*—Australian aboriginal populations

*Asiatic*—populations extending from Indonesia and Southeast Asia, to Tibet, China, Japan, Mongolia, and the native tribes of Siberia

*Indian*—populations of the subcontinent of India

*European*—populations of Europe, the Middle East, and Africa north of the Sahara; now world-wide

*African*—populations of Africa south of the Sahara

Coon, Garn and Birdsell (1950) propose also a classification involving a somewhat finer subdivision into thirty races and Garn (1961) into thirty-two races. I find it convenient to combine these two classifications, whereupon there emerges the following system of thirty-four races (also see Figure 10):

1. *Northwest European*—Scandinavia, northern Germany, northern France, the Low Countries, United Kingdom, and Ireland

2. *Northeast European*—Poland, Russia, most of the present population of Siberia

3. *Alpine*—from central France, south Germany, Switzerland, northern Italy, eastward to the shores of the Black Sea

4. *Mediterranean*—peoples on both sides of the Mediterranean, from Tangier to the Dardanelles, Arabia, Turkey, Iran, and Turkomania

5. *Hindu*—India, Pakistan

6. *Turkic*—Turkestan, western China

7. *Tibetan*—Tibet

8. *North Chinese*—northern and central China and Manchuria

9. *Classic Mongoloid*—Siberia, Mongolia, Korea, Japan

10. *Eskimo*—arctic America

11. *Southeast Asiatic*—South China to Thailand, Burma, Malaya, and Indonesia

12. *Ainu*—aboriginal population of northern Japan

13. *Lapp*—arctic Scandinavia and Finland

14. *North American Indian*—indigenous populations of Canada and the United States

15. *Central American Indian*—from southwestern United States, through Central America, to Bolivia

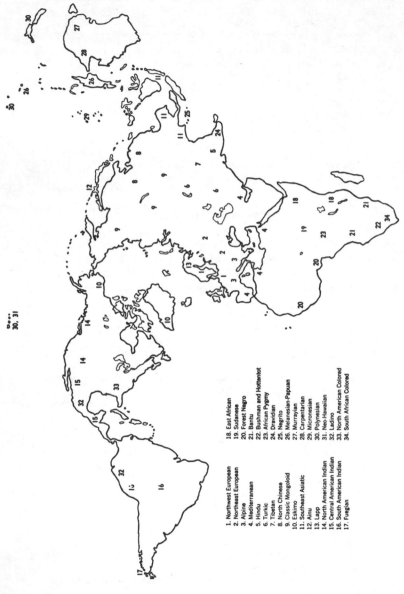

1. Northwest European
2. Northeast European
3. Alpine
4. Mediterranean
5. Hindu
6. Turkic
7. Tibetan
8. North Chinese
9. Classic Mongoloid
10. Eskimo
11. Southeast Asiatic
12. Ainu
13. Lapp
14. North American Indian
15. Central American Indian
16. South American Indian
17. Fuegian

18. East African
19. Sudanese
20. Forest Negro
21. Bantu
22. Bushman and Hottentot
23. African Pygmy
24. Dravidian
25. Negrito
26. Melanesian-Papuan
27. Murrayian
28. Carpentarian
29. Micronesian
30. Polynesian
31. Neo-Hawaiian
32. Ladino
33. North American Colored
34. South African Colored

*Figure 10.* The geographic occurrence of a majority of the thirty-four races of man.

16. *South American Indian*—primarily the agricultural peoples of Peru, Bolivia, and Chile

17. *Fuegian*—nonagricultural inhabitants of southern South America

18. *East African*—East Africa, Ethiopia, a part of Sudan

19. *Sudanese*—most of the Sudan

20. *Forest Negro*—West Africa and much of the Congo

21. *Bantu*—South Africa and part of East Africa

22. *Bushman and Hottentot*—the aboriginal inhabitants of South Africa

23. *African Pygmy*—a small-statured population living in the rain forests of equatorial Africa

24. *Dravidian*—aboriginal populations of southern India and Ceylon

25. *Negrito*—small-statured and frizzly-haired populations scattered from the Philippines to the Andamans, Malaya, and New Guinea

26. *Melanesian–Papuan*—New Guinea to Fiji

27. *Murrayian*—aboriginal population of southeastern Australia

28. *Carpentarian*—aboriginal population of northern and central Australia

29. *Micronesian*—islands of the western Pacific

30. *Polynesian*—islands of the central and the eastern Pacific

31. *Neo-Hawaiian*—an emerging population of Hawaii

32. *Ladino*—an emerging population of Central and South America

33. *North American Colored*—the so-called Negro population of North America

34. *South African Colored*—the analogous population of South Africa

There is an important difference between the Coon–Garn–Birdsell classification and numerous classifications proposed before them which makes theirs a pioneering venture. This is the explicit recognition that races are Mendelian populations that change in time, not abstract "types" or "components." Race classifications should reflect the state of affairs at a given time level and may have to be altered in the future. The origin of four out of the thirty-four races given above may be dated within the last 400 years or less. The North American Colored race (33) arose from a mixture of races 20, 21, 1, 3, 4, and probably some others; the South African Colored (34) from 21, 22, 1, and 3; Ladino (32) from at least 15, 16, 4, 20, and 21; and Neo-Hawaiian (31) from 30, 1, 9, and some 4, 8, and 11. Their recent hybrid origin makes these races no less real and natural than the others listed. Many or all of the old populations had mixed origins at various times in their histories. Already the Neanderthalians were differentiated into local races, some of which probably exchanged genes with races collectively labeled *sapiens* (Chapter 8).

A classification would oversimplify the actual situation if it implied that its categories, races or species or genera, are equivalent in all respects. Coon, Garn, and Birdsell made it clear that races are

of different kinds. Murrayians, Ainus, Negritos, Bushmen, Carpen-
tarians, and perhaps some others are relics of ancient populations,
which were more widely distributed in the past than they are at
present. Some of them are being submerged and assimilated by
intermarriage with their neighbors or becoming extinct. The new
races mentioned above are still in formative stages; their gene
pools, not clearly separated from those of their neighbors, are still
without internal coherence. For example, Ladinos are in reality a
social class in some Latin American countries, and in different
countries they constitute genetically different populations, which
have few or no genetic ties between them. Hindus are a complex
mosaic of caste populations which scarcely interbreed. North Chinese, Classic Mongoloids, and Southeast Asiatics (8, 9, 11) are huge
masses of humanity forming numerous geographically separated
Mendelian populations which could as well be treated as different
races or placed in a single race. The same is true of the populations
of Europe (races 1–4), which are well on the way to fusion into a
single race.

### Races, Subspecies, Varieties, Breeds, and Ethnic Groups

Boyd has recognized five, and Coon, Garn, and Birdsell nine or
thirty or thirty-two races. Does it follow that some of these classifications are necessarily wrong? No, all may be right; it should always be kept in mind that while race differences are objectively
ascertainable facts, the number of races we choose to recognize is
a matter of convenience.

Race studies serve a double purpose. Just as zoologists observe a
great diversity of animals, anthropologists are confronted with a
diversity of human beings. Classification and systematization are
devices used to make diversity intelligible and manageable. Classification in biology and in anthropology is as indispensable, and for
the same reason, as in a large library: A book misplaced may be as
useless as a book lost. Race studies serve a practical purpose—to
facilitate communication among students of man, who must be able
to indicate which peoples they have observed. But race is also the
subject of scientific study and analysis simply because it is a fact of
nature. We wish to understand, in Washburn's words, "the process
and the pattern of human evolution," and the place of human evolution in the evolution of life as a whole. Pragmatic and theoretic
race studies should be complementary and not rival. Unfortunately,

instead of serving a double purpose they have at times been at cross purposes.

Ideally, a race classification should take into consideration all variable traits. Blood types happen to be the traits genetically best understood; the more easily perceived traits, such as skin color, hair or nose or lip shape, etc., are polygenic and their analysis has not progressed anywhere nearly as far as that of the blood types. Classification is an art as well as a science, because, as pointed out above, different traits do not vary as accommodatingly together as a classifier might wish: classifications based on blood type or skin color or hair form will not coincide completely. A good classifier is one who can make the racial divisions in such a way that the least possible violence is done to any trait. Mathematical statisticians (Pearson, Fisher, Mahalanobis, and others) have devised techniques, called coefficients of racial likeness, discriminant functions, and generalized distance, which should decrease the art component and increase the scientific component in classification. These techniques are hopeful, but up to the present they have accomplished about as much for classification as the mechanical piano has for music.

It will, I think, be generally admitted that the ideal classification of the races of man is yet to be proposed. The existing ones are tentative, but they serve as cataloguing devices. Yet it does not follow that races are arbitrary and "mere" inventions of the classifiers; some authors have talked themselves into denying that the human species has any races at all! Let us make very clear what is and what is not arbitrary about races. Race *differences* are facts of nature which can, given sufficient study, be ascertained objectively: Mendelian populations of any kind, from small tribes to inhabitants of countries and continents, may differ in frequencies of some genetic variants or they may not. If they so differ, they are racially distinct.

With careful study most populations will be found to differ, at least slightly, in the frequencies of some genes. It does not, however, follow that we should multiply and subdivide races indefinitely. Race *names* are arbitrary; it is a matter of expediency how far a student of man wishes to go in naming the racially distinct populations. To recognize only the five Blumenbach races is not convenient because the fivefold division ignores some very distinctive populations; to have hundreds of named races is unwieldy.

Human races are neither more or less objective or "real" than races in other species, although they are more difficult to study. This fact should be stressed because it is obscured by terminologies. Darwin used "variety" in preference to "race," and the crux of his argument in *Origin of Species* was that species are merely strongly diverged and distinctive varieties. Darwin did not, however, stress as much as his successors that the varieties which may become incipient species are, at least in sexually reproducing and outbreeding organisms, those living in different territories. A polytypic species is a species differentiated geographically into local varieties or races. But "variety" is sometimes applied (or misapplied) also to distinctive forms within a population, in other words to polymorphs, as well as to strains (clones, pure lines) of asexually reproducing or self-fertilizing forms (e.g., "varieties" of fruit trees propagated by grafting or of wheat and barley which are mostly self-fertilizing). Because of this ambiguity, modern systematists generally avoid the term "variety" and refer to geographically separated, allopatric, races as "subspecies."

Human races are, then, subspecies of the species *Homo sapiens*. Subspecies of animals and plants are designated by Latin trinomials; thus also one might invent such names as *Homo sapiens africanus, Homo sapiens mongolicus,* etc., but this is not customary in studying man. Human subspecies are much more difficult to study than the zoological ones because the latter are practically always allopatric, while human races may also coexist in the same territory, social isolation replacing the geographic one. Nevertheless, zoologists often face quandaries with their subspecies very similar to those which anthropologists face with their races.

Into how many subspecies should a species be split? The little pocket gopher, *Thomomys bottae,* has some 150 named subspecies, which many zoologists regard as inordinate. It has been suggested (Mayr 1942) that describers of subspecies should abide by the so-called 75 per cent rule, i.e., that no subspecies are nameable unless one can classify 75 per cent or more of the individuals in one or the other subspecies. Wilson and Brown (1953) caused a storm in a teacup by pleading that no subspecies should be named at all. This set other systematists to arguing, at times passionately, the merits and demerits of naming subspecies. (See Edwards 1954 and Pimentel 1959 for further references.) Anthropologists will find these polemics not unfamiliar. But it must be kept clear that the dispute is about the advisability of naming subspecies, not about the existence of race differences!

Races of dogs, horses, cattle, and other domestic animals are usually referred to as "breeds." Like races of man and subspecies of wild animals and plants, breeds are Mendelian populations differing in frequencies of certain genes. The salient fact about breeds of domestic animals is that their reproduction is controlled by man: a puppy of a color "wrong" for a given breed will be "culled" in order to maintain the breed visibly distinct (in some breeds of horses a variety of coat colors is, however, permissible). Human control makes possible sympatric coexistence of several breeds of the same species without mixing. Replacement of geographic isolation by human control of reproduction in domestic animals has been likened to the social factors controlling human reproduction, which permit sympatric coexistence of two or more human races, but the analogy should not be stretched too far.

The term "ethnic group" was suggested for human races in the thirties, when anthropologists and biologists were anxious to dissociate themselves from the Hitlerian prostitution of the race concept. Whether a new name is of much use in combating race prejudice is questionable: one may hate an ethnic group as virulently as a race. But the propriety of using such subterfuges in science is questionable. Speak of ethnic groups if you like, but a statement such as "man has no races, he has only ethnic groups" is misleading. Ethnic groups are biologically the same phenomenon as races, subspecies, and breeds. To imply that if man had races, then race prejudice would be justified is to justify race prejudice.

I do not wish to maintain that all races of all species can be considered on an equal footing. Some species are more strongly and others weakly polytypic, and man is more likely in the latter than in the former category. Races may be incipient species, but man has preserved his specific unity ever since the australopithecine stage, at least in the sense that no more than one hominid species ever lived in any one place at any one time. Civilization causes race convergence, due to gene exchange, to outrun race divergence. In this sense, human races are relics of the precultural stage of evolution.

## Races as Products of Natural Selection

If the classification of human races is in an unsatisfactory state, the understanding of their origins and biological significance is still more so. These problems seemed simple to the pioneers of the study of man. Buffon, Blumenbach, and other eighteenth-century authors thought that people are modified by the environments in which they live and that the modifications are inherited. A Negro is a "child of the African sun"—his skin got dark because he was sun tanned for many generations. This is an attractively simple theory, and it was accepted explicitly or implicitly even to our day by many anthropologists who were oblivious of the unfortunate fact that the theory assumes inheritance of acquired modifications and thus contravenes modern biology.

Race differences might.have arisen through natural selection as adaptations to the environments, physical and social, in which people lived. If so, the distinguishing characteristics of each race must be directly or indirectly helpful for survival and/or reproduction in the respective environments of these races. This is not obviously so at any rate. For example, what difference does it make whether your hair is straight or wavy or curly? Darwin hesitated to ascribe human race differences either to natural selection or to the Lamarckian inheritance of acquired modifications. But there is still another possibility—sexual selection. Gentlemen may prefer curly-haired blondes or straight-haired brunettes; ladies may have preferences for tall and slender or for smallish and pudgy gentlemen. If tastes were unlike in different countries, and if those whose figures and features were popular with the opposite sex produced on that account more surviving progeny, then races could have become different in appearance even though the race "stigmata" were not in themselves useful or harmful. And finally race differences may be due to genetic drift—accidents of sampling from the gene pool (see p. 279).

Now, at present we unfortunately do not have the evidence that is required to discriminate between the above possibilities. To obtain it much painstaking work is doubtless needed. The really startling fact is that this work was not initiated until recently and even now not on a scale commensurate with its significance. This can only be explained by a failure to appreciate the importance of the issue. To believers in Lamarckian inheritance, any form of selection, natural or sexual, is rather inconsequential. To some anthropologists the classification must be based on traits which are neutral, i.e., neither useful or harmful to their possessors, in order to truly reflect the descent relationships of the races. The characteristics induced by the environment, either through natural selection or in a Lamarckian manner, are too labile to be dependable. The question of how neutral racial traits could have appeared and become established in the first place did not seem to have arisen or at least was not pressed.

Last but not least, the idea that human races differ in adaptively significant traits is emotionally repugnant to some people. Any inquiry into this matter is felt to be dangerous, lest it vindicate race prejudice. This attitude almost invariably goes hand in hand with the misunderstanding of the nature of biological heredity repeatedly dealt with above. To be different is not tantamount to being superior or inferior. Furthermore, the differential adaptations of the races of man are most probably concerned with environments of a remote past, largely superseded by the environments created by civilization, to which all races may be equally adapted or unadapted.

## Skin Color

Shocking though this may be, solid and conclusive evidence concerning the adaptive significance of racial traits in man is scant in the extreme, and the best that can be offered are plausible speculations and surmises! Speculations and surmises are necessary, however, if solid evidence is ever to be produced; such evidence will not appear without working hypotheses to stimulate observations and experiments. Coon, Garn, and Birdsell (1950), Schwidetzky (1952), Newman (1953), Coon (1954b, 1955, 1959), and Weiner (1954), among others, have provided such hypotheses.

Skin color is the most conspicuous, though not necessarily physiologically the most important, of race differences. The geographic distribution of heavily and lightly pigmented races is on the whole consistent with the assumption that dark skins are adaptive in climates with strong sunshine and clear skies and light ones in lands with cool and cloudy climates (Schwidetzky 1952, Reche and Lehmann 1959). The darkest people live in the savannas of Africa, south of the Sahara Desert but north of the equatorial rain forests. The forest-dwellers are lighter, and the aboriginal populations of South Africa (Bushmen) have yellowish-brown skin. Very dark people live also in Melanesia, New Guinea, and parts of southern India. Some of the Australian aborigines, though believed to be remote relatives of the white race, are also dark.

The center of "blondism" or "leucodermia" is northern Europe, with its notorious paucity of sunshine, and particularly that part of Europe which was covered by the Pleistocene ice sheet (Schwidetzky 1952). American Indians, however, fail to conform to the rule—those living in the tropics of Central and South America are on the average only slightly if at all darker than their relatives in temperate and cold parts. On the other hand, the Mongoloid peoples of northern Siberia and the Eskimos of arctic America seem to have more pigment than the climates of their lands warrant. Some plausible surmises have been offered to explain these last exceptions. Some of the arctic lands, particularly in Asia, are dry and rarely cloudy, making the snow glare very intense.

The Second World War forced many men to reside temporarily in climates not of their own choosing, and this stimulated some interesting research in the comparative physiology of different human subspecies. Excellent and highly critical reviews of the results have been provided by Barnicot (1959) and Newman (1961).

Since the acquired sun tan in generally light-skinned people protects them from painful sunburn, it is tempting to infer that the heavy pigmentation of the dark races is useful as a permanent protection. This situation turns out, however, to be rather complex. Sunburns are produced by the ultraviolet part of the solar spectrum, with wave-lengths in the neighborhood of 3,000 Ångstrom units, injuring the living cells of the subsurface (Malpighian and dermis) layers of the skin. Sun tan involves deposition of pigment granules in the cells of the Malpighian layer and a thickening of the outermost horny layer which consists of dead remains of the Malpighian cells, constantly rubbed off from the outside and renewed by cell multiplication from the inside of the skin. Now, it is chiefly the horny layer which absorbs the ultraviolet and prevents its penetration to and injury of the deeper living cells. Is it then the thickening of the horny layer rather than the pigmentation which protects from sunburns? It is both: a horny layer formed by pigmented cells is a more efficient absorber of ultraviolet radiation than that arising from unpigmented cells (see Blum 1959, 1961).

Protection against skin cancers is another advantage of dark pigmentation. Skin cancers are commoner in white persons than in darkly pigmented races habitually exposed to strong sunlight and greater on exposed parts of the body than on those protected by clothing. It is not clear, however, how strong the natural selection from this source is; sunlight-induced cancers in man are of low malignancy, and they occur mostly late in life (Blum 1959, 1961). The advantage of light pigmentation in countries with deficient sunshine is not firmly established either. It has been assumed to arise because it facilitates the production of the antirachitic vitamin D in living cells by absorbing the ultraviolet radiation. Anyway, these advantages have to be paid for. Dark Negro skin reflects less (10–20 per cent) in the visible sunlight spectrum than a light skin (40–50 per cent) and thus *increases* the heat load, a possible disadvantage under conditions of threatening heat stroke (Barnicot 1959). On the other hand, the disadvantage may be compensated for if the sweating is initiated at a lower temperature.

Cowles (1959) discounts the value of dark skin as a protection against sunburn. He surmises that heavily pigmented skin may be adaptive rather as a camouflage—a dark-skinned man is less conspicuous in the shade of a tropical rain forest than a light-skinned one. This, he supposes, might be advantageous for concealment from predators and from the game being stalked by a huntsman. The view is questionable because forest-dwellers tend, actually, to be less dark than those of tropical grasslands.

## Body Build and Climatic Adaptation

The comparative study of many species of animals has disclosed some rules which seem to be applicable also to human races. (Concerning these rules, see Mayr 1942, Rensch 1959a, Ray 1960.) One of the rules (Bergmann's) is that races which inhabit the warmer parts of the geographic range of a species tend to be smaller in body size than races living in colder parts. Another rule (Allen's) concerns the protruding body parts (extremities, ears, tails, etc.), which tend to be shorter relative to body size in colder parts of the species range. Both rules can be interpreted as adaptations for the conservation or dissipation of heat. If a body is increased proportionately in size, its surface grows as the square and its bulk as the cube of its linear dimensions. Since the dissipation of heat occurs by convection and radiation from the skin surface, small surface in relation to bulk is economical when heat needs to be conserved, and large surface relative to bulk is advantageous when heat must be thrown off. Anybody who ever exposed his ears or his fingers to a good frost knows how easily these protruding parts loose heat.

Newman (1953), Roberts (1953), and Baker (1958a) have analyzed the data accumulated in the anthropological literature on the stature and weight of inhabitants of many parts of the world. Table 23 shows a small sample of these data. Although the correlation is far from perfect, the stature : weight ratio tends to be lower in the inhabitants of cold countries and higher in those of hot. Certain facts deserve special emphasis. Some of the tallest (Batutsi, 176 cm average stature) and the shortest (Pygmies, 142 cm) people reside

TABLE 23

Stature (in cm), weight (in kg), and stature:weight ratio among inhabitants of different parts of the world *(after Baker)*

| Population | Stature | Weight | Ratio |
|---|---|---|---|
| CAUCASIAN | | | |
| Finland | 171.0 | 70.0 | 2.44 |
| United States (Army) | 173.9 | 70.2 | 2.48 |
| Iceland | 173.6 | 68.1 | 2.55 |
| France | 172.5 | 67.0 | 2.57 |
| England | 166.3 | 64.5 | 2.58 |
| Sicily | 169.1 | 65.0 | 2.60 |
| Morocco | 168.9 | 63.8 | 2.65 |
| Scotland | 170.4 | 61.8 | 2.76 |
| Tunisia | 173.4 | 62.3 | 2.78 |
| Berbers | 169.8 | 59.5 | 2.85 |
| Mahratta (India) | 163.8 | 55.7 | 2.94 |
| Bengal (India) | 165.8 | 52.7 | 3.15 |
| NEGROID | | | |
| Yambasa | 169.0 | 62.0 | 2.78 |
| Kirdi | 166.5 | 57.3 | 2.90 |
| Baya | 163.0 | 53.9 | 3.02 |
| Batutsi | 176.0 | 57.0 | 3.09 |
| Kikuyu | 164.5 | 51.9 | 3.17 |
| Pygmies | 142.2 | 39.9 | 3.56 |
| Efe | 143.8 | 39.8 | 3.61 |
| Bushmen | 155.8 | 40.4 | 3.86 |
| MONGOLOID | | | |
| Kazakh (Turkestan) | 163.1 | 69.7 | 2.34 |
| Eskimo | 161.2 | 62.9 | 2.56 |
| North China | 168.0 | 61.0 | 2.75 |
| Korea | 161.1 | 55.5 | 2.90 |
| Central China | 163.0 | 54.7 | 2.98 |
| Japan | 160.9 | 53.0 | 3.04 |
| Sundanese | 159.8 | 51.9 | 3.08 |
| Annamites | 158.7 | 51.3 | 3.09 |
| Hong Kong | 166.2 | 52.2 | 3.18 |

in equatorial Africa. The former are pastoralists living in open grasslands, the latter hunters in tropical rain forests. The stature : weight ratios are 3.09 in Batutsi and 3.56 in the Pygmies, both higher than in any European group. In ordinary language, the natives of hot and open countries are inclined to be tall and lanky or, which is more often, slight and slim. The natives in cold lands are likely to be bulky, large, and heavy or squat and thickset. They are inclined to accumulate fat, which is a highly efficient heat insulator. By the same token, subcutaneous fat is a disadvantage in hot environments and increases appreciably the danger of heat prostration.

The application of Bergmann's and Allen's rules to man has been criticized, particularly by Scholander (1955) and Scholander et al. (1950), on the ground that it is clothing, housing, and other cultural factors, not the shape of his body, that permit man to live in diverse climates. This is obviously true—our clothing maintains a "private" tropical climate over most of our body surface even in freezing outside temperatures. But it does not follow that the body build is immaterial in this regard, especially under critical stress conditions. It is also true that not all the differences in stature and weight listed in Table 23 are genetic. The stunted growth and the leanness of many peoples are due to inadequate nutrition. In a large sample of white American soldiers, Newman and Munro (1955) found a clear correlation between body weight and the winter temperature of their home states, northerners being appreciably heavier on the average than southerners. Even if this difference is entirely environmental, which should not be hastily assumed, it follows that cold climates modify the human physique differently than warm. Natural selection very frequently favors genetic fixation of traits which a given environment induces in the phenotype. (This is sometimes referred to as the Baldwin effect; see discussion in Waddington 1957.)

The insulating properties of subcutaneous fat lend plausibility to the suggestion, first made by Coon, Garn, and Birdsell (1950), that the characteristic features of the Mongoloid face may be a piece of thermal "engineering." While people working in the cold can protect their bodies by clothing, the face must often remain bare. Some (but by no means all!) Mongoloids inhabit parts of the world which have severe frosts and strong winds, and their flattened but well-padded faces should offer less target for frostbite and a smaller radiating surface than would a lean face with prominent

features. There is unfortunately no experimental evidence to test
the validity of this inference.

## Physiological Adaptation

Some beginnings have been made in the study of the comparative
physiology of human races, particularly in connection with climatic
adaptation. A nude person at rest is in thermal equilibrium with his
surroundings at temperatures 27–30°C (80–86°F); above this temperature he begins to sweat, the sweat evaporation helping to cool
the body. Sweating begins at lower external temperatures in men
doing physical work, since work generates more heat than rest does.
Below 27°C man must either cover himself or increase his heat production by exercise or by shivering. Now, contrary to popular belief, temperatures in the "torrid" equatorial zone rarely go above
30°C, with high relative humidities. In hot deserts, in the southwestern United States and elsewhere, temperatures frequently do
go much above 30°C, but the relative humidities are then low.

Most valuable experimental data have been published by Baker
(1958b). Groups of Negro and white soldiers matched for weight,
stature, and the amount of body fat, who had lived under similar
conditions, were made to rest or to do similar, more or less strenuous exercise, in sun or shade, clothed or nude. The experiments
were made under hot and humid conditions (in Virginia) and under
hot but dry desert conditions (near Yuma, Arizona). The body
(rectal) temperature and sweat production were measured. Negroes
proved to have a higher physiological tolerance in wet heat, but
whites were better off in dry heat. Under Virginia conditions, Negroes exposed to heat stress had an average rectal temperature of
100.0°F, whites an average of 100.4°F; Negroes a pulse rate of
119.4, whites of 122.4; Negroes a sweat loss of 873 g per hour,
whites of 912 g per hour. Under Yuma conditions there was little
difference in the temperature rise, but the sweat loss in Negroes
was appreciably greater than in whites.

When the body is threatened with excessive heat loss in cold
surroundings, the blood circulation in the skin and extremities is
diminished owing to constriction of the superficial blood vessels.
This permits the body surface to cool but maintains the temperature constant in the vital internal organs. Thus, a naked white
person at an air temperature of 23°C will have a rectal temperature
of 36.1° but his head will show 34.5°, trunk 34°, hands 30°, and

feet 25°C. However, when the extremities cool to between 5° and 10°C, the blood circulation in them is renewed to prevent the hands and feet from freezing (Coon 1954b).

The ability of some people to rest or sleep naked or nearly so in what seems like harsh cold is amazing. Darwin was greatly impressed by this ability in the natives of Tierra del Fuego, and his observation was amply confirmed by more recent observers (Bridges 1950). Scholander et al. (1958a) made some fascinating experiments, comparing their own ability and that of Australian aborigines to sleep naked on the ground between fires at temperatures close to freezing. The Australians slept soundly, although their extremities were colder than those of the experimenters who shivered violently and were unable to sleep.

The adaptedness of the Eskimos to the cold climate of their native lands has impressed numerous students. Much of this adaptedness is unquestionably a matter of their cultural specializations, but some of it may also be genetic. Probably genetic are the higher basal metabolic rates, which permit them to generate more body heat, and the high blood flow in the hands and forearms when immersed in cold water (Brown et al. 1952, 1954). Hammel (1960) and Coon (1961) have published preliminary descriptions of their fascinating experiments on the temperature regulation abilities of the Alakaluf, an Indian tribe related to the now almost extinct Fuegians. They live in southernmost Chile, a land with a cold, humid, and windy climate, and are often exposed to extreme cold because they get their food by diving naked in chilly waters, 6° to 8°C, in search of marine animals. The Alakaluf proved to have extraordinarily high basal metabolic rates, thus generating unusually large quantities of heat.

Caution is called for in interpreting data of the above sort. Human beings become acclimatized to heat or cold if they are exposed to them for more or less prolonged periods. This writer has found out by experience that he needs somewhat less than a week to become adjusted to a humid tropical environment after being transferred there from a New York winter. Scholander et al. (1958b) experimented on volunteer Norwegian students who lived for six weeks in Norwegian mountains without warm clothing or bedcovers. At first they were unable to sleep because of shivering, but eventually they became able to do so despite the shivering and maintained higher skin temperatures than at the beginning of the experiment. It has been surmised that the metabolic rates and the efficient blood circulation in the extremities of the Eskimos may also be due to long-term adaptations (Barnicot 1959).

## Other Forms of Selection

Though far from satisfactory in detail, the evidence discussed above adds up to a fairly convincing demonstration that some of the differences between the races of man are adaptive in the climates in which these races live or lived. It is not, however, possible to account for all race differences on this basis. Nor could this be expected, since the climate is only a part, and not even the most important part, of man's environment. Attempts to identify selective agents other than climate have not thus far emerged from the stage of speculation, albeit plausible speculation is needed to provide testable working hypotheses.

Selection by disease may have been one of the powerful agents in human evolution. This matter will be dealt with in the next chapter. It should suffice here to point out that the human species, like many animal and plant species, contains genetic variants more or less susceptible or resistant to many infectious and parasitic diseases, as well as to environmental breakdowns of various sorts. Human populations have been again and again decimated by epidemics, and by different epidemics in different parts of the world. Those who succumbed and those who survived the infections were most likely genetically different on the average, and this may have been a strong differentiating force in the course of time.

It is possible that the same genetic factors which confer immunity to a certain infection produce also visible bodily traits which are in themselves neutral, i.e., neither useful nor detrimental. It has been suggested that dark skin pigmentation may as a side effect give resistance to malarial fevers, but there is no evidence that this is so. The same may be said of the no less plausible ideas that different diets may favor different genetic constitutions with concomitant visible traits, or that deficiencies of various chemical trace elements in the soil may have acted as selective agents. For example, it has been surmised that some physical characteristics of the people of southeastern Asia may be connected with the use of rice as the principal staple food; that the squat and thickset body build and tendency toward obesity in some populations of northern Asia and parts of Europe may be adaptive when abundance of food alternates with its scarcity; and that the muscular and wiry body build was advantageous in those who lived by stalking and hunting game. All these surmises are in need of testing and confirmation.

The role of sexual selection in the development of race differences is uncertain. There is no doubt that popular tastes and ideas of what constitutes comeliness and sexual desirability have varied enormously with different peoples and at different times. Even within the confines of Western civilization there have been such divergent predilections for body forms as those of the painters El Greco and Rubens. A population in which corpulent Rubensian types are preferred as marriage partners might within a rather small number of generations come to look quite different from that which prizes El Greco's gaunt spirituality or Botticelli's elegant linearity.

Any such predilections will be genetically ineffective, however, if people with popularly esteemed lineaments and those with bodies of other shapes leave on the average equal numbers of surviving children and grandchildren. With many primitive cultures, the marriage rules are highly elaborate and leave little room for choice of a mate (see Murdock 1949, Levi–Strauss 1960): you simply have to marry somebody who stands in a given kinship relationship to yourself, and there may be just one such person in existence. Furthermore, in such cultures everybody is married and everybody can, and usually does, beget children (see, for example, Roberts 1956). There is no question that these circumstances will reduce the effectiveness of sexual selection, but sexual selection should not be hastily dismissed altogether as a possible factor of race differentiation. Even though the choice of the spouse is limited by custom, it may not be absent altogether, as when the prescriptive partner is absent and a substitute is to be picked instead. Furthermore, sexual promiscuity, in or out of wedlock, with or without the sanction of custom, probably occurs in most if not all peoples, making room for the operation of sexual selection. Once more, the problem requires the collecting of more evidence than is now available.

### Genetic Drift and Selection of Gene Systems

It would be dogmatic to insist that all race differences must have been produced by some form of direct or indirect selection. But what are the other possibilities? As pointed out above, many, in fact a majority, of racial traits in man seem to have no influence on the fitness of their carriers. Would you be better or worse off if your nose were a little longer or shorter or your lips a little thinner or thicker? One human polymorphism which has different incidence in different races is the ability (dominant) or inability (recessive) to taste phenylthiocarbamide (PTC), a chemical substance not known to occur in nature. What, then, was the gene for tasting or not tasting PTC doing in human populations before chemists synthesized this substance about forty years ago?

At this point we must proceed with the greatest caution. There is no gene "for" tasting this or any other chemical substance or "for" anything but causing the organism to develop in cooperation with all the other genes it has. The precise roles which different genes and their different alleles play in development are usually unknown, and our inability to detect easily the influence of certain genes on fitness does not mean that such influence does not exist. The story of the blood groups is instructive in this respect. For many years it seemed that people derived no advantage and suffered no disadvantage from the blood type they happened to possess. But it has been discovered that the incidence of O blood is slightly but significantly higher in persons with duodenal ulcers than in the controls (members of the same population who do not suffer from these ulcers); the incidence of A-type blood is higher in the victims of stomach cancer than in persons free of stomach cancer; and people who develop certain forms of goiters are nontasters of PTC more frequently than those without goiters. (See Fraser–Roberts 1957, 1959a,b, Mourant 1959a, and Sheppard 1959 for reviews of the already rather voluminous relevant literature.)

All this does not mean that we have now explained why different races differ in the frequencies of the blood groups and PTC tasting (as some people seem to have concluded a bit rashly). Not only are many O blood carriers free of ulcers, people with A blood without cancers, and nontasters of PTC without goiters, but these diseases also occur in the carriers of other genotypes. There is also no reason to believe that duodenal ulcers are less dangerous or less frequent in countries that have high frequencies of O blood than in those with low frequencies, or that it is any less dangerous to have a cancer of the stomach in countries in which A bloods are frequent than where they are rare. (Note added in proof: Vogel, Pettenkofer, and Helmbold, 1961, have made an interesting attempt to correlate the frequencies of A bloods in human populations with prevalence of epidemics of plague and of syphilis, and of O bloods with that of smallpox. This matter evidently requires further study.)

A possible mechanism bringing about differences in gene frequencies between populations is so-called random genetic drift. On page 219 we have seen that, if not acted upon by mutation or selection, the frequency of any gene in the gene pool of a population will tend to remain constant from generation to generation. It should now be added that an absolute constancy would be expected only in ideal, infinitely large populations: the smaller a population, the fewer breeding individuals it contains, the greater will be the "drift," the chance deviations, up and down, from a constant frequency in different generations. Genetic drift, worked out mathematically chiefly by Sewall Wright, is a rather abstruse matter in detail, but its principle can be explained very simply. Suppose that a person with a name as rare and outlandish as mine raises a family with ten sons. If this family continues to live in New York City the name will still be rare, but if the family happens to move to a country hamlet the name may become a relatively frequent one there. Conversely, one family called Smith moving out of the hamlet may make that name not represented there at all, while one Smith family leaving New York makes no appreciable difference in the frequency of Smiths in the city.

Early mankind was probably an array of more or less small endogamous bands or tribes, living as food gatherers or food collectors (see above). In some parts of the world, as in aboriginal Australia, such tribes still exist or recently existed. Some tribes may have been from time to time reduced by environmental hazards, starvation, or disease to small numbers of persons or may even have been annihilated entirely. Conversely, other tribes that happened to stumble upon favorable circumstances, such as an unoccupied territory, increased in numbers, spread, and gave rise to large populations and new tribes. Birdsell (1957b) made most interesting estimates of the probable rates of such expansion. The continent of Australia was most likely populated by small bands of people who entered from the north, the first invaders coming perhaps some thirty-two thousand years ago. Assuming that the original band numbered twenty-five persons, Birdsell reckons about twenty-two centuries as the time needed for their descendants to spread throughout the entire continent. Using a slightly different set of assumptions, he arrives at seventy-seven centuries for the expansion of the Australopithecines from their assumed ancestral home in South Africa to the rest of Africa, southern Asia, and Java.

A small band of migrants will evidently bring not the entire gene pool of the population whence they originated but only a small sample or slice of it. This sample may easily be atypical, like the rare surname in the above example: some genes of the original population may not be included in the sample, while others may be over-represented. The genes brought by the migrants will be impressed upon the new colony, tribe, and eventually, the race descended from the immigrant foundation stock. Just how great the differences between the original and the descended races caused by random genetic drift are likely to be has been disputed ground in evolutionary theory for nearly thirty years.

The dispute arose in large part through a misunderstanding. No one has seriously contended that genetic drift alone, without natural selection, can bring about major evolutionary changes. The model of the evolutionary process proposed some three decades ago by Sewall Wright has been that of a species subdivided into numerous isolated or semi-isolated endogamous colonies or bands, some of them with continuously small populations, say a few dozen families, and others reduced only from time to time to such small numbers. Random genetic drift together with natural selection among the colonies may lead to "evolutionary inventions," i.e., to the formation of new and adaptively valuable gene constellations. The evolutionary process in a species consisting of such colonies is likely to be more rapid and effective than in a large unitary species.

The form of genetic drift that may have been important in human evolution can be visualized as follows. A small band of people, coming upon an unoccupied territory, expands and forms a tribe, a group of tribes, and eventually a new race. A useful new technique or an invention may conceivably cause such expansion even without migration to new territories. As pointed out above, the sample of the gene pool contained in the expanding band or tribe may and, in fact, almost always will include only a fraction of the genetic variability present in the original race whence the migrants sprang. Now, we must remember that in organic development the genes do not act independently of each other; instead the genes of an individual or a population form an interdependent system.

For example, the adaptive value of a gene for muscularity or corpulence or A or B blood groups depends on what other genes an individual or a population contains and, of course, on the environment. A gene may be useful in combination with some, neutral with other, and harmful with still other genes. Natural selection acting on a population tends to bring about the most favorable composition of the gene pool. The gene variants present in a population must, therefore, be adapted not only to the environment but also to each other; they must form a *coadapted gene system*. When a small group gives rise to a new population or race, the process of coadaptation by natural selection leads to reconstruction and emergence of a new gene pool. It is possible that the genes for the O, A, and B blood groups have different frequencies in different human populations because they are more favorable in combination with the other genes of some of these populations than with genes in other populations.

The process of coadaptation of gene systems by natural selection has been observed in the experiments of Dobzhansky and Pavlovsky (1957) on the fly *Drosophila pseudoobscura*. Very briefly the story is as follows. Two geographic races of the fly (coming from California and from Mexico or from California and Texas) were intercrossed and second generation hybrids were obtained. Ten groups of twenty individuals each were taken at random and used as founders of new populations or "colonies." The populations were maintained for about a year and a half (about twenty fly generations) in specially constructed population cages under uniform laboratory environments. Because of the high fertility of the flies, the experimental populations, though descended from a small number, were not small—they fluctuated between about 1,000 and 4,000 adult individuals.

Natural selection acted on these populations, making them adapted to live in their, of course highly artificial, environment. The remarkable result was that the ten experimental populations were found to diverge genetically and at the conclusion of the experiment had different genetic constitutions. This seems at first sight a paradox. Why should a genetic divergence occur among populations derived originally from the same source and kept in a uniform environment? The answer is that each of the ten groups of twenty founder individuals contained a somewhat different assortment of genes. Natural selection did, so to speak, its best with the genetic materials at its disposal in each population. Since these materials were diverse, so were the results of the evolutionary changes induced by natural selection. Such a divergence may have easily been important in human evolution. Populations derived from small groups of founders or colonizers diverged genetically, because they received somewhat different gene complements.

## Levels of Technology and Gene Frequencies

Hulse (1955, 1957) has pointed out that in 1600 there were some three million persons of British stock, while at present there are at least 150 million, a fiftyfold increase. World population has increased only about sixfold during the same period. The parts of Europe containing high proportions of blond people held about three per cent of the world population in 1600, while at present people originating from this area comprise about twelve per cent of mankind. Hulse correctly points out that, racists to the contrary notwithstanding, these figures do not necessarily prove either a biological superiority of the Blond Beast, or a genetic excellence of the British stock. Technological progress or stagnation may enhance or reduce the frequencies of the genes of culturally active or sluggish groups of people no less effectively than more strictly biological advantages or defects.

Hulse calculates further that between 1600 and 1950 the populations of Eastern Europe (Russia and Poland) increased from 15 to 180 million, i.e., 1,100 per cent, while those of Central and Western Europe from 85 to 375 million, i.e., 341 per cent. Most of the former populations contain above 15 per cent of the gene for the B blood group and the latter usually less than 15 per cent. B blood has thus become increased in frequency. Hulse interprets the differential population growth in this case as a consequence of improvement of agricultural techniques and particularly the introduction of a new staple food—potatoes. Conversely, oppressed castes and races may fail to perpetuate their genes. Between 1792 and 1861 about 571,000 Negro slaves were imported in Cuba, and yet in 1861 there were only 603,000 persons of African descent on that island. The situation in Chile was even more extreme; Negro slaves were imported during the eighteenth and early nineteenth centuries, yet at present African genes are virtually nonexistent in that country. The chief reason is apparently that, because of the remoteness of the country from slave markets, almost exclusively male slaves, considered more valuable, were imported, and they were unable to find mates either among the white or the native Indian population.

Cultural factors have thus changed and continue changing the genetic composition of mankind. Caution is called for in interpreting these changes as due to natural selection of the usual biological sort. Such an interpretation would only be correct if it were shown that cultural and technological changes are in turn set on foot by genetic differences among populations. This is, of course, a widespread assumption, pleasing to some people but certainly not scientifically validated or even particularly probable on theoretical grounds. We must face the fact that the causes of genesis, advancement, and deterioration of civilizations remain unsolved, despite the efforts of some of the best intellects that mankind has produced. The possibility that genetic factors are involved in these phenomena should not be dismissed dogmatically, but it seems certain that they were not the only and not even the most potent determining factors involved.

## Race Equality vs. Sameness

That people may be equal without being alike has repeatedly been stressed in this book. Equality is a precept, similarity or dissimilarity a percept. Strictly speaking, science does not tell us whether people should or should not be equal, but it does show what consequences result from equality or inequality of opportunity, given the human diversity observed. We have faced this problem in the foregoing chapter in connection with the genetic polymorphism and caste and class distinctions. We concluded that denial of equality of opportunity stultifies the genetic diversity with which mankind became equipped in the course of its evolutionary development. Inequality conceals and stifles some people's abilities and disguises the lack of abilities in others. Conversely, equality permits (or rather, may permit, since a complete equality of opportunity has never existed except on paper) an optimal utilization of the wealth of the gene pool of the human species.

Race differences present really the same problem, albeit on a larger scale. Race bigots contend that the cultural achievements of different races being so obviously unlike, it follows that their genetic capacities for achievement must be just as different. And from this follows the moral that the nations and races who choose to consider their own capacities superior have the right and even duty to govern and lord it over those whom they regard as inferior to themselves. It is remarkable how many people have either welcomed this view or acquiesced in it. Those who found it abhorrent went too far to the other side in their protest: they countered with the suggestion that all people are as similar in their abilities and potentialities as identical twins.

The decisive point is, however, that nobody can discover the cultural capacities of human individuals, populations, or races until they have been given something like an equality of opportunity to demonstrate these capacities. Wisely or otherwise, most people prefer self-government even to good government. In the foregoing chapter arguments have been presented that educability, the capacity to learn and to profit from experience, is not concentrated in any one caste or class. It is not concentrated in any one race either. Members of yesterday's "inferior" and "subject" races now attend universities together with sons and daughters of the *ci-devant* masters, and many of the former do not do badly at all. It does not follow, however, that to demonstrate "equal" capacities for cultural achievement all races will have to reproduce copies of the civilizations and polities regarded as quintessences of enlightenment and discernment in Washington or Moscow. Given the opportunity, they may arrange their lives in different ways. One does not need to adopt the viewpoint of extreme cultural relativism, that any culture is as good as any other, to hope that mankind may eventually profit by this diversity more than it might have gained by monotonous sameness, even of the most "advanced" kind.

# 11. Evolution in Process

Considerate la vostra semenza:
Fatti non foste a viver come bruti
Ma per seguir virtute e conoscenza.
DANTE, *Inferno*

MAN HAS not only evolved; for better or for worse, he *is* evolving.
Our not very remote ancestors were animals, not men; the transition from animal to man is, on the evolutionary time scale, rather
recent. But the newcomer, the human species, proved fit when
tested in the crucible of natural selection; this high fitness is a
product of the genetic equipment which made culture possible.
Has the development of culture nullified the genes? Nothing
could be more false. Culture is built on a shifting genetic foundation. It is fairly generally admitted that genetic changes in the
human species are influenced by culture. But many people are
reluctant to credit that genetic changes may influence culture.
The reluctance comes from an almost obsessive fear that biological
influences on culture are somehow incompatible with democratic
ideals; social sciences must be guarded against the encroachment
of biology. Admittedly, most of the biologists' forays into the
realm of sociology warranted distrust. But the estrangement must
be overcome. Man's future inexorably depends on the interactions
of biological and social forces. Understanding these forces and their
interactions may, in the fullness of time, prove to be the main
achievement of science.

## Normalizing, Diversifying, Balancing, and Directional Selection

Mutations continue to arise in man, even as they have been
since the dawn of time. They were the raw materials from which
natural selection gradually built the genetic endowment of the
human species. Beneficial mutants are, however, a minority; a
great majority of the mutants are harmful. The simplest and most

obvious form of natural selection has been called "stabilizing" (Schmalhausen 1949) or "normalizing" (Waddington 1957) selection. It is a negative or conservative force; it counteracts the spread of detrimental mutants, hereditary diseases, and weaknesses of various sorts. The failure or at least weakening of normalizing selection in human populations leads many writers to fear that insidious processes of genetic decay are at work in the human species.

In Chapter 6 a beneficial mutant was compared to a needle in a haystack: it is hard to find. One has to examine very large numbers of individuals, place them in some rigorous or new environment, and apply a stringent natural or artificial selection. Should a beneficial mutant be as rare as one per billion "normal" individuals, it may still be found and isolated. This can be done in experiments with bacteria, but it cannot be done in man. Mutant genes are, however, not intrinsically beneficial or harmful; they become so when placed in certain environments. A gene harmful in one environment may be neutral or useful in another. The greater the variety of environments to which a population is exposed, the greater the chance that some mutants may be found useful in some environment.

Culture has made human environments endlessly diversified. One of the evolutionary mechanisms which enables life to become adapted to a variety of environments is "diversifying" selection (see p. 248) which brings about genetic diversification. A population, or species, abounding in genetic variety may have a better grip on the complex of environments with which it is confronted than would a genetically uniform population.

Physical (climate, soils, etc.), biological (diseases, parasites, available foods), genetic, and cultural environments must be considered. What is a genetic environment? It has been repeatedly pointed out above that the heredity of an organism is not a collection of "traits" independently produced by various genes. A person's development is the outcome of the interaction of that person's genes with his environment. A gene that is harmful in combination with some genes may be useful in combination with others. Diversifying selection maintains in populations, especially those facing diverse environments, such adaptively ambivalent genes.

An important kind of adaptive ambivalence is shown by genes which increase the fitness of their heterozygous carriers but are detrimental or even lethal in homozygotes. This is exemplified in man by the sickle-cell gene, discussed on pages 150–53. This gene causes an almost always fatal anemia in homozygotes but is believed to confer on its heterozygous carriers a relative immunity to certain kinds of malarial fevers. Individuals heterozygous for the sickle-cell gene enjoy hybrid vigor, heterosis, if they live in malarial countries and have no other means (such as modern medicine) of controlling the infection. Natural selection holds the "normal" and the sickle-cell genes in a balanced polymorphism in populations in malarial environments. This is the "balancing" form of natural selection.

In working with experimental animals or plants, biologists are often at pains to make the environment of their charges as uniform as possible. Devices are used to keep constant temperature and humidity, the animals are provided with uniform food and plants with uniform soil, etc. Let us suppose that the human species inhabits an environment at least as uniform as the ones used for laboratory animals. It is just conceivable that a genetic endowment might ultimately become selected which would be the best possible one for that particular environment. Any further genetic change could then only be harmful. The reality is otherwise. Not only do people follow different ways of life, engage in different occupations, have different duties and interests, but human environments change rapidly and most rapidly of all in technologically advanced societies. It cannot be overstressed that the ideal of equality of opportunity, the evolutionary consequences of which were considered in Chapter 9, does not necessarily envisage environmental uniformity; equality of opportunity may also mean freedom to choose among existing environments or to create new ones.

Environmental instability presents challenges to the organism—both to an individual and to a population or a species. To maintain itself in harmony with a changing environment, the organism must be not only adapted but also adaptable (Thoday 1953, 1955, Waddington 1957). A species should not only possess genetic variety but also be able to generate variety. It may then respond to changing environments by genetic changes. Some genetic variants may become less frequent or be eliminated; others may become more frequent and be fixed as the new "norm" of the population and the species. This is the "directional" form of natural selection. In the long run, directional selection may be the most important one. There is, however, no question that an understanding of all forms of natural selection is needed to assess the evolutionary status and perspectives of our species.

## Genetic Load and Genetic Elimination

It is most unlikely that the universal prohibition of incest was based on knowledge and understanding of the harmful effects of inbreeding. Such a knowledge did, however, accumulate through the experience of husbandmen and animal and plant breeders. Nevertheless, even thirty years ago it hardly occurred to most biologists that all or a great majority of Drosophila flies in natural populations are carriers of enormous genetic loads consisting of concealed genetic defects. The composition and dimensions of the genetic loads in human populations are still most inadequately known. The origin, maintenance, and biological functions of genetic loads present singularly complex problems which are far from resolved in a satisfactory manner.

There is no question that a lot of human ills are caused by the genetic load breaking through to the phenotypic surface and enfeebling, incapacitating, or killing its victims. The gross malformations and diseases listed in Table 8 do not, however, exhaust the manifestations of the human genetic load. It should be emphasized that genetic defects may have less dramatic but more insidious manifestations, such as loss of general vigor, debility, lack of resistance to stresses and infections, and physical, psychological, and even social maladjustment (Table 12).

Detrimental genes are produced by mutation and persist in the population for some generations, until eliminated by normalizing natural selection. Genetic equilibrium is established when the rate of the production of harmful genes by mutation is equal to their elimination by selection. At equilibrium, the income and the outgo, mutation and elimination, balance each other. Muller (1950, 1954, and other writings) refers to the elimination of detrimental genetic variants as genetic death. I prefer a less dramatic term—*genetic elimination*.

At equilibrium, the total genetic elimination must be equal to the total mutation rate. We have seen (p. 146) that probably no fewer than 10 per cent of the sex cells and 20 per cent of the progeny, of Drosophila flies and of humans, carry newly arisen mutants in every generation (and this is a minimum estimate)! It follows that human populations at genetic equilibrium must suffer at least 20 per cent of "genetic death" in every generation.

"Genetic death" is obviously an emotionally loaded phrase. It invites misunderstanding. Genetic death does not always produce a cadaver. To be sure, the demise of a victim of hemophilia, retino-blastoma, or sickle-cell anemia is both a death and a genetic death. But a person who remains unmarried or childless is genetically dead even if he lives to a ripe old age. Lethals and sterility genes equally bring about genetic elimination, the former through death and the latter through nonproduction of offspring. A mutant will be eliminated if its carriers produce one child fewer than they would have done had they not carried the mutant in question. The low fertility of achondroplastic dwarfs is a case in point (p. 144); none of these dwarfs need necessarily suffer premature death for a gene for dwarfism to be eliminated.

## Genetic Radiation Damage

Two of the factors which determine the magnitude of the genetic load a population will carry are mutation rates and selection rates. We have seen in Chapter 6 that the equilibrium frequency of a mutant gene with a harmful effect $s$ (selection coefficient) arising at a rate $u$ (mutation rate) will be $u/s$ if the mutant is dominant and $\sqrt{u/s}$ if it is recessive. In other words, the more often a mutant arises and the less rigorous is the selection against it, the higher will be its frequency in the populations. To reduce the genetic load one would have to lower the mutation rates and/or increase the elimination rates. What is actually happening in human populations is exactly the reverse—mutation rates tend to increase and selection rates to decrease.

One aspect of the problem of increasing mutation that has attracted a great deal of public attention in recent years is the genetic damage inflicted upon mankind by high-energy radiations, especially in connection with the use of atomic energy for peaceful purposes and its misuse for military purposes. The threat of genetic damage has been dealt with in the reports of special committees formed by, among others, the National Academy of Sciences (1956, 1960), the World Health Organization (1957), and the United Nations (1958); for a discussion of this problem see also Wallace and Dobzhansky (1959). Necessarily oversimplifying a situation that is far from simple, the following are the main guideposts.

All forms of high-energy or penetrating or ionizing radiation, from the "softest" X rays to gamma rays of radium and presumably to cosmic rays, increase the frequencies of mutations in all experimental organisms studied. Man is not one of those studied, but no informed person doubts that high-energy radiations are mutagenic also in man. There is no minimum or safe or threshold amount of radiation below which mutations would not be induced. Any increase, however small, of the amount of radiation to which living beings are exposed will augment the numbers of mutations that will arise (i.e., will increase the value $u$, mutation rate). The incidence of induced mutations is simply proportional to the radiation exposure, as measured by the ionization produced in the sex cells by the radiation (r-units, rem-units). Russell, Russell, and Kelly (1958) claimed, however, that "chronic" radiation (given slowly, over a long period of time) produces fewer mutations in mice than a similar amount of "acute" radiation (given rapidly). Traces of high-energy radiations are omnipresent in nature, in rocks, soils, and human bodies. However, only a fraction of the mutations that occur "spontaneously," i.e., in individuals not exposed to any particular mutation-inducing agents, can be ascribed to these "background" radiations. The spontaneous mutation rates are, as far as known at present, an irreducible minimum, to which may be superadded the mutations induced by exposure to radiation or any other "mutagenic" (mutation-inducing) agents.

Much discussion, some of it acrimonious, has arisen in connection with the testing of nuclear weapons. Do such tests and the resulting radioactive fallout induce harmful mutants which will result in the genetic death of many people? Or is the genetic damage so incurred negligible? The answer turns out to depend not on genetic but on ethical standards. Hurting, crippling, or killing just how many people is negligible? It is true that the increment of mutations which have arisen or are likely to arise as a result of exposure to fallout radiation is only a fraction of the mutations that would arise anyway, without radiation exposures. But it is also true that these extra, additional, mutations will continue to maim and murder human beings for many generations after our present conflicts, concerns, and follies will have been forgotten by everybody but historians.

Attempts have been made to calculate just how many additional cases of crippling hereditary disease will be induced in the human species by various radiation exposures. These are interesting mathematical exercises, but, the presently available knowledge of human population genetics being as limited as it is, the estimates obtained can hardly be trusted, even as to the order of magnitude. Some relative values are more dependable. The best available, though still very rough, estimate of the average amount of radiation exposure incurred by people from all "natural," or background, sources is about three rem per thirty years. Assuming that tests of atomic weapons will not be resumed, the radiation from this source will be about one third of one per cent of the "background." Radiation exposure from man-made sources other than weapon tests (diagnostic and therapeutic X rays, use of radiation in industry, scientific research, etc.) is quite variable from country to country, being of course much higher in technologically advanced than in underdeveloped countries. A rough estimate for the former is about three rem per thirty years. In other words, man has about doubled the exposure of his hereditary materials to radiations. (The calculations are made for thirty years because this is close to the average length of human generation, i.e., the average age of the parents when their children are born). There is no doubt that industrial civilization has a wholly unforeseen, unpremeditated, and unwanted effect—increase of mutation rates. How large this increase is compared to the mutation rates that prevailed in the past is an open question. Large or small, the increase is undesirable.

### The Threat of the Biological Twilight of Mankind

The flurry of public excitement over the genetic damage to human populations caused by radiation exposures has perhaps served a useful function. It may attract attention to a vastly greater problem of which genetic radiation damage is only a part, and at that a small part. Some biologists, among whom Muller (1950, 1954, 1959, and many other writings) is most authoritative and most indefatigable, are warning that the stabilizing or normalizing selection is faltering in human populations. They claim that the mutation rates are being increased not only by radiations but perhaps also by contact with and ingestion of some of the drugs to which almost everybody is exposed in this chemical age. And in the face of the rising mutation rates, the elimination of harmful mutants from human populations is no longer taking place as rapidly and effectively as it did in the past. The genetic loads are therefore rising in human populations. This dangerous situation occurs, strangely enough, because of the rapidly improving living conditions, in particular the increasing powers of modern medicine.

The argument runs as follows. Suppose that under primitive conditions, in the absence of medical help, a certain hereditary disease due to a dominant mutant gene reduced the Darwinian fitness of its carriers to half of normal: the spread of this disease was opposed by a natural selection with a selection coefficient $s = 0.5$. The equilibrium frequency of the gene for this disease in human populations was (see p. 144) $u/0.5$, or twice the mutation rate $(2u)$. Now assume that medical help enables most persons afflicted with this disease to live and to raise families so that their fitness is now nine-tenths normal: the selection coefficient has, thus, decreased to $s = 0.1$, and the frequency of the gene at equilibrium has increased to $u/0.1$, or ten times the mutation rate. The disease will, thus, be eventually five times more frequent than it was before medicine could help the victims.

It is not just one disease but many kinds of hereditary infirmities, disorders, and weaknesses that are "cured," relieved, or mitigated by treatments, remedies, drugs, or regimens. Medical care and sheltered and careful living spare many lives and by the same token increase the incidence of the same afflictions in the following generations. To be sure, the average length of human generation being close to thirty years, it will take centuries and even millennia before the genetic loads will increase to the new equilibrium values determined by the reduced normalizing selection. It is tempting to suppose that improved medicine and technology will in the future remedy all sorts of human ailments so that we can enjoy the present relaxation of natural selection, even though the respite is only temporary, and let our remote posterity take care of itself.

This is, alas, living in a fool's paradise. Relaxation of normalizing selection brings inexorably its nemesis—increasing, not decreasing, genetic loads. The more hereditary diseases are "cured" the more of them will be there to be cured in the succeeding generation, even if the mutation rates were not increasing. The fate toward which mankind is drifting is painted by Muller (1950) in very somber colors:

> The amount of genetically caused impairment suffered by the average individual, even though he has all the techniques of civilization working to mitigate it, must by that time have grown to be as great in the presence of these techniques as it had been in paleolithic times without them. But instead of people's time and energy being mainly spent in the struggle with external enemies of a primitive kind such as famine, climatic difficulties and wild beasts, they would be devoted chiefly to the effort to live carefully, to spare and to prop up their own feeblenesses, to soothe their inner disharmonies

and, in general, to doctor themselves as effectively as possible. For everyone would be an invalid, with his own special familial twists. . . . Our descendants' natural biological organization would in fact have disintegrated and have been replaced by complete disorder. . . . It would in the end be far easier and more sensible to manufacture a complete man de novo, out of appropriately chosen raw materials, than to try to refashion into human form those pitiful relics which remained.

This biological fire-and-brimstone prophecy certainly cannot be ignored. It rests on arguments at least a part of which are unassailable. There is no question that human populations contain some genetic variants that are unconditionally detrimental: dominant hereditary diseases and malformations, which weaken the health or reduce the vitality in all environments that we know of. Continued occurrence of such variants is doubtless due to recurrent mutation; there are good reasons to think that the mutation rates are rising throughout the world, and especially in technologically advanced countries. And since modern medicine and protected living increase the Darwinian fitness of the carriers of some of these diseases and malformations (though not necessarily their social desirability), their incidence will be increasing in future generations. But let us not accept the prophecy of doom as inevitable. There are several pieces missing from this puzzle. What part of the genetic load consists of unconditionally deleterious variants the supply of which is maintained by recurrent mutations? What are the social consequences of what is described dramatically as genetic death or more calmly as genetic elimination? Are all the evolutionary processes under way in modern mankind tending toward biological deterioration?

### Classical and Balance Theories of Population Structure

Drosophila flies are doing nicely in their natural habitats, despite the fact that they bear enormous genetic loads. The four lethal equivalents which constitute a person's average load (see above) let most of us enjoy reasonably good health and well-being for something close to three score and ten years. This is so because most of the genetic load remains concealed and unexpressed; it is concealed owing to recessivity or incomplete dominance of the potentially destructive genetic variants. The adaptive norm

(p. 126) of the human species consists of persons burdened with genetic loads. Nor is there anything new in this situation—all of human evolution occurred in populations that carried heavy genetic loads. A man or a fly free of genetic loads might perhaps be a superman or a superfly, but as far as anybody knows such a prodigy never walked the earth.

The question that logically arises is whether the genetic load is merely an inevitable evil or whether natural selection might somehow turn it to an advantage. Different answers to this question are returned by the classical and the balance theories of population structure, referred to briefly in Chapter 5. The modern version of the classical theory stems chiefly from Muller (1950, 1954, 1959, and other works). Individuals of a species are mostly homozygous for normal gene alleles, selected and established in the course of evolution. However, a minority of the genes are represented in populations by two or more variant alleles. One of these alleles is "normal" and desirable and the others are detrimental and components of the genetic load; the persistence in populations of the detrimental alleles is due to recurrent mutation.

Moreover, and this is an important assumption, there are few or no completely recessive mutants. An individual heterozygous for a mutant gene is not really normal and healthy; his fitness would be higher if he did not carry the mutant. The genetic load is thus never wholly concealed; it harms its carriers in subtle and insidious ways.

According to the balance theory (see, among others, Lerner 1954, Dobzhansky 1955, Wallace and Dobzhansky 1959), the adaptive norms of most sexual and outbreeding species, including man, are arrays of numerous and multiply heterozygous genotypes. Natural selection does not usually establish a single genetic endowment to the exclusion of all others. Diversifying and balancing selections promote a variety of genes *coadapted* to each other. Coadapted genes produce, in combination with many or most other genes present in the gene pool of a population, healthy and vigorous individuals, fit to survive and to reproduce in at least some of the environment which the population inhabits. Many genes occur more often in heterozygous than in homozygous condition. Natural selection promotes accordingly those genes which yield highly fit heterozygotes (see p. 150). Whether a gene is good also when homozygous becomes relatively unimportant.

Normal, highly adapted populations contain some genes held in a state of balanced polymorphism. The genetic loads that populations carry are, then, of at least two kinds. A mutational (classical) load consists of genes that damage heterozygotes as well as homozygotes, or if only the latter then at least do not benefit the heterozygotes. A balanced load consists of genes and gene combinations which are advantageous in heterozygotes as compared to their effects in homozygotes. Balanced loads are maintained chiefly by natural selection rather than by recurrent mutation.

Detailed discussion of the evidence for the classical and the balance theories would not be profitable here. Much of this evidence is highly technical and some is controversial. The solution of the problem must await accumulation of more evidence than is at present available. Evaluations of the biological meaning and social import of genetic loads are necessarily tentative.

The number of genes known with certainty to be in a state of balanced polymorphism in human populations is admittedly small. The classical case is the gene for sickle-cells, repeatedly mentioned above. There is good presumptive evidence of a similar adaptive advantage also for the heterozygous carriers of the gene for thalassemia (Mediterranean anemia). The homozygotes for this gene usually die young of a severe anemia, and yet the gene is common in populations of some highly malarial regions of southern Europe and Asia. The evidence is even less adequate for certain other genes that cause variations in the chemical structure of the hemoglobins in the red blood cells, but advantages of the heterozygotes suggest themselves. (For a review of the already voluminous and scattered literature on the hemoglobin variants, see Neel 1956, Rucknagel and Neel 1961.)

As shown in Chapters 8 and 9, most human populations are polymorphic for several genes that cause variations in the blood types. These variations proved to be most valuable for clarification of the race concept. It has been suspected for many years that the persistence of these polymorphisms may be due to superior fitness of the heterozygotes over the homozygotes for the blood type genes. Refined mathematical analysis by Morton and Chung (1959a) has validated this suspicion for the MN blood type in man. The physiological mechanisms which make the MN heterozygotes superior over the MM and NN homozygotes remain, however, obscure.

How frequent in human populations are the genes that benefit the heterozygotes but harm the homozygotes remains an open issue. They appear to be quite important in some organisms other than man. Lerner's brilliant analysis (1954, 1958) of the experience of animal breeders shows that peak performance and productivity in domestic animals, particularly in poultry, is often found in multiply heterozygous genotypes. Selection for high productivity maintains the heterozygosity, while relaxation of this selection in relatively small flocks often leads to a greater incidence of homozygotes and consequent losses of the productivity. A most impressive demonstration of the favorable effects of heterozygosity has been given by Wallace (1958). He treated with X rays some strains of Drosophila flies that were previously made homozygous for certain chromosomes and suffered a reduction of their fitness because of this homozygosis. The progenies of the irradiated flies had a slightly but significantly higher fitness than did the nonirradiated controls. Many of the induced mutations were evidently beneficial when heterozygous, although (as shown by separate experiments) detrimental when homozygous. (Note added in proof: Muller and Falk, 1961, and Falk, 1961, have claimed to have invalidated Wallace's results. Their experiments are however in no way repetitions of those of Wallace. The problem evidently awaits further study.)

To summarize—human populations carry genetic loads of at least two kinds, mutational and balanced. Some genes seem to be deleterious unconditionally, in heterozygotes as well as in homozygotes and in all genetic and external environments. Other genes are injurious under some but beneficial under other conditions. At a risk of oversimplification, it may be said that many of the genes that cause major hereditary diseases and malformations probably belong to the first class. The genes that produce differences of the sort we observe among healthy and "normal" people might fall mostly in the second category. The genes conditioning the variations in the appearance, physique, intelligence, temperament, special abilities—in short the genes making people recognizably different persons, really unique and nonrecurrent individuals—these genes may be maintained in human populations in balanced states, either because of being advantageous in heterozygotes or because of the action of diversifying selection. This problem needs a great deal of attention and study. It is of considerably more than academic interest. On its solution depends the evaluation of the present genetic predicament of mankind. Neither prophecies nor refutations of an imminent biological doom are convincing while our knowledge is in no way commensurate with the gravity of the problem at hand.

## Selection and Population Growth

Many discussions of natural selection (or of its alleged suspension) have a curious air of unreality because they tacitly assume that some genes are always harmful and ought to be eliminated, while others are perpetually useful and ought to be disseminated and fixed. True enough, to prevent the inroads of genetic decay normalizing selection should always be eliminating the unconditionally harmful mutant genes. This is, however, only a part of the story. The prime mover of evolutionary change is adaptation to the environment, and natural selection is the mechanism that translates the environmental challenges into genetic alterations (see p. 20). Now, man's environments are changing both rapidly and radically. The primitive simplicities of the way of life of our ancestors of ten thousand and even of one thousand years ago are utterly gone; we are facing instead the fantastic complexities of the jet age and of the incipient atomic age. Not even the few remaining "primitive" tribes can cling to their ancient ways.

Some of the most radical changes in human environments arise from there being more and more humans. Total populations and the population densities are growing almost everywhere in the world. Very rough estimates of the population growth are given in Table 24. A million years ago man (or the species ancestral to man) was a rare animal; Deevey (1960) guesses the total population to

TABLE 24

Estimated world populations, and population densities in persons per square kilometer *(after Deevy, 1960)*

| Years ago | Population | Density |
|---|---|---|
| 1,000,000 | 125,000 | 0.00425 |
| 300,000 | 1,000,000 | 0.012 |
| 25,000 | 3,340,000 | 0.04 |
| 10,000 | 5,320,000 | 0.04 |
| 6,000 | 86,500,000 | 1.0 |
| 2,000 | 133,000,000 | 1.0 |
| 310 | 545,000,000 | 3.7 |
| 210 | 728,000,000 | 4.9 |
| 160 | 906,000,000 | 6.2 |
| 60 | 1,610,000,000 | 11.0 |
| 10 | 2,400,000,000 | 16.4 |

have been about 125 thousand, living somewhere in Africa, with a density of 4.25 persons per 1,000 square kilometers. By 10,000 years ago (the Mesolithic stage) man is believed to have spread to all continents and to have increased to about 5 million, with a population density of about 4 persons per 100 square kilometers. At present (1960), the estimated population is close to 2,700 million and the population density close to 18.5 persons per square kilometer.

Braidwood and Reed (1957) give the following estimates of the population density in persons per square mile at different "developmental levels" in prehistoric southwestern Asia:

| | |
|---|---|
| Pleistocene "natural" food gatherers | 0.03 |
| More specialized food collecting of late Glacial and early post-Glacial times | 0.12 |
| Primary village–farming community, about 5000 B.C. | 25 |
| Primary urban community, Sumerian city states, about 3500 B.C. | 50 |

Comparable "levels" were reached, of course, at quite different times in different places. Southwestern Asia was one of the cradles of human civilization. The Australian aborigines were food gatherers when white men met them less than two centuries ago and their population density was about 0.08 per square mile (Birdsell 1957b). In the valley of the Nile in Egypt, high population densities were attained at the dawn of recorded history.

### The Population Explosion

Population growth depends upon a surplus of births over deaths. At present some 100 million babies are born yearly, but only about half as many people die annually. Man has not become more fertile than he was; in fact, nowadays populations expand in the face of declining birth rates. Populations increase because the human genetic endowment made possible the inception and evolution of culture which proved to be an adaptive instrument that enabled people to live longer and longer. Deevey (1960) gives the following estimates of the mean longevity (in years):

| | | | |
|---|---|---|---|
| Neanderthal | 29.4 | Classic Rome | 32 |
| Upper Paleolithic | 32.4 | England 1276 | 48 |
| Mesolithic | 31.5 | England 1376–1400 | 38 |
| Neolithic Anatolia | 38.2 | United States 1900–1902 | 61.5 |
| Classic Greece | 35 | United States 1950 | 70 |

Reductions of infant mortality have been most spectacular. Under primitive, or what some people are pleased to call "natural," conditions probably more than a quarter of the infants born died within a year. Infant mortality has declined in Mexico from 226 per 1,000 live births in 1920–24 to 95 per 1,000 in 1953. In Chile the corresponding decline was from 226 to 114 and in Ceylon from 192 to 71 (Bourgeois–Pichat and Pan 1956). In the United States the figure stood at 27.1 in 1958; the United Kingdom with 23.3, Australia with 20.5, and Sweden with 15.8 did still better. These last figures may be approaching a kind of irreducible minimum; the residual mortality may be due to elimination of genetically caused sublethal defects for which no therapy is possible.

Some of mankind's "well-wishers" are thrown into a panic by the sharp decline of the death rates which, they contend, suspends the action of natural selection in man. This is, however, not necessarily valid (see p. 160). A far greater and more present danger comes from the uncontrolled growth of human populations or, as the fashionable expression goes, from "the population explosion." Indeed, never before has mankind been faced with such a cruel paradox. Darwinian fitness is reproductive fitness; mankind has inherited the earth; having become so widespread and abundant the human species is an unprecedented biological success; and yet it is this very success which threatens to choke the advance of his culture and reduce him to starvation and misery. For the rate of the population growth is accelerating at an alarming rate (Table 25).

It requires no prophetic gift to foresee that, unless mankind annihilates itself by an all-out atomic war or a similar madness, the

TABLE 25

Estimated populations and population increases (*United Nations data, from Hauser 1960*)

| Area | Population (millions) | | | | |
|------|------|------|------|------|------|
|      | 1900 | 1925 | 1950 | 1975 | 2000 |
| World | 1,550 | 1,907 | 2,497 | 3,828 | 6,267 |
| Africa | 120 | 147 | 199 | 303 | 517 |
| North America | 81 | 126 | 168 | 240 | 312 |
| Central and South America | 63 | 99 | 163 | 303 | 592 |
| Asia | 853 | 1,020 | 1,380 | 2,210 | 3,870 |
| Europe (including U.S.S.R.) | 423 | 505 | 574 | 751 | 947 |
| Oceania | 6 | 10 | 13 | 21 | 29 |

task of controlling population size will overshadow all else within at most a century and probably much sooner. The urgency of this task surpasses that of the control of the accumulation of deleterious mutant genes and the alleged suspension of natural selection.

The genetic implications of the population "explosion" are several. One is the vision of doom conjured by C. G. Darwin (1953 and other writings). Compressed in a few sentences, his argument runs as follows. Reduction of the birth rates is necessary if the population growth is to be contained. Family planning and limitation are not, however, likely to be undertaken by everybody simultaneously. Those who practice such controls will contribute to the following generations fewer genes in proportion to their number than those who do not. Fewer and fewer people will, therefore, be inclined to limit their families as the generations roll by. The human flood, rising higher and higher, will overwhelm a multitudinous but degenerate mankind. The assumption implicit in this argument is, of course, that the craving for perpetuation of one's seed is uncontrollable by reason and education and that people will go on spawning progeny, even knowing that it is destined to be increasingly miserable. This assumption need not be accepted, even admitting that a solution of the population problem is not yet in sight.

### Selection of and by Infection

Now that pestilences and epidemics are held in check, the severity of these scourges in former days is not easily appreciated. For example more than half the population of England and about twenty-five million persons in Europe died during the plague of the mid-fourteenth century. Unsurprisingly, these visitations were ascribed to supernatural causes. Actually it can be surmised that man's relations to infections went through a cycle: increased population densities, emergence of villages and then of more and more crowded cities, created opportunities for epidemics to spread, often at rates high enough to exterminate whole tribes and perhaps even nations. These disasters checked the population growth, or at least slowed it down. Then the belief that filthiness is akin to holiness gave way to the view that cleanliness is akin to godliness, the infections retreated, and the populations surged upward.

The fascinating story of the spread and transformation of the myxomatosis disease in wild rabbits in Australia will serve as a paradigm (Fenner, Day, and Woodroofe 1956, Fenner and Marshall

1957, Fenner 1959). The European rabbit *(Oryctolagus cuniculus)* was brought to Australia by white settlers about a century ago. It multiplied to become a pest of major proportions. Attempts to control the pest were not successful until 1950 when myxomatosis, a virus disease, was introduced into the Australian rabbit population. The myxoma virus occurs naturally in the Brazilian wild rabbit *(Sylvilagus brasiliensis)*, in which it causes a relatively mild and nonlethal skin disease. When artificially transferred into the European–Australian rabbit it causes a severe, generalized, and almost invariably fatal infection. Between 1950 and 1957 myxomatosis spread over the whole of the rabbit-infested area of Australia and reduced the rabbit population to between one and two per cent of the premyxomatosis level. (The infection is transferred from ill to healthy rabbits by mosquito bites, but the virus does not multiply in mosquitoes—the insects act merely as "flying needles."

As early as 1955 it was noticed in Australia that the disease was becoming less severe: more and more infected rabbits recovered from the disease, and where the disease was fatal the time interval between the infection and death lengthened considerably. The magnificently executed experiments of Fenner and his collaborators showed that Australian rabbits were becoming more and more resistant to the disease and the virus was becoming less and less virulent. It is easy to see how the resistance develops—resistant rabbits survive and become parents of the next generation more often than the nonresistant ones. The advantage to the virus of a reduced virulence is a more subtle matter. Death of the host means death of the parasite: the longer an infected rabbit remains alive the greater the chance that a mosquito will transfer the virus it contains to another rabbit. Natural selection favored a mutual accommodation between the virus and the Australian rabbit; the situation observed in the Brazilian rabbit is perhaps a result of such an accommodation.

## Ebb and Flow of Resistance to Diseases

The survivors of a disease are likely to be genetically different from those who fail to survive. The repeated epidemics through which mankind has gone changed its genetic endowment. And the changes were not limited to increases in resistance to particular diseases. It is a common experience of animal and plant breeders that selection for any one quality brings changes, often unexpected and unwelcome, in other qualities. This happens, first, because the genes for a disease resistance may be associated (linked) in the chromosomes with genes for sundry other qualities. Second, the genes "for" the resistance to a given disease may have other, perhaps less obvious but nevertheless very real, effects on all kinds of characteristics (Haldane 1949, Coon, Garn, and Birdsell 1950, and others).

The evidence for such changes in human populations is meager. This is not surprising since the reliability of even not-so-old medical statistics is often questionable, and the environmental and genetic factors of the susceptibility to a disease are hard to disentangle. Dubos and Dubos (1952), Dubos (1958, 1959a,b), Motulsky (1960), and Simon (1960) have critically sifted the available data, and I take their works as my guide in this field. Crowded populations were often ravaged by tuberculosis. During the past century tuberculosis was the most important cause of death among young adults in Europe and in North America. It appears, however, that the disease went through a cycle. There is good evidence that it existed in prehistoric man but became especially prevalent when people started to live in crowded villages, towns, and cities. During the eighteenth and nineteenth centuries it reached a peak, with an annual mortality of about 500 per 100,000, and then declined, long before vaccination or chemotherapy were used. According to Grigg (1958), the peak was reached in the population of London before 1750, in large cities of western Europe probably during the first half of the nineteenth century, and in eastern Europe mostly a few decades later, in the eastern United States around 1800, in northern and midwestern states around 1860, in southern around 1880, and in western ones around 1910. The peaks in the rural areas of the respective countries trailed those in the cities by twenty to sixty years.

The course of the tuberculosis epidemic has been well studied among the Plains Indians who went to live in the Qu'Appelle Valley reservation in Saskatchewan, Canada. The annual death rate, which was about 1,000 per 100,000 in 1881, reached 9,000 per 100,000 in 1886. The disease was not only widespread but also highly virulent, causing extensive glandular involvements, meningitis, bone and joint disease, and rapid fatality. By 1921 the disease was usually chronic and localized in the lungs, glandular involvement became rare, and mortality rates fell to values usual among non-Indian populations (Ferguson 1955).

The history of tuberculosis in human population strikingly parallels that of myxomatosis in Australian rabbits. Ancient human populations probably contained many genotypes which made their carriers highly susceptible to tuberculosis. When population densities increased and people came to live in crowded places, epidemics broke out and resulted in calamitous mortalities. The fall of the virulence and the death rates in recent times were, then, brought about not only by the improved living conditions and better medical services but also by higher, genetically conditioned, resistance levels.

What of the present situation and the prospects for the future? The introduction in 1945–46 of penicillin, and soon thereafter of streptomycin and isoniazid therapy, decreased the mortality rates from tuberculosis to a fraction of what they were formerly. In the United States, the rate stood at 45.2 per 100,000 in 1939, 34.9 in 1946, 22.5 in 1950, and 7.5 in 1957. So effective are these therapeutic methods that the populations of the parts of the world in which tuberculosis is still rampant (some of the "underdeveloped" countries) need not go through the cruel process of eliminating susceptible genotypes by death. Natural selection against these genotypes has certainly relaxed. But let us not quickly conclude that the susceptibility to tuberculosis must rapidly increase in the generations to come. The situation has many unknowns and calls for caution.

The proximate cause of tuberculosis is infection with Koch's bacteria. The susceptibility to the infection has, however, an important genetic component. Thus, Planansky and Allen (1953) found the following morbidity rates in their 308 "twin index families" (in per cent):

| Mates | 7.1 | Siblings | 25.5 |
|---|---|---|---|
| Parents | 16.9 | Fraternal twins | 25.6 |
| Half-siblings | 11.9 | Identical twins | 87.3 |

In twenty pairs of identical twins and six pairs of fraternal twins which were concordant as to the disease, the illness appeared at the same age (within a year); in twenty-three pairs of identicals and twenty-four pairs of fraternals the ages of onset were separated by more than a year. There is much evidence that the susceptibility to tuberculosis goes together with certain kinds of body build. In fact, already the pioneer physicians in ancient Greece knew of a "phthisic habitus," or body build, which went together with, and presumably indicated a heightened susceptibility to, the tubercular infection. (Surprisingly enough, Sheldon et al. 1949 found no correlation between tuberculosis and their "somatotype" classification; see p. 93.)

A hereditary endowment may confer upon its carriers some advantages but hamper them in other ways. The Darwinian fitness of a genotype is determined by the sum of these advantages and disadvantages in a certain environment. The "phthisic habitus" was for some centuries under a handicap because it carried a susceptibility to tuberculosis under crowded and unhealthy living conditions. It has not necessarily become selectively neutral now that the risk of the infection has become reduced. We simply do not know enough about the influences on fitness of most human genes in present-day environments, let alone in environments that may be contrived in the future. The genes for susceptibility to tuberculosis may increase in frequencies or may become stabilized or may become rare. This will depend on their effects on traits other than the disease resistance, as well as on their mutation rates.

Similar reasoning applies, of course, to genes which made their carriers resistant to infections other than tuberculosis (see Swellengrebel 1940). When these infections become rare or are eliminated, the resistance genes may or may not become adaptively superfluous or undesirable. The susceptibility to infections may grow with time, yet, on the other hand, this growth may be counteracted by natural selection because of undesirable effects of these genes on traits other than the lowered resistance to the infections. No sane person will advocate that people should not be protected from infections, or be cured once they contract a disease. The changes in the genetic endowments of human populations must, however, be carefully watched and before all else must be studied in order that their possible consequences may be correctly understood. Mankind may or may not be standing on the threshold of a medical utopia (Dubos 1959b,c).

## Increasing Severity of Natural Selection

The dangers of the alleged suspension of natural selection in the human species have been often and stridently proclaimed, so much so that it becomes worth while to point out that this is not the whole story. With respect to some genetic variants natural selection in civilized societies has become more, not less, rigorous.

A neat example, though admittedly unimportant on the species-wide scale, is the dominant gene which causes porphyria. This is a metabolic anomaly, diagnosable because of the excretion in the urine and feces of excessive amounts of porphyrin, a breakdown product of the hemoglobin molecule. The porphyria gene is present in about one per cent of the Afrikaner (Dutch) populations of South Africa. Its carriers suffered little discomfort, other than developing minor skin abrasions, when they lived in conditions of rustic simplicity on farms and in villages. But they happen to be acutely sensitive to barbiturates and certain other drugs, and not a few of these people died because they were given medical treatments which would have benefited "normal" people but were poisonous to the porphyrics (Dean 1957, Dean and Barnes 1958).

It may be asked why the porphyric gene is so frequent among the Afrikaners. This appears to be a case of random genetic drift, or an accidental increase of the frequency of an adaptively neutral gene. The Afrikaners are descended in the main from a rather small number of immigrants from Europe—almost 1,000,000 persons have the family names of only forty original settlers. Dean's painstaking research traces many of the porphyrics to a single immigrant who came to South Africa in 1686. But while the porphyric gene may have been harmless in the past, it turns out to be detrimental, in fact lethal, in certain environments created by modern medicine!

Another recently discovered gene, this one a recessive carried in the sex-determining X-chromosome, causes a biochemical anomaly of the red blood cells: a reduced activity of an enzyme with the formidable name of Glucose-6-phosphate dehydrogenase. You may carry this gene without being aware of anything unusual, but it can be detected by a suitable chemical test, and it becomes very important under the following circumstances. First, if a person with the enzyme defect has a hearty meal of fresh fava beans *(Vicia faba)* he may develop an anemia owing to the destruction of many of his red blood cells. This disease has long been known as "favism," and its cause was hard to understand. Second, a severe anemia develops after administration of certain drugs, among them primaquine, a very useful medicament for prevention or cure of malarial fevers in "normal" persons. (A review of the literature is in Motulsky 1960a.)

Although the evidence available is fragmentary, it is certain that the gene for the enzyme deficiency causing favism is quite common in many populations. It has been found in 9–11 per cent of American Negroes, 6–28 per cent of Congolese Negroes, 2 per cent of

South African Bantus, 1–2 per cent of Bushmen, 13 per cent of Filipinos, 3–8 per cent of Indians, 8 per cent of Iranians, 60 per cent of Kurdish Jews, and also among Portuguese, Spaniards, Italians, Greeks, Chinese, Burmese, and Javanese. (All the percentages given above are for males; the deficiency is found less frequently in females, as expected for a sex-linked, recessive trait.)

The trait is rare or absent in natives of central and northern Europe, Japan, and in some American Indian tribes. What cause has brought about so wide a distribution of the gene concerned is a matter of speculation. The evidence points toward the enzyme deficiency giving, as the abnormal hemoglobins mentioned above, some protection against certain forms of malarial fevers (Motulsky 1960a). We have, then, a splendid example of a gene subject to conflicting selective forces. It is, or was, favored because it conferred a protection against one of the most deadly perils to which the inhabitants of many tropical, subtropical, and Mediterranean countries were exposed—malarial fevers. It was unfavorable because it made a certain kind of food unsuitable for its carriers. And it has become dangerous because its carriers suffer from certain drugs which may be given to them if their genetic peculiarity is unknown.

With respect to some genetic variants natural selection grows in severity. The situations indicated for porphyria and the enzyme deficiency causing favism are straws in the wind. Some genes that were favored or tolerated in the environments which were "natural" for our ancestors are detrimental in our present environments. This aspect of the situation has received insufficient attention because too many students of human evolution were busy prognosticating biological damnation. So little is known about it that the best one can do now is to ask questions and to suggest directions for further inquiries.

Living in, to use the popular phrase, "the ulcer belt cities" imposes emotional strains, states of anxiety, and nervous tensions that are less common or less acute in those who have elected the joys of suburban domesticity or the idyllic cares of tillage and harvest. Now, the carriers of some genotypes are likely to break under tensions which others take in their stride. The triumphal progress of our industrial civilization thus redounds to lessen the Darwinian fitness of some genetic constitutions, which become discriminated against by natural selection. The evidence bearing on these points is at the same time abundant and unsatisfactory. I am referring here to the whole field of studies on physiological stress and on psycho-somatic disorders, effectively popularized in recent years by Selye (1956) and Dunbar (1955).

"In its medical sense, stress is essentially the rate of wear and tear in the body. Anyone who feels that whatever he is doing—or whatever is being done to him—is strenuous and wearing, knows vaguely what we mean by stress" (Selye 1956). The body responds to stress by a set of changes in the endocrine (hormone-producing) glands, primarily by an increased activity of the pituitary gland and the adrenal cortex. The hormones produced by these glands mobilize the resources of the body needed to deal with the stress situation. This mobilization is, of course, a beneficial, adaptive reaction. Chronic or oft-repeated stress is something else, however. It overtaxes the body's stamina and may lead to nervous and physical breakdowns and finally to death. Deevey (1958, 1959) argues persuasively that excessive population growth and population densities result in inordinate stresses which cause high mortalities and partial or complete sterility. This is one of the factors that checks immoderate expansion of animal populations in nature. The number of human disorders and diseases known or suspected to be caused by psychic factors is considerable. The unfortunate gap in the evidence is, from our point of view, the lack of data on the differential susceptibility of different constitutions to maladies of this kind.

One would like to see adequate data on the incidence of mental disorders in people living under different circumstances and engaged in different occupations. There is, unfortunately, a lack of mutual understanding between some representatives of the medical profession, particularly psychoanalysts, and biologists interested in this problem. The psychoanalytic schools, stressing the importance of emotional strains and anxiety-producing and traumatic experiences in the lives of their patients, concluded that the role of the genetic variables must therefore be negligible. Conversely, discovery of genetic factors is taken by some to mean that environmental agencies are unimportant. The two misconceptions are, indeed, worthy of each other! If mental disorders are really more frequent among city dwellers than among country folk, are we to conclude that people with such disorders are prone to migrate to cities or that living in cities causes them to crack up under stress? If the frequencies of mental disorders increase with time, does this mean that the genes for such disorders are becoming more frequent or that their carriers are now more likely to break down than they were in "the good old days"?

The last point which we may discuss under the rubric of increasing severity of natural selection concerns certain forms of heart disease. In the past the human race was always preoccupied with finding enough to eat. The ability to wring from the available food the last bit of nourishment conferred, therefore, a tremendous adaptive advantage on man, as it does on most animals. So does the ability of the camel to store in the hump on his back some of the nutriment available in times of plenty for use in times of want. Man is in this respect different from a camel in that he tends to develop his hump in a more ventral location.

A new and unprecedented situation has, however, arisen in our day. It affects, to be sure, a minority of humanity. Some tens of millions, or possibly a hundred million people have too much, not too little, to eat: their trouble is overeating, not undernourishment. Now, because this trouble is so new, natural selection has not provided our bodies with means to cope with it. This problem has attracted a great deal of attention, especially in the United States in recent years, and resulted in a mass of publications. (See Gertler and White 1954, Keys and White 1956, and Friedman and Rosenman 1957 for further references.) Although different investigators disagree sharply on many points, the aspects that are interesting to a student of human evolution may perhaps be summarized tentatively as follows.

Degenerative heart diseases (those of the coronary arteries are most important) at present account for roughly half of all the deaths in the United States. This is due in part to increased longevity, since heart disease afflicts predominantly, though by no means exclusively, older people. The death rates from heart disease per 100,000 persons of a given age group in the United States were about as follows (in 1950):

| Age Group | Men | Women |
|---|---|---|
| 35–39 | 67 | 28 |
| 45–49 | 313 | 103 |
| 55–59 | 878 | 331 |
| 65–69 | 1,939 | 1,056 |

Unenviably, the United States holds the world record for the incidence of death from heart disease. In other countries the rates, for similar ages, vary from about the same values as in the United States (Scandinavia) down to much lower values among Italians,

Japanese, Bantus, and Navajo Indians (Keys and White 1956, Page, Lewis and Gilbert 1956). The problem of disentangling the environmental and the genetic factors of this situation is not an easy one. Both are almost certainly involved. The incidence of heart disease is highest in countries with the most generous diets, but it appears that the quality of the diet is equally or more important than the quantity. The proportion of fats in the diet has attracted most attention. People who consume much fat tend to show high concentration of substances called cholesterol and cholesterol-bearing lipoproteins in their blood serum and to have an elevated incidence of coronary artery disease. There are good reasons to suspect that intake of animal fats is more conducive to heightened cholesterol levels than that of vegetable fats.

Though important, diet and age are not the sole factors predisposing to coronary heart disease. Still another is sex—the incidence is appreciably higher, age for age, in men than in women. And individual susceptibility is also considered to be important. Although slim people are not immune to coronary heart disease, those overweight or obese are much more likely to be victims (Dawber, Moore, and Mann 1957). The slimness or obesity are in part environmental, due to scant diets or overeating, but in part they are almost certainly genetically conditioned. The matter has been stated best by Neel (1958b):

> It is difficult to avoid the speculation that increasing levels of animal fat consumption as well as an increase in total caloric intake, coupled with decreasing physical activity, have rendered important an agent of natural selection which formerly affected only a "favored" few. To the extent that there is a genetic determinant in the ability to handle relatively high dietary fat loads without developing atherosclerosis, then biological natural selection should be at work in a society such as ours where one-fifth of the population over age 30, or about 15,000,000, are overweight.

It may, of course, be argued that natural selection has little to do with genetic conditions that increase or decrease the risk of heart disease or senile dementia; as pointed out above, natural selection does not directly control the situation of the postreproductive ages. But in the first place, heart disease affects also some young people. More important still, the condition of the superannuated members of the family often affects the welfare of the children and young adults indirectly, via the economic and social consequences. It may be that the Darwinian fitness of human genotypes is measured more adequately by their relative contributions to the gene pool of the generation of their grandchildren, rather than to that of their children.

### Intelligence, Social Position, and Fertility

Methods of contraception are neither novel inventions nor monopolies of technologically advanced societies. They were known to and utilized by preliterate peoples. What is new is the relative efficacy, acceptability, and safety of these methods. Their increasingly widespread use has ushered in a trend toward lower birth rates. In Europe the decline of fertility started early in some countries—in France and in Ireland by the mid-nineteenth century. Elsewhere in northwestern Europe it began by about 1870, in Spain and Italy early in the current century, in eastern Europe and in Japan around 1920. The birth rate in the United States was about 55 per 1,000 in 1800; it declined to a low point of 18 in 1933 and rose somewhat in the postwar "baby boom." Elsewhere in the world the decline has merely begun or is yet to commence (United Nations 1953). The trend toward lower birth rates is a salutary one, in view of the deadly menace of runaway population growth. One hopes that this trend will become universal. And yet it provokes serious misgivings.

Populations of different parts of the world grow at unequal rates. As shown in Table 25, the population of Europe will about double during the twentieth century, that of North America and of Asia will quadruple, and that of Central and South America will increase by a factor of more than nine. Habits of prejudice, fears of competition, and specious "scientific" arguments make some people alarmed when they discover that the group to which they belong is not the fastest growing. Hence such shibboleths as "the yellow peril," "the rising tide of color," etc. One may as well accept the fact that the future will contain a relatively greater proportion of descendants of some than of other races. Anyway, no useful purpose will be served by what has been described as a "passionate protest against the meek inheriting the earth."

Another facet of the situation is perhaps more genuinely disturbing but not necessarily irremediable. In technologically advanced societies the business of propagation seems to be entrusted largely to people with mediocre to inferior qualifications for parenthood. The fact that the prosperous are less fertile than the poor and that city and town dwellers tend to have fewer children than do rural people was first noticed in Europe as early as the seventeenth and eighteenth centuries (United Nations 1953). This has been since confirmed by numerous studies. As birth rates declined, they fell more rapidly among the higher than among the lower social classes. This is true regardless of how one defines "higher" and "lower"—by social position, income, education, etc. As shown in Table 26, fertility is inversely related to educational status. The more schooling a person has, the fewer children he tends to produce. The low fertility of college graduates, particularly women graduates, was until recently notorious (see however p. 317).

TABLE 26

Schooling and the mean numbers of children ever born to American white women aged 45–49 years (after the 1940 U.S. Census, from Osborn)

| Schooling completed | Children per woman | Children per married woman |
|---|---|---|
| None | 3.95 | 4.97 |
| Grade school | | |
| 1–4 years | 4.33 | 4.54 |
| 5–6 " | 3.74 | 3.97 |
| 7–8 " | 2.78 | 3.04 |
| High school | | |
| 1–3 years | 2.37 | 2.61 |
| 4 " | 1.75 | 2.03 |
| College | | |
| 1–3 years | 1.71 | 2.07 |
| 4 or more | 1.23 | 1.83 |

This situation is undesirable, irrespective of any genetic considerations. People who should be able to provide the best environment for the physical and mental development of their children produce fewest progeny. Genetic consequences cannot, however, be ignored. They have been debated in many ways by many biologists, psychologists, sociologists, and political propagandists. Many dreadful prophecies and strident proclamations have been made. It cannot be gainsaid that there is a predicament here which should cause concern. The argument given runs somewhat as follows.

Poorly educated people include both those who lacked the opportunity for better education and those deficient in the capacity for such education. The genetic endowment for whatever it is that makes people able to profit by education is less common among the poorly trained than among the well educated. And the incidence of talent, ability, or whatever it takes to achieve success (however defined in a given society) is lower among the unsuccessful than among the successful. This may sound as blatantly undemocratic as Galton's speculations criticized in Chapter 3. But there is a difference which should allay the qualms of even the most compulsive egalitarians. It is recognized that many people deficient in education were fully capable of profiting by it; that many have-nots and failures are no less gifted than the haves and the successes; that in different environments and under different social systems the present failures might be successes and the successes failures; and that equality of opportunity must be striven for not because people are alike but precisely because they are different (p. 244). We should not, however, be lured into disregarding the fact that in any environment and under any social system, be it democracy or a dictatorship of the right or the left, people will differ in achievements, and this variability is in part genetically conditioned.

Now, the differential fertility described above makes those who achieve less mundane success achieve most success in reproduction. Therefore it happens that each following generation is descended in greater proportion from the less well endowed strata of the preceding generation. This amounts to a selection favoring lower endowment. Many investigators, not satisfied with this finding, make brave attempts to predict just how rapidly human abilities will deteriorate. Estimates of the expected decline of intelligence as measured by IQ techniques are the favorite targets of such predictions.

The methods used are really simple and at first sight convincing. Suppose that single children have a certain average IQ and that families with two, three, four, and higher numbers of children have progressively lower mean IQs. A well-conducted census will show the proportions of families with different numbers of children in the population. This tells us what proportions of the individuals of the next generation will be descended from families with different numbers of children and with different intelligence levels. The degree of the heritability of intelligence is estimated by various methods, such as comparisons of identical and fraternal twins (Chapter 4). The predicted rates of decline of the average intelligence in American and British populations varies from one to four IQ points per generation. A grim prospect indeed! Cook (1951) believes:

> As this process continues, the fortunate combinations of many plus-genes in one individual occur less frequently; the average level of intelligence and the proportion of gifted individuals declines. Should the feeble-minded level be reached, most of the plus-genes will have been eliminated. But before this time growing inefficiency and incompetence would cause a collapse of modern industrial society.

### Are People Becoming Less Intelligent?

The somber prognosis of declining intelligence has called forth a number of investigations designed to test its validity. By far the most significant of these are the surveys conducted by the Scottish Council for Research in Education (1949, 1953). In 1932, and again in 1947, an intelligence test was administered to all eleven-year-old children that could be reached in Scotland. About 88 per cent of the estimated children of that age in the country were actually tested; the remainder were absent from school on the days of the testing or could not be tested because of some bodily handicaps. The fifteen-year interval between 1932 and 1947 corresponds to at least half of the average length of a human generation. Has, then, the intelligence of the Scottish children dwindled during this time? Far from it, the average score has slightly but significantly increased! A similar situation was found in the United States: the soldiers drafted for the Second World War scored on the average higher than those in the First World War (Tuddenham 1948).

This result causes some embarrassment to the prophets of doom. Indeed, in Scotland, as elsewhere, the intelligence of children is negatively correlated with family size (in the 1947 survey a correlation coefficient —0.28 was obtained). The average score of single children was 3.7 points above that in families with three children, 11.1 points above families with six children, 14.0 above families with nine children, and 17.7 above families with twelve or more children. The investigators who conducted the surveys honestly admit that they expected a decline, not a rise. Among the explanations offered are improved health of the children and increasing "test sophistication," i.e., a greater familiarity with the kinds of tasks employed in the tests. It is amusing that some writers use these explanations to argue that the Scottish surveys have borne out the predictions that the intelligence is declining! Truly, they let no inconvenient fact interfere with their predilections.

An excellent critical analysis of the intelligence–fertility problem has been made by Anastasi (1956, 1959; these papers contain extensive references to other relevant publications). Most investigators have compared the average intelligence of single children with that of children having one or more siblings, not the intelligence of children with that of their parents. This is important because the amount of attention a child gets from his parents is on the average less in large than in small families; the development of the child's verbal faculties is, therefore, likely to be retarded in large families, and this will influence adversely the IQ scores. Data comparing the intelligence test scores of parents and their children with family sizes are scanty. The few published studies of this kind have yielded much less impressive correlations than the studies in which only the intelligence of the children and the size of the family were investigated. One would like to compare the scores of parents and children in families of the same size, but such data are scarce or unavailable.

These strictures undercut the overconfident calculations of the expected rates of the decline of intelligence. But it would be as hasty to conclude that the genetic basis of intelligence is in no danger of erosion. The consequences of the greater fertility of the less intelligent members of the population remain in need of elucidation. A suggestion well worth investigating further has been made by Penrose (1949, 1950a). Decreased fertility of the possessors of genetically-conditioned superior intelligence is compatible with preservation of a constant intelligence level in the population, provided that it is matched by a low fertility of the least well endowed members of the same population. In other words, people of middling intelligence may produce most children, while very intelligent and very unintelligent people have small families. One of the possible mechanisms to bring about such a situation would be a balanced polymorphism, mediocrities being the heterotic heterozygotes and the superior and the inferior people representing the two kinds of homozygotes.

Penrose has made a study of the parental origins of 1,194 mentally deficient patients in a hospital in England. As shown in Table 27, the matings in which one or both parents are low-grade defectives produce smaller families than normal parents do. Moreover,

TABLE 27

Mean number of siblings per an institutional mental defective
*(after Penrose 1949)*

| Parents | Cases observed | Siblings (mean) |
|---|---|---|
| Superior x normal | 9 | 2.89 |
| Normal x normal | 798 | 4.72 |
| Normal x dull | 196 | 5.45 |
| Normal x feebleminded and dull x dull | 113 | 4.52 |
| Normal x imbecile and dull x feeble-minded | 54 | 3.82 |
| Dull x imbecile and feebleminded x feebleminded | 24 | 3.58 |

there is evidence of assortative mating (the tendency for people of similar degree of intelligence to marry), and many defectives do not marry at all. This matter certainly needs further study. It may turn out that the intelligence level is under the control of a normalizing natural selection (p. 131), mediocrity being favored above superior intelligence as well as above wretched stupidity.

A lucid analysis of the changing patterns of differential fertility in the United States is given in a short paper by Kirk (1957). His data come mainly from a study of the families of men in *Who's Who*, which aims "to include the names, not necessarily of the best, but rather of the best known, men and women in all lines of useful and reputable achievement." These men have had smaller families than the general population of their generation. However, "the difference is progressively narrowing, and the younger men listed in *Who's Who* may approximate or exceed the national average in completed family size for their age groups. Men in *Who's Who* marry later, but more of them marry and they have fewer childless marriages than the general population of comparable age."

Kirk finds, in agreement with investigators of other population groups, that fertility is negatively related to social mobility. Those who have an inherited social status have more children than do the "self-made" men who had to struggle for comparable status. Large families may obviously act as impediments in such a struggle. "If present trends continue, the genetic qualities of men in *Who's Who* will be biologically perpetuated in the future at least in their numerical proportion to the general population. This is in marked contrast to the situation prevailing for at least two generations in the past." This again agrees with a more general trend. The birth rates in the United States have increased during the postwar period in all social strata; however, the greatest relative increases have been in those socially favored groups which had been characterized earlier by deficient fertility.

It may well be that the situation in which the economically more successful and, also, the more intelligent (which is certainly not the same thing) strata of the population failed to produce their proportional quota of children was only a temporary one. It may have arisen, especially in the West, because some people became familiar with efficient methods of progeny limitation before others. It is interesting in this connection that the patterns of differential fertility in at least some underdeveloped and non-Western countries favored greater families in economically more prosperous strata. This seems to have been the situation in China (Ho 1959b, Hsu 1959).

The direction of natural selection in the human species has certainly been shifting in the environments created by cultural changes. Have these changes and shifts been on the whole beneficial or injurious? Asking this is really another way of posing the question whether man must accept the "natural" drift of evolution as something preordained and inevitable. The alternative to such acceptance is pitting the forces of man's knowledge and wisdom against the forces of nature. The concluding chapter attempts to approach this fateful problem.

# 12. The Road Traversed and the Road Ahead

Man needs the unfathomable and the
infinite just as much as he does the
small planet which he inhabits.
DOSTOEVSKY

PEOPLE used to talk about the march of history. Marching, i.e., walking, was a suitable metaphor. Nowadays history bestrides a motor vehicle or maybe an airplane (thank goodness, not yet a rocket). Anybody in mid-life or older has witnessed great changes. Has not the "unchanging East" changed greatly? Where are the ancient European monarchies and their loyal subjects? Even in "primitive" societies people no longer live as they used to. A few years ago I heard a young Papuan, grandson of a cannibal, whistle the Toreador song from *Carmen* in the Owen Stanley Mountains of New Guinea!

Most of these changes evidently occurred not because human populations were altered genetically, but because they were altered culturally. The human species is biologically an extraordinary success, precisely because its culture can change ever so much faster than its gene pool. This is the reason cultural evolution has become adaptively the most potent extension of biological evolution. For at least 10,000 and perhaps for 1,000,000 years man has been adapting his environments to his genes more often than his genes to his environments. And the supremacy of culture in adaptation doubtless will continue in the foreseeable future. In this sense, but in this sense only, it may be said that man has escaped from the clutches of his biological past and has become to some extent the master, rather than a slave, of his genes.

The craving of the human mind for either-or categories is, however, a powerful one (perhaps genetically so?). Hence the widespread belief that the evolution of culture has suspended and superseded biological evolution. Since we live in the world of culture, it is, allegedly, a derogation of human dignity to say that we live in the biological world as well. But the biological world is not such a bad place in which to keep a toehold; it contains many joys for which no fit substitutes have yet been devised. Not only do we live in both worlds, but the world of culture can endure only so long as most of mankind possesses genetic equipments which are favorable for culture. Conversely, most of these genetic equipments are now such that their carriers probably could not survive without the benefit of culture. So, interdependence should be the watchword.

## Is the Biological Evolution of Man Completed?

Far-reaching cultural transformations have manifestly taken and are taking place. Do genetic changes accompany the cultural ones? White (1949) believes that "in the man–culture equation over a period of a million years, we may assume some absolute increase in magnitude of the biological factor. But during the last hundred, or even the last fifty thousand years, we have no evidence of an appreciable increase in mental ability." The assumption of the psychic unity, or uniformity, of mankind is probably pivotal in the working philosophy of a majority of anthropologists, psychologists, sociologists, and of not a few biologists. They maintain that biological evolution has achieved the genetic basis of culture and run its course; it is now a matter of the past. The genetic basis of culture is uniform everywhere; cultural evolution has long since taken over.

Up to a point the above view is justified. All healthy individuals of *Homo sapiens* have a capacity to learn a language, any language, and to acquire a culture, any of the cultures any group of people have anywhere. This capacity is one of the biological universals of our species, like walking erect, the approximately nine-month pregnancy term, or the nonopposable big toe. There are no genes for the French or Chinese or Hottentot language or culture. Our genotype confers on us a remarkable plasticity of cultural development. It cannot be too strongly emphasized that this plasticity is itself a species trait, formed by natural selection in biological evolution (Dobzhansky and Ashley Montagu 1947).

It is, however, a fallacy to think that specific or ordinal traits do not vary or are not subject to genetic modification (see p. 56). Phenotypic plasticity does not preclude genetic variety. There may be variations in the degree of plasticity; or some of the functions or roles which exist within a culture may be more congenial, and hence more easily learned, than others.

White (l.c.) is on firm ground when he denies that an "appreciable" change in the "biological factor" of human mental ability during the last fifty thousand years can be rigorously proven. If anything, he is overgenerous when he concedes that such change is proven for the last million years. There is no way to make the experiments necessary to secure such a proof. We cannot plant some identical twins to be reared by Peking man or by the Neanderthalians and leave cotwins to grow up in a modern society. We cannot give IQ tests to a sample of Cro-Magnons or, for that matter, to contemporaries of Plato or Charlemagne. The "proof" has to be based on inference. It cannot be otherwise, since what is at issue is whether certain historical events have or have not occurred. Anti-evolutionists have said again and again that evolution is not "proven." We cannot reproduce in the laboratory the changes which transformed the three-toed horse into the one-toed one or those which led from *Australopithecus* to *Homo*. It is an inference (and at that, one questioned by some competent authorities) that the bones of our ancestors were once upon a time not very different from those of *Australopithecus*. Darwin did not claim to have observed evolution, except that under domestication. He claimed that evolution can be inferred from what he did observe.

Emergence and development of culture makes adaptation to changing environments by means of genetic changes less binding than it was in precultural times. Man did not need to grow warm fur to cope with cold climates, because he donned warm fur garments. But there is really no way for culture to ward off genetic change altogether. Culture does not make human environments stable and uniform; far from it. The tempos of environmental changes have grown and are growing. Given environmental flux, the necessary and sufficient condition for genetic change is availability in populations of genetic variants, some of which are better and others less well adapted to shifting environments. Natural selection will do the rest—it will multiply the favored variants and depress or eliminate the unfavorable ones. The crux of the problem is, thus, how much genetic variance is available in human populations. This can be established by observation and experiment.

The diversity of human beings is seemingly endless. Granted that our senses are better trained to perceive differences between humans than between sheep, sparrows, or Drosophila flies, the human species must be regarded an extraordinarily variable one. What parts of the variance are genetic and what environmental is inadequately known. Human genetics has much to learn. This much is, however, certain: whenever the matter has been studied, both genetic and environmental components of the variability have usually come to light. And this is what one might have expected on theoretical grounds.

### The Feedback between Genes and Cultures

The fundamentals of the nature–nurture problem have been discussed in Chapters 2 to 5. No modern geneticist thinks that there existed in our ancestors or that there appeared by mutation some special genes "for culture." The transformation of the prehuman ancestral species into the "political animal" involved mutational changes in most or perhaps in all gene-loci. It is the whole genetic system which makes us human. However, many, or most, genes are represented in human populations by two or by several alleles. Has this genetic variability any relevance to culture? I believe that it has. Discussions of this matter are often plagued by a sheer misunderstanding. Some people are looking for a one-to-one correspondence between genetic and cultural traits. They find no such correspondence: there are no genes to make you a painter or statesman, or gangster; the Negro race is not homozygous for a nonexisting gene for jazz music, nor are the Balinese genetically dancers or the Jews merchants. The matter is considerably more subtle.

Genes create the setting for cultural traits, but they do not compel the development of any particular ones. An imaginary, extreme but, I hope, instructive illustration has been given in Chapter 1— if mankind consisted of individuals of one sex only, countless cultural changes would follow. In Chapter 9 the suggestion of Brues (1959) was referred to—the way of life of settled agriculturists favored and was favored by different bodily constitutions than the cultures based on hunting and pursuing game. It was also shown that rigid caste structure has genetic consequences different from and less desirable than those of social systems which accord to their members a rough equality of opportunity. Indeed, any major social or political change is bound to be reflected in an alteration of the gene pool of the population subjected to such change. This is a consequence of the fact that the magnitude as well as the direction of natural selective pressures depends on the environment, and the environment that exerts a decisive influence on the human species is the social environment.

The changes taking place in our modern world need rethinking in the light of genetics as well as that of sociology and politics. From the beginning of human history until recently, countless multitudes endured scarcity, hunger, disease, exposure to the elements, and misery of all kinds. Privations were believed to be the order of nature. Industrial and scientific revolutions have taught people otherwise. People learned that misery is unnecessary, that the world has the means for providing a decent living to all. There will be no return to the old beliefs, not even if the "population explosion" would result in a real shortage of the wherewithal for decent living. In one way or another, people will check the uncontrolled population growth and will secure what they now regard as their just right.

Certain consequences seem probable, not to say inevitable. Instead of most of the world producing raw materials and a few countries arrogating to themselves the roles of industrial and cultural centers, industrialization on a global scale is assured. Technical and scientific training will be widespread if not universal. Urbanization, more and more people living in urban communities, will continue. Now, city life favors a different kind of relation between people than does rural existence. Rural folk were traditionally members of communities in which everybody knew everybody else and everybody felt morally obligated to give and entitled to receive help in case of need from other members of their community. Urban life favors replacement of the desire for neighborliness by the desire for privacy: many an inhabitant of New York City neither knows nor cares to know who is living on the other side of a partition wall. It is chiefly, if not exclusively, from members of one's nuclear family that one hopes to receive assistance and succor when in need.*

A Russian adage had it that "God is too high, the Czar is too far." But nothing is too far with modern means of communication. While expecting little from their immediate neighbors people expect more and more from their states, nations, and governments. Democratic or totalitarian, governments will assume greater and greater responsibilities for the welfare of their citizens. Demands for a closer approach to an equality of opportunity for all citizens

*After this and the following paragraphs were outlined, I heard A. Inkeles, of Harvard University, expound somewhat similar but much more thoroughly argumented ideas at the Conference on Evolution, organized by the American Academy of Arts and Sciences in November 1960 (see *Daedalus*, Summer 1961).

of a state, and eventually for all citizens of the world, will be irresistible. The advice of a high church authority to the poor, "to take delight in the prosperity of elevated persons and to expect confidently their assistance," is unlikely to be accepted, least of all by members of a society atomized to a multitude of nuclear families. With relationships between members of a community becoming more and more impersonal, people expect and indeed demand assistance from the state. And everybody feels equally entitled to such assistance.

Now, we have seen in Chapter 9 that equality of opportunity has genetic consequences different from those of hierarchical, stratified, and caste societies. Equality decreases the wastage of the genetic potential of the human species. It favors manifestation of talents which remain hidden in societies that let high culture and refinement flourish while a great majority of people live in misery and ignorance. We need not raise here the difficult question of the role of the individual in history. It will be generally conceded that persons like Leonardo, Newton, Beethoven, Darwin, Dostoevsky, or Einstein have made priceless contributions to the treasury of culture of our species. And although this cannot be proven rigorously, it is extremely probable that these individuals carried rare and precious constellations of genes. (See, however, pp. 74–75 for a contrary opinion.) Now, if these gene constellations had appeared among Indian untouchables or Negro slaves or even in the slums of our cities, their carriers might not have accomplished much. Humanity would be the loser.

Equality of opportunity is an ideal not uniformly appealing to everyone. Continuation of hereditary privileged classes has found an outspoken and highly articulate defender in the poet T. S. Eliot (1948 and other writings). To Eliot, equality of opportunity endangers the refinements of civilization. In his view, a culture must be an "organic" whole, while equality of opportunity presupposes "an atomic view of society"; only an entrenched aristocracy can guarantee continuity of culture from generation to generation. (See Williams 1958 for a temperate but critical discussion of these views.) Hardin (1959) fears that as class competition decreases, competition between individuals increases in intensity and vindictiveness. "The complete elimination of classes would mean the installation of a dog-eat-dog society." He insists that mankind's biological as well as cultural welfare demands competition of many separate class or race populations; some of these will become extinct, while others will survive and repopulate places "left vacant by those that have succumbed."

The basic error of these views lies, it seems to me, in the implied assumption that equality of opportunity and mitigation or elimination of inter-group competition is tantamount to uniformization, leveling, disappearance of genetic and cultural variety. But this is not necessarily the case at all. Genetically, the gene exchange between Mendelian populations leads to their fusion in a single population, but there will be much greater inter-personal variability, and, I suspect, a greater number of nervous breakdowns, in that single population than there was in the previously isolated, separate populations. The variety of human genotypes, and hence of inclinations and abilities, is increased, not decreased, by hybridization. I suppose the same is true on the cultural level also. A large and complex society should be better able to provide for specialized talent and to tolerate unconformity than a small homogeneous group. I, for one, do not lament the passing of social organizations that used the many as a manured soil in which to grow a few graceful flowers of refined culture.

## Of Rats and Men

The failure of some nations and races to evolve high cultures is often taken as evidence of their genetic incapacity. Unfavorable environment is at least as likely to be responsible. Cultural advancement is hamstrung in populations where most people are infected with malaria, hookworm, or other infectious or parasitic diseases. The state of public health inevitably has repercussions in the cultural sphere. Populations in which the life expectancy is twenty-five years offer different cultural settings from those with a life expectancy of seventy years. Hereditarians as well as environmentalists will be well advised to remember that health is conditioned by environmental as well as genetic variables. However, as medicine and hygiene reduce or eliminate environmental hazards, the importance of genetic variables will loom larger and larger.

The National Health Education Committee (1959) estimates that about 17 million people in the United States suffer from some form of mental disease, about 4.8 million are mentally retarded, about 70 million have eye defects, 345 thousand are blind, etc. It is at present futile to try to estimate what proportion of these afflictions are genetic and what environmental. As pointed out repeatedly, these are not discrete categories. One may hope that, at least in the long run, only a fraction, perhaps a small fraction, of this human misery will remain incurable. Myopia is an eye defect which often has a genetic basis, yet it is corrected environmentally—by wearing glasses. The magnitude of the genetic load may, nevertheless, be influenced by culture and may influence culture at least by speeding up or applying a brake to its progress.

Richter (1959) is one of the writers who foresees the biological twilight of human evolution brought about by the influences of culture. His argumentation may be taken as representative of a school of thought having many adherents. Our ancestors lived the wholesome lives of wild animals. They struggled and fought for survival; natural selection held full sway; the strongest and cleverest survived; the rest succumbed. This has resulted in the development of man's finest qualities. In technologically advanced societies natural selection has come to a halt: birth and death rates being low, necessities of life assured to everybody, environmental hazards and epidemics controlled—the unfit survive and reproduce their kind. According to Richter, the process that has transformed the wild rat into the domesticated laboratory rat is also working in human evolution.

Norway rats *(Rattus norvegicus)* have been kept in laboratories since sometime between 1840 and 1850. The modern laboratory rat belongs to a well-defined variety that differs from its wild progenitor in many ways. The laboratory rat is entirely dependent on "the protected state of the laboratory where food, water, mates, and shelter are provided, and the struggle for survival no longer exists." Among other differences, laboratory rats have smaller adrenal glands and less resistance to stress, fatigue, and disease than wild rats. Thyroid glands have also become less active in laboratory rats, while, on the contrary, sex glands develop earlier and permit a greater fertility. They have smaller brains and are tamer and more tractable than the active and aggressive wild rats.

The genetic changes which occurred in the laboratory rat would, undeniably, make them unable to compete successfully with wild rats in the environments in which the latter normally live. But it does not follow that laboratory rats are decadent and unfit; nor does it follow that the "welfare state" is making man decadent and unfit—to live in a welfare state! What Richter has overlooked is the obvious fact that the laboratory rat is manifestly fit to live in its environment—which is the laboratory cage. Indeed, laboratories maintain stocks of laboratory rats, not of wild rats. The laboratory rat is not a decadent product of the absence of natural selection, it is a product of rigid natural selection in laboratory environments. Being tame, tractable, unaggressive, and fecund confers upon it a high fitness. And inasmuch as these qualities depend upon the lessened activity of the adrenal and thyroid glands, having these glands less active than in the wild rat is also a part of the high fitness. The contention that civilization or the "welfare state" set aside natural selection in man is not necessarily true either.

## Muller's Bravest New World

Utopias are seldom used as blueprints for action, even when their authors intend them for this purpose. Utopias may, however, fire the popular imagination and goad people to action, or they may indicate the intellectual climate at the time when they are composed. The genetic utopia painted by Muller (1935, 1959) will have an interest of at least this latter kind.

We have seen in Chapter 11 that Muller is the leading advocate of the view that the genetic loads which human populations carry are unconditionally deleterious, that civilization increases the mutation and decreases the selection rates, and that the genetic load of mankind threatens to swell until it becomes too heavy to carry. One can hardly contemplate a prospect of doom without looking for an escape. Muller has attempted to find one. He recognizes that the measures which he advocates run counter to the mores of all human societies. The decision to have or not to have children (and when and how many) is a prerogative of the individual; attempts, even benevolent ones, to dictate or sermonize on these matters evoke resentment. He thinks, however, that people will have to "recognize a duty on the part of individuals to exercise their reproductive function with due regard to the benefit or injury thereby done to society." This would make possible the introduction of the measures which Muller discusses under the headings of "Presently available genetic techniques," "Technical advances in the offing," and "More distant prospects."

Although frowned upon by some legal and ecclesiastic authorities, artificial insemination of human females is practiced on a small scale in the United States at present. It is applied mostly to women whose husbands produce no functional spermatozoa; the sperm donors are not, however, chosen with genetic or eugenic considerations. Therefore, "here is an excellent opportunity for the entering wedge of positive selection, since the couples concerned are nearly always, under such circumstances, open to the suggestion that they turn their exigency to their credit by having as well-endowed children as possible," and this can be done by "choosing as donors individuals of the most outstanding native mental ability." Muller endorses also a plan credited to Dr. R. Meir, which, in his opinion, "does not involve as radical a departure from present day customs and attitudes as does artificial insemination." This is for "couples of high native endowment" to "be willing to bear more children than they could bring up and give them out for adoption." Since this would presumably mean that the highly endowed parents would have a part of their progeny brought up by less highly endowed ones, the former must be very eugenical-minded indeed.

Animal semen (at least bull semen) can be frozen and kept for a long time at low temperatures, presumably without deterioration. Muller visualizes preserving the semen of outstanding men for future use in artificial insemination. Then when they will have long been dead a mature and dispassionate judgment of their real value could be reached. In the first version of his utopia (1935) Muller believed that no woman would refuse to bear a child of Lenin, but in the more recent one (1959) he nominates Einstein, Pasteur, Descartes, Leonardo, and Lincoln. Furthermore, with the passage of years the real value of the progenies begotten by these men in their lifetime by the more old-fashioned methods would also become clear. This is the technique of "progeny testing" which is known and widely employed in animal breeding.

If using the semen of select fathers with the egg cells of unselected mothers will lead to racial improvement, utilizing selected eggs as well as selected sperm should be even more successful. The number of children produced by a human female is limited not so much by the number of the egg cells she matures as by the total length of the pregnancies. It is estimated that the ovaries of a normal woman can shed several hundred egg cells. Techniques could be developed to flush these at present wasted egg cells from the reproductive tracts of outstanding women and to fertilize the eggs by spermatozoa of well-endowed men. The fertilized eggs thus obtained could then be implanted into the uteri of eugenically less desirable females, develop there, be born in the old-fashioned manner, and be brought up by the foster parents as though they were the biological parents.

When people will be enlightened enough to accept the foregoing, still better techniques could be evolved. Would not humanity profit enormously if instead of one Leonardo, one Einstein, or one Pasteur numerous individuals could be manufactured having genetic endowments *precisely* similar to those of the above great men? Not even having available for use the germ cells of the actual parents of these persons would make it possible to obtain replicas of their genotypes. For gene recombination takes place when the germ cells are formed, and it is, alas, well known that some of the progeny of outstanding parents fall short of the parental standards. It is, however, perfectly imaginable that techniques may be invented to dispense with sexual reproduction altogether, by implanting nuclei of body (somatic) cells into enucleated eggs and making them develop without fertilization (parthenogenetically).

Suppose then that we have available body cells of truly great men and women, preserved in special cultures or in deep-frozen condition, and that a technique is available to make these cells develop into whole organisms. One could at any time bring into the world any number of persons who would resemble the respective donors of the cells as much as if these donors had identical twin brothers or sisters. The limit would be to select the ideal man, or the ideal woman, and to have the entire population of the world, the whole of mankind, carry this ideal genotype. All men (or all women—one could, if desired, have individuals of one sex only) would then be born not only equal but indeed genetically alike. If this would seem too monotonous, the (perhaps unreasonable?) craving for diversity could be gratified by engineering environmental differences. The resulting people would be as different as identical twins reared apart (see Chapter 4).

Nor are still greater advances in human evolution excluded. "The biological distance from apes to men is a relatively slight one, yet how potent! Our imaginations are woefully limited if we cannot see that, genetically as well as culturally, we have by our recent turning of an evolutionary corner set our feet on a road that stretches far out before us into the hazy distance."

It might be argued that the only fair way to criticize a utopia is to compose a substitute. I am not prepared to do so. Muller's sweep of imagination is so great that his utopia has a certain romantic appeal. To point out difficulties, such as the possibility that detrimental mutations might arise in the germ cells or the somatic cells of the outstanding persons during their storage, would seem almost picayune. Such difficulties probably could be overcome; if only a fraction of the money and effort now being wasted on bombs and missiles were to be invested in biological research, new and remarkable techniques would certainly result. However, are we, "hastily made-over apes," ready to agree what the ideal man ought to be like? Granted that mankind would profit immeasurably from the birth of more persons with the mental stamina of Einstein, Pasteur, and even Lenin, do we really want to live in a world with millions of Einsteins, Pasteurs, and Lenins? Muller's implied assumption that there is, or can be, *the* ideal human genotype which it would be desirable to bestow upon everybody is not only unappealing but almost certainly wrong—it is human diversity that acted as a leaven of creative effort in the past and will so act in the future.

### Social Costs of Variant Genes

Among the biological problems which mankind has to face, that of the management and direction of the biological evolution of our species is second in urgency only to the awesome problem of overpopulation. This problem, in turn, has two fairly distinct aspects: the alleged failure, or weakening, of normalizing natural selection and the improvement of the present genetic endowment of humanity by directional selection.

Muller's utopia envisages a radical solution for the management of our evolution. The trouble with this solution is not only that it gives short shrift to the deepest of human emotions. It may be doubted that we know enough genetics to plan so ambitious a program. The situation cries out for more research in what Wright (1960) so aptly describes as "the unpopular and scientifically somewhat unrewarding borderline field of genetics and social sciences."

It is plain that normalizing selection does not act at present as it did in the Stone Age. The carriers of some genotypes who would have had no chance to survive then do survive and reproduce now. It is often forgotten that the reverse is also true—with respect to some genotypes selection has increased in severity (see p. 306). Natural selection is conditioned by the environment; its direction and intensity cannot remain constant when people adopt new ways of life. The selection is now as "natural" as it was a hundred thousand years ago, but it cannot be relied upon to do what is best in our—human—estimation: selection tends to increase Darwinian fitness; Darwinian fitness is reproductive fitness, not necessarily fitness for social progress.

It is uncertain how much genetic change there has been in mankind owing to the shifting direction of normalizing selection. Modern man might or might not be able to survive, even if properly trained, in the environments of his ancestors of one hundred thousand years ago. Or if he survived, he might not be as efficient or as happy in those environments as his ancestors were. We do not know for sure. It is often alleged that modern women experience greater difficulties in childbirth than did their great grandmothers, that more people suffer from weak teeth, etc. This is unproven. But it is a fallacy to conclude that what is unproven did not occur. In point of fact, it probably did.

Medicine, hygiene, social agencies, technology, and civilization save many lives which would otherwise be extinguished. This situation is here to stay; we would not want to alter it even if we could. Now, some of the lives thus saved carry genes which will engender other lives that will need to be saved in the generations to come. What are the consequences? No one has stated the principles on which the assessment of this problem must be based more clearly than Wright (1960).

Wright rejects the basic assumption of the classical theory of population structure (see p. 296) that there is, or can be, a single best, optimal, normal, or typical homozygous human genotype, all deviations from which would be detrimental and would be selected against. We have seen that the corollary of this assumption is that for each mutation there must be on the average one elimination (genetic death), and that a population must suffer, at equilibrium, a number of eliminations equal to that of mutations which arise. Equating the effects of all mutations is unrealistic. The elimination of a lethal mutant which causes the death of an embryo before implantation in the uterus is scarcely noticed by the mother or by anyone else. But grief and suffering accompany the elimination of a mutant, such as retinoblastoma, which kills an infant apparently normal at birth. Mutants such as hemophilia, sickle-cell anemia, and Huntington's chorea cripple, maim, and kill children, adolescents, or adults, cause misery to their victims, and disrupt the lives of their families. There is no way to measure precisely the different amounts of human anguish and woe, yet one may surmise that the painful and slow death of the victims of so many hereditary diseases is a torment greater than that involved in the elimination of a gene for achondroplasia owing to the failure of an achondroplastic dwarf to marry and beget children.

Looked at from the angle of the costs to the society, the non-equivalence of different mutants is no less evident. Myopia, or rather a predisposition to myopia, is believed to be inherited as a recessive trait. Being myopic is advantageous perhaps only under some exceptional circumstances; increases of the frequencies in populations of the gene for myopia are undesirable. Yet only a fanatic would advocate sterilization of the myopics or other radical measures to prevent the spread of this gene. Society can tolerate some more myopics: many of them are very useful citizens, and their defect can rather easily be corrected by a relatively inexpensive environmental change—wearing glasses. The effort that would be needed to eradicate or reduce the frequency of myopia would exceed that requisite to rectify the defect environmentally.

Diabetes mellitus, a rather widespread defect also believed to be inherited as a recessive (see p. 115), is, given the present level of medicine and technology, more difficult and expensive to correct than myopia. The incidence of diabetics may creep up slowly in the generations to come. How long it would take to be doubled, for example, we do not know—probably centuries or millennia. This prospect is not pleasant to contemplate, but insulin injections may, conceivably, have to be as common in some remote future as taking aspirin tablets is at present. Let us face this fact: our lives depend on civilization and technology, and the lives of our descendants will be even more dependent on civilized environments. The remedy for our genetic dependence on technology is more, not less, technology. You may, if you want, feel nostalgic for the good old days of our cave-dwelling ancestors, but the point of no return was, in the evolution of our species, passed many millennia before anyone could know what was happening.

It does not, however, follow that we may sit idly by, hoping that our posterity will learn how to correct any and all genetic defects. Timely surgery may save the lives of the carriers of retinoblastoma genes, but it leaves them blind (see p. 137). Should not these people be warned that if they reproduce, approximately half their children will inherit the defect? If all the retinoblastomatics were saved and had the same number of children as do other people, the frequency of retinoblastoma would after $n$ generations be approximately $2nu$, where $u$ is the mutation rate (and half the present frequency) of retinoblastoma.

Retinoblastoma is one of the many genetic defects which, unfortunately, are serious enough to make their correction too costly

and incomplete, if possible at all. We cannot sacrifice our fundamental ethic, which commands that lives, no matter how wretched,
be saved if at all possible, even though this frustrates normalizing
natural selection. The only solution open is replacement of natural with artificial selection. Persons known to carry serious hereditary defects ought to be educated to realize the significance of this
fact, if they are likely to be persuaded to refrain from reproducing
their kind. Or, if they are not mentally competent to reach a decision, their segregation or sterilization is justified. We need not
accept a Brave New World to introduce this much of eugenics.

Mention must be made of the distant possibility of a radically
different solution. A method may some day be discovered to induce
directed mutations, i.e., to change specific genes in desired ways.
This would enable one to alter certain genes in the sex cells or in
the body cells, and thus "cure" hereditary diseases by removing
their causes. Now, if the history of science has taught us anything,
it is the unwisdom of declaring that certain things will never be
discovered. I must nevertheless concur with Muller's opinion
(1959): the problem of the management of human evolution should
not be postponed until the conjectural time when directed mutation in man will have been discovered.

## Social Contribution and Social Cost

The social fitness of human phenotypes and genotypes is even
more difficult to evaluate than their Darwinian fitness. Wright
(1960) suggests that the problem may be treated in terms of the
balance between the contributions to the society and the social
costs of the different genotypes. He distinguishes, very tentatively
of course, the following categories:

1. A rough balance between contribution and cost, both at relatively modest
levels. This category includes the bulk of the population, the much-maligned
"mass man": the ordinary, orderly workingman or bourgeois—the humble or
the not-so-humble citizen.

2. A balance between contribution and cost, but at relatively high levels.
This includes professional men and women, technicians, experts, and specialists
of average competence, but with an education and a standard of living above
the average of the whole population.

3 and 4. This is the intellectual and technological elite: top artists or experts, creative and seminal minds, persons of genius who make extraordinary
contributions, either at a low cost (3) or at a high cost (4) to the society.

5. Persons whose capacities are those of class 1 or 2 (rarely 3 or 4) but who
repay the society much less than the costs of their maintenance. Possessors of

unearned wealth, nobles, aristocrats, and personages whose social contribution consists chiefly of high life and conspicuous consumption.

6. Criminal and antisocial persons of otherwise normal mental capacity.

The above categories, at least 1–5, correspond to the adaptive norm of the human species, as defined on page 126. Even at a risk of belaboring the obvious, it must be stressed that these categories embrace a great multitude of genotypes. Moreover, many or most of these genotypes are not fated to produce persons of any one of these categories. People whom we meet are what they are because of their genotypes and their environments. Surely, some (but probably not all) of these distressing fellows we see choosing the vulgar, the inane, and the banal instead of the beautiful, the rational, and the original could have been egg-heads and members of the avant-garde had they had the chance to learn the difference. And equally certainly, some of the snobs who are contemptuous of the plebeians are better endowed financially than genetically. Genetic equipments of classes 3 and 4 may arise among the children of the parents whose phenotypes place them in other categories.

The remaining categories, in which the social costs outweigh the returns, may be regarded as manifestations of the genetic load, provided, of course, that the phenotypic traits observed are genetically conditioned.

7. Subnormal physical constitution and health.

8. Low intelligence, but sufficient to take care of self under the existing social conditions.

9 and 10. Normal to maturity, but early physical or mental breakdown. Here belong many of the hereditary diseases, mentioned in Chapter 5 and elsewhere in this book, in which the ages of onset and incapacitation fall in youth or adulthood, thus interfering with self-realization and productive life. Many mental diseases, such as schizophrenia, belong to this category (except, of course, childhood schizophrenia).

11. Physical or mental incapacitation throughout a life of more or less normal duration.

12. Death before maturity, too early for any appreciable contribution to society.

13. Death at or before birth.

Categories 11–13 include some of the hereditary diseases mentioned in Chapter 5, as well as many lethal mutants which cause early or late abortions, miscarriages, or neonatal deaths. Although mutant genes which cause early fetal deaths involve, in general, graver disturbances than those which kill later, the attendant distress is probably smaller the earlier the death. With categories

5–13, the social costs outweigh the social contributions. These categories may be said to constitute the social load. Wherever the genetic variables are more or less strongly implicated, the genetic and social loads coincide.

## Biological Flaws in Man's Nature

In 1691 John Ray saw "the Wisdom of God Manifested in the Works of Creation," in that living beings show "the admirable contrivance of all and each of them, the adapting all the parts of animals to their several uses" (quoted in Greene 1959b). For a century and a half this idea dominated biology. In 1858 Darwin and Wallace advanced a different idea, better attuned to the spirit of their time, and of ours. The adaptedness is a product of natural selection.

Natural selection is, however, neither a stern master nor a benevolent guide. Selection does often bring about ostensibly purposeful results—genetic changes that increase the probability of survival and reproduction. Yet natural selection is automatic, mechanical, planless, and opportunistic. The adaptedness of organic structures and functions, though a source of wonder and fascination, obviously falls short of perfection.

A flagrant example of imperfection is the genetic load. Adaptation involves genetic elimination of countless ill-adapted variants. The welfare of the species is paid for by the misery of many individuals. Another example is the debility and infirmity of old age. As pointed out on page 125, natural selection may promote the welfare of the postreproductive age groups only if by so doing it benefits the reproductive ages. Indeed, Darwinian fitness of a genotype is measured by the contribution its carriers make to the gene pool of succeeding generations. To be sure, animals and humans may go on living for some time after their youngest children have been born. A homely analogy with cheap watches, which are "guaranteed" to function properly for a year or some other specific period, may be helpful here. Most of these watches work longer than the period of the guarantee. A watch that would stop running immediately after the expiration of the guaranteed period would have to be a high-precision mechanism, difficult and expensive to make. Spry and healthy oldsters are like the watches that go on ticking beyond their appointed time. Yet "the thousand natural shocks that flesh is heir to" in old age are, indeed, "natural" biological shortcomings. Painless death willingly accepted in the fullness of age would be preferable, if death can be accepted at all.

It may seem paradoxical that adaptively useless and harmful traits are not uncommonly established in evolution as specific and group characteristics. The principle of the utilitarianism of natural selection is not thereby negated. Natural selection perpetuates or eliminates genes and genotypes, not traits; what survives and reproduces, or dies or remains sterile, is an organism, not a characteristic. Useless and harmful traits are often by-products of the same genetic constitutions which also yield useful traits. Evolutionary transformations of living bodies succeed or fail as wholes, not as aggregates of traits in isolation from each other. Evolutionary success may, therefore, be due to the excellence of the organism in only one or in a few important respects. Similarly, evolutionary failure, extinction, may be caused by a breakdown of some one important function.

The more general and radical a transformation, the more likely it is to contain weaknesses in particulars. Now, "man is an entirely new kind of animal in ways altogether fundamental for understanding of his nature" (Simpson 1949). As a product of evolution, man is only roughhewn: he lacks the biological polish that comes from a long and slow adaptive improvement through natural selection. Among the pioneers of evolutionism, Mechnikov devoted most attention to the "disharmonies" in man's biological organization. The difficulty of childbirth in the human female is perhaps the most striking example of such disharmony.

Darwinian fitness is reproductive fitness; birth is a biological function obviously of prime importance. One would expect the performance of this function to become as safe, if not individually as pleasurable, as the similarly important function of copulation. And yet, "in sorrow thou shalt bring forth children." In the human female, and apparently in her alone among mammalian females, parturition is attended by intense pain and suffering. And as though this were not enough, the process of childbirth exposes both the mother and infant to risks of accidents and infections. From two to twenty per cent of the mothers were dying of puerperal infections in some hospitals during the seventeenth, eighteenth, and early part of the nineteenth centuries. What a strange miscarriage of natural selection!

Consider, however, that man is a mammal walking erect. Erect posture has necessitated considerable alterations in the body struc-

tures. As Coon (1954b) puts it, "in many respects man's shift to
erect walking is comparable to the development of organs of flight
in birds." Man's spinal column has an S-shaped curvature instead
of being arched, the pelvis has become massive enough to support
the whole weight of the upper part of the body, and the organs of
the abdominal cavity have changed their positions with respect to
the gravity pull. The difficult childbirth may be one of the components of this pattern of change. The pattern as a whole is highly
adaptive. Freeing the hands from walking duties has facilitated
tool-making and hence the process of "hominization" (see Chapter
7). But the female of *Homo faber* has to bring forth children in
"sorrow." This is one of the payments for the unrequited debt of
being human. The human species is, however, able to afford this
payment from the proceeds of its humaneness.

## Self-Awareness and the Fall of Man

*Cogito ergo sum*—I think hence I am. This was what Descartes
(1596–1650) found he could not doubt when he resolved to doubt
everything. This famous formula has withstood the efforts of most
resolute doubters, even to Sartre with his "being-in-itself." Self-
objectivation is a late product of evolution. When and at what stage
of the evolutionary development it entered upon the scene is conjectural. Rensch (1959b) finds its rudiments in some animals, but
affirms emphatically that a fully developed self-awareness is diagnostic of humanity. Teilhard de Chardin (1955) writes: "The animal knows, of course. But certainly it does not know that it knows."

For a generation (about 1910–1940), many psychologists found
it possible "to write psychology" without using such words as self-
awareness, self-objectivation, consciousness, or ego. More recently
these words were legitimized. No one has set forth the adaptive significance of self-awareness more clearly than Hallowell (1953,
1960):

> The attribute of self-awareness, which involves man's capacity
> to discriminate himself as an object in a world of objects other
> than himself, is as central to our understanding of the pre-
> requisites of man's social and cultural mode of adjustment as
> it is for the psychodynamics of the individual. A human social
> order implies a mode of existence that has meaning for the
> individual at the level of self-awareness. A human social order,

for example, is always a moral order. . . . It is man's capacity for and development of self-awareness that makes such unconscious psychological mechanisms as repression, rationalization, and so on of adaptive importance for the individual. . . . Man, unlike his animal kin, acts in a universe that he has discovered and made intelligible to himself as an organism not only capable of consciousness but also of self-consciousness and reflective thought. . . . An organized social life in man, since it transcends purely biological and geographical determinants, cannot function apart from communally recognized meanings and values, or apart from the psychological structuralization of individuals who make these their own.

The meaning of the acquisition of self-awareness in human evolution is expressed beautifully in the biblical symbol of the Fall of Man. Self-awareness is a blessing and a curse. Through self-awareness man attained the status of a person in the existential sense: he became conscious of himself and of his environment. He is able to form mental images of things and situations which do not yet exist but which may be found, brought about, or constructed by his efforts. Man can create in his imagination worlds different from the actual one and can visualize himself in these imaginary worlds. Before you build a house, construct a machine, write a book, or go on a vacation, you have already built, constructed, or written them, or gone vacationing in your mind. The adaptive value of forethought or foresight is too evident to need demonstration. It has raised man to the status of the lord of creation.

Self-awareness and foresight brought, however, the awesome gifts of freedom and responsibility. Man feels free to execute some of his plans and to leave others in abeyance. He feels the joy of being the master, rather than a slave, of the world and of himself. But the joy is tempered by a feeling of responsibility. Man knows that he is accountable for his acts: he has acquired the knowledge of good and evil. This is a dreadfully heavy load to carry. No other animal has to withstand anything like it. There is a tragic discord in the soul of man. Among the flaws in human nature, this one is far more serious than the pain of childbirth.

It would not do for a student of human evolution to ignore the tragic human predicament, although scientists in general have prudently avoided coming to grips with such problems. Here we arrive close to that ill-defined line which is the boundary of science, at least of science as at present understood and constituted. Let us simply acknowledge that on the other side of the line there exist profound insights into human nature, the nature we know to be an outcome of the evolutionary process. The psychoanalytic schools have attempted to describe this nature in quasi-scientific terms. Their conclusions are stamped with deep pessimism. The view of Freud (1930) is characteristic:

> In all that follows I take up the standpoint that the tendency to aggression is an innate, independent, instinctual disposition of man, and I come back now to the statement that it constitutes the most powerful obstacle to culture. [But the evolution of culture is] the struggle between Eros and Death, between the instincts of life and the instincts of destruction, as it works itself out in the human species.

Plato and Plotinus, St. Augustine and Luther, Kierkegaard and Nietzsche, Shakespeare and Dostoevsky, and many others have explored the abyss of human nature. It is a dark abyss, but the greatest of the explorers discerned a bright light shining up from it.

> Reason is only reason, and it satisfies only man's reasoning capacity, while the desire is a manifestation of the whole life, of human life in its entirety, including the reason as well as all the quirks. . . . I, for example, quite naturally want to live in order to satisfy my entire capacity to live and not in order to satisfy only my rationality, which may amount to only one-twentieth of my entire capacity to live.

But the same Dostoevsky who wrote the above wrote also that "beauty will save the world." It is a sad fact that man has always been able to depict hell more convincingly than paradise, and not even Beato Angelico and Dostoevsky were exceptions to this rule.

And yet, man has also risen, not only fallen. We are, in Muller's words (see p. 330), "hastily made-over apes." The evolutionary process has managed, the haste notwithstanding, to do more than equip the made-over ape for mere survival. It implanted in us extraordinary strivings for self-actualization and self-transcendence, for beauty, and for rectitude. *Homo sapiens* is not only the sole tool-making and the sole political animal, he is also the sole ethical animal.

### Evolution and Ethics

Almost two centuries ago, Kant pointed out that ethics are exclusively human possessions. Animals as well as man obtain, via their sense organs, information about the states of their bodies and their surroundings. But only man distinguishes what is from what ought to be. Man has normative as well as cognitive faculties. Darwin and Wallace agreed that evolutionary changes are brought about by natural selection. But they parted company when it came to the evolution of the human brain and its faculties. Wallace felt it necessary to invoke supernatural agencies, which Darwin considered uncalled for. (See Eiseley 1955, 1958 for very readable accounts of this controversy.)

The origin of ethics had been happy hunting ground for speculation long before Darwin. Not even a brief review of these speculations can be given here. Supernatural sanctions for ethics have been looked for most frequently. However, Spinoza (1632–1677) attempted an *Ethica more geometrico demonstrata*—ethics proved like a series of theorems of geometry. Spencer (1820–1903) started working on his theory of evolutionary ethics even before Darwin published his great books and continued for many years thereafter. The influence of Spencer's philosophy on his contemporaries was enormous; Keith's anachronistic *New Theory of Human Evolution* (1949) is the most recent incarnation of this philosophy.

Essentially Spencer thought (1896) that life is good and death is bad, that general evolution and the evolution of man are progressive, that progress and evolution enhance life and are therefore good. Ethical conduct is that which helps to promote life and hence the evolutionary progress. All this sounds reasonable, but unfortunately difficulties develop. Evolutionary progress arises, so Spencer thought, from the struggle for existence and the survival of the fittest. In the human species, the struggle for existence gave rise to a "code of amity" which operates between members of the same family, clan, or nation, but it also produced a "code of enmity" between different groups. Although human progress is believed to make amity more widespread than enmity, Spencerian ethics are clearly tinged with Social Darwinism.

A devastating critique of evolutionary ethics was given by T. H. Huxley in his famous Romanes Lecture, in 1893 (Huxley and Huxley 1947). However much we may admire what evolution has produced, "there is a general consensus that the ape and tiger methods of the struggle for existence are not reconcilable with sound ethical principles." Huxley never faces the problem of where these sound ethical principles come from, but establishes the sad fact that "what we call goodness or virtue involves a course of conduct which, in all respects, is opposed to that which leads to success in the cosmic struggle for existence." Accordingly, "cosmic evolution may teach us how the good and evil tendencies of man have come about; but, in itself, it is incompetent to furnish any better reason why what we call good is preferable to what we call evil than we had before."

The force of these strictures has never been overcome, although Julian Huxley (1941, 1953, 1960, Huxley and Huxley 1947), Waddington (1942, 1960), and Leake and Romanell (1950) have made valiant efforts to deduce evolutionary ethics from our modern conceptions of evolution. What T. H. Huxley called "the gladiatorial theory" of the struggle for existence is, indeed, no longer a part of our understanding of how natural selection operates in evolution. Social Darwinism really never had sound biological roots, even though it was, and in some places continues to be, an ideological prop of laissez-faire capitalism. Not only organisms which are the products of evolution but also the mechanisms of evolution itself evolve. The ways of the apes and tigers are not incumbent upon men because human evolution entered a new phase when it evolved culture; ethics are products of evolution which themselves evolve.

Julian Huxley believes:

> Ethics *must* be based on a combination of a few main principles: that it is right to realize ever *new* possibilities in evolution, notably those which are *valued for their own sake;* that it is right to respect human individuality and to encourage its fullest development; that it is right to construct a mechanism for further social evolution which shall satisfy these prior conditions as fully, efficiently, and as rapidly as possible [emphasis supplied].

And he also maintained that "anything which permits or promotes open development is right, anything which restricts or frustrates development is wrong. It is a morality of evolutionary direction."

Unfortunately, as Simpson (1953) and Raphael (1958) have convincingly shown, these ideas have no greater validity than those which T. H. Huxley criticized in 1893. It is, indeed, right to realize

possibilities which are valued for their own sake, whether they be
new or old; but what is there to show that new possibilities will be
most valuable; and, anyhow, from where are the criteria of value
to come? How do you prove from what we know of evolution that
human individuality is more valuable than human society? Societies are biologically newer than individuals, and they presumably
have more possibilities for "open development." And yet we do feel
that individuals should not be sacrificed for attainment of social
aims. As Simpson has observed: "All trend ethics demand the postulate that the trends of evolution, or some particular one among
those, is ethically right and good. There is no evident reason why
such a postulate should be accepted." Attempts to find evolutionary
ethics have at best "produced partial answers which are indeed
ethically good although not achieving a general and firmly based
evolutionary ethics."

### Evolution, Values, and Wisdom

It is certainly possible that natural selection may have favored
in human evolution the establishment of certain patterns of behavior which we regard as "ethical" or "unethical." The disposition
of the parents, and particularly of mothers, to protect and care for
their offspring, even to the point of self-abnegation and self-sacri-
fice, seems to us admirable, whether it is found in man, a bird, or
any other animal. We are apt to forget that in an animal this behavior is really "forced"; the animal cannot choose to behave
otherwise, while man can and occasionally does. Just the same, the
disposition is a built-in feature and is basically genetic.

Haldane showed long ago (1932) that genes for "altruistic behavior" may have spread when mankind was divided into many small
endogamous groups, but are unlikely to do so in a large undivided
species. Indeed, such a "gene" may depress the Darwinian fitness
of its carriers, if the latter sacrifice themselves for the benefit of
their fellows in ways which jeopardize their chances of leaving
progeny. Nevertheless, a small tribe containing genes for altruism
may gain an advantage through the sacrifice of some of its members and hence may multiply and spread. In large societies natural
selection is likely to operate in the reverse direction and eliminate
the genes for altruism. Conversely, a gene for selfish or criminal
behavior, which benefits its carriers and their progenies, is likely
to be eliminated if it appears in a small tribe, but may spread in
a large society.

It is unlikely that many of the human values could have become established in human societies by means of selective processes similar to those envisaged for "altruistic" and "criminal" genes. It is true that certain value judgments and ideas may further, and others hamper, the success, including the biological success, of the society in which they appear and are entertained. Several authors saw here analogies with mutations and gene combinations perpetuated or eliminated by natural selection. Analogies are interesting, yet to think that a mutant gene may not only make a person an inventor or entertainer of ideas but also determine which ideas he will invent or entertain, seems hardly compatible with the present trends in human genetics, anthropology, and psychology. For the crucial adaptation in human evolution has been the ability to learn a great variety of ideas and to make a variety of inventions, not to learn fixed ideas and only a certain invention. It seems to me on the whole more likely that natural selection has established in man a drive toward what Maslow (1954) denotes as "self-actualization" and avoided fixation of the means whereby the self-actualization may be achieved.

Waddington (1960) steers clear of the pitfalls in which previous theories of evolutionary ethics were trapped. He recognizes that natural selection has provided man not with ethics and values but with a capacity to acquire ethics and values. Values are products of human culture, not of the human genotype. But in order to become an "ethicizing being" man must be an "authority acceptor," a receiver of socially transmitted information. Waddington makes good use of the findings of psychoanalysts who describe the processes whereby a newborn child develops an "authority-bearing system." He finds, however, that these processes have adaptive as well as unadaptive aspects. The former concern the development of the "superego"; a successfully socialized infant grows to become an effective member of his society. The latter leads to the curious result of "producing ethical authorities which have the qualities of other-worldliness and absoluteness that we find in our ethical feelings, as well as guilt and anxiety which are another of their unexpected but obtrusive characteristics."

All this goes to explain how we develop our belief that certain things are good and others evil; it does not explain why we *ought* to regard them good and evil respectively. However, Waddington believes: "The framework within which one can carry on a rational discussion of different systems of ethics, and make comparisons of their various merits and demerits, is to be found in a consideration of animal and human evolution." The process of evolution has produced a human species capable of entertaining ethical beliefs; the biological function of ethics is to promote human evolution; ethics may consequently be judged by how well they fulfill this function. This Waddington calls the criterion of biological "wisdom." He compares the biological "wisdom" of ethics with the "wisdom" of eating. The function of eating is to promote healthy growth; if somebody would say that he prefers to grow in an unhealthy and abnormal manner, one can only tell him that he is "out of step with nature." Similarly, the "wisdom" of evolution cannot be doubted; evolution is "wise" by definition.

This solution is too easy. Do we always know what is and what is not in step with nature? Is, for example, Muller's utopia discussed above in step with nature? Some people think that all would be well with man if natural selection operated freely, but we have seen that this is at most a half-truth, since the kind of "natural" selection which operated in the Stone Age would be unnatural in modern man. "Wisdom of the body" and "wisdom of evolution" are good metaphors, but they are not synonymous with wisdom which is the source and validation of ethics. This has been stated splendidly by Simpson (1953): "The means to gaining right ends involve both organic and human evolution, but human choice as to what *are* the right ends must be based on human evolution. . . . The old evolution was and is essentially amoral. The new evolution involves knowledge, including the knowledge of good and evil."

I do not think (and neither does Simpson) that understanding of evolution, biology, or science is irrelevant to wisdom. Wisdom is itself evolving, and it includes the insights derived from cumulative knowledge, which subsumes biology. As Bronowski (1956) put it: "Science is nothing else than the search to discover unity in the wild variety of nature—or more exactly, in the variety of our experience." But wisdom includes also other insights. St. Augustine said: *Surgunt indocti et rapiunt coelum*—ignorants come and grasp the heavens. This is not an apologia for ignorance or even for the irrational man. Waddington himself asks for something more than the wisdom of biology when he writes:

I would not say that the scientific ideal alone is a wholly adequate foundation for the good life of the individual or the highest civilization of society. . . . It needs, in my view, to be supplemented by the ideal of the creative artist—an ideal which expresses itself in thought processes which move in a different dimension to those of logic and experiment.

We do not know whether it is a by-product of the aesthetic faculty (see p. 214) or of the more fundamental faculty of self-awareness (see p. 337) which confers upon some persons a quality of wisdom which seems curiously unrelated to their mastery of cumulative knowledge. In *War and Peace,* Tolstoi makes his aristocratic and cultured hero learn wisdom from an ignorant peasant turned soldier. And the highest wisdom of all was at one time entrusted to a group of unlettered Galilean fishermen.

Human values and wisdom are products of cultural evolution, conditioned of course by biological evolution, yet not deducible from the latter. In point of fact, man will not be dissuaded from the arrogant aspiration to query whether the biological and cosmic evolutions, which produced him among countless other things, do or do not conform to his wisdom and his values. I know no better criterion of wisdom and values than that proposed by the ancient Chinese sage (cited after Herbert Muller, 1957):

> Every system of moral laws must be based upon the man's own consciousness, verified by the common experience of mankind, tested by due sanction of historical experience and found without error, applied to the operations and processes of nature in the physical universe and found to be without contradiction, laid before the gods without question or fear, and able to wait a hundred generations and have it confirmed without a doubt by a Sage of posterity.

## Man, the Center of the Universe

Civilization has helped most of mankind to change from ignorance, undernourishment, and filth to education, at least relative abundance, and sanitation. That these changes are to the good is unquestionable. Yet in the process of change man has also lost and failed to recapture some things of inestimable value. Man no longer enjoys the certitude that he stands at the center of a universe created especially for his sake or the twin certitude that this universe is presided over by a Power which can be implored or propitiated and which cares for man, individually and collectively. Copernicus and Galileo suddenly broke the news that the world does not revolve around man but man, instead, revolves around the world. And in this world, vast and merciless instead of snug and familiar, man is incidental and almost superfluous. The feeling of schism between man and nature was expressed with unsurpassed poignancy by Pascal (1623–1662):

> When I consider the short duration of my life, swallowed up in the eternity before and after, the little space which I fill, and even can see, engulfed in the infinite immensity of spaces of which I am ignorant, and which know me not, I am frightened, and am astonished at being here rather than there; for there is no reason why here rather than there, why now rather than then. . . . The eternal silence of these infinite spaces frightens me.

Attempts have been made to relieve man's alienation from the world he inhabits. Descartes thought that while animals were machines man possessed an immortal soul; Locke pointed out, however, that there is nothing in man's mind that did not enter there via the sense organs. Romantics revolted against the tyranny of mechanistic science, trusting the poet's inspiration more than the scientist's plodding toil; but it was physics, not poetry, that led to the industrial revolution, to the abundance of material goods, and eventually to the frightening power of atomic energy. Nothing succeeds like success, and the man in the street became convinced that material power is to be admired above intellectual power. To many Darwin seemed to have delivered the heaviest blow, making the schism in man's soul irreparable: far from the world having been made for man, man himself proved to be merely one of some two million biological species, a result of material processes of a rather unedifying sort, called struggle for existence and survival of the fittest, and a relative of creatures as disreputable as monkeys and apes. With Freud the depreciation of the human condition reached the lowest level. Freud mocked man's pretensions to spirituality, by denying him not only spirituality but rationality as well.

The most important point in Darwin's teachings was, strangely enough, overlooked. Man has not only evolved, he is evolving. This is a source of hope in the abyss of despair. In a way Darwin has healed the wound inflicted by Copernicus and Galileo. Man is not the center of the universe physically, but he may be the spiritual center. Man and man alone knows that the world evolves and that he evolves with it. By changing what he knows about the world man changes the world that he knows; and by changing the world in which he lives man changes himself. Changes may be deteriorations or improvements; the hope lies in the possibility that changes resulting from knowledge may also be directed by knowledge. Evolution need no longer be a destiny imposed from without; it may conceivably be controlled by man, in accordance with his wisdom and his values.

An inspiring attempt to sketch an optimistic philosophy of the cosmic, biological, and human evolutions has been made by Teilhard de Chardin (1955, 1959). I must, however, gainsay the admonition which the author makes in the opening sentence of the Preface to his remarkable book: "If this book is to be properly understood, it must be read not as a work on metaphysics, still less as a sort of theological essay, but purely and simply as a scientific treatise." The book must be read as science, and as metaphysics and theology, and, furthermore, as something its author does not mention at all, namely poetry (though this last named component has been sadly mauled in the English translation).

> Is evolution a theory, a system, or a hypothesis? It is much more—it is a general postulate to which all theories, all hypotheses, all systems must henceforward bow and which they must satisfy in order to be thinkable and true. Evolution is a light which illuminates all facts, a trajectory which all lines of thought must follow—this is what evolution is.

Teilhard de Chardin saw that the evolution of matter, the evolution of life, and the evolution of man are integral parts of a single process of cosmic development, of a single and coherent history of the whole universe. Furthermore, he saw in this history a clear direction or trend. Regrettably, he described this trend as "orthogenesis," but if I understand him aright, he did not mean to imply that evolution is an uncreative unfolding of preformed events (see pp. 15–17); unfortunately he lacked familiarity with modern biology.

He chose to designate the direction in which evolution is going as "The Point Omega." This is

> a harmonized collectivity of consciousnesses, equivalent to a kind of superconsciousness. The Earth is covering itself not merely by myriads of thinking units, but by a single continu-

um of thought, and finally forming a functionally single Unit of Thought of planetary dimensions. The plurality of individual thoughts combine and mutually reinforce each other in a single act of unanimous Thought. . . . In the dimension of Thought, like in the dimension of Time and Space, can the Universe reach consummation in anything but the Measureless?

Such grand conceptions are patently undemonstrable by scientifically established facts. They transcend cumulative knowledge; it is sufficient that this one is not contradicted by this knowledge. To modern man, so forlorn and spiritually embattled in this vast and ostensibly meaningless universe, Teilhard de Chardin's evolutionary idea comes as a ray of hope. It fits the requirements of our time. For

Man is not the centre of the universe as was naively believed in the past, but something much more beautiful—Man the ascending arrow of the great biological synthesis. Man is the last-born, the keenest, the most complex, the most subtle of the successive layers of life. This is nothing less than a fundamental vision. And I shall leave it at that.

# Bibliography

Adler, A. (1927) 1957. *Understanding human nature*. New York, Premier Books, Fawcett.

Aguirre, E. 1959. Aspectos filosoficos y teologicos de la evolution. *Rev. Univ. Madrid, 8:* 445–531.

Allee, W. C. 1951. *Cooperation among animals*. New York, Schuman.

Allison, A. C. 1954a. Protection afforded by sickle cell trait against subtertian malarial infection. *Brit. Med. J., 1:* 290–92.

———— 1954b. Notes on sickle cell polymorphism. *Ann. Human Genetics, 19:* 39–57.

———— 1955. Aspects of polymorphism in man. *Cold Spring Harbor Symp. Quant. Biol., 20:* 239–55.

———— 1959. Metabolic polymorphisms in mammals and their bearing on problems of biochemical genetics. *Am. Nat., 93:* 5–16.

Anastasi, A. 1956. Intelligence and family size. *Psychol. Bull., 53:* 187–209.

———— 1958. *Differential psychology*. 3rd Ed. New York, Macmillan.

———— 1959. Differentiating effects of intelligence and social status. *Eugenics Quart., 6:* 84–91.

————, and R. F. Levee. 1959. Intellectual defect and musical talent: a case study. *Amer. J. Mental. Defic., 64:* 695–703.

Arnheim, R. 1954. *Art and visual experience*. Berkeley, Univ. of California Press.

Bagehot, W. 1873. *Physics and politics*. New York, Appleton.

Baker, P. T. 1958a. The biological adaptation of man to hot deserts. *Am. Nat., 92:* 337–57.

———— 1958b. Racial differences in heat tolerance. *Am. J. Phys. Anthropol., 16:* 287–305.

Barnicot, N. A. 1952. Albinism in southwestern Nigeria. *Ann. Eugenics, 17:* 38–73.

———— 1957. Human pigmentation. *Man, 144:* 1–7.

———— 1959. Climatic factors in the evolution of human populations. *Cold Spring Harbor Symp. Quant. Biol., 24:* 115–29.

Bartholomew, G. A., and J. B. Birdsell. 1953. Ecology and the protohominids. *Am. Anthropol., 55:* 481–98.

Barzun, J. 1937. *Race, a study in modern superstition*. New York, Harcourt Brace.

———— 1941. *Darwin, Marx, and Wagner*. Boston, Little, Brown.

Bateman, A. J. 1948. Intra-sexual selection in *Drosophila*. *Heredity, 2:* 349–68.

Bateson, B. 1928. *William Bateson, F.R.S.* Cambridge University Press.

Beach, F. A. 1945. Current concepts of play in animals. *Am. Nat., 79:* 523–41.

―――― 1948. *Hormones and behavior.* New York, Hoeber.

Benedict, P. K., and I. Jacks. 1954. Mental illness in primitive societies. *Psychiatry, 17:* 377–89.

Benedict, R. 1934. *Patterns of culture.* Boston, Houghton Mifflin.

―――― 1946. *The chrysanthemum and the sword.* Boston, Houghton Mifflin.

―――― 1949. Child rearing in certain European countries. *Am. J. Orthopsychiatry, 19:* 342–50.

Bergounioux, F. M. 1958. "Spiritualité" de l'homme de Néandertal, pp. 151–66. *In Neanderthal Centennary*, Utrecht, Kemink.

Birch, L. C. 1957. The meaning of competition. *Am. Nat., 91:* 5–18.

Birdsell, J. B. 1951a. The problem of the early peopling of the Americas as viewed from Asia. *Physical Anthropology of the American Indian.* New York, Viking Fund.

―――― 1951b. Some implications of the genetical concept of race in terms of spatial analysis. *Cold Spring Harbor Symp. Quant. Biol., 15:* 259–314.

―――― 1953. Some environmental and cultural factors influencing the structuring of Australian aboriginal populations. *Am. Nat., 87:* 171–207.

―――― 1957a. On methods of evolutionary biology and anthropology. *Am. Scientist, 45:* 393–400.

―――― 1957b. Some population problems involving Pleistocene man. *Cold Spring Harbor Symp. Quant. Biol., 22:* 47–69.

Bloomfield, P. 1955. *Uncommon people.* London, Hamish Hamilton.

Blum, H. F. 1959. *Carcinogenesis by ultraviolet light.* Princeton, Princeton Univ. Press.

―――― 1961. Does the melanin pigment of human skin have adaptive value? *Quart. Review Biol., 36:* 50–63.

Bolk, L. 1926. *Das Problem der Menschenwerdung.* Jena, Fischer.

Böök, J. A. 1953. A genetic and neuropsychiatric investigation of a north-Swedish population. *Acta Genetica, 4:* 1–100.

Bose, N. K. 1951. Caste in India. *Man in India, 31:* 107–23.

Boule, M., and H. V. Vallois. 1957. *Fossil men.* New York, Dryden.

Bourgeois-Pichat, J., and C. L. Pan. 1956. Trends and determinants of mortality in underdeveloped areas. *Trends and Differentials in Mortality.* New York, Milbank Mem. Fund.

Boyd, W. 1939. Blood groups. *Tabulae Biologicae, 17:* 113–240.

―――― 1950. *Genetics and the races of man.* Boston, Little, Brown.

―――― 1953. The contributions of genetics to anthropology, pp. 488–506. *In* A. Kroeber, *Anthropology today,* Chicago, Univ. of Chicago Press.

Braidwood, R. J. 1958. Near Eastern prehistory. *Science, 127:* 1419–30.

―――― 1960. Levels of subsistence-settlement types, multilinear evolution, environment, and diffusion, in human prehistory, pp. 143–51. *In* S. Tax, *Evolution after Darwin,* Vol. 2. Chicago, Univ. of Chicago Press.

――――, and C. A. Reed. 1957. The achievement and early consequences of food production. *Cold Spring Harbor Symp. Quant. Biol., 22:* 19–31.

Breitinger, E. 1955. Das Schadelfragment von Swanscombe und das "Praesapiens Problem." *Mitteil. Anthropol. Ges. Wien, 84–5:* 1–45.

——— 1957. Zur phyletischen Evolution von Homo sapins. *Anthropol. Anz.*, *21:* 62–83.

Bridges, E. L. 1950. *The uttermost part of the earth.* New York, Dutton.

Brinton, C. 1953. *The shaping of the modern mind.* New York, New Amer. Library.

——— 1959. *A history of western morals.* New York, Harcourt Brace.

Bronowski, J. 1956. *Science and human values.* New York, Messner.

Brown, G. M., J. D. Hatcher, and J. Page. 1952. Temperature and blood flow in the forearm of the Eskimo. *J. Appl. Physiol., 5:* 410–20.

———, G. S. Bird, L. M. Boag, D. J. Demhaye, J. E. Green, J. D. Hatcher, and J. Page. 1954. Blood volume and basal metabolic rate of Eskimos. *Metabolism, 3:* 247–54.

Brozek, J. 1953. Measuring nutriture. *Am. J. Phys. Anthropol., 11:* 147–80.

Brues, A. 1954. Selection and polymorphism in the A–B–O blood groups. *Am. J. Phys. Anthropol., 12:* 559–97.

——— 1959. The spearman and the archer—an essay on selection in body build. *Am. Anthropol., 61:* 457–69.

Carpenter, C. R. 1942. Societies of monkeys and apes. *Biol. Symposia, 8:* 177–204.

——— 1954. Tentative generalizations on grouping behavior of nonhuman primates. *Human Biol., 26:* 269–76.

Carstairs, G. M. 1958. *The twice-born.* Bloomington, Indiana Univ. Press.

Carter, H. D. 1935. Twin similarities in emotional traits. *Character and Personality, 4:* 61–78.

Cassirer, E. 1944. *An essay on man.* New Haven, Yale Univ. Press.

Cattell, R. B., D. B. Blewett, and J. R. Beloff. 1955. The inheritance of personality. *Am. J. Human Genet., 7:* 122–46.

———, G. F. Stice, and N. F. Kristy. 1957. A first approximation to nature-nurture ratios for eleven primary personality factors in objective tests. *J. Abnorm. and Soc. Psychol., 54:* 143–59.

Cavalli-Sforza, L. L. 1958. Some data on the genetic structure of human populations. *Proc. X. Intern. Congr. Genet., 1:* 389–407.

Ceppellini, R. 1957. I meccanismi evolutivi nelle popolazioni umane. *La Ricerca Sci., Suppl., 27:* 1–23.

Chetverikov (Tschetwerikoff), S. S. 1926 (1961). On certain features of the evolutionary process from the viewpoint of modern genetics. *J. Exp. Biol., 2:* 3–54. [In Russian] Translation in: *Proc. Am. Philos. Soc., 105:* 167–95.

——— 1927. Über die genetische Beschaffenheit wilder Population. *Verh. V. internat. Kongr. Vererbungsw., 2:* 1499–1500.

Childe, G. V. 1951. *Social evolution.* New York, Schuman.

Chung, C. S., and N. E. Morton. 1959. Discrimination of genetic entities in muscular dystrophy. *Am. J. Human Genet., 11:* 339–59.

———, O. W. Robinson, and N. E. Morton. 1959. A note on deaf-mutism. *Ann. Human Genet., 23:* 357–66.

Clarke, C. A., and P. M. Sheppard. 1960. Supergenes and mimicry. *Heredity, 14:* 175–85.

Clausen, J. 1951. *Stages of the evolution of plant species.* Ithaca, Cornell Univ. Press.

————, D. D. Keck, and W. M. Hiesey. 1940. Experimental studies on the nature of species. I. *Carnegie Inst. Washington, Publ. 520.*

————, ————, ————. 1948. Experimental studies on the nature of species. III. *Carnegie Inst. Washington, Publ. 581.*

Comfort, A. 1956. *The biology of senescence.* New York, Rinehart.

Conrad, H. S., and H. E. Jones. 1940. A second study of familial resemblance in intelligence. *39th Yearb. Nat. Soc. Study Educ.,* Part 2: 97–141.

Cook, R. C. 1951. *Human fertility; the modern dilemma.* New York, Sloane.

Coon, C. S. 1939. *The races of Europe.* New York, Macmillan.

———— 1954a. *The story of man.* New York, Knopf.

———— 1954b. Climate and race. *Smithsonian Report for 1953:* 277–98.

———— 1955. Some problems of human variability in climate and culture. *Am. Nat., 89:* 257–59.

———— 1959. Race and ecology of man. *Cold Spring Harbor Symp. Quant. Biol., 24:* 153–59.

———— 1961. Man against the cold. *Natural History, 70:* 56–69.

————, S. M. Garn, and J. B. Birdsell. 1950. *Races.* Springfield, Thomas.

Count, E. W. 1950. *This is race.* New York, Schuman.

Cowles, R. B. 1959. Some ecological factors bearing on the origin and evolution of pigment in the human skin. *Am. Nat., 93:* 283–93.

Crow, J. F. 1958. Some possibilities for measuring selection intensities in man. *Human Biol., 30:* 1–13.

———— 1961. Selection. *Symp. Methodology in Human Genetics* (in press).

Czekanowski, J. 1928. Das Typenfrequenzgesetz. *Anthrop. Anz., 4:* 335–59.

———— 1939 (1950). The anthropological structure of Europe as seen from the results of Polish research, pp. 593–607. *In* E. W. Count, *This is race,* New York, Schuman.

Darlington, C. D. 1953. *The facts of life.* London, Allen & Unwin.

———— 1959. *Darwin's place in history.* Oxford, Blackwell.

Darwin, C. G. 1953. *The next million years.* New York, Doubleday.

Davenport, C. B. 1913. Heredity of skin color in Negro-white crosses. *Carnegie Inst. Washington, Publ. 188.*

Davis, K. 1940. Extreme social isolation of a child. *Am. J. Sociol., 45:* 554–65.

———— 1947. Final note on a case of extreme isolation. *Am. J. Sociol., 52:* 432–37.

Dawber, T. R., F. E. Moore, and C. V. Mann. 1957. Coronary heart disease in the Framingham study. *Am. J. Publ. Health, 47,* No. 4.

Dean, G. 1957. Pursuit of a disease. *Sci. American, 196:* 133–42.

————, and H. D. Barnes. 1958. Porphyria: a South-African screening experiment. *Brit. Med. J., 5066:* 298–301.

Deevey, E. S. 1958. The equilibrium population, pp. 64–86. *In* R. G. Francis, *The population ahead,* Minneapolis, Univ. of Minnesota Press.

———— 1959. The hare and the haruspex; a cautionary tale. *Yale Review, 49:* 161–79.

———— 1960. The human population. *Sci. American, 203:* 195–204.

Dennis, W. 1938. Infant development under conditions of restricted practice and of minimum social stimulation. *J. Genet. Psychol., 53:* 149–57.

———— 1940. Does culture appreciably affect patterns of infant behavior? *J. Soc. Psychol., 12:* 305–17.

Dobzhansky, Th. 1944a. On species and races of living and fossil man. *Am. J. Phys. Anthropol.*, 2: 251–65.

—— 1944b. Chromosomal races in *Drosophila pseudoobscura and Drosophila persimilis. Carnegie Inst. Washington, Publ. 554:* 47–144.

—— 1948a. Genetics of natural populations. XVI. *Genetics, 33:* 158–76.

—— 1948b. Genetics of natural populations. XVIII. *Genetics, 33:* 588–602.

—— 1952. Genetics of natural populations. XX. *Evolution, 6:* 234–43.

—— 1955. A review of some fundamental concepts and problems of population genetics. *Cold Spring Harbor Symp. Quant. Biol.*, 20: 1–15.

—— 1956. What is an adaptive trait? *Am. Nat., 90:* 337–47.

—— 1958. Evolution at work. *Science, 127:* 1091–98.

——, and M. F. Ashley Montagu. 1947. Natural selection and the mental capacities of mankind. *Science, 106:* 587–90.

——, and O. Pavlovsky. 1957. An experimental study of interaction between genetic drift and natural selection. *Evolution, 11:* 311–19.

——, and B. Spassky. 1954. Rates of spontaneous mutation in the second chromosomes of the sibling species, *Drosophila pseudoobscura* and *Drosophila persimilis. Genetics, 39:* 899–907.

Dubos, R. J. 1958. The evolution of infectious diseases in the course of history. *Canadian Med. Assoc. J., 79:* 445–51.

—— 1959a. The evolution and the ecology of microbial diseases, pp. 14–27. *In* R. J. Dubos, *Bacterial and mycotic infections,* 3rd Ed., Philadelphia, Lippincott.

—— 1959b. Medical utopias. *Daedalus, 88:* 410–24.

—— 1959c. *Mirage of health.* New York, Harper.

——, and J. Dubos. 1952. *The white plague: tuberculosis, man, and society.* Boston, Little, Brown.

Dunbar, F. 1955. *Emotions and bodily changes.* New York, Columbia Univ. Press.

Dunn, L. C. 1957a. Studies of genetic variability in populations of wild mice. *Genetics, 42:* 299–311.

—— 1957b. Evidence of evolutionary forces leading to the spread of lethal genes in wild populations of house mice. *Proc. Nat. Acad. Sci., 43:* 158–63.

Durkheim, E. 1915. *The elementary forms of the religious life: a study of religious sociology.* London, Allen & Unwin.

East, E. M. 1916. Inheritance in crosses between *Nicotiana langsdorfii* and *Nicotiana alata. Genetics, 1:* 311–33.

Edwards, J. G. 1954. A new approach to infraspecific categories. *Systematic Zool., 3:* 1–20.

Eiseley, L. 1955. Fossil man and human evolution. *Yearbook of Anthropology:* 61–78. New York, Wenner-Gren Foundation.

—— 1958. *Darwin's century.* New York, Doubleday Anchor.

—— 1959. Charles Darwin, Edward Blyth, and the theory of natural selection. *Proc. Am. Philos. Soc., 103:* 94–158.

Eliot, T. S. 1948. *Notes towards the definition of culture.* New York, Harcourt.

Emerson, R. A., and E. M. East. 1913. The inheritance of quantitative characters in maize. *Nebraska Agr. Exp. Sta., 2:* 1–120.

Etkin, W. 1954. Social behavior and the evolution of man's mental faculties. *Am. Nat., 88:* 129–42.

Falconer, D. S. 1960. *Introduction to quantitative genetics.* Edinburgh, Oliver & Boyd.

Falk, R. 1961. Are induced mutations in Drosophila overdominant? II. Experimental results. *Genetics, 46:* 737–57.

Fenner, F. 1959. Myxomatosis in Australian wild rabbit—evolutionary changes in an infectious disease. *Harvey Lectures, 1957–58:* 25–55.

———, M. F. Day, and G. M. Woodroofe. 1956. Epidemiological consequences of the mechanical transmission of myxomatosis by mosquitoes. *J. Hyg., 54:* 284–303.

———, and I. D. Marshall. 1957. A comparison of the virulence for European rabbit *(Oryctolagus cuniculus)* of strains of myxoma virus recovered in the field in Australia, Europe, and America. *J. Hyg., 55:* 149–91.

Ferguson, R. G. 1955. *Studies in tuberculosis.* Toronto, Univ. of Toronto Press.

Firth, R. 1955. Function, pp. 237–58. *In Yearbook of Anthropology,* New York, Wenner-Gren Foundation.

Fischer, J. L. 1960. The role of religion as viewed by the science of man, pp. 216–41. *In* H. Shapley, *Science ponders religion,* New York, Appleton-Century.

Fisher, R., and J. Vaughan. 1939. Surnames and blood groups. *Nature, 144:* 1047.

Fisher, R. A. 1930. *The genetical theory of natural selection.* Oxford, Clarendon.

Fiske, J. 1909. *The meaning of infancy.* Boston, Houghton Mifflin.

Forssman, O., and B. Lindegard. 1958. The post-coronary patient. *J. Psychosomatic Research, 3:* 89–169.

Freedman, L. Z., and A. E. Roe. 1958. Evolution and human behavior, pp. 455–79. *In* A. Roe and G. G. Simpson, *Behavior and evolution,* New Haven, Yale Univ. Press.

Freud, S. 1913 (1931). *Totem and taboo.* New York, New Republic.

——— 1930 (1951). *Civilization and its discontents.* London, Internat. Psychoanalytical Library, No. 17, Hogarth.

Friedman, M., and R. H. Rosenman. 1957. Comparison of fat intake of American men and women: possible relationships to incidence of clinical coronary artery disease. *Circulation, 16:* 339–47.

Frisch, J. E. 1959. Research on primate behavior in Japan. *Am. Anthropol., 61:* 584–96.

Frisch, K. v. 1955. *The dancing bees.* New York, Harcourt Brace.

Fromm, E. 1951. *The forgotten language.* New York, Grove Press.

Fuller, J. L., and J. P. Scott. 1954. Heredity and learning ability in infrahuman mammals. *Eugenics Quart., 1:* 28–43.

———, and W. R. Thompson. 1960. *Behavior genetics.* New York, John Wiley.

Galton, F. 1869. *Hereditary genius.* London, Macmillan.

——— 1876. The history of twins as a criterion of the relative powers of nature and nurture. *J. Anthropol. Inst., 5:* 391–406.

——— 1883. *Inquiries into human faculty and its development.* London, Macmillan.

Gandhi, M. 1959. *All men are brothers.* New York, Columbia Univ. Press.

Garn, S. M. 1961. *Human races.* Springfield, Thomas.

Gartler, S. M., Th. Dobzhansky, and H. K. Berry. 1955. Chromatographic studies on urinary excretion patterns in monozygous and dizygotic twins. II. *Am. J. Human Genet., 7:* 108–21.

Gates, R. R. 1948. *Human ancestry from a genetical point of view.* Cambridge, Harvard Univ. Press.

Gentry, J. T., E. Parkhurst, and G. V. Bulin, 1959. An epidemiological study of congenital malformations in New York state. *Am. J. Public Health, 49:* 1–22.

Gertler, M. M., and P. D. White. 1954. *Coronary heart disease in young adults.* Cambridge, Harvard Univ. Press.

Gesell, A., and C. S. Amatruda. 1941. *Developmental diagnosis.* 2nd Ed. New York, Hoeber.

———, and H. Thompson. 1941. Twins T and C from infancy to adolescence: a biogenetic study of individual differences by the method of co-twin control. *Genet. Psychol. Monogr., 24:* 3–121.

Ghurye, G. S. 1957. *Caste and class in India.* 3rd Ed., Bombay, Popular Book Depot.

——— 1959. *The scheduled tribes.* 2nd Ed. Bombay, Popular Book Depot.

Gieseler, W. 1959. Die Fossilgeschichte des Menschen, pp. 951–1109. *In* G. Heberer, *Die Evolution der Organismen,* Vol. 2. Stuttgart, Fischer.

Goddard, H. H. 1946. What is intelligence? *J. Soc. Psychol., 24:* 51–69.

Gorer, J. 1948. *The American people.* New York, Norton.

———, and J. Rickman. 1950. *The people of Great Russia.* New York, Chanticleer.

Goto, G. 1958. The mechanism of inheritance of poliomyelitis. *J. Heredity, 49:* 38–9.

Goudge, T. A. 1957. Is evolution finished? *Univ. Toronto Quart., 26:* 430–42.

Greenacre, P. 1949. Infant reactions to restraint, pp. 390–406. *In* C. Kluckhohn and H. A. Murray, *Personality in nature, society, and culture,* New York, Knopf.

Greene, J. C. 1959a. Biology and social theory in the nineteenth century: Auguste Comte and Herbert Spencer. *In* Clagett, *Critical problems of the history of science,* Wisconsin, Madison.

——— 1959b. *The death of Adam.* Ames, Iowa Univ. Press.

Grigg, E. R. N. 1958. The arcana of tuberculosis, with a brief epidemiological history of the disease in the U.S.A. *Am. Rev. Tuberc. and Pulmonary Disease, 78:* 151–72, 426–53, 583–603.

Hadas, M. 1959. *Hellenistic culture.* New York, Columbia Univ. Press.

Haldane, J. B. S. 1932. *The causes of evolution.* London, Longmans Green.

——— 1949. Disease and evolution. *La Ricerca Sci., 19, Suppl.:* 68–76.

——— 1959. Natural selection. *In* P. R. Bell, *Darwin's biological work; some aspects reconsidered.* Cambridge Univ. Press.

Hall, C. S., and G. Lindzey. 1954. Psychoanalytic theory and its applications in the social sciences, pp. 143–180. *In* G. Lindzey, *Handbook of social psychology,* Cambridge, Wesley.

Hallowell, A. I. 1953. Culture, personality, and society, pp. 597–620. *In* A. L. Kroeber, *Anthropology today,* Chicago, Univ. of Chicago Press.

——— 1956. The structural and functional dimensions of a human culture. *Quart. Rev. Biol., 31:* 88–101.

——— 1960. Self, society, and culture in phylogenetic perspective, pp. 309–371. *In* S. Tax, *Evolution after Darwin,* Vol. 2. Chicago, Univ. of Chicago Press.

Hammel, H. T. 1960. Response to cold by the Alacaluf Indians. *Current Anthropol., 1:* 146.

Hammond, W. H. 1957a. The constancy of physical types as determined by factorial analysis. *Human Biol., 29:* 40–61.

——— 1957b. The status of physical types. *Human Biol., 29:* 223–41.

Hardin, G. 1959. *Nature and man's fate.* New York, Rinehart.

Harlow, H. F. 1958. The evolution of learning, pp. 269–90. *In* G. G. Simpson and A. Roe, *Behavior and evolution,* New Haven, Yale Univ. Press.

Harris, H. 1950. The familial distribution of diabetes mellitus: a study of the relatives of 1241 diabetic propositi. *Ann. Eugenics, 15:* 95–119.

——— 1959. *Human biochemical genetics.* New York, Cambridge Univ. Press.

Hauser, A. 1951. *The social history of art.* New York, Knopf.

Hauser, P. M. 1960. Demographic dimensions of world politics. *Science, 131:* 1641–47.

Hayes, C. 1951. *The ape in our house.* New York, Harper.

Hayes, K. J., and C. Hayes. 1954. The cultural capacity of chimpanzee. *Human Biol., 26:* 288–303.

Heberer, G. 1951. Grundlinien in der pleistocänen Entfaltungsgeschichte der Euhominiden. *Quartär, 5:* 50–78.

——— 1956. Die Fossilgeschichte der Hominoidea. *Primatologia, 1:* 379–560.

——— 1959a. Die subhumane Abstammungsgeschichte des Menschen, pp. 1110–42. *In* G. Heberer, *Die Evolution der Organismen,* Vol. 2. Stuttgart, Fischer.

——— 1959b. The descent of man and the present fossil record. *Cold Spring Harbor Symp. Quant. Biol., 24:* 235–44.

Henry, G. W. 1955. *All the sexes.* New York, Rinehart.

Herbert, S. 1910. *The first principles of heredity.* London, Blacks.

Herre, W. 1959. Domestikation und Stammesgeschichte, pp. 801–56. *In* G. Heberer, *Die Evolution der Organismen,* Vol. 2. Stuttgart, Fischer.

Hess, E. H. 1959. Imprinting. *Science, 130:* 133–41.

Hirsch, N. D. 1930. *Twins: heredity and environment.* Cambridge, Harvard Univ. Press.

Ho, Ping-ti. 1959a. Aspects of social mobility in China, 1368–1911. *Comp. Studies in Soc. & Hist., 1:* 330–59.

——— 1959b. *Studies on the population of China, 1368–1953.* Cambridge, Harvard Univ. Press.

Hoch, P. H., and J. Zubin. 1949. *Psychosexual development in health and disease.* New York, Grune & Stratton.

Hockett, C. F. 1954. Chinese versus English: an exploration of the Whorfian theses. *In* H. Hoijer, *Language in Culture,* Am. Anthropol. Assoc., Mem. No. 79.

——— 1959. Animal "languages" and human language, pp. 32–9. *In* J. N. Spuhler, *The evolution of man's capacity for culture,* Detroit, Wayne Univ. Press.

Hofstadter, R. 1955. *Social Darwinism in American thought.* Boston, Beacon.

Hoijer, H. 1954. Language in culture. *Am. Anthropol. Assoc., Mem.* No. 79.

Hook, S. 1959. *Psychoanalysis, scientific method, and philosophy.* New York, New York Univ. Press.

Hooton, E. A., and C. W. Dupertuis. 1955. *The physical anthropology of Ireland.* Cambridge, Peabody Museum Papers, Harvard Univ. Press.

Howell, F. C. 1951. The place of Neanderthal man in human evolution. *Am. J. Phys. Anthropol., 9:* 379–416.

———— 1957. The evolutionary significance of variation and varieties of Neanderthal man. *Quart. Rev. Biol., 32:* 330–47.

———— 1958. Upper Pleistocene men of the Southwest Asian Mousterian, pp. 185–98. *In Neanderthal Centennary,* Utrecht, Kemink.

———— 1959. The Villafranchian and human origins. *Science, 130:* 831–44.

Howells, W. W. 1952. A factorial study of constitutional type. *Am. J. Phys. Anthropol., 10:* 91–118.

———— 1955. Universality and variation in human nature. *Yearbook Anthropol.:* 227–36. New York, Wenner-Gren Foundation.

Hsia, D. Y. Y. 1959. *Inborn errors of metabolism.* Chicago, Year Book Publ.

Hsu, F. L. K. 1959. The family in China: the classical form, pp. 123–45. *In* Ruth N. Anshen, *The family. Its function and destiny,* 2nd Ed., New York.

Huizinga, J. 1955. *Homo ludens.* Boston, Beacon.

Hulse, F. S. 1955. Technological advance and major racial stocks. *Human Biol., 27:* 184–92.

———— 1957. Some factors influencing the relative proportions of human racial stocks. *Cold Spring Harbor Symp. Quant. Biol., 22:* 33–45.

Hunt, E. E. 1959. Anthropometry, genetics, and racial history. *Am. Anthropol., 61:* 64–87.

————, and W. H. Barton. 1959. The inconstancy of physique in adolescent boys and other limitations of somatotyping. *Am. J. Phys. Anthropol., 17:* 27–35.

Hurzeler, J. 1958. *Oreopithecus bambolii Gervais:* a preliminary report. *Verh. Naturf. Ges. Basel, 69:* 1–48.

Hutchinson, G. E. 1959. A speculative consideration of certain possible forms of sexual selection in man. *Am. Nat., 93:* 81–91.

Huxley, J. S. 1941. *The uniqueness of man.* London, Chatto & Windus.

———— 1953. *Evolution in action.* New York, Harper.

———— 1960. The evolutionary vision, pp. 249–61. *In* S. Tax, *Evolution after Darwin,* Vol. 3. Chicago, Univ. of Chicago Press.

Huxley, T. H., and J. S. Huxley. 1947. *Touchstone for ethics.* New York, Harper.

Imanishi, K. 1957. Identification: a process of enculturation in the subhuman society of Macaca fuscata. *Primates, 1:* 1–29.

———— 1960. Social organization of subhuman primates in their natural habitat. *Current Anthropol., 1:* 393–407.

Inkeles, A., and D. J. Levinson. 1954. National character: the study of modal personality and sociocultural system, pp. 977–1020. *In* G. Lindzey, *Handbook of social psychology,* Cambridge, Wesley.

Jarvik, L. F., A. Falek, F. J. Kallmann, and I. Lorge. 1960. Survival trends in a senescent twin population. *Am. J. Human Genet., 12:* 170–79.

————, F. J. Kallmann, A. Falek, and M. M. Klaber. 1957. Changing intellectual functions in senescent twins. *Acta Genet. Stat. Medica, 7:* 421–30.

Jenkins, I. 1958. *Art and human enterprise.* Cambridge, Harvard Univ. Press.

Johannsen, W. 1909. *Elemente der exakten Erblichkeitslehre.* Jena, Fischer.

———— 1911. The genotype conception of heredity. *Am. Nat., 45:* 129–59.

Jones, E. 1955–1957. *The life and work of Sigmund Freud.* New York, Basic Books.

Juda, A. 1953. *Hochstbegabung.* München, Urban & Schwarzenberg.

Jung, C. G. 1933 (1955). *Modern man in search of a soul.* New York, Harcourt Brace.

Kallmann, F. J. 1952. Twins and susceptibility to overt male homosexuality. *Am. J. Human Genet., 4:* 136–46.

———— 1953. *Heredity in health and mental disorder.* New York, Norton.

———— 1957. Twin data on the genetics of aging. *Ciba Found. Coll. on Ageing, 3:* 131–43.

Keith, A. 1949. *A new theory of human evolution.* New York, Philosophical Library.

Kempthorne, O. 1957. *An introduction to genetic statistics.* New York, John Wiley.

Kettlewell, H. B. D. 1956. Further selection experiments on industrial melanism in the Lepidoptera. *Heredity, 10:* 287–301.

———— 1958. A survey of the frequencies of Biston betularia L. and its melanic forms in Great Britain. *Heredity, 12:* 51–72.

Kety, S. S. 1959. Biochemical theories of schizophrenia. *Science, 129:* 1590–96.

Keys, A., and P. D. White. 1956. *Cardiovascular epidemiology.* New York, Hoeber-Harper.

Kimball, O. P., and A. H. Hersh. 1954. The genetics of epilepsy. *Acta Genet. Med. Gemel., 4:* 131–41.

Kinsey, A. C., W. B. Pomeroy, and C. E. Martin. 1948. *Sexual behavior in the human male.* Philadelphia, Saunders.

————, ————, ————. 1953. *Sexual behavior in the human female.* Philadelphia, Saunders.

Kirk, D. 1957. The fertility of a gifted group: a study of the number of children of men in *Who's Who. Milbank Mem. Fund, 1956 Ann. Conf.:* 78–98.

Klineberg, O. 1935. *Race differences.* New York, Harper.

———— 1954. *Social psychology.* 2nd Ed. New York, Henry Holt.

Klopfer, P. H. 1959. An analysis of learning in young Anatidae. *Ecology, 40:* 90–102.

Kluckhohn, C. 1949. *Mirror for man.* New York, McGraw Hill.

———— 1954. Culture and behavior, pp. 921–76. *In* G. Lindzey, *Handbook of social psychology,* Cambridge, Wesley.

————, and W. H. Kelly. 1945. The concept of culture, pp. 78–106. *In* R. Linton, *The science of man in the world crisis,* New York, Columbia Univ. Press.

————, and H. A. Murray. 1949. *Personality in nature, society, and culture.* New York, Knopf.

Koenigswald, G. H. R. v. 1958. Der Solo Mensch von Java: ein tropischer Neanderthaler. *Neanderthal Centennary,* pp. 21–6. Utrecht, Kemink.

Köhler, W. 1921. *The mentality of apes.* New York, Harcourt Brace.

Kratchman, J., and D. Grahn. 1959. *Relationships between the geologic envi-ronment and mortality from congenital malformation*. U.S. Atomic Energy Commission, Washington.

Kretschmer, E. 1951. *Körperbau und Charakter*. 20th Ed. Berlin, Springer.

Kroeber, A. L. 1917 (1952). The superorganic. *Am. Anthropol., 19:* 163–213. *Reprinted in* A. L. Kroeber, *The nature of culture*, Chicago, Univ. of Chicago Press.

—— 1939 (1952). Totem and taboo in retrospect. *Am. J. Sociol., 45:* 446–51. *Reprinted in* A. L. Kroeber, *The nature of culture*, Chicago, Univ. of Chicago Press.

—— 1960. Evolution, history, and culture, pp. 1–16. *In* S. Tax, *Evolution after Darwin*, Vol. 2. Chicago, Univ. of Chicago Press.

Krogh, C. v. 1959. Die Stellung der Hominiden in Rahmen der Primaten, pp. 917–50. *In* G. Heberer, *Die Evolution der Organismen*, Vol. 2. Stuttgart, Fischer.

Kropotkin, P. 1902 (1955). *Mutual aid. A factor of evolution*. Boston, Extend-ing Horizons.

Krutch, J. W. 1957. *The great chain of life*. Boston, Houghton Mifflin.

Kurlander, A. B., S. Abraham, and J. W. Rion. 1956. Obesity and disease. *Human Biol., 28:* 203–16.

Kurth, G. 1960a. Zinjanthropus boisei aus dem Unterpleistozän von Oldoway, Ostafrika. *Naturwissen., 47:* 265–74.

—— 1960b. Les restes humains wurmiens du gisement de Shanidar, Nord-Est Irak. *L'Anthropologie, 64:* 36–63.

La Barre, W. 1954. *The human animal*. Chicago, Univ. of Chicago Press.

Lack, D. 1947. *Darwin's finches*. New York, Macmillan.

Leake, C. D., and P. Romanell. 1950. *Can we agree?* Austin, Univ. of Texas Press.

Leakey, L. S. B. 1959. A new fossil skull from Olduval. *Nature, 184:* 491–93.

—— 1960. The origin of the genus Homo, pp. 17–32. *In* S. Tax, *Evolution after Darwin*, Vol. 2. Chicago, Univ. of Chicago Press.

Lee, D. D. 1949. Being and value in a primitive culture. *J. Philosophy, 46:* 401–15.

—— 1956. Linguistic reflections on Wintu thought. *Explorations, 6:* 6–14.

Le Gros Clark, W. E. 1955. *The fossil evidence of human evolution*. Chicago, Univ. of Chicago Press.

—— 1959. The study of man's descent, pp. 173–205. *In* S. A. Barnett, *A century of Darwin*, London, Heinemann.

Lehrman, D. S. 1953. A critique of Konrad Lorenz's theory of instinctive be-havior. *Quart. Rev. Biol., 28:* 337–63.

—— 1955. The physiological basis of parental feeding behavior in the ring dove *(Streptopelia risoria). Behavior, 7:* 241–86.

Lenneberg, E. H. 1960. Language, evolution, and purposive behavior, pp. 871–93. *In* S. Diamond, *Culture in History*, New York, Columbia Univ. Press.

Lerner, I. M. 1950. *Population genetics and animal improvement*. Cambridge, Cambridge Univ. Press.

—— 1954. *Genetic homeostasis*. New York, John Wiley.

—— 1958. *The genetic basis of selection*. New York, John Wiley.

Lerner, M. 1957. *America as a civilization*. New York, Simon & Schuster.

Levi-Strauss, C. 1960. The family, pp. 261–85. *In* H. L. Shapiro, *Man, culture, and society*, New York, Oxford Univ. Press.

Li, C. C. 1955. *Population genetics*. Chicago, Univ. of Chicago Press.

Lindegard, B. 1956. Body-build, body function, and personality. *Lunds Univ. Årsskrift, 52*.

Linton, R. 1955. *The tree of culture*. New York, Knopf.

Lorenz, K. Z. 1943. Die enbegorenen Formen moglicher Erfahrung. *Zeits. Tierpsychol., 5:* 235–409.

———— 1952. *King Solomon's ring*. New York, Crowell.

Lorimer, F. 1954. *Culture and human fertility*. Paris, Unesco.

Lovejoy, A. O. 1936 (1960). *The great chain of being: a study of the history of an idea*. Cambridge, Harvard Univ. Press and New York, Harper Torchbooks.

Malinowski, B. 1927a. *Sex and repression in savage society*. New York, Harcourt Brace.

———— 1927b. *The father in primitive society*. New York, Norton.

Malzberg, B. 1955. Trends of mental disease in New York state 1920–1950. *Proc. Am. Philos. Soc., 99:* 174–83.

Mandel, S. P. H. 1959. The stability of a multiple allelic system. *Heredity, 13:* 289–302.

Mark, J. C. 1953. The attitudes of the mothers of male schizophrenics towards child behavior. *J. Abnorm. and Soc. Psychol., 48:* 185–89.

Marks, H. H. 1956. Body weight: facts from life insurance records. *Human Biol., 28:* 217–31.

Marshall, A. J. 1954. *Bower-birds, their displays and breeding cycles*. Oxford, Clarendon.

———— 1960. Bowerbirds. *Endeavour, 19:* 202–08.

Maslow, A. H. 1954. *Motivation and personality*. New York, Harper.

Mather, K. 1943. Polygenic inheritance and natural selection. *Biol. Reviews, 18:* 32–64.

———— 1951. *Biometrical genetics*. 2nd Ed. London, Methuen.

———— 1955. Polymorphism as an outcome of disruptive selection. *Evolution, 9:* 52–61.

Mayr, E. 1942. *Systematics and the origin of species*. New York, Columbia Univ. Press.

———— 1950. Taxonomic categories in fossil hominids. *Cold Spring Harbor Symp. Quant. Biol., 15:* 109–18.

Mead, M. 1953. National character, pp. 642–67. *In* A. Kroeber, *Anthropology today*, Chicago, Univ. of Chicago Press.

———— 1954. The swaddling hypothesis: its reception. *Am. Anthropol., 56:* 395–409.

Mettler, F. A. 1956. *Culture and the structural evolution of the neural system*. New York, Am. Museum Nat. Hist.

Millicent, E., and J. M. Thoday. 1960. Gene flow and divergence under disruptive selection. *Science, 131:* 1311–12.

Miyadi, D. 1959. On some new habits and their propagation in Japanese monkey groups. *Proc. 15th Internat. Congr. Zool.* (London): 857–60.

Mollison, T. 1941. Der Aufbau des Arteiweisses in Stammesgeschichte und Einzelentwicklung. *Scientia, 35:* 154–65.

Montagu, Ashley. 1955a. *The direction of human development.* New York, Harper.

—— 1955b. Time, morphology, and neoteny in the evolution of man. *Am. Anthropol., 57:* 13–27.

—— 1959. *Human heredity.* Cleveland & New York, World Publishing Co.

Mørch, E. T. 1941. Chondrodystrophic dwarfs in Denmark. *Opera ex Domo Biol. Hered. Hum. Univ. Hafniensis, 3:* 1–200.

Morris, D. 1961. Primate's aesthetics. *Nat. History, 70:* 22–9.

Morris, M. D. 1960. Caste and the evolution of the industrial workforce in India. *Proc. Am. Philos. Soc., 104:* 124–33.

Morton, N. E., and C. S. Chung. 1959a. Are the MN blood groups maintained by selection? *Am. J. Human Genet., 11:* 237–51.

——, and ——. 1959b. Formal genetics of muscular dystrophy. *Am. J. Human Genet., 11:* 360–79.

——, J. F. Crow, and H. J. Muller. 1956. An estimate of the mutational damage in man from data on consanguineous marriages. *Proc. Nat. Acad. Sci., 42:* 855–63.

Motulsky, A. 1960a. Population genetics of glucose–6–phosphate dehydrogenase deficiency of the red cell. *Proc. Conf. Genet. Polymorphisms,* U.S. Dept. Health: 258–92.

—— 1960b. Metabolic polymorphisms and the role of infectious diseases in human evolution. *Human Biol., 32:* 28–62.

Mourant, A. R. 1954. *The distribution of the human blood groups.* Oxford, Blackwell.

—— 1959a. Human blood groups and natural selection. *Cold Spring Harbor Symp. Quant. Biol., 24:* 57–63.

—— 1959b. The blood groups of the Jews. *Jewish J. Sociology, 1:* 155–76.

——, A. C. Kopec, and K. Domaniewska-Sobczak. 1958. *The ABO blood groups: comprehensive tables and maps of world distribution.* Oxford, Blackwell.

——, and I. M. Watkin. 1952. Blood groups, anthropology, and language in Wales and the Western counties. *Heredity, 6:* 13–36.

Movius, H. L. 1948. The lower Palaeolithic cultures of southern and eastern Asia. *Trans. Am. Philos. Soc., 38:* 329–420.

—— 1953. Old World prehistory: Palaeolithic, pp. 163–92. *In* A. L. Kroeber, *Anthropology today,* Chicago, Univ. of Chicago Press.

Muller, H. J. 1935. *Out of the night: a biologist's view of the future.* New York, Vanguard.

—— 1950. Our load of mutations. *Am. J. Human Genet., 2:* 111–76.

—— 1954. The nature of the genetic effects produced by radiation, pp. 351–473. *In* A. Hollaender, *Radiation biology,* Vol. 1. New York, McGraw Hill.

—— 1959 (1960). The guidance of human evolution. *Persp. Biol. Med., 3:* 1–43. Also pp. 423–62 *in* S. Tax, *Evolution after Darwin,* Chicago, Univ. of Chicago Press.

——, and R. Falk. 1961. Are induced mutations in Drosophila overdominant? I. Experimental design. *Genetics, 46:* 727–35.

Muller, Herbert J. 1957. *The uses of the past.* New York, Oxford Univ. Press.

Murdock, G. P. 1945. The common denominators of cultures, pp. 123–42. *In* R. Linton, *The science of man in the world crisis,* New York, Columbia Univ. Press.

——— 1949. *Social structure.* New York, Macmillan.

——— 1959. Evolution in social organization, pp. 126–43. *In Evolution and anthropology. A centennial appraisal,* Washington, Anthropol. Society.

Murphy, G. 1958. *Human potentialities.* New York, Basic Books.

McCown, T. D. 1950. The genus *Palaeoanthropus* and the problem of super-specific differentiation among the Hominidae. *Cold Spring Harbor Symp. Quant. Biol., 15:* 87–94.

———, and A. Keith. 1939. *The stone age of Mount Carmel.* Oxford, Clarendon.

National Academy of Sciences, U.S.A. 1956. *The biological effects of atomic radiation. Summary Report.* Washington, D.C.

——— 1960. *The biological effects of atomic radiation. Summary Report.* Washington, D.C.

National Health Education Committee. 1959. *Facts on the major killing and crippling diseases in the United States today.* New York.

Neel, J. V. 1956. The genetics of human hemoglobin differences. *Ann. Human Genet., 21:* 1–30.

——— 1958a. A study of major congenital defects in Japanese infants. *Am. J. Human Genet., 10:* 398–445.

——— 1958b. The study of natural selection in primitive and civilized human populations. *Human Biol., 30:* 43–72.

———, and W. J. Schull. 1954. *Human heredity.* Chicago, Univ. of Chicago Press.

Nesturkh, M. F. 1958. *The origin of man* [in Russian]. Moscow, Acad. Sci. USSR.

Newman, H. H. 1940. *Multiple human births.* New York, Doubleday.

———, F. N. Freeman, and K. J. Holzinger. 1937. *Twins: a study of heredity and environment.* Chicago, Univ. of Chicago Press.

Newman, M. T. 1953. The application of ecological rules to the racial anthropology of the aboriginal New World. *Am. Anthropol., 55:* 311–27.

——— 1961. Biological adaptation of man to his environment: heat, cold, altitude, and nutrition. *Ann. N.Y. Acad. Sci., 91:* 617–33.

Newman, R. W., and E. H. Munro. 1955. The relation of climate and body size in U.S. males. *Am. J. Phys. Anthropol., 13:* 1–17.

Niebuhr, R. 1941. *The nature and destiny of man.* New York, Scribner's.

Nilsson-Ehle, H. 1909. *Kreuzungsuntersuchungen an Hafer und Weizen.* Act. Univ. Lund.

Nissen, H. W. 1951. Social behavior in primates, pp. 423–57. *In* C. P. Stone, *Comparative psychology,* 3rd Ed., New York, Prentice Hall.

Northrop, F. S. C. 1950. Evolution in its relation to the philosophy of nature and the philosophy of culture, pp. 44–84. *In* S. Persons, *Evolutionary thought in America,* New Haven, Yale Univ. Press.

Oakley, K. P. 1954. Skill as a human possession, pp. 1–37. *In* C. J. Singer, *History of technology,* Vol. 1. New York, Oxford Univ. Press.

——— 1956a. The earliest tool-makers. *Antiquity, 30:* 4–8.

——— 1956b. The earliest fire-makers. *Antiquity, 30:* 102–07.

——— 1957. Tools makyth man. *Antiquity, 31:* 199–209.

———— 1958. Use of fire by Neanderthal man and his precursors, pp. 267–69. *In Neanderthal Centennary*, Utrecht, Kemink.

Ogburn, W. F., and N. K. Bose. 1959. On the trail of the wolf-children. *Gen. Psychol. Monogr., 60:* 117–93.

Okladnikov, A. P. 1958. The establishment of man and society [in Russian], pp. 121–53. *In Problemy Razvitia v Prirode i Obshchestve,* Moscow–Leningrad, Acad. Sci. USSR.

Osborn, F. 1951. *Preface to eugenics.* New York, Harper.

Osborn, R. H., and F. V. DeGeorge. 1959. *Genetic basis of morphological variation.* Cambridge, Harvard Univ. Press.

Page, I. H., L. A. Lewis, and J. Gilbert. 1956. Plasma lipids and proteins and their relationship to coronary disease among Navajo Indians. *Circulation, 13:* 675–79.

Parnell, R. W. 1954. Somatotyping by physical anthropometry. *Am. J. Phys. Anthropol., 12:* 209–39.

Pastore, N. 1949. *The nature-nurture controversy.* New York, King's Crown.

Patterson, B. 1954. The geologic history of nonhominoid primates in the Old World. *Human Biol., 26:* 191–209.

Pearl, R. 1922. *The biology of death.* Philadelphia, Lippincott.

Pearson, K. 1904. On the laws of inheritance in man. II. *Biometrica, 3:* 131–90.

————, and A. Lee. 1903. On the laws of inheritance in man. I. *Biometrica, 2:* 357–462.

Penfield, W., and L. Roberts. 1959. *Speech and brain-mechanisms.* Princeton, Princeton Univ. Press.

Penrose, L. S. 1949. *The biology of mental defect.* London, Sidgwick & Jackson.

———— 1950a. Genetical influences on the intelligence level of the population. *Brit. J. Psychol., 40:* 128–36.

———— 1950b. Propagation of the unfit. *Lancet, 259:* 425–27.

Philipchenko, J. 1934. *Genetics of soft wheats* [in Russian]. Moscow–Leningrad, State Publ. House.

Pimentel, R. A. 1959. Mendelian infraspecific divergence levels and their analysis. *Syst. Zool., 8:* 139–59.

Piveteau, J. 1957. *Traité de Paléontologie. Primates. Paléontologie humaine.* Paris, Masson.

Planansky, W., and G. Allen. 1953. Heredity in relation to variable resistance to pulmonary tuberculosis. *Am. J. Human Genet., 5:* 322–49.

Pontecorvo, G. 1958. *Trends in genetic analysis.* New York, Columbia Univ. Press.

Popenoe, P. B., and R. H. Johnson. 1918. *Applied eugenics.* New York, Macmillan.

Popham, R. M. 1953. The calculation of reproductive fitness and the mutation rate of the gene for chondrodystrophy. *Am. J. Human Genet., 5:* 73–5.

Portmann, A. 1944. *Biologische Fragmente zu einer Lehre vom Menschen.* Basel, Schwabe.

Rank, O. 1952. *The trauma of birth.* New York, Brunner.

Raphael, D. D. 1958. Darwinism and ethics, pp. 334–59. *In* S. A. Barnett, *A century of Darwin,* London, Heinemann.

Ray, C. 1960. The application of Bergmann's and Allen's rules to the poikilotherms. *J. Morphol., 106:* 85–108.

Reche, O., and W. Lehmann. 1959. Die Genetik der Rassenbildung beim Menschen, pp. 1143–91. *In* G. Heberer, *Die Evolution der Organismen,* Stuttgart, Fischer.

Rensch, B. 1947 (1959a). *Neuere Probleme der Abstammungslehre.* Stuttgart, Enke. Trans.: *Evolution above the species level.* London & New York, Methuen & Columbia Univ. Press.

———— 1957. Aesthetische Faktoren bei Farb- und Formbevorzugungen von Affen. *Zeits. Tierpsychology, 14:* 71–99.

———— 1958. Die Abhängigkeit des Struktur und der Leistung tierischer Gehirne von ihrer Grösse. *Naturwissenschaften, 45:* 145–54.

———— 1959b. *Homo sapiens. Vom Tier zum Halbgott.* Göttingen, Vandenhoeck & Ruprecht.

———— 1960. Trends towards progress of brains and sense organs. *Cold Spring Harbor Symp. Quant. Biol., 24:* 291–303.

————, and G. Dücker. 1959. Versuche uber visuelle Generalization bei einer Schleichkatze. *Zeits. Tierpsychologie, 16:* 671–92.

Richter, C. P. 1959. Rats, man, and the welfare state. *Am. Psychologist, 14:* 18–28.

Risley, H. H. 1915. *People of India.* 2nd Ed. Calcutta, Thaker Spink.

Rife, D. C., and L. H. Snyder. 1931. Studies on human inheritance. *Human Biol., 3:* 547–59.

Roberts, D. F. 1953. Body weight, race, and climate. *Am. J. Phys. Anthropol., 11:* 533–58.

———— 1956. A demographic study of Dinka village. *Human Biol., 28:* 324–49.

Roberts, J. A. Fraser. 1957. Blood groups and susceptibility to disease. *Brit. J. Prev. Soc. Med., 11:* 107–25.

———— 1959a. Some further observations on association between blood groups and disease. *Proc. X Internat. Congr. Genet., 1:* 120–28.

———— 1959b. Some associations between blood groups and disease. *Brit. Med. Bull., 15:* 129–33.

Robinson, J. T. 1954. The genera and species of the *Australopithecinae. Am. J. Phys. Anthropol., 12:* 181–200.

Roheim, G. 1950. *Psychoanalysis and anthropology.* New York, Internat. Univ. Press.

Rucknagel, D. L., and J. V. Neel. 1961. The hemoglobinopathies. *On press in* A. Steinberg, *Progress in medical genetics,* New York, Grune & Stratton.

Russell, W. L., L. B. Russell, and E. M. Kelly. 1958. Radiation dose rate and mutation frequency. *Science, 128:* 1546–50.

Sahlins, M. D., and E. R. Service. 1960. *Evolution and culture.* Ann Arbor, Univ. of Michigan Press.

Sanghvi, L. D. 1953. Comparison of genetical and morphological methods for a study of biological differences. *Am. J. Phys. Anthropol., 11:* 385–404.

Sapir, E. 1921 (1949). *Language.* New York, Harcourt Brace.

Sarton, G. 1952. *A history of science: Ancient science through the golden age of Greece.* Cambridge, Harvard Univ. Press.

———— 1959. *A history of science: Hellenistic science and culture in the last three centuries B.C.* Cambridge, Harvard Univ. Press.

Schaeffer, L. E., D. Adlersberg, and A. G. Steinberg. 1958. Heredity, environment, and serum cholesterol. *Circulation, 17:* 537–42.

Schmalhausen, I. I. 1949. *Factors of evolution*. Philadelphia, Blakiston.

Schneirla, T. C. 1955. Interrelationships of the "innate" and the "acquired" in the instinctive behavior, pp. 387–452. *In L'instinct dans le comportement des animaux et de l'homme*, Paris, Masson.

Scholander, P. F. 1955. Evolution of climatic adaptations in homeotherms. *Evolution, 9:* 15–26.

—— 1958. Studies on man exposed to cold. *Federation Proc., 17:* 1054–57.

——, H. T. Hammel, J. S. Hart, D. H. Le Messurier, and J. Steen. 1958a. Cold adaptation in Australian aborigenes. *J. Appl. Physiol., 13:* 211–18.

——, ——, K. Lange Andersen, and Y. Loyning. 1958b. Metabolic acclimatization to cold in man. *J. Appl. Physiol., 12:* 1–8.

——, R. Hock, W. Waters, L. Irving, and F. Johnson. 1950. Body insulation, heat regulation, and adaptation to cold in arctic and tropical mammals and birds. *Biol. Bull., 99:* 225–71.

Schull, W. J. 1958. Empirical risks in consanguineous marriages: Sex ratio, malformations, and viability. *Am. J. Human Genet., 10:* 294–343.

Schultz, A. H. 1950. The physical distinctions of man. *Proc. Am. Philos. Soc., 94:* 428–49.

—— 1956. Postembryonic age changes, pp. 887–964. *In* Hofer–Schultz–Starck, *Primatologia*, Vol. 1.

Schwidetzky, I. 1952. Selektionstheorie und Rassenbildung beim Menschen. *Experientia, 8:* 85–98.

Scottish Council for Research in Education. 1949. *The trend of Scottish intelligence*. London, Univ. of London Press.

—— 1953. *Social implications of the 1947 Scottish mental survey*. London, Univ. of London Press.

Selye, H. 1956. *The stress of life*. New York, McGraw Hill.

Sheldon, W. H., C. W. Dupertuis, and E. McDermott. 1954. *Atlas of men*. New York, Harper.

——, E. M. Hartl, and E. McDermott. 1949. *Varieties of delinquent youth*. New York, Harper.

——, and S. S. Stevens. 1942. *The varieties of temperament*. New York, Harper.

——, ——, and W. B. Tucker. 1940. *The varieties of human physique*. New York, Harper.

Sheppard, P. M. 1959. Blood groups and natural selection. *Brit. Med. Bull., 15:* 134–39.

Simon, H. J. 1960. *Attenuated infection*. Philadelphia, Lippincott.

Simpson, G. G. 1944. *Tempo and mode in evolution*. New York, Columbia Univ. Press.

—— 1945. The principles of classification and a classification of mammals. *Bull. Am. Museum Nat. Hist. 85*.

—— 1949. *The meaning of evolution*. New Haven, Yale Univ. Press.

—— 1953. *The major features of evolution*. New York, Columbia Univ. Press.

Singer, R. 1954. The Saldanha skull from Hopefield, South Africa. *Am. J. Phys. Anthropol., 12:* 345–62.

Singh, J. A. L., and R. M. Zingg. 1942. *Wolf-children and feral man*. New York, Harper.

Siniscalco, M., M. d'Agostino, and A. Iannaccone. 1953. Contributo al problema genetico del diabete mellito. *La Ricerca Sci., Suppl. 23:* 71–80.

Sinnott, E. W., L. C. Dunn, and Th. Dobzhansky. 1958. *Principles of genetics.* 5th Ed. New York, McGraw Hill.

Sjögren, T. 1957. The genetics of schizophrenia. *Rep. 2nd Internat. Congr. Psychiatry, 1:* 312–18.

Slater, M. K. 1959. Ecological factors in the origin of incest. *Am. Anthropol., 61:* 1042–59.

Snyder, C. R. 1958. *Alcohol and the Jews.* New Haven, Yale Univ. Press.

Sorsby, A. (Ed.) 1953. *Clinical genetics.* London, Butterworth.

Spassky, B., N. Spassky, O. Pavlovsky, M. G. Krimbas, C. Krimbas, and Th. Dobzhansky. 1960. Genetics of natural populations. XXIX. *Genetics, 45:* 723–40.

Spiess, E. B. 1958. Effects of recombination on viability in *Drosophila. Cold Spring Harbor Symp. Quant. Biol., 23:* 239–50.

Spuhler, J. N. 1959. Somatic paths to culture. *Human Biol., 31:* 1–13.

―――― 1962. Empirical studies on quantitative human genetics (in press).

Steinberg, A. 1959. The genetics of diabetes. *Ann. New York Acad. Sci., 82:* 197–207.

―――― , and R. M. Wilder, 1952. A study of the genetics of diabetes mellitus. *Am. J. Human Genet., 4:* 113–35.

Stephens, F. E. 1943. An achondroplastic mutation and the nature of its inheritance. *J. Heredity, 34:* 229–35.

Stern, C. 1953. Model estimates of the frequency of white and near-white segregants in the American Negro. *Acta Gen. Stat. Medica, 4:* 281–98.

―――― 1960. *Human genetics.* 2nd Ed. San Francisco, Freeman.

Steward, J. N. 1953. Evolution and process, pp. 313–26. *In* A. L. Kroeber, *Anthropology today,* Chicago, Univ. of Chicago Press.

―――― 1960. Evolution and social typology, pp. 169–86. *In* S. Tax, *Evolution after Darwin,* Vol. 2. Chicago, Univ. of Chicago Press.

Stewart, T. D. 1960. Form of the pubic bone in Neanderthal man. *Science, 131:* 1437–38.

Stolyhwo, K. 1924 (1950). Fundamental and secondary types in Europe, pp. 351–53. *In* E. W. Count, *This is race,* New York, Schuman.

Stone, C. P. 1951. Maturation and "instinctive" functions, pp. 30–61. *In* C. P. Stone, *Comparative psychology,* 3rd Ed., New York, Prentice Hall.

Strandskov, H. H. 1954. A twin study pertaining to the genetics of intelligence. *Atti IX Congr. Internat. Genetica, 2:* 811–13.

Straus, W. L. 1949. The riddle of man's ancestry. *Quart. Rev. Biol., 24:* 200–23.

―――― , and M. A. Schön. 1960. Cranial capacity of *Oreopithecus bambolii. Science, 132:* 670–72.

Sutter, J. 1958. Recherches sur les effets de la consanguinité chez l'homme. *Biologie Médicale, 47:* 563–660.

Swellengrebel, N. H. 1940. The efficient parasite, *Proc. 3rd Internat. Congr. Microbiol.:* 119–27.

Tappen, N. C. 1953. A mechanistic theory of human evolution. *Am. Anthropol., 55:* 605–07.

Tax, S. 1960. The celebration, a personal view, pp. 271–82. *In* S. Tax, *Evolution after Darwin,* Vol. 3. Chicago, Univ. of Chicago Press.

Teilhard de Chardin, P. 1955. *Le phénomène humain*. Paris, Du Seuil.
—— 1959. *The phenomenon of man*. New York, Harper.
Thoday, J. M. 1953. Components of fitness. *Symp. Soc. Exp. Biol., 7:* 96–113.
—— 1955. Balance, heterozygosity, and developmental stability. *Cold Spring Harbor Symp. Quant. Biol., 20:* 318–26.
—— 1959. Effects of disruptive selection. I. Genetic flexibility. *Heredity, 13:* 187–203.
——, and T. B. Boam. 1959. Effects of disruptive selection. II. Polymorphism and divergence without isolation. *Heredity, 13:* 205–18.
Thorpe, W. H. 1956. *Learning and instinct in animals*. London, Methuen.
Thurstone, T. G., L. L. Thurstone, and H. H. Strandskov. 1953. *A psychological study of twins. Psychometr. Labor., Univ. N. Carolina*, No. 4.
Tinbergen, N. 1951. *The study of instinct*. Oxford, Clarendon.
—— 1953. *Social behavior in animals*. London, Methuen.
—— 1959. Behaviour, systematics, and natural selection. *Ibis, 101:* 318–30.
Todd, G. F., and J. I. Mason. 1959. Concordance of smoking habits in monozygotic and dizygotic twins. *Heredity, 13:* 417–44.
Tuddenham, R. D. 1948. Soldier intelligence in world wars I and II. *Am. Psychol., 3:* 54–6.
Turresson, G. 1922. The genotype response of the plants species to the habitat. *Hereditas, 3:* 211–350.
United Nations. 1953. *The determinants and consequences of population trends*. New York, Population studies.
—— 1958. *Report of the United Nations scientific committee on the effects of atomic radiation*. New York.
Vandenberg, S. G. 1956. The hereditary abilities study. *Eugenics Quart., 3:* 94–9.
Verschuer, O. F. v. 1954. *Wirksame Faktoren im Leben des Menschen*. Wiesbaden, Steiner.
—— 1957. Über den genetischen Ursprung der Begabung. *Jahrb. 1957 Akad. Wissen. Literatur:* 230–46.
Vogel, F., H. J. Pettenkofer, and W. Helmbold. 1961. Uber die Populationsgenetik der ABO Blutgruppen. *Acta Gen. Stat. Med., 10:* 267–94.
Waddington, C. H. 1942. *Science and ethics*. London, Allen & Unwin.
—— 1957. *The strategy of the genes*. London, Allen & Unwin.
—— 1960. *The ethical animal*. London, Allen & Unwin.
Wallace, B. 1948. Studies on "sex-ratio" in *Drosophila pseudoobscura. Evolution, 2:* 189–217.
—— 1958. The average effect of radiation-induced mutations on viability in *Drosophila melanogaster. Evolution, 12:* 532–56.
——, and Th. Dobzhansky. 1959. *Radiation, genes, and man*. New York, Holt.
Washburn, S. L. 1950. The analysis of primate evolution with particular reference to the origin of man. *Cold Spring Harbor Symp. Quant. Biol., 15:* 67–78.
—— 1953. The strategy of physical anthropology, pp. 714–27. *In* A. L. Kroeber, *Anthropology today*, Chicago, Univ. of Chicago Press.
—— 1959. Speculations on the interrelations of the history of tools and biological evolution. *Human Biol., 31:* 21–31.

————, and V. Avis. 1958. Evolution of human behavior, pp. 421–36. *In* A. Roe and G. G. Simpson, *Behavior and evolution*, New Haven, Yale Univ. Press.

————, and F. C. Howell. 1960. Human evolution and culture, pp. 33–56. *In* S. Tax, *Evolution after Darwin*, Vol. 2. Chicago, Univ. of Chicago Press.

Watson, J. B. 1924. *Behaviorism*. New York, Norton.

Watson, J. D., and F. H. C. Crick. 1953. The structure of DNA. *Cold Spring Harbor Symp. Quant. Biol., 18:* 123–31.

Weckler, J. E. 1954. The relationships between Neanderthal man and *Homo sapiens*. *Am. Anthropol., 56:* 1003–25.

Weidenreich, F. 1946. *Apes, giants, and man*. Chicago, Univ. of Chicago Press.

Weiner, J. S. 1954. Nose shape and climate. *Am. J. Phys. Anthropol., 12:* 615–18.

White, L. 1949. *The science of culture*. New York, Grove Press.

———— 1959. The concept of culture. *Am. Anthropol., 61:* 227–51.

Whorf, B. L. 1956. *Language, thought, and reality*. New York, John Wiley.

Wile, I. S., and R. Davis. 1949. The relation of birth to behavior, pp. 297–314. *In* C. Kluckhohn and H. A. Murray, *Personality in nature, society, and culture*, New York, Knopf.

Wilkie, J. S. 1959. Buffon, Lamarck, and Darwin: the originality of Darwin's theory of evolution, pp. 262–307. *In* P. R. Bell, *Darwin's biological work*, Cambridge, Cambridge Univ. Press.

Willey, G. R. 1960. Historical patterns and evolution in native New World culture, pp. 111–42. *In* S. Tax, *Evolution after Darwin*, Vol. 2. Chicago, Univ. of Chicago Press.

Williams, G. C. 1957. Pleiotropy, natural selection, and the evolution of senescence. *Evolution, 11:* 398–411.

Williams, R. 1958. *Culture and society*. New York, Columbia Univ. Press.

Williams, R. J. 1953. *Free and unequal*. Austin, Univ. of Texas Press.

———— 1956. *Biochemical individuality*. New York, John Wiley.

Wilson, E. O., and W. L. Brown. 1953. The subspecies concept and its taxonomic application. *Syst. Zool., 2:* 97–111.

Wingfield, A. N. 1928. *Twins and orphans: the inheritance of intelligence*. London, Dent.

Wittgenstein, L. 1953. *Philosophical investigations*. Oxford, Blackwell.

Woodworth, R. S. 1941. Heredity and environment: a critical survey of recently published material on twins and foster children. *Soc. Sci. Research Council, Bull. 47*.

World Health Organization. 1957. *Effect of radiation on human heredity*. Geneva.

Wright, S. 1931. Evolution in Mendelian populations. *Genetics, 16:* 97–159.

———— 1960. On the appraisal of genetic effects of radiation in man. *In The biological effects of atomic radiations*, Washington, Nat. Acad. Sci.

Yerkes, R. M. 1939. Social dominance and sexual status in the chimpanzee. *Quart. Rev. Biol., 14:* 115–36.

———— 1943. *Chimpanzees. A laboratory colony*. New Haven, Yale Univ. Press.

————, and A. W. Yerkes. 1929. *The great apes*. New Haven, Yale Univ. Press.

Zeuner, F. E. 1958. The replacement of Neanderthal man by *Homo sapiens*, pp. 312–15. *In Neanderthal Centennary*, Utrecht, Kemink.

Zirkle, C. 1946. The early history of the idea of the inheritance of acquired characters and of pangenesis. *Trans. Am. Philos. Soc., 35:* 91–151.

——— 1959. *Evolution, Marxian biology, and the social scene.* Philadelphia, Univ. of Pennsylvania Press.

Zuckerman, S. 1954. Correlation of change in the evolution of higher primates, pp. 333–52. *In* Huxley, Hardy, and Ford, *Evolution as a process,* London, Allen & Unwin.

# Index